Labour and liberalism in nineteenth-century Europe

Labour and liberalism in nineteenth-century Europe

Essays in comparative history

JOHN BREUILLY

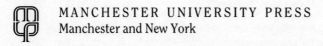

MANCHESTER UNIVERSITY PRESS
Manchester and New York

distributed exclusively in the USA and Canada by St. Martin's Press

Copyright © John Breuilly 1992

Published by Manchester University Press
Oxford Road, Manchester M13 9PL, England
and Room 400, 175 Fifth Avenue, New York, NY 10010, USA

Distributed exclusively in the USA and Canada
by St. Martin's Press, Inc., 175 Fifth Avenue, New York, NY 10010, USA

A catalogue record for this book is available from the British Library

Library of Congress cataloging in publication data
Breuilly, John. 1946–
    Labour and liberalism in nineteenth-century Europe: essays in
comparative history / John Breuilly.
        p. cm.
    ISBN 0–7190–2590–7 (hardback)
    1. Labor movement—Europe—History—19th century.   2. Liberalism—
Europe—History—19th century.   I. Title.   II. Title: Labor and
liberalism in nineteenth-century Europe.
HD8376.B74   1991
331.88'094'09034—dc20   91–16345

ISBN 0 7190 2590 7 *hardback*

Photoset in Linotron Clearface
by Northern Phototypesetting Co. Ltd, Bolton.
Printed in Great Britain
by Biddles Ltd, Guildford & King's Lynn

Contents

Preface

This book draws together for the first time my comparative studies on labour and liberalism in the nineteenth century. The essays which have been previously published have all been considerably revised and updated, while the opening and concluding essays, as well as the essay on liberalism in Britain and Germany, see their first publication in this volume.

The essay on the labour aristocracy originally saw life as a paper given at a conference held in Bad Homburg in November 1982. I am indebted to the participants at the conference for their comments, especially Ulrich Engelhardt and Jürgen Kocka. It also gave me a chance to meet with and talk to the late Werner Conze who has had such a major influence on modern German social history. In 1983 I gave a revised version of the paper at a conference at the University of East Anglia and then in May 1983 to a seminar at the Institute of Historical Research. The latter occasion was especially stimulating because the audience included Geoff Crossick, Robbie Gray and Eric Hobsbawm, all of whose work figure centrally in this essay. The essay here draws upon and revises the slightly different English and German versions which have been published as well as the very differently organised review article on the same subject.

In 1982 a section of the German Historikertag held in Münster dealt with comparisons of the nineteenth-century European labour movement. Jürgen Kocka invited me to contribute an additional essay to the book which subsequently appeared. This was the essay on 'Liberalism or social democracy?'. I subsequently gave talks on the subject to the Centre for the Study of Social History at the University of Warwick and a German version to the Institut für Europäische Geschichte in Mainz. The essay here revises heavily both the German and English language versions which have been published before.

I first gave a paper comparing British, French and German artisans at a conference held in 1981 at the University of East Anglia. This was one of a series of conferences supported by the then SSRC and organised by Richard Evans. Like many modern German historians I am indebted to Richard Evans for the energy he has put into bringing German and British historians together at conferences. It was then a great personal pleasure to be able to revise this for publication in a book dedicated to Gwyn A. Williams, an inspirational teacher who first made me want to be an historian, and who had himself published a comparative study of artisans. The essay published here is extensively revised and expanded.

The essay on law originates from a paper I gave at a conference in June 1984 at the Historisches Kolleg in Munich. I am especially indebted to Jürgen Kocka as conference organiser, and to Gerhard A. Ritter as leader of the section in which my paper appeared, for comments and criticisms. The revised essay published here has tried particularly to take account of more recent work on liberalism and the middle classes.

In May 1988 Arno Herzig and Günther Trautmann organised a conference in Hamburg on the subject of Hamburg and the European labour movement as one of a number of events to mark the 900th 'birthday' of the port of Hamburg. I gave a paper comparing liberalism and socialism in mid-nineteenth-century Hamburg and Manchester. Apart from the comments made by participants at the conference, which mainly concerned the Hamburg side, I am indebted to my Manchester colleagues Patrick Joyce, Frank O'Gorman, Iori Prothero and Tony Taylor for their criticisms of that paper. I have considerably revised the original published form of this essay, especially taking into account my involvement in a research project with Iori Prothero, Patrick Joyce and Sally Taylor which compares the cultural history of mid-nineteenth-century Hamburg, Lyon and Manchester.

I gave a paper comparing liberalism in mid-nineteenth-century Germany and Britain to a conference entitled *'Bürgertum und Liberalismus im 19. Jahrhundert: Deutschland im europäischen Vergleich'* held at the Zentrum für Interdisziplinäre Forschung at the University of Bielefeld in the Federal Republic of Germany in February 1987. I am especially indebted to Dieter Langewiesche who organised the conference and who has written so effectively on both German liberalism and European liberalism more generally.

The section of the introductory essay concerned with labour history draws upon a paper I gave at a conference to mark the 30th anniversary of the Society for the Study of Labour History held at Birkbeck College, London, in February 1990. A revised version (drawing upon the changes made for publication here) was given to the Economic History Conference held in Manchester in April 1991.

The conclusion is utterly new.

I provide details of the publication of earlier versions of these essays and acknowledge with thanks the editors, publishers and journals mentioned.

'Arbeiteraristokratie in Großbritannien und Deutschland. Ein Vergleich', in *Handwerker in der Industrialisierung: Lage, Kultur und Politik vom späten 18. bis ins frühe 20. Jahrhundert*, edited by Ulrich Engelhardt (Ernst Klett Verlag, Stuttgart, 1984), pp. 497–527.

'The labour aristocracy in Britain and Germany: a comparison', *Bulletin of the Society for the Study of Labour History*, 48 (1984), pp. 58–71.

'The labour aristocracy in Britain and Germany, 1850–1914: a review of the literature', in *Geschichte der Arbeiterschaft und der Arbeiterbewegung. Die internationale Forschung*, edited by Klaus Tenfelde (Oldenbourg, Munich, 1986), pp. 179–226.

'Liberalismus oder Sozialdemokratie? Ein Vergleich der britischen und deutschen politischen Arbeiterbewegung zwischen 1850 und 1875', in *Europäische Arbeiterbewegungen im 19. Jahrhundert*, edited by Jürgen Kocka (Vandenhoeck & Ruprecht, Göttingen, 1983), pp. 129–166.

'Liberalism or social democracy?: a comparison of British and German labour politics, c.1850–1875, in *European History Quarterly*, 15/1 (1985), pp. 3–42.

'Artisan economy, artisan politics, artisan ideology: the artisan contribution to the nineteenth-century European labour movement', in *Artisans, Peasants and Proletarians, 1790–1860: essays presented to Gwyn A. Williams*, edited by Clive Emsley & James Walvin (Croom Helm, London, 1985), pp. 187–225.

'Civil Society and the Labour Movement, Class Relations and the Law: a comparison between Germany and England', in *Arbeiter und Bürger im 19. Jahrhundert*, edited by Jürgen Kocka (Oldenbourg, Munich, 1986), pp. 297–318.

'Liberalismus und Arbeiterschaft in Hamburg und Manchester in der Mitte des 19. Jahrhunderts', in *'Der kühnen Bahn nur folgen wir'. Ursprünge, Erfolge und Grenzen der*

Arbeiterbewegung in Deutschland. Bd.2. Arbeiter und technischer Wandel in der Hafenstadt Hamburg, edited by A. Herzig & G. Trautmann (Reider Verlag, Hamburg, 1989), pp. 29–72.

The essays published here indicate a shift of interest from 'labour' and 'labour history' in a fairly conventional sense to artisans as a distinct group, and then on to relationships between labour and middle-class groups and the character of liberalism. Nevertheless all these essays are the product of a consistent concern to use comparison to understand better the various national histories of nineteenth-century western Europe, especially in relation to the character of the labour movement and of liberalism. The themes overlap or complement one another. In the revising process I have been able to exploit this by referring to arguments developed in greater detail in other parts of the book. On that basis I felt able to add an introduction which analysed the nature of comparative history and outlined the way in which I think it should be practised. It also enabled me to put forward some ideas in the concluding essay about national peculiarities.

As a consequence, I think that this is one case of a book of essays where the whole is greater than the sum of its parts.

1

Introduction: making comparisons in history

The practice of comparative history

The great strength of historical study is its attention to the particular. It is necessary to use general concepts and terms in the investigation of the past, but the purpose of the historian is to understand particular events, not to test the validity of such concepts or terms. What is meant by 'particular event' varies greatly: one historian may study an incident in a battle while another writes the history of warfare. To handle a very large number of actions and events will undoubtedly call for the more explicit employment of concepts and terms which will enable the historian to define and classify events. But in principle a history of the world and a history of one incident in a battle both involve the same concern with the particular.

The position is different for the practice of comparative history. Comparative history involves comparing and contrasting two or more particular events or sets of events. Again, it does not matter in principle how large or small scale are the particular events (although one cannot, by definition, write a comparative history of the world as there is only one case).

In comparative history the historian's concern is not to understand *the* particular, because there is now more than one particular. Comparison which begins by regarding one particular case as the norm against which comparisons are made with other cases is flawed from the outset. As we shall see, labour history, especially at the macrohistorical level, is well-supplied with notions of norms and exceptions. Why was there no socialist movement in the United States? Why did an Independent Labour Party take so long to develop in Britain? Why did it develop so quickly in Germany? Why did French trade unions remain so hostile to reformism up to 1914?

There are two problems with posing questions in these implicitly comparative terms. First, they assume that the contrasting event to that referred to in the question is the norm; what they are considering is the exception. That itself requires further examination. Second, they assume simple outcomes which can be compared (independent labour party or not, socialism or not, reformist trade unionism or not). As we shall see in the next section such simple conceptions of macro-level outcomes, enabling the comparative technique to be turned quickly from descriptive to explanatory purposes, cannot be sustained. At this stage, however, I want above all to insist that the comparative approach cannot privilege one of the cases it compares over the others, whether as norm or its corollary, exception.

When this illegitimate path is taken, usually one of two procedures are then followed. One involves imposing the framework used for the case in which the historian is really interested upon the other case or cases. For example, one can ask how far 'industrialisation' in other countries differed from that of British industrialisation. Undoubtedly one will find that this differed in numerous ways, but as the historian will have developed his idea of industrialisation as a way of understanding the particular British case, he will not be comparing Britain with other cases, but rather comparing procedures which work for the British case with other cases for which the procedures clearly do not work.

The second error is of the opposite kind. This involves taking over from other cases the ways their historians have studied them. For example, a political ideology such as liberalism or socialism will be defined and studied in different ways by historians of different countries. An historian of British liberalism may focus on the concern with classical political economy and the limitation of state power. An historian of German liberalism, on the other hand, may rather focus upon the concern to enforce the rule of law upon the operation of the state. A comparison between British and German liberalism which accepted such approaches would not be comparing two particular examples of the same kind of event, but actually two different kinds of events which simply happen to have the same general label.

The worst error of historical comparison is when these two false approaches are compounded. For example, one might take French history, with its series of revolutions, as establishing the 'norm' for how old forms of class rule are replaced by new forms. One can then ask how far 'revolutions' in British or in German or in Russian history also allow for the movement from one kind of class rule to another. The problem is not only that French history is used as the norm by which to judge other cases, but also that the historian takes as equivalents of one another, whatever events that British or German or Russian historians define as a 'revolution'. To try to compare directly the 1640s (or even more absurdly 1688) in Britain with the 1790s in France, or 1917 in Russia with 1918–19 in Germany is pointless. At best one will note that the events were rather 'different' from one another. At worst one will conclude that one set of events was a 'failure' by comparison with the other.

The first requirement of a proper comparative history is to be equally interested in all the cases under consideration. This means that no one case can set the terms by which comparisons are made. The second requirement of comparative history is that one must be comparing cases which can meaningfully be analysed using the same methods. This means that one cannot simply compare cases with the same general labels while silently accepting the very different definitions and concerns used by the historians of the various cases.

Taken together this indicates that the comparative historian must start with some general question which extends beyond any of the particular cases. The way in which each of the cases is then approached will be related to how the historian sets about answering that general question. This may well involve defining and approaching those cases in very different ways from that of the 'normal' historical treatment.

Proper comparative history is difficult to practise precisely because of this need to ask general questions and to develop explicitly a general framework for the consideration of the particular cases. What can one hope to gain from such an exercise which one could not gain from 'normal' history? I think there are two major benefits to be had.

The first is that comparative history is the nearest equivalent that the historian has to the experimental method. The historian cannot re-run his events with some alteration to one specific element in order to test for the significance of that element. He cannot, in advance, set up a number of comparable events in which slight differences are built into the initial situation in order to gauge the significance of those differences. In a way comparison is a mental experiment which tries to compare particular events in this way. The benefit to be gained from this is that in a negative sense some accounts offered of particular events by normal history can be questioned. For example, some historians have attributed the political stability of post-1850 Britain to prosperity. Others have emphasised the importance of the emergence of a 'labour aristocracy'. Examination of other cases may show that prosperity or the existence of a labour aristocracy was not accompanied by political stability. This does not in any straightforward way 'disprove' the original account offered. However, it should compel the historian to question the way in which the role of prosperity or a labour aristocracy had been employed in earlier accounts of political stability.

In the end, a 'full' account can only be offered by normal history. Comparative history necessarily involves a radically selective treatment of particular cases in order to ensure common treatment of all the cases which are being compared. There is no point in studying events which have nothing in common but nor is there in studying events which do not differ significantly. Where the 'experimental' aspect can come in is when one can show that apparently different events can be related to similar conditions (which means that those conditions cannot explain the difference of events) or that apparently similar events can be related to different conditions. Having eliminated certain possible explanations, comparative history has to hand over to normal history to take further those possible explanations which remain.

So comparative history can be used to help deepen the understanding of particular cases. It also has a rather less specific but more positive benefit. As a European historian I have always been struck by the extent to which national boundaries shape historical study. Historians are trained in different ways from one state to another. Most of those historians then study their own country. The few who study the history of other countries generally take over the questions and methods employed by indigenous historians; sometimes, more interestingly but not necessarily any more comparatively, they introduce the concerns of their own national historiographies into their study of another country. In turn those questions and methods are shaped by the acceptance of the nation as the unit within which historical study proceeds. This has a different significance according to the length of time a nation-state has existed or whether it exists at present, but generally historians accept state boundaries (which from the nineteenth century are increasingly taken to be also national), indeed often anachronistically projecting this equation of state and national boundaries into earlier periods. The acceptance of such boundaries may be accompanied by certain assumptions about national history which shape the particular object of study. Even where, as in the case of regional or local history, the national unit is not the defining one, these regions and locales are bound within the confines of the nation-state. The historiography which informs the approach of such historians is usually a national one, and most historians are only able to gain some perspective on their particular field of study by at best making comparisons with other cases within the national unit. This can be especially limiting in those cases where the most appropriate boundaries extend beyond that of the nation-state – for example, in considering the history of a great river or a major coal field. At times the assumption that the nation-state provides the boundary definition of a subject – for example that of economies – may mean forcing together what should be studied separately and forcing apart what should be studied together.[1]

For all these reasons I think it is vital to find ways of transcending nation-state barriers. One way, of course, is to write European history, but that necessarily involves selecting large-scale historical events, and one is still largely dependent on the differing approaches and results of historians operating within national frameworks. Certain types of history – economic and demographic history for example – have sufficiently explicit and well-developed general theory to enable them to transcend national boundaries either by means of comparison or by taking larger units of study. Other types of history, for example political, social and intellectual history tend to find this more difficult. There are, of course, exceptions. Barrington Moore and Theda Skocpol both provide examples of how to practice comparative political history on a large scale.[2] They both ask a general question. Barrington Moore's question is one about a long-run historical relationship – namely that between agrarian class structures and the emergence of modern democracy and dictatorship. There is a problem about the way in which he then tends to become absorbed by the current historiography for the different national cases considered, but nevertheless the book transcends national boundaries. Skocpol has a less explicit question in that she is not looking for the kind of historical relationship Barrington Moore investigates. Rather she is interested in how one goes about understanding major revolutions. On the other hand, she develops a much more explicit general framework for the analysis of each case, and this enables more rigorous comparison to be undertaken. The result is a study which both deepens our understanding of the particular cases and of revolutions as a major kind of event.

Nevertheless, these and other studies have tended to take the modern state as the basic unit of analysis.[3] For the social or intellectual or cultural historian, particularly those concerned with rather smaller-scale events than the development of modern states, this is not appropriate. Furthermore, the larger the scale of comparison, the more radically selective one has to be in the treatment of particular cases. My own interests in nineteenth century European labour and liberal movements require rather smaller-scale comparisons. I have also found that the comparison of two or three cases enables one to consider a wider range of features for each case. Finally, there were often actual connections between the various cases I wish to consider.

Labour and liberalism in nineteenth-century Europe

My major interest as a 'normal' historian is in modern German history. My research has been primarily into nineteenth-century German labour history. However, as an Englishman,[4] trained and working in the British university system, I could not but be aware that my outlook and interests were rather different from those of my German colleagues. Furthermore, I had a natural interest in modern British history. For these reasons alone I would at the very least have made casual comparisons between Germany and Britain.

To these reasons one must add the openess of German historians to foreigners studying German history (a piece of good fortune for we foreigners) and their concern to understand German history within a wider perspective. This has much to do with recent German history. Intellectual exiles from the Third Reich learnt much from (and also taught much to) European and American social scientists. Germany was necessarily opened to influence from outside, with defeat, occupation, and division after 1945. A new generation of German historians grew up in the Federal Republic concerned to understand why Germany had fallen prey to national socialism and this has involved trying to work out what was special about German history.

This concern with German 'uniqueness' automatically carries with it a comparative implication. However, whether one accepts some idea of uniqueness or not, there is the danger that such comparison is made from within the framework established by German historians for the study of German history.[5] German 'failure' is set against the 'success' of others – usually the liberal democracies of western Europe and the areas of overseas European settlement, especially the United States. When that comparison is questioned it is usually done so on the basis of questioning that understanding of *German* history rather than developing another strategy of comparative history.[6] It is sometimes suggested that perhaps these other countries have not been as successful as German historians have assumed, but this has rarely been taken beyond the level of suggestion. Sometimes it is suggested that a different approach which considered Germany as just one variant within a general framework would be better. For example, instead of asking why Germany 'failed' to have a bourgeois revolution in the way that England, France or the United States had, it is suggested that one re-define the concept of 'bourgeois revolution' so as to draw attention to similarities between Germany and these other countries.[7] But these have never got beyond the status of suggestions. It is easier to plead for proper comparative history than to practise it.

If German history is especially open to comparison, there are impulses in British history which also imply comparisons. In a series of famous articles written in the early 1960s Perry Anderson and Tom Nairn unfavourably compared British history with that of France.[8] E.P.Thompson responded with a brilliant essay 'The Peculiarities of the English' which managed simultaneously to debunk comparison that took the form of measuring one history against the norm of another history and to suggest the need for a more general framework to enable proper comparison.[9] But as with the critique by Eley and Blackbourn of ideas of German uniqueness, it was the first point which was made most effectively.

Certain of the specific problems which I was considering as a research historian seemed to relate to the problems that were being debated in this more general way. For example, the question of why Germany so rapidly developed an independent labour party implied a comparison with Britain or France or the United States where such an event took place somewhat later or not at all. British labour historians sometimes posed that question in reverse: why did Britain take so long to develop an independent labour party? In both cases the answers were also related to how far liberalism could develop as a popular political movement which inhibited the growth of class-based politics. Another closely related set of questions revolved around the extent to which industrialisation destroyed one kind of labour force and created another, thereby generating both reactionary and progressive tendencies within the labour movement, or depending upon the speed of the disruption allowing different degrees of continuity in labour traditions. There have often been assumptions about 'national character' which are beyond testing, but can be related to more meaningful questions about differences in political structures and cultures. In all these cases a comparative and focused approach is really the only way more understanding can be gained.

Questions of this kind cannot easily be answered within one single comparative framework. Rather one needs to develop different frameworks to answer these different questions. However, in all cases it is necessary not to allow one case to set the terms on which comparisons are made. This requires posing general questions and then seeing how results within existing historiography bear upon those questions, and then seeing if rather different kinds of research are needed to take the matter further.

The appropriate form for such inquiry seems to me to be that of a series of essays in comparative history. Each essay can attack a particular problem without the claim to definite results that one would expect of a monograph or or a single article in a scholarly journal. Yet an essay should go rather more deeply than a 'think-piece' at a conference or in a journal. Definite frameworks can be sketched out and some evidence provided to support the approach taken. By having a number of essays with overlapping concerns, one can complement and reinforce points made in individual essays.

Before moving on to explore some of the themes I have mentioned, it is necessary to say rather more about how comparative history should be pursued. I will consider the practice of comparison within labour history. From this consideration I will draw more general conclusions about strategies of comparative history.

The subject of labour history

Introductory remarks

First, I will consider the problem that the interests of labour historians are diverse and have shifted in emphasis over the last few decades and that this, coupled with different national historiographical traditions and sources as well as the fact that national *histories* are varied, creates serious difficulties about what it is that is to be compared. After that I will suggest that there are a range of scales on which comparisons can be made – beginning with what might be termed 'comparative historical macroanalysis'[10] which compares long-term patterns of change on a cross-national base, moving on to more limited cross-national comparisons of various kinds, then considering comparisons of particular cases within different national units, and finally comparisons between cases within a single nation unit. I will try to say something at each of these levels about the problems confronting comparative labour history and the benefits of engaging in such comparison.

The varieties of labour history

Labour history is a term that covers a very diverse range of historical practices. In order to establish just how diverse it has been and is becoming I have combed through issues of the *Labour History Review* (LHR) (formerly the *Bulletin of the Society for the Study of Labour History*) and of the major west German labour history journal, *International Wissenschaftliche Korrespondenz zur Geschichte der deutschen Arbeiterbewegung* (IWK), in order to see the range of subjects on which substantive essays have been written, and the characteristic shifts in interest which have taken place over the last fifteen years.

Looking through LHR backnumbers makes one realise just how diverse labour history has become. Leaving aside the 'professional' preoccupation with archives and libraries, the two hardy perennials are biographical and organisational studies. Generally there is something of a trend from the biography of the leading figures and activists to more humble figures (but usually activists) in the labour movement. So far as organisations are concerned there has been a slight shift from trade unions and political organisations to such organisations as schools, welfare and leisure institutions, and cooperatives, though not so much as I had expected to find. Both these shifts indicate a turn from the 'commanding heights' of the labour movement to the 'lowlands'. This in part is linked to the increased interest of labour historians in women, colonial labour movements, and ethnic minorities.

Methodologically more innovative perhaps is the shift away from labour institutions, whether high or low, and activists, whether leaders or rank-and-file, to more diffuse subjects. An interest in the beliefs of working people is evidenced by recent conferences and publications on workers and religion. One also finds patterns of working-class housing and consumption used to explore beliefs rather than to gauge 'objective' standards of living; and patterns of relatively informally organised collective behaviour such as strikes and food riots used to try to reconstruct labour mentalities. Labour festivals are likewise studied less with a view to understanding their political purposes but rather, by considering their language, imagery, iconography, timing and much else, to gain further understanding of labour culture.

Turning to IWK, and again leaving aside material on archives and libraries, one gains a slightly different impression. Biographical studies of various kinds were most numerous, followed by accounts of political organisations or significant political events. There were far more studies of 'ideology' in the sense of the programmes of labour organisations and leading activitists and the debates to which such programmes gave rise than one finds in LHR. There were rather fewer studies of trade unions or industrial relations. However, the influence of British labour history has given rise, from the late 1970s, to an interest in strikes as one aspect of protest studies. Most cultural studies were concerned with formal educational institutions and activities within the labour movement.

In both cases there were a few studies on such subjects as government treatment of labour, emigration, and labour views on social policy. What also struck me was the comparative paucity, in both journals, of studies of the family in working-class life (nothing under this heading in the LHR index 1975–85; one essay in IWK from 1974–90) or of attempts at any broad characterisation of the working class as part of a class structure. It may be because these lend themselves to a more extended monographic treatment which will not be registered in essay form, and I will come back to some studies of these kinds later in this essay.

To some extent these more recent interests pose grave problems for the comparative historian. First, insofar as comparison has often been seen as a way of helping to explain *already established but varying outcomes*, it was important to have already established what those outcomes were (e.g. an independent labour party or popular liberalism, reformism or radicalism, etc.). This new work throws up two problems. First, there are no clear 'outcomes' for which a comparative scrutiny of possible explanations can then be undertaken. Second, these new forms of work actually cast doubt on the 'data' established before. Thus, for example, if a study of strike activity as an index of class militancy reveals that British workers, by this index, were more militant than their French or German counterparts in the years immediately before the First World War, then a set of comparative explanations designed to explain the lack of British militancy which had been read off from the official policy of leading labour organisations such as unions and parties, will automatically be called into question.

It may also be that some of this newer work, with its attention to fine detail in the investigation of such matters as worker beliefs, and its use very often of a narrative, descriptive mode, would make it very difficult to construct frameworks within which comparison can be made. The kind of work in these journals which more easily lends itself to comparative study is labour history as the study of organised activity – economic, political, and to a lesser extent cultural – rather than of beliefs and styles of life.

Types of comparative labour history

Long-run macroanalysis

a) The choice of long-run periods

At its most ambitious level this involves taking the 'total' subject of labour history, understood as the working-class under capitalism in all its manifestations, noting comparatively the different patterns of developments between national cases, and then seeking to bring out the crucial variables which can explain this diversity along with certain similarities.

For the period up to 1914 such analysis most usually is confined to the four major countries of Britain, France, Germany and the United States. This can be defended on the grounds that these four countries produced about 80 per cent of the industrial output of the world by 1914 and, with something between 35–45% of their labour forces employed in the manufacturing sector broadly defined, they were the only major societies in which the working class had become of central importance.[11] Furthermore, the absence of any major upheavals through war and revolution between 1815 and 1914 (with the major exception of the Civil War in the United States and the more limited cases of the wars of German unification) would make it appear possible that long-run patterns could be traced and variables which might explain differences in those patterns identified through comparative analysis. I will come back to concentrate upon this period for these reasons.

A recent publication also argues that, at least for European labour history, the period 1919–45 can also be treated as a meaningful one, with the common impact of war, the establishment of states with mass labour participation, the experience of the depression and then again of war.[12] Arguably the integration of industrial capitalist economies in a United States dominated bloc after 1945 creates another meaningful period. There is, however, only scope within this introduction to consider the period 1815–1914, which is in any case the period within which the subjects of the essays that follow are located.[13]

b) The period 1815–1914: the making of a working class

The most common theme which allows of comparison between the four major countries on a macro-level for this period is that of the 'making of the working class'. In all four cases one can establish the clear growth in the labour force of a wage-labour force in the manufacturing sector. On that basis it might be assumed that there will be a limited array of consequences in terms of the patterns of life and beliefs within that labour force, its forms of organisation, and its relationships to other social groups and to the state.

In looking at this the comparative historian has to avoid, as I have already stressed, the ideas of 'norms' or 'exceptions'. Rather it will be necessary to build up, first of all at a descriptive level, comparisons between the way that an industrial labour force and its dependents develop in the different countries.

This is not a simple descriptive task. First, it is clear that the notion of the 'making of a working class' operates at different levels and that historians arrive at different conclusions according to which level they consider. For some historians it has been the imperative of the transformation into the commodity of labour–power under the conditions of capitalism which has forced the process of working-clas formation. For others it has been the political and intellectual effort of trying to think and act in class terms which has been of central importance, and in which economic circumstances have acted as little more than a backdrop to this dramatic history.

Usually these two approaches have operated with the two notions of what might be called 'class in itself' and 'class for itself'. In comparative perspective it does appear that historians focusing on the latter usually concentrate on a rather earlier period. The clearest example is the work of E.P.Thompson with his stress on action, consciousness, culture, the idea that the working class *made itself*.[14] The major criticisms of Thompson have been from those who might be said to take a 'class in itself' approach, who argue that the objective processes of working-class formation either were still in their infancy in the period Thompson considers, or that there was at best a rather tangential connection between that process and the groups considered by Thompson. Thompson, it might be argued, rather considers radical artisans, proletarianised outworkers, and the declassé from the middling ranks of society to be found in journalism, shopkeeping, law, the world of entertainment, business, etc. The class language is then not so much the expression or a component of working-class formation, but rather just part of the criticisms aimed at the rich and the powerful, the superficial grafting of social categories upon an older language of radicalism.[15] Furthermore, one might go on to argue that without an adequate sense of the structures in which class is formed, Thompson and those who follow him have no means of connecting what they are studying to class as a category within a system of class relations.

The other approach, in the British context, focuses much more upon the later nineteenth and early twentieth centuries. Here the emphasis is laid upon the diffusion of industrial wage-labour across wider sectors of the economy, the growth of trade union and other forms of occupational organisation and collective action, and the growth of clear working-class districts in industrial areas with a distinctive social and cultural character. Political effects are seen as secondary, and increasingly in terms of movements which have accepted the rules of the new industrial society and are concerned principally with maximising their own interests within that society.[16]

There are problems about how the two phases are related to one another and also how labour historians deal with the intervening period. I will return to that intervening period in the essay which considers the concept of the labour aristocracy.

I do not want to discuss the relative merits of these two approaches. I simply want to stress that from within an international comparative perspective, one finds similar contrasts in the labour history of other countries. However, because the actual course of events was rather different, the results of these two approaches differ from the British case.

In the French case a much greater degree of continuity is stressed compared to Britain. There is again a first phase, up to around 1848, which is seen in terms of action, organisation, language. The labour movement considered is artisan-dominated and it is politically radical. Much of the work of French labour historians has been to try to understand this connection, especially if it is argued that the social vision of such artisans was conservative. However, in the French case it is often assumed that the prominence of these kinds of movements was related to the limited development of industrial capitalism in this period. This 'relative backwardness' is considered to continue into the later 19th century and the break in artisan radicalism is connected more with political repression between 1848 and 1871 than with marked shifts in economic and social structures. There were, it is conceded, some 'modern' forms of development in certain regions, e.g. in textiles and mining in parts of northern France, and this helped give rise to a more modern working class and also can explain the development of more reformist political attitudes within the labour movement, or at least a more progressive kind of socialism represented by Guesde. But many of these changes are seen as becoming really important only in the post-1918 period.

Much of this approach has been subjected to criticism – because of its tendency to treat artisans as a single, pre-industrial grouping, its failure to take seriously the growth and change in the French economy, and its attempt to read off from political programmes the attitudes of broad groups of workers.[17] However, it seems to me that there is still a powerful hold in the idea of looking at labour history in terms of class 'in itself' and 'for itself', with the great emphasis in France being on the latter and on continuities.

In the German case there is much less of an early labour movement combining artisan dominance with political radicalism. One can find such a movement in the period before and during 1848 but not on the same scale as in France or Britain. However, if one regards this just as 'pre-history', and the first real phase in the making of a working class is dated from the 1860s, then a different view can be developed. This was the period of very rapid industrial growth which also saw the radical reconstruction of the political framework, brought about by the wars of unification.

Most labour historians have focused upon the political responses to these changes, above all in the formation of political parties but recently also in terms of trade unions and strikes. The stress again is on the making of a working class, measured in the development of independent political action within class boundaries and the use of class language. Again, as with Britain and France, it is recognised that only a minority of the working class is involved, but this is seen as a crucial precursor to the more widespread formation of a working class. The story then is of how this politics can be accommodated to the growth of an industrial working class 'in itself' under the Second Empire. As with France the story is one of continuity from the first to the second phase, but with the stress on the precocity and advanced character of the German working-class movement rather than on its relative backwardness.[18] It should be stressed that this understanding has been vigorously criticised, but I think this general picture still predominates.

We can see that despite the different stories that are told, there is a similar contrast between class as action, politics, and language, and class as an objective process of economic and social formation. Two things soon become clear. First, historians rightly turn to the problem of connecting together these two different levels or understandings of class. Second, there appear to be insuperable obstacles in the way of making satisfactory connections.

One reason is that the two-level distinction is too crude. Recently Katznelson has tried to distinguish between four levels on which class can be understood; the structural level (that is the formation of a working class in relation to other classes);

the development of common ways of life; the formation of common dispositions; and the engagement in collective action.[19] In their different ways certain West and East German historians had operated with a similar approach, distinguishing between an economic, a social, and a political-cum-ideological level of analysis.[20] Naturally there is a strong tendency to treat these levels as moving from the more to the less basic, although it is apparent that a teleological or determinist treatment of relations between the different levels soon breaks down.

One advantage of this approach, however, is just at the descriptive level. If we cannot 'read off' a class response at one level as signifying class at another one, then two kinds of dangers can be avoided. First, we will avoid reading off, say, class 'dispositions' on the basis of political and ideological actions by labour organisations; or assuming that the growth of an industrial labour force automatically creates an homogenous social class; or that the political expression of solidary class attitudes means that there are clear class divisions in everyday life. It is increasingly clear that often the opposite is the case. Class attitudes have more stubbornly persisted at the 'disposition' level in twentieth century Britain than in twentieth century Germany, although 'class' appeared to have a much stronger and solidary expression at the political level in Germany by 1914. That, of course, also takes us to the story of the converse of the 'making of the working class', namely the 'unmaking of the working class'. Unfortunately there is not space to consider this question.[21]

The second danger is the tendency to look for one clear outcome, or at least a dominant outcome, for each country. There is a great pressure to do this, and I have succumbed to it myself (e.g. in terms of liberalism *or* social democracy, different kinds of political-legal cultures). That in turn tends to work most persuasively for the political level, because at least there is national-level organisation which can be compared, and pushes historians to try then to read back from that level to other levels. Also one can forget that yet more possibilities exist which are clearer in third and further cases (e.g. working class allegiance to ethnic or confessional parties or fragmented support for a range of other parties or working-class populism).

Once one moves away from those dangers, then the whole task of looking for a decisive phase of working-class formation is called into question. Comparisons will have to work firstly at the different levels indicated. Furthermore, at each of those levels, one will need to work out further differentiating concepts – e.g. about different patterns of industrialisation, about different forms of residence and social contacts both within and across class boundaries. At the political level too I think more should be done not so much to try to *explain* supposedly different outcomes, but rather to describe comparatively such matters as the political sociology of labour parties and trade unions, the types of negotiations they engage in with employers, other political groups and the state.[22]

Because the class levels I have indicated tend to give an analytic if not a causal priority to economic structures, then social relationships, then dispositions, and finally political organisations and the construction of formal political programmes, they do also pose a difficulty for the general tendency to locate an initial phase of working-class formation at the level of politics and ideas. One way around that, of course, is to repudiate such a sense of analytical or causal priority, either by abandoning any kind of class approach and/or by insisting not merely on the autonomous but on the creative impact of political traditions and culture on the way whole social groups act and think. The recent work on an enduring radical tradition, on the creative role of language in shaping political movements, on the powerful impact of various traditions of political action and symbolism – all point in this direction.[23] I would only say that it is difficult to see how this can be fitted as yet into some alternative, large-scale comparative framework, especially as it is still unclear how it is being developed for particular national cases. Along the way also a clear definition of 'labour' as the subject of the historian is being lost.

Whether one proceeds in that way or in terms of differentiating more within a class model, the historian engaged in comparisons will have to focus on more specific issues and periods in a comparative way, and these will often also take the historian beyond the particular concern with class which does appear at present the only effective way of engaging in very large-scale comparisons in labour history. We need to consider how these rather smaller-scale comparisons can proceed.

More specific cross-national comparisons

a) The industrial labour force as a whole

As I indicated in the previous section, one can focus on one particular level of labour/class history. For long-run analysis the subjects which most obviously lend themselves to such a treatment are the growth of a wage-labour force and the development of certain kinds of collective economic action and organisation amongst such workers.

So far as I know. there has not been a great deal of systematic comparative work on the first of these subjects. Clearly one finds in individual cases work on the rate of growth of such a labour force and its distribution over different sectors and occupations. Usually this has focused on the issue of an *industrial* labour force, concentrating on statistics which indicate concentrations of workers into larger units of production employing machinery and steam, later electrical power. Rather less systematic has been the kind of work undertaken by Kocka for Germany which focuses on the development of wage labour rather than the size and technology of production units.[24] Yet the recent trend towards stressing the continued growth and development of small workshop production (either independently organised or transposed into larger production units), of rural industry, and of domestic production in conjunction rather than direct conflict with factory production suggests that this is precisely the kind of comparative descriptive work that is needed.[25]

Clearly there will be problems. For example, different industrial censuses operated with different definitions (which also makes long-run analysis of particular cases difficult) which renders cross-national comparison impossible.

Even a fairly simple stage model of industrialisation requires one to recognise that comparison must be between comparable stages, not the same chronological period for different cases. However, such models have themselves been questioned. The idea, for example, of the need for an 'agrarian revolution' preceding industrial development has been put into doubt for some cases.[26] The need for capital accumulation as a prior stage is also not applicable to all cases: in Germany, for example, the problem was rather one of concentrating and directing such capital into industrial investment.[27] Industrialisation is no longer regarded as a brief and hectic period of economic transformation dominated by factory and machine production. Instead, the stress has been upon quite different patterns of industrialisation and capitalist growth. For example, if successive cases of industrialisation generally involve the need to concentrate larger amounts of capital, and if these alter the pattern of firm size and of management, and if these are also related to lower skill levels and much more first-generation industrial employment, then one would expect quite different kinds of labour forces to be formed with very different capacities for collective action.[28] If this was accepted it is difficult to see what specific processes and periods of industrial or wage-labour formation are comparable. So again one is forced to rather narrower scales of comparison. It may be that later one could return to larger-scale comparisons for particular cases, once it had been established that there were certain parallels in the pattern of industrialisation.

Related to the issue of comparing the formation of the industrial labour force in different countries is that of comparing their experiences and patterns of behaviour. Two clear and related subjects can be considered comparatively: strike activity and trade unionism, as well as the complex relations between these two.

Strikes can be approached in a way which lends itself to comparative treatment if it is possible to construct a statistical base in terms of numbers of strikes, strikers, duration of strikes, distribution over time, region and industrial sector and occupation, classes of demand, etc. Sometimes such work has been fitted into certain broader models of different types of protest. Geary, for example, operated with a broad typology moving from pre-industrial forms of protest through to the initial responses to industrial development and then the 'maturation' of patterns of protest.[29] The most ambitious work on this scale has been undertaken for France, but unfortunately there are no really comparable sets of data for other industrial countries, so systematic comparison is difficult.[30]

Of course, this kind of long-run analysis again depends on the assumption that we are comparing like with like. Geary ran into problems, for example, when facing the emergence of apparently 'archaic' patterns of protest in post-1918 Germany (food riots) whereas some historians of eighteenth century artisans have pointed to quite 'advanced' forms of strike activity. Kocka did try to show at a macro-level that there were certain types of shift, e.g. between 1800 and 1870 strikes were more class-bounded (fewer masters were involved) and increasingly concerned with wages and hours rather than other concerns, but beyond that it was difficult to generalise.[31] Even that generalisation has to face the objection that it is the broader scale of action which explains this shift of concern (because wages and hours are the lowest common denominator amongst the larger number of workers involved in a strike action).[32] Feldman has pointed out that trends identified before 1914 break down in the post-1918 situation, partly with the rise of labour parties to governmental power, partly in the face of new kinds of employer and state strategies, partly with a reversal of the general economic advances since the mid-nineteenth century.[33] General models of a steadily modernising pattern of behaviour seem therefore to be rather shaky, especially when even longer time-spans than that of 1815–1914 are used. One could, however, argue that it is enough if such models help us grasp comparable changes over that century.

Yet in that period the comparative approach also points to great variations, even between similar groups of workers. It is clear that these cannot always be explained mainly in terms of economic factors, but raise such issues as the role of the state, something on which Geary placed great emphasis in his comparisons. Finally one should note that some historians have used strikes to conduct a very different kind of analysis from the kind I have been considering. There has been a rather more qualitative approach in order to explore the 'dispositions' and capacities for collective action amongst workers.[34] They can also be used to explore the history of a particular industry and its workers, being linked to many other issues rather than being singled out as a particular category for study.[35] Study of strikes can also be used to bring out *sectional* divisions amongst workers as much as solidarity.[36] Much of this qualitative work does not easily lend itself to comparison; at the very least one would have to break the subject down further, for example in to particular industries and occupations. Thus, it is not merely a question of selecting a subject for comparison, but also approaching that subject in a way which (a) allows comparable bodies of data to be built up for each case (descriptive task) and (b) enables some hypothesis to be advanced about the main trend or reasons for variations (explanation).

The same points can be made about trade unionism so there is no need to repeat this general argument with further examples from this field of study.

In both of these cases then it is often difficult, if not impossible, to obtain comparable bodies of data. There is therefore a trend towards a more qualitative rather than quantitative treatment of these matters, and a good deal of doubt has been cast upon the basic economic framework (stages and types of industrialisation; stages of traditional to modern collective labour action) within which data might be assembled and hypotheses advanced. For all these reasons there is little scope here for long-run comparative macroanalysis across national boundaries. Rather work has to focus on more specific types of comparisons which also involve bringing in qualitative aspects.

b) Sectoral comparisons

Within the subject matter I have just considered, namely strike activity and trade unionism it is possible to move to much more limited comparisons. Aggregate strike data at a national level might not in fact mean very much because it is a sum total of a very diverse range of industries. Clearly one could go on to look at strike activity or patterns of trade union formation in particular industries or occupations. Some work of this kind has been done and I will focus on a couple of examples of such work. I deliberately choose what seem to me to be good studies because any weaknesses in those studies would suggest problems with the entire approach.

The first example takes some studies by Rimlinger comparing patterns of labour protest of British and German miners.[37] Rimlinger engaged in a long-run study though the main focus was upon the period 1850–1914. He concluded that two different patterns emerged. In the British case lack of status traditionally made it easier for miners under more organised capitalist conditions to develop trade unions which insisted on independent bargaining rights and made demands, first for wages to be related to profits and later for a living wage. By comparison he argued that German miners had a traditional status which inhibited the development of independent organisation, that they continued to rely upon petitions and appeals, and even when unions were formed, they tended to rely upon external guidance, e.g. from the socialists or the catholics.

This is an important and in many ways persuasive account, but there are many problems with the comparative strategy Rimlinger adopts. Examining these can bring out the difficulties of making long-run comparisons, even of fairly specific subjects. First, Rimlinger is forced to deal with aggregate outcomes – the 'strike pattern' of the 'British' and the 'German' miner, even if sometimes this is qualified as being the 'dominant tendency'. Second, in order to carry through a long-run analysis he has radically to reduce and simplify the range of factors considered. For example, there is nothing on the internal work organisation of mining, on the levels of capital investment and average size of pits, on the rate of expansion of the labour force and the nature of labour recruitment. A long-run analysis finds it difficult to be sensitive to context and tends to provide an 'internalist' analysis in which such factors as 'tradition' and 'independence' are stressed.[38] Dispositions are read off from formal expressions of grievances – for example, petitioning is seen as expressive of a 'subordinate' mentality. One could, however, interpret that rather differently, and it is worth bearing in mind that the petitioning Rimlinger considers, that of Ruhr miners in 1889, was accompanied by the most extensive strike action yet undertaken, an action which made a major contribution to the downfall of Bismarck. One might well argue that the major obstacles in the way of independent organisation were not so much traditions of subordination, but rather the rapid rate of growth of an ethnically and religiously divided first-generation mining labour force confronting highly cartellised managements who practised a range of anti-union strategies. One could also note that another study, by Barrington Moore, saw in tradition a major resource for creating expectations of just treatment and stimulating collective action and organisation to enforce such expectations.[39]

To summarise, the problem with this type of long-run comparison of whole sectors is that it can create over-simple and contrasted outcomes which then lead on to an excessively internalist analysis considering a very restricted range of factors in order to identify those variables that would explain the different outcomes. To have a context-sensitive comparison one must take a much shorter timespan. There needs to be more attention paid to a pattern of comparative research to produce balanced comparative *descriptions* which bring out similarities as well as differences, rather than comparing two rather monolithic and questionable outcomes. Only then can one turn to look for variations which might help explain the firmly established differences in the pattern of strike or trade union activity.

A more recent and detailed comparative study of trade unions is that provided by Christiane Eisenberg.[40] It is impossible in short compass to summarise a complex argument based on research into primary sources on such matters as the organisation of urban tailoring in the late eighteenth and early nineteenth centuries,[41] and which employs sophisticated distinctions in order to understand different patterns of organisation. At this level – and I would stress that comparative *description* is itself a very demanding task which is too often short-circuited – Eisenberg's book works very well. But she also feels the need to relate this work to a major difference in outcome by the end of her chosen period (in this case the 1860s) and then to search for a key variable which might help us understand this difference of outcome. In her case the difference in outcome is the well-worn comparison between trade union sectionalism and non-independent labour politics in Britain and more general trade unionism tied more closely to the rapid emergence of independent labour politics in Germany. Eisenberg rather originally finds the key variable in the nature of workshop social organisation, arguing that wage-earners in Britain, in trades such as tailoring, developed a much more independent social network than their German counterparts. This is seen by Eisenberg as creating the basis for a vigorous craft unionism. The relative failure of German craftsmen to build up such social networks (partly due to the inibiting legacy of the guilds, partly to more rapid patterns of economic change) reduces the sectional organisation of craft trades and also the workplace based strength of such workers. As a consequence, political action and a stress on more general identities – industrial and class – can penetrate more deeply and earlier into the labour movement.

It is an ingenious and very well constructed argument but also suffers from some crucial weaknesses that in turn illustrate problems in comparative history. There is a jump from the descriptive material on trades such as tailoring to the treatment of outcomes a few decades later and in which craft unionism was more significant in other sectors. There is again a tendency to stress internal factors, though instead of a vacuous notion of tradition, we do at least have specific material on worker organisation in the workplace.

Partly the comparison between these two pieces of work registers a shift in the depth of research in more recent labour history and a new concern with workplace organisation rather than formal organisations and broad patterns of industrial relations. But the similar defects – above all in the search for a basic contrast and then the search for a crucial internal variable to explain that contrast – suggest endemic problems.

Rather than seeing comparison furnishing one with the key variable in an explanation, I think one should see it as compelling a re-examination of explanations offered by conventional single-case history. To begin with it is necessay to establish through disciplined comparative description that there really is, within a single general framework, some significant variation to explain. Then, rather than initially searching for a key variable, one should examine the kinds of explanations which are offered from within the conventional, single-case historical treatments. Only if this historiography is inadequate should one go further and bring in other possibilities.

I think this will almost inevitably involve reducing the timespan covered because single case histories are usually very sensitive to context and it is difficult to do justice to this aspect of historical accounts in long-run comparisons. I think there has to be a clear comparability in the subject matter and this probably cannot be through the rather dubious procedure of simply looking at what happens in comparable 'stages' (e.g of industrialisation or transition to political democracy). There are ways of getting round this, for example in Skocpol's work on revolution and ancien regimes, though typically that succeeds more because of a disciplined and innovative comparative methodology that built up comparable descriptions rather than because of a novel explanatory idea.

This will also mean trying to integrate qualitative with quantitative – e.g., one has to explore not merely strike statistics but also what it meant to strike and see if these are comparable between cases.

More specific cross-national comparisons

On this kind of basis I have tried myself to carry out comparative work. I can see weaknesses in that work but would defend the general approach. For example, in the essay 'Liberalism or social democracy', I try to establish that there *was* a significant difference of outcome in the trend in German and English labour politics between 1850 and 1875, although it must not be exaggerated. Comparability was important also in the sense that the *other alternative* was consciously posed in both cases rather than being posited just by the historian.

Having established a difference of outcome, I do not so much try to *explain* that difference as point to deficiencies in some of the arguments offered by the normal historiography. Only then do I move on to suggest which variations between the two cases should be stressed in understanding the differences in outcome. My conclusion is that the role of political action has been underplayed, above all the degree to which one could reasonably expect to bring about desired changes in coalition with others, and the significance of operating within a stable or a radically changing institutional framework. In the essay on the labour aristocracy I compare an historiograpical idea rather than a pattern of events. Again I devote a good deal of time to building up a comparative description of this idea. Only then do I move on to try to explain the differences that have then been established. I have tried to proceed in similar ways in the essays on liberalism, the law and artisans. I think these essays all share in certain general features. There is a similar concern with fairly specific focus in period and subject matter. The question or problem concerning that subject matter is put initially in general terms so that each case is treated even-handedly. There is an attempt to demonstrate that there really *are* variable conditions or outcomes of significance in the different cases, and there is a close scrutiny of the range of accounts which have been offered within normal historiography to explain those variations. Finally there are suggestions as to which appear to be the key variations.

There is a problem in that all of these essays involved aggregating from a range of material a single dominant national tendency which became the subject of comparison. The criticism could be made that this aggregate, this 'national' sum of many parts, is itself a fiction. Actually this criticism can be levelled at all comparisons, no matter how much more specific the focus is, since there is always empirically another level of detail to which one can move. If one compares a problem in two regions of the same country, it could be argued that each 'region' is itself an aggregation of smaller units. Nevertheless, I think there is a lot to be said for trying to move comparison from the national towards the regional or local because it can help one cut away from the constraints posed by national histori-ography. That is why I include in this collection an essay which compares liberalism in Hamburg and Manchester, seeing in this a useful complementary approach to that of the essay comparing liberalism on a national scale.

From cross-national to intra-national comparisons

What I have found happens with this narrower focus of comparison is that very soon any specifically 'labour history' subject disappears. This may partly be because I personally am less interested in studying a group called 'workers' and more interested in studying, within a fairly narrowly defined boundary such as that of a city, the different ways groups are defined and people act in relation to one another in a 'society'. But I think it is also because as one extends the range of matters which are systematically described, so one becomes aware that only under extraordinary conditions in the development of industrial–urban societies are there very stably defined working classes whose economic, social, political and cultural experiences all mutually reinforce one another both across any internal class divides and within a class boundary. What is more one also becomes aware of the importance of experiences which are relatively remote from the direct work situation or class position. Take for example the question of religion. We have some good suggestive comparative work on religion and labour between Britain and Germany by Hugh MacLeod,[42] good in part because he does not opt for 'single contrasted outcomes' but provides a more subtle, balanced picture, and also because he does not read off from an institutional, formal level (e.g. church attendances, the religious utterances of labour leaders) conclusions about class dispositions.

A particular interest of mine is in the relative weakness of a popular dissenting Protestant tradition within the German labour movement. That in turn was related to the varying strengths of popular liberalism in the two cases. Immediately I was falling into the two major traps I have mentioned. First, I was assuming rather than first establishing by detailed description that there was this contrast in outcome. That would require not merely more descriptive material but an attention to internal variations within each country. Second, I tended almost subconsciously to look to long-term 'internal' factors such as the cultural character of Protestantism and its relationship to the national working class, insofar as I wished to explain these differences.

The concern with the 'character' of Protestantism I now think was misplaced and underestimated short-run factors. I have tried to focus on two cities – Manchester and Hamburg, where evidence does suggest far less religiosity in the latter case amongst the labouring classes. However, one thing which I would now emphasise is the degree to which a popular dissenting tradition *was* in fact developing in the 1830s and 1840s in parts of Germany. This suggests some similarities with the pattern of development in some English regions. It also points to important connections across class boundaries. In this context what comes to seem very important is the failure of the revolution of 1848 in Germany. The counter-revolution identified dissenting religion as politically dangerous and repressed such movements. It was this short-run, 'contextual' variation between the English and German cases which is as important in explaining the lack of a cross-cutting dissenting tradition after 1848 in Germany as any long-run emphasis upon the nature of German Protestantism. With an approach like this one is inevitably moving away from a specifically labour focus to consider, for example, the way in which state action, permissive or repressive, can help or hinder cultural movements which in turn shape the extent to which people turn to class and secular values for a sense of identity.

However, comparison of this kind in turn raises the issue of the 'typicality' of the cities chosen. To defend against this criticism and also to complement this very specific cross-national comparison, one can take up comparisons within one national case which bring out internal variations. For example, the comparative work of A.D. Taylor on post-Chartist radicalism in Manchester and London, has established, amongst other differences, the relative unimportance of a dissenting Protestant tradition in popular movements in London compared to Manchester.[43] One should stress this is only one strand in a systematic comparative description which builds up a picture of a different kind of radicalism in the two cities. In Manchester one encounters a radicalism which feeds into popular liberalism and a rhetoric of class cooperation. In London, rather there is a more independent and explicit radicalism with stronger connections to the Chartist period and which is associated with a more independent working class politics. The value of comparisons of this sort is that the very systematic and detailed character of the descriptions already points compellingly to ways of understanding observed differences. It is not so much a case of isolating a separate set of 'explanations' as of providing a full description which in itself makes intelligible the variations in what it describes. The 'explanation' is simply a more extended part of the context in which certain patterns of activity are fitted. What is more, the similarity between London and what might be regarded as the dominant German tendency (secularism and independent radicalism) tends to reinforce some of the original comparative arguments. The next step should be to find some German areas in which a dissenting Protestantism did continue to be important amongst working class groups and then to see what were the political implications of this. Of course, there still will be a 'national' level to consider, not merely as an aggregate of local cases but also in its own right.[44]

These are other good examples of this kind of intra-national comparison exploring differences. Crew's comparison of different levels and patterns of collective action in the foundry and mining industries of Bochum provides a nice example of how a large variety of factors can be examined to help understand a clearly established difference of outcome.[45] Offermann has brought out interesting features of Prussian liberalism after 1850 by comparing the Rhenish and Berlin regions.[46]

Another type of interesting intra-national comparison involves pointing to *similar* outcomes in varying situations which suggest that variables which were automatically considered significant for shaping those outcomes now have to be looked at again. James Vernon has compared radical politics in a number of English towns with very different social and economic features.[47] He established, by means of systematic description, that similar kinds of political action and organisation nevertheless develop. This suggests that common factors are at work at the political level which shape politics irrespecitve of major social and economic differences. Vernon then went on to pay close attention to the way in which political language and tradition, seen at work in the symbolic activity of politics in such areas as timing and character of meetings and demonstrations, can give a similar political shape to varying social and economic concerns and also help create and sustain a common range of political values.

In both cases, whether the logic of comparison is from different outcomes to varying circumstances or from similar outcomes to similar circumstances, what first gives such comparison its value and persuasiveness is the build up of systematic descriptions which carry their own explanatory weight.

Conclusion

Macro-level comparison over a long run has been concerned with the making of a working class. To move beyond the very unsatisfactory models which just considered class as an economic or political category (broadly class in itself and class for itself), the class idea needed to be broken down into further levels. But this has created problems even for the study of individual countries because the sheer variety of connections between these variables cannot be contained within a single concept: that of the working class. Even when one turns to some more specific subjects such as the formation of an industrial labour force, it turns out that the lack of acceptance of any single model of development, along with the fact that any such broad process occurs at different times in different countries, means that it is difficult to establish a framework (be it the same chronological period or the same 'stage of development' within which comparison can be conducted.

Even when the subject matter is narrowed down to a more specific area, such as long-run patterns of strike activity in a particular industry, insuperable problems are encountered. The long-run perspective requires one to assume very simple and contrasted outcomes. Furthermore, the inability to be sensitive to changes of context tends to force the comparison towards a consideration of a few, internal factors to explain the contrast in outcomes. Unless there are powerful theories which can substitute for that context (e.g. an accepted 'stage' theory of industrialisation or the modernisation of patterns of protest), I doubt whether these kinds of comparisons will ever work.

At the other extreme, very detailed and individualised treatments of the kind which are becoming increasingly popular in labour history hardly lend themselves to the explicit use of general concepts which are a *sine qua non* for any proper comparative history.

This suggests the need to focus on medium-level work, operating over a few years, at most a couple of decades, concentrating on a specific issue such as a social group, a type of politics, a certain relationship, a historiographical idea, or an ideological current. The problem concerning this issue must be stated in general terms. One needs to employ a systematic method to build up a full comparative description of the various cases. It is also necessary to have some point to such a description, perhaps to try to assess the weight of one particular strand in producing particular outcomes. However, it is necessary to establish clearly through the descriptions that these *really* are the outcomes. Once that has been done persuasively, one will often find there is no need for a separate search for 'explanations' of those outcomes. The very full context which the descriptive account has furnished will itself carry an explanatory charge. Such accounts can then be used to look critically at the explanations offered by conventional, single-case history. One should employ the different strategies of comparisons at the national level and then more specific comparisons between and within national cases. These strategies will enable one to develop fresh ways of contextualising particular cases which can in turn provide 'normal' history with new and worthwhile questions. That, I would suggest, is the most important purpose that can be served by the practice of comparative history.

Notes

1 The introduction in Jacobs, 1986 brilliantly criticises much of modern economic theory for its acceptance of the unit of the 'national economy'.

2 B. Moore, 1969; Skocpol, 1979.

3 See also Grew (ed), 1978, which shows how a number of historians can collaborate to provide a basis for good comparison by being set a standard set of general questions and ways of approaching those questions.

4 I use the term deliberately. Being female of of Celtic origin would probably have made a good deal of difference to my attitudes towards history.

5 For survey of the idea of German uniqueness or *Sonderweg* see Grebing, 1986.

6 Blackbourn & Eley, 1984.

7 *Ibid.*

8 Anderson, 1964 and 1965; Nairn, 1964a, 1964b and 1964c.

9 Thompson, 1965.

10 Zolberg, 1986, p. 401.

11 Zolberg, 1986.

12 Salter & Stevenson, 1990.

13 I make some comparative comments on Britain and Germany in the post-1918 period in Breuilly, 1989a.

14 Thompson, 1963.

15 Jones, 1984a.

16 I develop these points a little more in Breuilly, 1989a.

17 I consider some of these problems in the essay on artisans.

18 I consider issues raised here further in the essay on liberalism and social democracy.

19 Katznelson & Zolberg, 1986.

20 Breuilly, 1987a. Whether they will continue to do so, now that Germany has been unified, especially so far as Marxist approaches are concerned, remains to be seen.

21 See Tenfelde, 1988; Jones, 1984b; the various contributions in Herzig & Trautmann (eds), 1989a in

the sections 'Sozialdemokratie, Gewerkschaften und sozio-politischer Wandel' and 'Ende der Arbeiterkultur?'; and Johnson, 1985.

22 I discuss these possibilities in more detail in the section of the essay on the labour aristocracy, considering the treatment of officials in labour institutions as labour aristocrats.

23 Joyce, 1991; Jones, 1984a; Sewell, 1980. There is not much to cite on the German side as yet. I have not had the chance to read Zerwas, 1988, which looks as if it might be of interest.

24 Kocka, 1983; and Kocka, 1990a and 1990b.

25 See the essay on artisans for further consideration of these issues.

26 Goodman & Honeyman, 1988; Wehler, 1987b.

27 Wehler, 1987b.

28 Much of this is implied in Gerschenkron, 1976, although this still retains the possibility of a 'stage' model, but with the nature of the stages varying according to the relationship of a particular case of industrialisation to other cases.

29 Geary, 1981 and 1986.

30 Perrot, 1987; Tilly & Shorter, 1974.

31 Kocka, 1983, especially pp. 154ff. See also Tenfelde & Volkmann (eds), 1981. I do not know of any work of synthesis for British strikes of this period.

32 In which case the shift to the language of class which Kocka, 1983 relates to the patterns of strike activity could be seen as a function of the scale of action rather than reflecting the emergence of a new collective identity. Of course, once a particular kind of terminology has been used effectively it can help generate a new sense of identity.

33 Feldman, 1981.

34 Machtan, 1983; and some of the studies in Tenfelde & Volkmann (eds), 1981.

35 For example, Burgess, 1975 where the 1851 lock-out is seen as a crucial event in the history of industrial relations in the British engineering industry. In some cases even the absence of strikes has been interestingly explored in order to demonstrate that this emphatically did *not* mean an absence of conflict and tension. Vetterli, 1978 and 1981.

36 Reid, 1980, who also extends this to trade unionism.

37 Rimlinger, 1959 and 1967.

38 It is interesting that Moore, 1978, taking a long-run view of German miners, also operates in this way.

39 Moore, 1978; Tenfelde, 1981; Hickey, 1985; Crew, 1979. For regions other than the Ruhr see Schofer, 1975 and Mallmann, 1981. The coalminers are the most intensively researched of all industrial occupations.

40 Eisenberg, 1986.

41 The archival research conducted for both cases makes this book a rarity in the field of comparative history.

42 McLeod, 1981, 1982, 1984 and 1986.

43 Taylor, forthcoming. Some of these ideas have been sketched out in Breuilly, Niedhart & Taylor (eds), forthcoming.

44 For example, repression in the Hamburg case was closely related to the pressure placed on the city-state by Prussia. The counter-revolution was a 'national' process which penetrated every region, albeit in differing ways.

45 Crew, 1979.

46 Offermann, 1988.

47 Vernon, 1991.

2

The labour aristocracy in Britain and Germany: a comparison

The concept of an aristocracy of labour has been central to the way in which historians have interpreted the nineteenth century British labour movement. It has been less important and rather differently employed by German labour historians. The contrast has as much to do with the different aims and methods of British and German historians as it has with the different pasts they study. Systematic comparison can show how much a concept comes to play a central role in historical writing. It can also show how the interactions between historians, their present concerns and the materials with which they work, bring about changes in the way an historical concept is used and how it can come to be marginalised or even discarded.

The idea of a labour aristocracy up to 1945

Survey

In the period 1850–1914 contemporaries had often noted differences within the growing class of manual wage labourers in the manufacturing sector of the economy.[1] One difference that was frequently noted was that between those in relatively skilled, secure and well-paid occupations and all other workers. This difference was sometimes associated with a rather aloof or 'aristocratic' attitude on the part of such better-placed workers towards other workers. Coach-makers, millwrights, book-printers, and workers in luxury trades such as jewellery, bespoke tailoring and shoemaking, fancy foods, watchmaking and engraving were the sorts of workers mentioned in this way.[2] Sometimes the occupations were quite traditional, sometimes, as in engineering and printing, they could be associated with technological and organisational innovation. Particular groups of workers often had their own reasons for drawing attention to these distinctions. Guild journeymen would deplore the work of non-guild and 'improperly' trained workers when asking governments to enforce or restore guild privileges.[3] German guild vocabulary contains a choice selection of terms of abuse for 'botchers' (Pfuscher) and 'cowboys' (Bonhasen).[4] In England defence of proper apprenticeship accompanied such attitudes. In these cases it was the importance of skill which was emphasised. However, such apparently objective differences were in turn related to moral evaluations about sobriety, education, family-life, reliability and much else. The skilled man was the respectable man.

Generally speaking, however, the observation was a fairly casual one. Even where one finds it used in a more systematic analysis of the working classes, it figures as just one difference amongst many, and by no means the most important one. Thomas Wright, for example, who wrote three important studies between 1867 and 1873 under the *nom de plume* of 'A Journeyman Engineer' distinguished between occupational groupings but also recognised that the important difference between those who drank and those who did not (at least not excessively) could cut across such occupational distinctions.[5] Henry Mayhew often used such behavioural categories rather than sociological ones to differentiate between workers, although he also identified occupations as the basis of virtually separate communities.[6] Furthermore, the distinction between the skilled and the others was rarely used to explain different political reactions. Even Marx and Engels, in 1848 and 1850, did not seek to explain the political failure of the working class in terms of such differences but rather in the simple and general terms of economic recovery.[7]

By 1850 the problem of how the working classes would act politically was beginning to concern those higher up the social scale. This involved also thinking about how working men should be treated by society and by governments and how they might respond. Once people began to accept that one could not continue with a simple exclusion of all workers from the political system then it became necessary to look more closely at workers and the differences amongst them. By the 1860s the question came to be discussed in terms of political participation. The central issues were how far to extend the scope of parliamentary government and how extensive should be the right to vote or stand in election to parliament. In both Germany and Britain political organisations of workers, sometimes in association with other social groups, pressed for political reforms along these lines. In Germany the *Allgemeine Deutsche Arbeiter Verein* (ADAV) and the *Verband der deutschen Arbeitervereine* (VDAV), both established in 1863, pressed for universal manhood suffrage. Some liberals supported them.[8] In Britain the Reform League, set up in 1865, aimed '. . . to procure the extension of the elective franchise to every resident and registered adult male person of sound mind and unconvicted of crime'.[9] The leaders of the League worked closely with liberals.[10] Whereas 'respectable' opinion had considered such demands to be out of the question when put by Chartists between 1838 and 1848 (and even during the 1850s) or by radicals during the revolutions of 1848, there was now a greater preparedness to contemplate at least moves in this direction in the 1860s. There are many reasons for this change of mood which cannot be considered here. However, one reason was to do with a new perception of workers as forming a complex and differentiated group, rather than a simple and dangerous mass.

This became clear in the debates in Britain on the franchise question between 1865 and the passing of the Second Reform Act in 1867.[11] The question was which, if any, groups of workers were fit to be trusted with the right to vote? It was this debate which crystallised the first version of the labour aristocracy idea.[12] The argument in favour of enfranchising a special group of 'respectable' workers was two-pronged. Positively, one could expect that these workers would use their votes 'sensibly'. This could strengthen support for the existing political system as well as benefit whichever party could best appeal to these new voters.[13] Negatively, the effect of such a concession would be to prevent this group of workers taking up a hostile position to the established political system and possibly leading a more general working-class opposition. This idea of labour aristocrats as potential leaders of a radical working-class movement who are instead incorporated into the established system so that this potential radicalism is undermined is an argument frequently associated with the concept of the labour aristocracy.

The debate took a rather different form in Germany. Here the working class was a much smaller proportion of the population, parliaments had less powers than in Britain, and much attention was focused on the question of establishing a national state. In these circumstances attention was devoted to such issues as rivalry between Austria and Prussia, the balance between unitary and federal elements within a national state, and the powers to be granted to the various institutions of that national state. In this situation the particular question of enfranchising workers appeared even to many sympathetic liberal nationalists as one of minor importance. Furthermore, when the question of an extensive franchise was raised, the crucial matter to consider was how the lower-class majority living in the countryside would behave. This helps explain why many liberals and workers active in the democratic and nationalist movement were anxious about too rapid a move to universal manhood suffrage and also why a bold conservative like Bismarck was prepared to make such a move.[14] For these reasons the issue was not how workers would act if they had the vote, but rather how the peasants and agricultural workers would act.[15]

In the event, franchise reform proceeded in very different ways in Britain and Germany. This had the effect of increasing the preoccupation with differences within the working class in Britain but ensuring this remained a marginal issue in Germany. The Reform Act of 1867 increased the electorate by about 80% and more than doubled the urban electorate. In this new situation the two major parties were able to alter their organisations, policies, and styles in such a way as to be able to attach most of the enlarged electorate to themselves and to prevent any new party emerging.[16] The Liberal Party generally did better in competition for urban workingmen's votes, though precise measurement is difficult and one should not exaggerate liberal superiority.[17] The Liberal Party obtained the cooperation of the Reform League in the General Election campaign of 1868 which led to the return of a Liberal Government.[18] The contribution of this to the development of a 'Lib–Lab' politics is considered in the essay 'Liberalism or social democracy?'.

The election seemed to confirm the arguments of those who had favoured giving 'respectable' workers the vote. Taken together with such images as that of respectable trade union testimony to the Royal Commission on Trade Unions in 1867–69, on the expansion of savings institutions supported by better-off workers, and in improvements in the education, housing and recreations of these workers – this appeared to demonstrate that one element in the stability of the mid-Victorian period was the integration of the labour aristocracy into the values and material advances of liberal capitalism.[19] The argument even convinced observers like Engels who deplored what was happening. He saw workers as having been corrupted by prosperity and bought off by limited reforms. This corruption and bribery applied especially to those skilled workers able to organise in unions and to protect their own sectional interests. Engels' analysis is often unclear or inconsistent. Sometimes he asserts that it was working-class leaders who were bought off, as in his judgement of the Reform League leaders in the 1868 General Election. Sometimes he stresses the simple effect of prosperity rather than any distinct process of ideological or political manipulation. Sometimes it is the pliability of the working class as a whole which matters rather than that of a particular section. Nevertheless, many of the themes attached to the concept of a labour aristocracy were sketched out by Engels, such as divisions within the working class, the role of British imperialism in creating prosperity and inducing nationalist sentiments amongst workers, a reformist accommmodation between an upper section of the working class and their social superiors and apostasy of labour leaders.[20]

In 1867 Bismarck had granted the vote to all males over twenty-five for elections to the parliament (Reichstag) of the North German Confederation. This right was extended to the lower house – the Reichstag – of the imperial parliament established in 1871. The importance of this measure as a step towards parliamentary democracy has to be qualifed when one notes the small, rather negative role accorded to the Reichstag at the imperial level, the many important powers retained by state governments, and the weighted or restricted franchises retained for many state parliaments (most notably the Prussian lower house – the Landtag – with its notorious three-class system) as well as local insitutions such as city councils. However, one consequence of these reforms was the emergence of an independent socialist political movement hostile to both conservative and liberal parties and which claimed to speak for the whole working class even if its electoral support initially was limited.[21] As the working class grew in size and as the working-class vote grew even faster, so this movement, formed into a single party by 1875, became the major beneficiary of those votes. In such a situation the concept of a labour aristocracy which concentrated upon divisions within the working-class and the alliance between labour aristocrats and their social superiors had little relevance. Independent and apparently united working class political behaviour (leaving aside the quite different distinctions between Catholic and non-Catholic workers as well as that between German-speakers and those who spoke other languages) could be regarded as one manifestation of a working class whose separation from other classes was of far greater importance than any internal divisions.

This contrast between Britain and Germany continued up to about 1900, underpinned by the dominance of Lib–Lab politics in Britain and the growth of mass working-class support for the socialist party in Germany. It was as some convergence took place between the two countries in the last decades of the nineteenth century that a rather different version of the labour aristocracy could be elaborated. In Britain the expansion of unions including less skilled workers and the events leading to the setting up of a Labour Party with at least some socialist tinges signalled the end of Lib–Lab politics, both in practical and ideological terms. This in turn could lead to a reduced interest in the idea of the labour aristocracy or the idea that it had ceased to have the importance it had previously possessed. In Germany the similar growth of trade unions and pressures within the SPD to overcome its isolation from society and government also meant that mass, organised working-class activity and the need to balance concerns with opposition and socialist transformation with those of achieving reforms became the central issues.

Furthermore, the growth of such organisations was associated with new problems. Larger memberships, the work of publicity, the running of welfare and advisory services, the party machinery for election campaigns, the proper support of parliamentary and other representatives, the preparation and management of large-scale negotiation with employers or government agencies – all this required larger numbers of functionaries such as journalists, secretaries, legal and financial experts, researchers, and administrators. It also called for more elaborate and bureaucratic organisation.[22]

It was only to be expected that conflicts and tensions would arise within these organisations. In the SPD there were disagreements over the basic policies of the party and some have argued that these intensified to the point of near-schism by 1914.[23] There was also increased pressure from the major Free Trade unions upon the SPD over such issues as political strikes, as well as disputes within those unions about questions such as strike policy.[24] In Britain there were arguments between the socialists of the Independent Labour Party (ILP) and more pragmatic trade unions leaders as to the direction the Labour Party should take.[25] There were also disputes between trade union officials and members about the calling and conduct of strikes.[26]

Radicals opposed to what they perceived as reformist or accommodating tendencies could identify the more powerful trade union organisations as well as the increasingly bureaucratised leadership of the SPD as a new kind of labour aristocracy. There had now developed a new division between the permanent officials at the centre of these labour organisations and the ordinary members. Organisation came to be seen as a force which could develop its own goals and impose them upon its members. In 1902 Lenin elaborated this notion in terms of the revolutionary party which has the mission of injecting true socialist consciousness into the working class and leading it in a revolutionary direction.[27] However, the labour aristocracy variant worked in the opposite direction, with the organisation eliminating the class-conscious and revolutionary tendencies within the membership. Robert Michels argued that large labour organisations produced conservative bureaucratic elites whose major concern was the maintenance of their organisations rather than the achievement of the original purposes of those organisations.[28] On the other side attention was drawn to unofficial strikes, support for syndicalism, and 'spontaneous' action as evidence of the resistance of the ordinary members to the policies of labour officialdom.[29] Thus a concept of the labour aristocracy as an oligarchy came to take on some significance.

These arguments tended to have a greater appeal in Germany than Britain. In Germany organisation was larger and more bureaucratic, it had developed more dramatically, and it stood in much sharper contrast to the radical traditions of the socialist movement. As a consequence there was a much clearer discrepancy between the traditional ideals of the movement and the policies which officials were now seeking to pursue. These arguments reached their peak with the outbreak of war and the decision of the SPD and FTU leaders to support the German war effort. Again, the less committed position of leading activists of the British labour movement made it less urgent to find an explanation for such apostasy. Lenin, who was deeply shaken by the news of what the SPD had done, argued that there had developed a deep divide between the party leadership and the working class as a whole. He generalised the idea to include many other labour parties which had behaved in a similar way. However, like Engels, Lenin used different ideas in an eclectic fashion. Sometimes the responsibility was attributed to an organisational elite, sometimes to a privileged section of the working class, and sometimes even to a whole national working class bribed by the profits of imperialism. These kinds of arguments were continued after 1918 with communist criticisms of social democracy in western Europe.[30] Later the critiques were institutionalised and coordinated through the Communist International, taking on particularly crass forms with the development of the notion of 'social fascism'.[31]

Within Comintern the Soviet Union increasingly turned historical interpretation and ideological debate into instruments of official policy. There is no need to dwell on this phase of intellectual bankruptcy.[32] Some critics did, however, see in the rise of a Stalinist bureaucratic state further proof of the capacity of organisations to master the class on which they were supposedly based and to develop and pursue their own interests.[33] On the other hand, those close to western European social democracy had little inclination to take the critical approach implied by the idea of a labour aristocracy towards the 'pioneers' of the early trade unions and reformist labour parties. The pioneers would only be seen as aristocratic in the sense of being the vanguard of a broader movement rather than a section divided from the rest of the working class. Labour history tended to take on a 'celebratory' character, focusing on the pioneer personalities and institutions and usually written by activists in the contemporary movement.

There were some intellectual developments in the inter-war period which could influence the idea of a labour aristocracy. These centred above all on the work of Gramsci, as well as other Marxists, who were concerned to give much more weight to the role of ideology and culture in persuading workers to accept capitalism, rather than explaining this solely in terms of prosperity or simple manipulation.[34] However, this work remained largely unknown until after 1945. In any case, it was as likely to stress the impact of ideological and cultural incorporation and containment upon the whole working class as to focus on the particular role of a labour aristocracy.

Comments

The idea of a labour aristocracy had a particular appeal to those trying to explain certain patterns of working-class political behaviour. It tended to be adopted by those who were critical of the failure of the working class to display independent and/or sufficiently radical and class-conscious political action. It could, however, also be employed by those arguing for a gradual integration of workers into the status quo, beginning with those respectable workers who were ready to use political rights sensibly.

For these reasons the idea was particularly well developed in Britain in the decades after 1850. For liberals facing what still seemed to them a largely uncivilised class, an alliance with respectable workers pointed to divisions within that class. For radicals, critical of that very alliance and the price workers paid for it, a similar division was indicated although given a different evaluation. For socialists, although in the period 1850–80 these were far less important than those standing in the Chartist–radical tradition, the failure of workers to turn to their creed could also be accounted for in terms of the influence of better-off workers. Given that in Germany politics took the form which such socialists and many radicals approved of and which liberals and conservatives deplored, there was no point in using an idea which explained the lack of class unity. From about 1900, however, as disputes arose over the policies of independent and well-organised labour parties and unions, radical critics now began to focus again on divisions within the working class, though now as much in relation to those organisations as to occupational distinctions.

It should be emphasised that these ideas were rather poorly worked out. They were more the stuff of polemic than of serious historical investigation. Engels and Lenin, for example, took the idea up at one point and dropped it at another, and presented the notion of divisions within the working class in varied and often contradictory ways. Lenin's idea, for example, that workers are naturally immured in trade union consciousness until exposed to revolutionary leadership would seem to render redundant any explanation of reformism in terms of the manipulations of trade union officials. Those officials would rather simply be expressing the 'natural' working-class position. (They might, of course, be particularly adept at preventing radicals from exercising influence over workers, and in that sense have a more active counter-revolutionary function. It was that sense of frustration which perhaps really explains why radicals so vehemently attacked the principle of organisation.) Again, if as was sometimes suggested by Engels, Lenin and Bukharin, a whole national working class was corrupted by the profits of imperialism, it would appear superfluous also to explain that corruption in terms of the work of a section of the working class.

Apart from fluctuating, inconsistent and contradictory uses of the idea of a labour aristocracy, there were also no clear views, even less agreement, on the reasons for the formation of a labour aristocracy. One can think of a wide range of possible explanations such as technological changes, the nature of the division of labour, social engineering, divisive political reform, different bargaining strengths, and organisational capacities. There was also little clarity on how to provide a definition of the labour aristocracy which could guide and be tested by empirical investigations, for example, by making skill, earnings, life style, organisation or some other characteristic the defining feature of a labour aristocracy. It was unclear what was the relationship of a labour aristocracy to other sections of the working class – aloof and exclusive or actively leading, possessing influence indirectly as a model or directly as an elite. Nor was the relationship to other classes clear – imitating middle-class values, seeking entrance into the middle classes as individuals, or developing a collective ethos even if this was one of accommodation with social superiors.

The scholarly history of the labour movement before 1945 tended to be written by those active in labour parties, unions and cooperatives. It usually took on an institutional or biographical character and rarely sought to place that history within an empirically supported sociological analysis of the working class as a whole. However, only in that way could the idea of a labour aristocracy really be employed and tested.[35] On the other hand, broader investigations by historians detached from the labour movement tended to focus on such issues as recruitment and adaptation to industrial life[36] or the nature of poverty.[37] In such cases it was the nature of industrial society or the standard of living rather than the sociology of the working class which was the focus of attention. Only in the organisational sociology developed by Weber and applied by Michels to the SPD does one find a version of the labour aristocracy concept being employed in an empirical investigation.[38]

It was only after 1945 when social and economic history sought to investigate broad social groups rather than institutions and individuals, that more attention came to be paid to ideas which stressed attitudes, life-styles, and divisions within the workplace and the community. When historians in turn sought to relate such investigations to the politics of the labour movement, then the idea of the labour aristocracy came to play a central role in properly researched labour history.

The labour aristocracy in historical writing since 1945

Introductory comments

The interests of historians since 1945 in the use of the idea of a labour aristocracy have generally paralleled those of contemporaries. The idea of a new and distinctive social grouping in mid-Victorian Britain – an aristocracy of labour – has been one major concern. There is no real parallel in German labour history covering the same period. Conversely, much of British labour history in the late nineteenth century up to 1914 and beyond has been linked to the 'decline' of the labour aristocracy. In a way there has been a German parallel here because writing on such subjects as the rise of a mass labour movement or of an *andere Arbeiterbewegung* certainly implies the prior existence of something like an aristocracy of labour. Finally it has been in German labour history that the idea of a 'labour oligarchy' has had the most importance for the 1900–14 period, although there are faint British parallels.

There are two very different ways in which one can analyse this historiography. One is historical, that is considering the changing emphases in historical writing and the differences also according to whether it is the period c.1850–80 or 1880–1914 that is under consideration. That is a more appropriate treatment for a review article and I would refer the interested reader to an essay of mine which proceeds in this manner.[39] The other treatment is conceptual, considering different forms that the concept of the labour aristocracy has taken, irrespective of the period treated or the precise time at which the historian in question was writing. That is the approach that is adopted here. First I will distinguish between two purposes which labour aristocracy concepts serve and then three distinct forms in which those concepts can be framed.

Purposes of the labour aristocracy concept

a) Political

The brief review of pre-1945 use of the idea has made clear that the major attraction of the idea of an aristocracy of labour was to explain certain patterns of working-class politics. For British labour historians it was not merely that the period 1850–80 was dominated by Lib–Lab politics, but that the periods before and after appeared in such marked contrast. The 1830s and 1840s had been a period of tension, with agitations against poor law reform, factory and trade union reform and culminating in the mass movement for the People's Charter, a radical demo-cratic programme. The period afterwards was marked by the formation of general trade unions including a high proportion of less skilled workers, the break-up of the Liberal Party, and the re-emergence of political organisations claiming to speak independently for the interests of labour. By contrast the intervening period appeared as an 'age of equipoise'.[40]

Between the second and third quarters of the nineteenth century, the co-operative move-ment did pass from community-building to shopkeeping; the Trade Unions did become less like 'schools of war' and more like the workman's equivalent to the public school; the importance of political activity did decline as compared with that attached to promoting social and industrial movements and, as this happened, so did the vigorous insistence upon an independent class basis for such activity diminish; working-class politics became less of a 'knife and fork' and more of a 'collar and tie' question.[41]

In the change that took place repression or other dramatic political change appeared to be of litle importance. Historians, therefore, were inclined to seek 'deeper' explanations in social, economic, and ideological terms. The emergence of more powerful trade unions of skilled workers and the ways in which references to 'respectable working men' were used to justify political reform suggested that it was social and economic changes within the working class that were of central impor-tance. The danger for historians is that they might take over contemporary references to 'respectable' workers – labour aristocrats – without a full understand-ing of the *different* political purposes such references might serve. On occasions the reference was prescriptive, that is it constructed a model of how it was thought workers should conduct themselves. Sometimes the reference was an expression of hope. Sometimes it was a justification. For instance providing certain workers with the vote or providing trade unions with certain legal rights was justified on the basis of the responsible way in which it was thought such rights would be exercised. Sometimes the point was one of advocacy, that is when working men or those speaking on their behalf argued that they should be granted certain rights *because* they were respectable. The problem with all these references is that what looks like a statement about social reality is rather a political claim. The same point applies to the polemic surrounding the actions of large trade unions and labour parties in the decade or so up to 1914. It is, of course perfectly legitimate to seek sociological explanations for political behaviour, but one should be clear that this *is* the purpose of certain lines of social historical inquiry and that the explanation must work *from* the social to the *political* rather than deducing social reality from political behaviour (and then, by sleight of hand, reversing the relationship in the form of an explanation).

Use of the labour aristocracy concept for this political purpose involves two steps: the identification of a particular stratum of workers as a labour aristocracy and the connection of the interests and actions of this stratum of workers to a certain type of politics. In many cases where the concept is used for this political purpose, the underlying assumption appears to be that politics in an industrial and capitalist society revolves around class identities, interests and conflicts. Any tendency away from this 'natural' state of affairs and towards political allegiances that cut across or through classes, therefore, needs to be explained in terms of some particular factor that inhibits or suppresses the politics of class. The aristocracy of labour can be seen as such a factor. It can be seen to prevent the development of working-class political organisations or, where such organisations do take shape, the pursuit of independent working-class policies. Clearly one could explain matters such as working-class liberalism or labour party nationalism in other ways. One could abandon the assumption that class is the natural basis of politics. One could be more flexible about what might be regarded as working-class interests. One could see accommodation taking place between classes generally rather than highlighting the role of a particular section of the working class. But all these options can create problems for those who wish to retain class and class conflict at the centre of their attention. It is for this reason that the political purpose of the labour aristocracy concept has had a particular appeal within Marxist historical writing. However, one should note that the concept has also been taken up by non-Marxist historians and that there are Marxist historians who seek to explain these patterns of labour politics without resorting to the labour aristocracy concept.[42]

b) The sociological purpose

Any sociology of the working class must draw attention to differences within that class and the ways in which those differences change over time. One also needs to consider the relationship of different elements within the working class both to one another and to other classes. There are a variety of differences based on criteria such as gender, skill, earnings, occupation, organisation, regional or social origin, ethnicity, and religion. One possible distinction (which may involve some of the criteria listed) is that between a minority of labour aristocrats and the rest of the working class. A sociological analysis should first identify those characteristics which mark off such a minority and should then go on to see whether this group displays distinctive attitudes and patterns of behaviour which would justify particular attention.

Clearly there are close connections between the two purposes of the labour aristocracy concept. The political explanation can only be sustained if one can independently establish the existence of a minority of workers who are the bearers of the distinct type of political behaviour to be explained. However, the political explanation would also need to go further than such a sociological account in order to explain the influence of that minority beyond their own ranks. The sociological account can only be justified if it can show that the labour aristocracy does exist as a group which behaves in a distinctive way and attention to political behaviour might be an important part of making such a case. However, the concept might be useful if it could help account for aspects of labour conduct other than political behaviour, for example attitudes towards work, or family, or leisure. So although the two purposes overlap, they remain distinct.

Definitions and uses

a) Introductory comments

Beier has usefully distinguished between three kinds of labour elite: *Leistungselite*, *Funktionselite*, *Wertelite*.[43] The idea can be adapted to draw attention to three different contexts in which one can focus attention in distinguishing between labour aristocrats and other workers. The first context is that of work; the second, that of the community; the third, that of labour organisations. Particular applications of the labour aristocracy concept often shift from one context to another, or try to connect the contexts to one another, but usually one of these contexts is the focus of attention.

b) Leistungselite: the labour aristocracy in the context of work

There are in turn two aspects of work on which one can focus: on the worker in the production process or on the worker as income earner.

(i) The worker as income earner The first important attempt to put the concept of the labour aristocracy on a firm basis by defining it clearly and then providing evidence for its existence and importance was made by Hobsbawm.[44] In his essay 'The labour aristocracy in nineteenth century Britain' Hobsbawm focused above all on the earnings of labour aristocrats relative to other workers. This is how he defined a labour aristocracy

First, the level and regularity of a worker's earnings; *second*, his prospects of social security; *third*, his conditions of work, including the way he was treated by foremen and masters; *fourth*, his relations with the social strata above and below him; *fifth*, his general conditions of living; *lastly*, his prospects of future advancement and those of his children. (273)

Hobsbawm's principal concern in this essay was to establish empirically the existence of a labour aristocracy. In attempting to do this he came to focus largely upon the first of his criteria, that of earnings, and even here tended to concentrate upon level rather than regularity. This was the most manageable indicator because it allowed one to establish the degree of wage differentials and to place workers from different regions and occupations into income groups. In considering the data on wages (data which improves greatly in both reliability and informativeness from the 1890s for both Britain and Germany) Hobsbawm argued that there *was* a labour aristocracy, consisting of some 10–20 per cent of the labour force, which could earn some two to three times more than general labourers. He argued that this group became relatively better established in the period from the 1870s to the 1890s, and that its position was secured in periods of reasonable prosperity, reduced economic fluctuation, and low or falling prices. The 'classical age' for this group was the 1840s to the 1890s. Preceding that had been the period of the industrial revolution which saw '. . . the birth of the modern working class' and succeeding it '. . . we enter the age of imperialism and monopoly capitalism, and technically speaking, of the development of mass production, and the great expansion of secondary and tertiary industries'.[45]

Hobsbawm clearly recognised the complexities of this 'classical age'. There were marked shifts of importance between declining and growing industries, but Hobsbawm argued that the continuing importance of cotton and the growing metal industries ensured that labour aristocrats continued to be an important element in the labour force, and that new labour aristocrats could replace those who disappeared with the decline of craft-based industries. Hobsbawm also recognised that there were intermediate labour groups between aristocrats and unskilled labourers. Hobsbawm also added some important contextual points which would make it difficult to extend his arguments beyond Britain. He saw in the new trade unions, in links with the lower middle class, and in the predominance of the industrial working class within the lower social strata (unlike most of continental Europe where a large agricultural population prevented a secure and stable differentiation within the working class) features which were unique to Britain in allowing an important labour aristocracy to take shape. Finally, although Hobsbawm's work was clearly motivated by the concern to explain the temporary eclipse of an independent labour movement, he did not seek explicitly to link the formation of this labour aristocracy to particular patterns of political behaviour.

There have been many comments and criticisms of Hobsbawm's work and he has responded to some of these.[46] To return to points made earlier one can see in principle two areas in which a critique can be made. The first concerns the definition of the labour aristocracy and the proof within the terms of this definition that such a group exists. The second concerns the worth of this concept in explaining certain actions and attitudes.

In his more recent defences Hobsbawm does not seem to want to go beyond the first area.His main justifications are that contemporaries constantly refer to this stratum of workers and one cannot simply disregard this testimony; that data on wages supports the point; and that income is the most important criteria for differentiation amongst workers because it is this which permits other differences to develop. Without extra income it is impossible to have a decent home and furniture, to buy books, to keep a wife at home as a non-earner. Criticisms of Hobsbawm and those who have followed him which argue in relation to the political behaviour of labour aristocrats are, in this regard, beside the point because Hobsbawm accepts that such workers could be active in radical and socialist movements and indeed frequently played a leading role in those movements.[47] I am not sure that Hobsbawm would wish to argue that income differentials within the working class have *no* bearing upon political behaviour, but that does seem to be the position towards which his defence of his labour aristocracy concept is taking him.

If we briefly turn to the principal case, that of wage differentials, there have been a number of criticisms. Some historians have criticised the reliability of the sources used by Hobsbawm.[48] Others have argued that, even if this wages data is reliable, a snap-shot of the full-time earnings of adult males is not a very good indicator of relative livingstandards among workers. Such data fails to take account of industry-specific patterns of unemployment. Certain occupations with high levels of earnings suffered from high accident or illness rates or required physical strength which only a young adult male could furnish.[49] Other occupations such as building, tailoring and shoemaking suffered from seasonal fluctuations.[50] In some of these occupations there was also a good deal of sweated or casual employment. Mayhew reckoned for mid-century London that in many skilled trades only about one-third of the workers were fully employed at any one time, while another third were only partially employed, and the final third had no employment within the trade.[51] Regional differences of earnings within particular occupations were often greater than the differences between occupations.[52] A different line of criticism is that one should consider household rather than head of household earnings and expenditure. Schomerus has studied the importance of differences in household expenditure for groups with different average ages of marriage and numbers and timing of children. She has related this to the 'career' pattern of earnings for particular occupations to produce the powerful but simple concept of a *Lebensverdienstkurve* (life time earnings curve) which reveals differences in the standard of living between workers, at variance with those indicated by a snapshot of adult male earnings.[53] Even then this data tends to qualify the import of such earnings. However, also of importance are opportunities for supplementary earnings. In textile regions women and children had more chance to earn for the household than they did in engineering or coal-mining districts. Women's work was notoriously understated in contemporary surveys and statistics.[54] In some mining areas an important supplementary income could be earned from the land, again using family labour.[55]

I am not sure, however, that these important criticisms really undermine Hobsbawm's case once it is limited to the claim that there *is* a group of workers who are generally better-off than all other workers. Many of the points would seem actually to reinforce the argument – the more aristocratic trades or sectors within a trade tended to enjoy the best conditions and employment patterns; part of the life-style of the labour aristocrat was the ability to maintain a non-earning wife. In some cases the points seem designed to muddy the waters rather than present a clear critique. However, they do raise questions which Hobsbawm recognises are important about the size, composition and significance of the labour aristocracy.

Obviously to argue that this group was only 5 per cent or as much as 40 per cent of the working class is to present a case very different from that which sets it as 10–15 per cent.

Nor is there much force in the case that *all* workers in Victorian Britain lived a life of uncertainty, that no-one could take economic security for granted, and that even the group of better-off workers was constantly changing as individual members fell upon hard times. As Hobsbawm has subsequently argued, precisely such change and uncertainty could increase the preoccupation with restrictive unionism and a sense of exclusiveness.[56] However, there is a danger of retreating to dependence on such exclusive unionism as the prime evidence for the existence of a labour aristocracy rather than using earnings data.

Far more important criticisms concern the merits of a labour aristocracy/others distinction, focusing on a particular period, and seeing the labour aristocracy as peculiarly British. It is these arguments that implicitly smuggle back in a political purpose.

Pelling, amongst others, has argued that Hobsbawm paid insufficient attention to that large section of the working class between labour aristocrats and unskilled general labourers, and that if one takes this into account, then the working class will come to be seen in terms of a continuum of earnings groups.[57] This can then be linked to arguments that the strategy of exclusion can be found below the level of the so-called labour aristocracy. What then develops is an argument for endemic sectionalism within the working-class. The presumption now is one of disunity and the real puzzle is how any moves to working class unity can take place. This reverses the logic of the labour aristocracy arguments.[58] The comparative point becomes significant here. Once one has severely criticised the actual size of the 'labour aristocracy' group, then the more mundane point that some workers earn more than others would seem to apply also to Germany.[59] This criticism would also put into question the argument that there is something special about the period *c*.1840 to 1880 in Britain. Musson has stressed the continuity of high-earning, 'aristocratic' trades both before and after this period in Britain.[60]

Increasingly it appears that, insofar as the argument has any political purpose, attention needs to shift from data on income which is not as conclusive as Hobsbawm has argued, to concern with how workers organised. Above all, the apparent dominance of exclusive craft unionism within the British labour movement in this period would seem to require further attention. It is perhaps no accident that the work which most explicitly applied Hobsbawm's ideas to a particular case was Turner's study of cotton industry trade unions.[61] But one cannot simply identify such trade unionism with a distinct higher income stratum within the working class. It is necessary to go on to look at the position such workers occupied within the workplace.

(ii) The worker in the workplace The recent interest in this aspect of labour history

has been stimulated by industrial sociology which has drawn attention to the differences amongst workers induced by complex divisions of labour, different kinds of work, and different methods of management.[62] The study by Braverman had an especial influence, arguing that under the conditions of monopoly capitalism the labour force was stripped of skill and of control over work.[63] Much of the subsequent research has tended to argue against this position whilst stressing the central importance of a 'struggle for control' between employers and workers.

The idea of control can begin with the image of the skilled craftsman under pre-industrial conditions.[64] This craftsman possesses a wide range of skills acquired over a number of years, both through formal training and job experience. He may well own the tools with which he works. He, often collectively with other craftsmen, may have a good deal to say about the methods of recruiting and training new workers. His range of skills may mean that there is no complex division of labour *between* workers but rather that the same worker carries out a great variety of processes. This will tend to make it difficult for the employer to set very clear task definitions and will give to the craftsman a great deal of discretion about how he achieves the goals set by the employer. Such a craftsman may well be the principal authority over younger or less qualified workers, including making payments to them and even hiring and firing. In such a situation the employer can appear as little more than the supplier of materials, funds, and orders for goods, likely to have more authority as a co-worker (as with a master in his own workshop). In the terminology that has come to be used – such an employer only possesses 'formal' control of the labour process by virtue of the wage-relationship, but does not have 'real' control. The development of industrial capitalism, it has been argued, shifts real as well as formal control increasingly towards the employer, or his agents such as foreman and managers.[65]

This can happen in a number of ways. The introduction of machinery and more complex divisions of labour can lead to the narrowing and even the destruction of skills. This makes it more difficult for workers to control training and recruitment. The concentration of production into larger units can lead to the formation of a special class of supervisory workers and a much closer control over work tasks. The more explicit and tighter definition of the wage relationship can lead to the employer taking much more firmly into his hands control of hiring and firing.[66]

Few would argue that industrialisation destroys the 'all-round' skill of the craftsman as an important and differentiating feature of labour, but there is some force to the argument that hallmarks of this development are skill specialisation, closer supervision, and a tighter and more direct employer/wage labourer relationship, rather than the actual levelling of the labour force to a semi- or un-skilled mass. Also, it is often recognised that a change of this kind cannot be characterised simply in terms of the transition from workshop or domestic production to the factory. Some groups of workers possess a good deal of autonomy under factory conditions, and masters or merchants can often exercise a great deal of close control in workshop or domestic production. Finally, the change should not be seen in absolute terms, but rather in terms of where the balance of control between workers and employers is struck. This has tended to mean that historical research has focused on particular industries and/or regions and has often drawn attention to very specific processes such as the introduction of new management techniques, or new methods of payment such as piece-rates.[67]

In the British case this argument can be fitted into a broad interpretation of British economic history after the mid-century. This begins by claiming that there was a shift towards exporting industries such as engineering as well as to the export of capital. At the same time there was, certainly in comparison with other, more recently industrialising countries, a slowdown in the rate of capital investment in new technology which would save on labour costs and in particular displace skilled labour with semi or un-skilled labour.[68] In many sectors of the economy skilled labour, often hand labour, continued to be in high demand.[69] Growth industries such as engineering required more, not less, skilled labour and for various reasons it did not seem appropriate to invest in new technology instead of recruiting skilled labour.[70] At the same time, the decline of the agricultural sector eliminated one great reservoir of low-paid, unskilled labour which might have stimulated investment in technology which could use such labour.[71] However, simultaneously, the skills required of workers were more narrowly defined, set within more elaborate divisions of labour, and subjected to closer supervision. In this way the 'artisan' or 'traditional craftsman' figure gave way to the 'skilled worker'. This figure could be seen as the typical labour aristocrat of the mid-Victorian period.

The clearest arguments along these lines have been applied to the cotton and engineering industries. In the cotton industry it was the mule-spinner who could be seen in these terms.[72] This worker had rather limited skills. He was able, however, to retain some control over the way in which his machines were used and also some managerial control over his assistants. Associated with this was the formation of fairly exclusive and powerful trade unions which also acted to suppress organisation amongst other workers. Although tough trade union bargainers, these workers accepted the authority of the employers and, indeed, were rather conservative in their political attitudes.

So far as engineering is concerned, an important change has been identified following the defeat of workers in the great lock-out of 1851.[73] Although turners and fitters continued to exercise their skills with little technological innovation threatening them until the very end of the century, they lost much control over recruitment and training. Again they came to concentrate their attention on trade union and benefit society organisation, practised exclusive unionism, above all in the Amalgamated Society of Engineers (ASE), and largely accepted the authority of the employer.

Less clear and convincing arguments have been advanced for the building and mining industries. In building there was little of the technological change associated with engineering and cotton.[74] Work gangs and subcontracting remained important. There was no marked shift to the supply of ready-made materials to the site. Some studies have emphasised continuity, with very fluid employer/employee relationships.[75] On the other hand, Price has seen in the rise of the 'general contractor' and more formal methods of collective bargaining an erosion of worker control in the building industry.[76] Even here, however, Price has stressed the degree of struggle which went on, often in violent forms, and which can hardly be compared with the more peaceful pattern of industrial relations in engineering and cotton.[77] Nevertheless unions representing carpenters and join-ers, and a figure like Robert Applegarth, have been taken as representative of the new, respectable workingman of the mid-Victorian period.[78]

In the coal-mining industry Foster has argued that the checkweighman, the worker who checked the quality and amount of the miners' loads, became a 'labour aristocrat' figure, but this argument has been largely rejected by others who have examined it.[79] There was little change in the division of labour or technology of coal mining. Team work at the coal-face and down the pit generally reduced the degree of managerial supervision. Control through the checkweighman, through piece-rate payments, and through the greater employment control which came with larger and deeper pits employing more workers, (often under the control of combines owning a number of pits) were important but they do not lend much support to any labour aristocracy case. Few contemporaries or historians have treated coal-miners in the same way as engineers or cotton spinners (or indeed, any other occupation). However, as with the building industry, it was the case that at times the British mining industry produced unions and union leaders who seem to epitomise the labour aristocrat.[80]

The reasons advanced for these changes at the workplace vary. Most historians see it as an unintended consequence of fairly rational decisions by employers and workers in the national and international economic setting of the period when Britain did not need to invest massively in new technology to maintain comfortable growth rates. Foster, almost alone, has argued that employers deliberately created a class of dependent, skilled workers who helped impose their authority on the labour force as a whole. But whatever the explanation offered, the general conclusion is that a new kind of skilled worker came to have central importance in the most important industrial sectors, more dependent on the employer than the older type of all-round craftsman, more concerned with maintaining wage-levels and wage-differentials than control over work,[81] and who accordingly organised powerful trade unions on exclusive lines while accepting the authority of the employer and the values of a free-market economy.[82]

There has been a great deal of debate about these arguments. One issue is how far the strength of such workers was based upon objective skills which employers required or how far it was the organisation and determination of those workers and/or the policy of employers which enabled relatively modest levels of skill to obtain quite high rewards.[83] Some historians have disputed that there was a marked shift of the kind indicated in the British economy around the mid-century.[84] Some historians have argued that craft controls of various kinds continued after 1850 along the same lines as earlier.[85] It can also be argued that although one can trace changes which signify some 'loss of control', the timing and character of these changes varied enormously from one industry to another.[86] Furthermore, it could be argued thatconflicts between workers and employers over issues of 'control' were no more nor less important than conflicts over wages, and indeed that it is frequently impossible to distinguish such conflicts from one another. The payment for a job was dependent on how the job was defined.[87] The focus on wages and hours could be seen as due not to the growth of a more 'materialist' labour force, but as a function of organisational expansion. As trade union officials bargained on behalf of larger and more dispersed groups of workers, so they had to focus on the lowest common denominator on which all those workers could agree. This tended to be issues of hours and wages, because more 'qua-lititative' matters varied from one workplace and group of workers to another. But that is not to say that those qualitative issues did not retain as much importance as earlier. Finally, it has been argued that while the stabilisation of the relationship between capital and skilled labour may well have been an important feature of the British economy after 1850, the result was not a clear-cut division between labour aristocrats and others, but rather one of endemic sectionalism in which various groups of workers carved out positions of advantage for themselves and battled with fellow workers as well as employers in order to defend those positions.

This important counter-argument is forcefully advanced by Alistair Reid, both in his detailed research into Clydeside shipbuilding as well as more generally. It would be useful here to focus on the main points of this argument before turning to the German case. Reid demonstrates the continuity of craft skills, controls and wage differentials and connects this to the endemic sectionalism of workers rather than to any bi-polar division between labour aristocrats and others. Skill is treated as something which exists along a continuum rather than being a quality which workers either do or do not possess. It is bound up with negotiations and compromises between employers and particular groups of workers. Trade union representation develops out of and plays a part in such negotiations. However, trade unions do not represent skill groups in any clear or direct way. Some unions consisted of coalitions of different sorts of workers. Conversely workers with similar skills were often divided between different unions. Reid persuasively rejects the view that somehow these unions failed to represent their members and helped to subvert a web of 'informal' worker controls. Disputes about control of work and wage bargaining are closely linked and of equal importance. There is no clear trend towards less control over work and so any changes in the patterns of labour politics have to be sought elsewhere. Reid especially emphasises the importance of state intervention which took a markedly different and stronger form after 1914.

What this amounts to is a complete rejection of any form of labour aristocracy argument. The argument is rejected on sociological grounds in favour of a situation of endemic sectionalism. This in turn implies that there is no 'natural', 'objective', 'pre-political' class base to labour politics which might, at times, be undermined by the formation of a distinct labour aristocracy. Instead the explanation of working-class politics has to be found in the political sphere itself. The tendency of such argument is then to stress the role of state intervention, especially with the onset of war in 1914, as the major contributor to labour unity at the political level.

Reid's research was into the shipbuilding industry and this raises the problem of typicality. This industry produced what was possibly the most complex item of manufacture of the time – the large steel ship – and one would expect an especially complex division of labour in that industry. His own work does suggest some increase in supervisory and planning powers in shipbuilding which one could argue undermined the control over production of all shipyard workers. Reid and others who follow him have focused on the division of labour and the conflicts this produced both between workers and employers and amongst workers. They have not looked at other issues at work (e.g. trade union recognition, safety, hours of work) to anything like the same extent. Nor have they considered the social relationships between workers outside work, something I will look at in the next section of this essay. It could be argued that the assertion that sectionalism is the dominant fact about the working class represents a rather sweeping generalisation based on one particular aspect of work experience. Reid and others also tend to posit a rather mysterious 'autonomy' of the state, although in part the state responds to class pressures from below. One unfortunate effect of this could be to re-establish the traditional division of labour between the economic historian of labour at work, the social historian of labour at home or at play, and the political historian looking at labour politics. It would be unfortunate if innovative research into precisely what happens at work revived a narrow political approach to labour politics. In any case, the argument that the 'state' held aloof until 1914 and then intervened, and this produced something like a 'class' response is itself rather implausible. The state had an important role to play, for example in enforcing particular understandings of the labour contract, in placing limits on hours and conditions of work, and in providing certain kinds of welfare. At the very least Reid, Zeitlin and others have to provide a much fuller account of the relationship between the state and labour before their alternative approach can be taken seriously.

German labour history has also begun to pay more attention to the work situation, although not in relation to the concept of a labour aristocracy.[88] Rather the purpose has been to explain strike activity or trade union development or simply to find out more about workers at work.[89] The way in which this material can be related to the labour aristocracy debate is by looking at how historians have asked if the first phase of industrialisation (c.1850–80) was associated with certain patterns of differentiation within the working class at work.

German historians have certainly been concerned with the general question of differentiation. One form this concern has taken is with the issue of the survival of *Handwerk*. At one time it was generally assumed that the much more rapid industrialisation of Germany was associated with the rapid decline of the *Handwerk* sector. Terms associated with *Handwerk* came to be attached to a backward and reactionary class of master artisans, placed outside and resistant to the industrialising sector. This was compared to Britain where artisanal terminology and traditions continued to play a much more important role within the ranks of skilled labour in industrial work.[90]

It is now recognised that Handwerk was far more adaptive than had often been understood previously.[91] 'Survival' did involve considerable adaptation, but historians have demonstrated the continued importance of small workshop production with high levels of skill and low levels of mechanisation.[92] However, this does not really bear comparison with the British approach which has identified skilled workers with less independence working in larger industrial establishments as the labour aristocrats. Clearly the survival of small craft workshops was relevant because much of the skilled factory labour force was recruited from those workshops and often moved back and forth between small workshops and larger factories.[93] However, what is crucial is what happened to those skilled workers in the factory.

Various German historians have pointed to the considerable differentiation within the factory labour force. Fischer has demonstrated the continuity of wage and status differentials in the factory.[94] Workers were often referred to in wage lists as masters and journeymen. Wage data exhibits considerable variations in earnings both within and between industries related to differences in skill, status and organisational capacity.[95] Engineering is a clear case but one can also find similar patterns in mining, building, iron and steel as well as other industries.[96] There is nothing peculiar about Britain in these respects, although the degree of difference (which is very difficult to measure) may be important. One also finds that the workers who managed to form unions in the period 1850–80 in Germany were usually drawn from skilled occupations earning above average wages and with fairly narrowly defined concerns.[97]

Furthermore, in a way similar to British work, some historians have also shown how craft traditions and controls have had an important bearing on the capacity of workers to organise and to secure certain advantages for themselves. Tenfelde and others have shown the importance of corporate traditions and team work organisation for the collective strength of miners.[98] By comparison, where such traditions had been less important or mine owners were able to crush them, one generally found lower strike rates, lower levels of organisation, lower wages, and higher turnovers of labour.[99]

Research into the engineering industry has also shown the continuity of skills from an earlier period, the existence of an elite of turners and fitters, and the importance of craft controls in the factories which often turn out, on closer inspection, to have been organised as a series of small, semi-autonomous workshops.[100] In the building industry, the more modestly skilled groups such as masons and carpenters retained certain collective work practices on which they could base organisation.[101] Where skill levels were lower, the division of labour more complex, the labour force correspondingly more fragmented – levels of organisation, collective action, occupational identity, and wages appear to have been much lower, as in iron and steel and much of the textile industries.[102]

Generally German historians have not however seen these better-placed workers as a labour aristocracy. Rather other differences such as between industries or regions appear to be much more important. For example, Ruhr, Upper and Lower Silesia and the Saar mining areas display very great differences from one another. With high levels of migration developing within what was a highly regionalised society, historians have been struck by differences based on language, religion and pre-existing social and economic features.[103]

German historians have also been more interested in the issue of *integration* rather than *differentiation*. Collective work practices, for example at the coal-face, could integrate workers with different functions, skills and levels of earnings. What is more, workers in this industry could expect to change jobs (both in terms of employment and occupation) and so would not tend to identify themselves exclusively in occupational terms.[104] In areas like the Ruhr attempts by the employers to tie workers (or at least a core labour force) to the enterprise by means of company housing and pension schemes and other measures could create solidarity amongst workers with different functions, whether this worked for or against the employer.[105] Alternatively it could produce a difference based less on skill and occupation and more upon the differential treatment of the employer.[106] Equally, employer intransigence towards *all* their workers (e.g. refusing union recognition to all groups) could have such an integrating effect.[107]

German historians have also been more concerned to study trade unions less in sectional terms and more for their role in politicising workers. This in turn has been linked to the role of the state in relation to labour where arguably it helped generate solidarity amongst different groups of workers. Finally, the interest in integration has also taken into account the way new arrivals were brought into a working-class community.

The problem is whether this indifference to identifying a labour aristocracy at work is simply due to other, often more politically focused concerns. It may be that the pattern of industrial change in Germany did leave less scope for the emergence of stable and well-placed groups of skilled workers. Certainly the major difference between Germany and Britain appears to be one of numbers – especially when one compares how many workers were able to unionise in the two countries. By the mid-1870s perhaps 1.2 million British workers were unionised whereas the German figure had probably not yet reached 100,000. Arguably more skilled and unionised workers in Britain were partly an expression of different workplace situations.[108] This in turn made it more sensible for employers and the state to compromise with these labour interests in Britain whereas it was more rational to prevent further organisation developing in Germany. Such preventive measures in turn led to smaller but less sectionalised and more radically-minded trade unions.

There are also some indications that even in similar industries it was more difficult for a section of skilled workers to establish a firm position for themselves in Germany. I have already considered at some length what Reid has said about British shipbuilding where he certainly demonstrates the importance of sectionalism and entrenched organisations amongst those with skill, even if not in terms which support the labour aristocracy concept. It is interesting that studies of German ship-building suggest that employers there were able to impose their will much more completely and to undermine the position of certain occupations, for example the old shipwrights who had to adapt to metal shipbuilding.[109] That in turn can be related to the more important role of capital investment and heavy industry in Germany's industrialisation drive, although there are also more specific features such as the tendency of German shipbuilders to produce smaller and more uniformly designed ships which perhaps reduced the significance of some skill groups.

There is something in this argument, although it can perhaps exaggerate the speed and character of German industrialisation.[110] Nevertheless, it is clear that attention to differences within the workplace points far more towards either endemic sectionalism where there is a complex division of labour or to integration where there is job mobility and/or similar treatment by employers. The ability of some workers to organise more effectively and obtain better wages and conditions cannot easily be related to specific features of the work situation which point to a labour aristocracy/others distinction. At the economic level one is forced back instead to wage levels and unionisation. This points to a more important grouping of better-placed workers in Britain than in Germany between 1850 and 1880, but without attempting the misleading precision of the workplace studies. What is more, such a focus can disarm many of the powerful criticisms emanating from historians such as Reid which show just how sectionalised are workers *in the workplace*. However, the small move from the situation as producer to that as earner does not really explain how skilled workers might come to see themselves as labour aristocrats. There is still too much concern with sharply-defined material interests which alone cannot explain political attitudes or how groups with similar material interests but who are divided from one another can constitute themselves as a political and cultural and social force. For that we have to turn to the third aspect of labour aristocracy studies, namely the place of the labour aristocrat within the community.

c) A labour aristocracy in the community

A working-class or an occupational community may be *defined* in terms of the work situation and the economic relationship to the market and other classes. However, an important part of how such workers and their families come to identify themselves as belonging to a certain group and sharing certain values will be shaped by what happens outside the workplace. A number of historiographical and methodological developments have made it possible for historians to investigate this in some detail and this has produced major contributions towards the labour aristocracy debate.

First, there has been the increased awareness since the 1960s of the way in which social mobility and improvements in living standards can erode traditional working-class identities. This first led to a concern with *embourgeoisement*, a process whereby workers came to think of themselves as consumers rather than producers. Although the most important British contribution to this subject, *The Affluent Worker in the Class Structure*[111] did have a great deal to say about work processes and experiences in this change, the most influential part of that work was to do with patterns of housing, living standards, and social and geographical mobility.

So long as these were conceived of as a new set of processes working on traditional working-class solidarity, such a view did not seriously question the class understanding of earlier labour history. However, insofar as the labour aristocracy concept itself is a means of explaining occasional aberrations from that class position, the methods used by sociologists could in limited ways be applied by historians. A second influence has come about through an increased preoccupation of Marxist historians with the way in which cultural and political processes shape social consciousness. The concern of the Italian communist Antonio Gramsci with the way in which the institutions of civil society and the ideologies generated and diffused by those institutions can help integrate the working class into capitalist society has led some historians to consider how a labour aristocracy might be formed which succumbs to bourgeois 'hegemony' and in turn exercises some cultural and political sway over other segments of the working class.[112] Again, insofar as this is treated as a way of explaining the absence of solidary and combative working-class consciousness in what remains a class divided society, such ideas can contribute directly towards an elaboration of the concept of the labour aristocracy.

Such ideas can be taken further, however, to question the idea of using class divisions as the norm of social analysis. Some historians have projected back into at least the inter-war period the image of a working class broken up by the pursuit of consumer goods and individual and familial improvement.[113] German labour historians have there the rather special case of the Third Reich to consider, with its forcible destruction of the institutions of labour, but they have also asked whether in positive as well as purely negative ways, inter-war Germany did not see the erosion of traditional working-class solidarities.[114]

For some time the focus of such work was upon the post-1920 and even more the post-1945 period. There was frequently the assumption that something like a unitary working class had taken shape in the decades up to 1914, and had possibly persisted through the inter-war period. This was particularly the case for work which focused on the social character of working-class life – on working-class districts and housing and leisure – and linked the making of a working class to the spread of industrial life rather than the rise of labour parties.[115]

However, this view has been attacked for the period before 1914. One line of attack has been to focus on an 'under-class' which was never integrated into what is often seen as 'mainstream' working-class culture.[116] Another line of attack is to look at what was happening to workers at the 'top' rather than the 'bottom' of the working class. For Britain I will focus on the work of Crossick, Gray and Foster.[117] There is other relevant work but concentrating on a few major studies will enable me to bring out the sorts of evidence and arguments involved.[118] I will then compare this work with Crew's study of Bochum, Zwahr's on Leipzig, Ditt's on Bielefeld and Schomerus's on Eßlingen.[119] Although these are not concerned to advance a labour aristocracy thesis along the lines of Crossick and Gray, they are among the few German works with a similar focus on the workforce outside work.

The first concern of such studies is to establish the existence of the labour aristocracy as a distinct social stratum. This involves establishing certain 'social facts' that distinguish members of this group from other labour groups and showing that members of this group displayed specific and distinctive patterns of behaviour.

The first social fact is that of income. In order to have different consumer patterns from other workers it was necessary for labour aristocrats to earn more. (One might object that different people can spend the same earnings in different ways. When average earnings are well above subsistence level, this is a valid point. When, as in this period, average earnings barely cover food and housing costs, the idea of constructing different life styles from those earnings hardly applies. It is having a little extra that is the most important difference.) Gray and Crossick spend a little time on this subject.[120] However, higher than average earnings are treated as no more than a necessary condition for the existence of a labour aristocracy. Much more attention is devoted to other social indicators. Quite quickly, therefore, the focus of this work shifts to other matters which Hobsbawm mentioned in his original work on the labour aristocracy but did not really consider any further.

Neither Gray nor Crossick present much evidence on residence patterns. Foster did spend some time considering patterns of neighbourhood to try to see if labourers and skilled workers lived more or less closely together than a random settlement pattern would suggest for the three towns concerned (Oldham, Northampton, South Shields).[121] However, at this stage in his argument Foster was mainly concerned to show a degree of class solidarity rather than differentiation in

Oldham in the period 1830–50, which he went on to relate to political radicalism and working-class unity in this period. Although later in his work Foster sought to show that a process of differentiation took place after 1850 which produced a labour aristocracy, he shifted his attention at this point from community patterns to relationships at work.[122] It should also be noted that Foster's evidence and arguments concerning class solidarity in the community have been subjected to strong and, in my view, persuasive criticism.[123] In a slightly different tack Gray also produced some evidence which indicated that better-off workers tended to occupy rather better housing than less well-off workers and also occupied more rooms.[124] However, the arguments for a labour aristocracy defined in terms of location or type of residence in contrast to other workers have only been weakly developed.

More attention has been paid to patterns of marriage and social mobility. Crossick argues that rates of upward social mobility from the working class were much higher when a man's father came from a skilled occupation than when he came from an unskilled occupation. He also argues that bridegrooms from skilled working-class backgrounds were much more likely to marry into skilled working-class or non-manual occupation families than were bridegrooms from general labourer backgrounds.[125] Gray argues a similar case for Edinburgh in the 1850s and 1860s.[126] This certainly suggests that skilled workers have closer social ties to non-working-class groups than do unskilled workers. Whether the ties are stronger between skilled workers and non-working-class groups than they were between skilled and unskilled workers is a rather more debatable matter. If one could argue that they were, this would certainly fit in with Hobsbawm's arguments concerning the greater openness of the labour aristocracy to groups above rather than groups below them.But again it seems to me that this case is less clear-cut than the simpler and unsurprising one that skilled workers are higher up the social ladder than unskilled workers.

Both Crossick and Gray go on to argue that there is also a distinctive pattern of leisure time activity on the part of labour aristocrats which marks them off from other workers. The evidence for this is sought in the membership of voluntary associations such as savings clubs, friendly societies, educational associations, churches, trade unions, and militias. It is clear that associations like these were important to many skilled and respectable workers. Analyis of membership details shows the low participation of unskilled workers. Of greater importance is the participation of members of higher social groups, though this is more central to Gray's evidence and argument than it is to Crossick's.[127]

The next step in the argument is to show that these labour aristocrats shared a distinct set of values and that this helps explain why they favoured a politics of reform and accommodation between classes, rather than opposition and class conflict. A crude approach to this question might be to see the labour aristocrats as simple opportunists whose 'values' were simply shaped by prospects of prosperity, security and social advancement open to them. Engels and Lenin, as argued earlier, sometimes took this line. Less crude but still fairly simple is the idea that such labour aristocrats came genuinely to accept the laissez-faire liberal values of the day, though whether through direct contacts with middle-class advocates of these values or more indirectly is unclear.[128]

It is one of the strengths of the work of Crossick and Gray (but not of Foster) that they do not take up these simple but actually untenable arguments. The problem is that these arguments fail to take account of the continuity of great social differences between even the skilled Victorian worker and his social superiors, the very real conflicts which still took place across class boundaries, and the persistence of a consciousness and resentment of social inequality amongst skilled workers. Instead they, as well as other historians, have stressed the distinctiveness and autonomy of labour aristocrat values and ways of thinking.[129] They do, however, argue this case in interestingly different ways. Crossick sees the values and beliefs of labour aristocrats as being grounded in the traditions and experiences of artisans. Stress upon the virtues of thrift, respectability, independence and social advancement are seen as a continuation of those traditions rather than an accept-ance of new-fangled ideas worked out by middle-class Victorians. What is more, such virtues are placed within a more collectivist, solidary context than the individualist version of middle-class liberalism. Examples are the idea of skill as a kind of property which can legitimately be protected by collective action such as regulation of apprenticeship and recruitment to an occupation, or the concern to punish by collective action those employers who fail to pay a proper rate. Such labour aristocrats might well stress the dignity of manual labour and portray the work of the shopkeeper or clerk (let alone the doctor or the clergyman) as effete and in some sense unproductive. In these ways the labour aristocrat could come to display a strong group (but not class) ethos and pride that could come into conflict with the type of liberalism dominant within middle class circles. However, given the reasonable position of these labour aristocrats in mid-Victorian Britain, it was the experience of success and advance that prevailed amongst them, and led them to stress what they shared with middle-class liberals rather than what divided them. Certainly there was a stress upon 'self-help' even if this was with a collective rather than an individualist slant.[130]

Gray is rather more concerned with the relationship between labour aristocrats and middle-class groups. This may be because Edinburgh displays rather more contacts across class boundaries than Kentish London. But there is also a different approach involved. Crossick places the stress upon the *traditions* and *experiences* of the artisan community. Gray places it upon the *ideological relationship* between skilled workers and the bourgeoisie. To explore this approach Gray uses the concept of 'hegemony' first propounded by Gramsci. This concept is outlined by Gray as follows

Class hegemony is a dynamic and shifting relationship of social subordination, which operates in two directions. Certain aspects of the behaviour and consciousness of the subordinate classes may reproduce a version of the values of the ruling class.But in the process value systems are modified, through their necessary adaptation to diverse conditions of existence; the subordinate classes thus follow a 'negotiated version' of ruling class values. On the other hand, structures of ideological hegemony transform and incorporate dissident values, so as effectively to prevent the working through of their full implications.[131]

Gray's procedure, therefore, is to start from the views of the world that the middle classes sought to diffuse throughout society, then to see how these were accepted by labour aristocrats, albeit with some typical modifications to suit their own circumstances. This sort of treatment has been subjected to a number of criticisms.[132]

First, the communities studied by Crossick and Gray are not centres of manufacturing but national capitals, and may therefore display peculiar features of social structure not encountered elsewhere. Of course, one can respond that there is no such thing as a 'typical' town or city. However, one would expect to find a much higher proportion of skilled workers providing goods and services to a large professional and administrative bourgeoisie in these two towns than most other parts of Britain. Perhaps the divisions of industrial society would be less obvious than in more industrial centres.

Second, the focus is upon social and cultural spheres of action. There is nothing wrong with that in itself, but only loose connections are made with political and economic behaviour. Evidence which might enable one to make such connections is frequently not available. But it does mean that we do not know how far these labour aristocrats favoured gradualist and reformist politics or avoided confrontation with their employers.

Third, there is the problem of establishing what the 'values' or 'ideology' of these labour aristocrats actually were. Are statements in favour of certain virtues associated with virtuous conduct? Does virtuous conduct in one sphere of life mean belief in what is virtuous, and does it mean virtuous conduct in other spheres of life? One must remember that the evidence upon which historians fasten usually consists of reflective statements made to particular audiences, often with a view to influencing the attitudes of that audience.[133] There are dangers in generalising from that language and those situations.

Apart from the problems of establishing *what* labour aristocrats believed and how this affected their behaviour, there is the further problem of explaining *why* they believed what they did. Crossick's emphasis upon experience as the basis of beliefs can be criticised for failing to grasp that experiences can take place only through the mediation of certain values and beliefs. One is then liable to enter a circular argument for which it is difficult to extricate oneself. A simple emphasis upon tradition working upon new experience demonstrates the same problems. Gray avoids this sort of criticism by explicitly making labour aristocrat ideology a product of certain class relationships and associated ideologies. However, his emphasis upon incorporation as a product of ideological hegemony assumes the ever-present possibility of successful opposition to that hegemony. This is clear from the passage quoted by Gray above. The degree of incorporation and hegemony is measured by the potential in 'dissident values' and the 'working through of their full implications'. It would seem that one requires a model of 'true class consciousness' (both of the dominant and the subordinate classes) as a necessary basis upon which to work. If this is not to be dismissed as an arbitrary assumption, it would seem important to be able to show that such a true class consciousness or something near to it is frequently to be found in societies, and that it operates as a real standard by which some historical actors at least make judgements. The problem for the historian of Britain is that this is very difficult to assert: classes seem to spend most of their time harbouring illusions about their true nature. Given that then, the very basis upon which Gray's arguments rest appears arbitrary and immune to empirical testing.[134]

When one turns to German social and cultural history of the working class in the period up to about 1880, one can see a good deal of work using similar methods to some of the work for Britain just described. However, the notion of a labour aristocracy does not play a central part in that historical writing.

Historians of the German Democratic Republic were, of course, committed to an orthodox Marxist position, whether sincerely or not. Much of the work concentrated upon ideology and politics in relation to a very narrowly defined concern with the emergence of a class conscious (i.e. Marxist) party of the working class. The unity of the working class has often operated simply as an assumption upon which such work is based. At its worst, assertions about social position have been derived from an evaluation of political position and are not based on independent investigation.

However, there are studies which go beyond this. The most important historian in this regard is Hartmut Zwahr.[135] In his labour history work Zwahr was committed to an orthodox Marxist position and his main concern was to demonstrate the way in which the development of industrial capitalism produced a working class. However, he did wish to *demonstrate* and not merely assert this. Furthermore, Zwahr recognised that class has to be understood as including economic, social and political–ideological aspects. The historian must separate these different aspects, study the development of class at these three levels, and then seek to establish the relationships between those levels. He works on the principle that the analysis must move from the most basic or objective level, that of the economy, to the most subjective level, that of politics and ideology. Put simply: a working class is first formed within the economic structure of capitalism, with factory workers becoming increasingly central within that class. Such a class comes to take on a distinct social character through common situation, inter-marriage and declining social contacts with other classes. Finally this class begins to develop a conscious sense of identity as well as to understand its situation and the way it must act to end its subordination. This is a clear framework. Furthermore, Zwahr is inventive in working out ways of examining sources such as applications for citizenship in Leipzig in order to show how these processes actually developed between 1830 and 1870.

So far as the labour aristocracy concept is concerned, two things can be noted. First, Zwahr does draw attention to differences within the emergent working class of Leipzig. However, these differences tend to be presented in terms of types of industry (domestic, workshop, factory) or social origins rather than in terms of skill or social levels. Second, Zwahr's main concern is to argue that over the period 1830–70 such differences decline in importance and that by the end of the period a fairly unified working class, with an 'hereditary proletariat' at its centre, had taken shape. Although one can dispute some of Zwahr's arguments, it is clear that a quite different approach would be needed if one wished to examine any concept of a labour aristocracy.[136]

For work produced in the Federal Republic I will focus upon that by Schomerus and Ditt.[137] The work by Schomerus was undertaken within the *Arbeitskreis für moderne Sozialgeschichte* at Heidelberg which was established by Werner Conze. Generally the concern of this group has been with the socio-economic position of urban workers and how industrial development has altered that situation and the attitude of those affected. There is rather less concern with the complex of problems that interested Zwahr concerned with capitalism, class identity and class conflict.[138]

Schomerus has been able to use particularly rich evidence which enables her to connect information about the property and family circumstances of individuals with that concerning their employment situation in the engineering factory which is the focus of her attention. She has developed sophisticated techniques involving the use of a computer and some powerful analytical concepts such as that of the 'life-time earnings curve' in order to produce something quite novel in the way of understanding how people come into the world of industry and how, over generations, they adapt to that world. Schomerus draws attention to differences within the labour force, but in a way which is not only unconcerned with the idea of a labour aristocracy but which implicitly undermines that idea.

Schomerus certainly shows that there are substantial differences in earnings within the factory labour force and that skilled engineering workers occupied something of an elite position. But this point is rather lost amongst more salient findings. First, Schomerus shows how important were the social origins of workers for influencing how they adapted to their new circumstances. Social origins affected how much they possessed upon marriage, how long they worked at the factory, how frequently they changed jobs, how early they married and, related to the age of marriage, how many children they had. That in turn is related by Schomerus to the pattern of earnings over a life-time to produce a rich and complex account of the determinants of living standards in which it is difficult to see a simple labour aristocracy/others distinction fitting. Schomerus also shows how firm festivals and forms of employer parternalism helped create a sense of solidarity in the labour force. Finally Schomerus shows that there is a pattern of adaptation to the industrial world which takes two to three generations to complete (though it varies with social origins) and which produces something of a convergence amongst originally widely differing groups.

Ditt is rather more concerned to relate a history of the working class to that of the labour movement. He also pays close attention to differentiation within the labour force in the first phase of industrialisation up to about 1875. He argues in contrast to Zwahr, that differentiation if anything *increases* during this period when one looks at factors such as social origins and mobility. But the major differentiations to which Ditt draws attention are not simply those between skilled and unskilled workers, but even more importantly between domestic workers (above all, the weavers) who dominated in pre-industrial Bielefeld and the new group of factory workers. In this account it is the weavers who became an increasingly closed, 'hereditary' group. By contrast the positions of farm labourer – unskilled worker – skilled worker – non-worker became a social ladder. The ladder was difficult to climb but there was no particularly sharp closure at the divide between unskilled and skilled workers. Again, this work provides little support for any argument about a labour aristocracy.[139]

A final study to which I would draw attention is that by Crew dealing with Bochum.[140] This study also displays a great interest in patterns of regional and social mobility, though strongly influenced in this case by American work and a concern to see whether mobility really was much less in Europe. That, of course, could be linked to arguments about the greater salience of class in European labour forces.[141] At some point this fairly straightforward analysis became diverted by concern with the work situation of miners and foundry workers, how this in turn explains different patterns of strike activity, and the way in which capitalists in Germany could be highly illiberal.[142] The two concerns sometimes sit a little uneasily with one another but in one area they do come together in a very effective way: when Crew argues that the miners developed an 'occupational community' based both on collective work practices under worker control and neighbourhood and inter-marriage. Interestingly, Crew argues that the one apparent exception to this – namely evidence that miners were more likely to escape beyond the manual working class than were foundry workers – actually strengthens his case. Miners who were injured or ill could not find work in the mines and sometimes established small shops which depended upon the custom of their fellow miners. Foundry workers might get promotion to supervisory positions where they would be likely to come into conflict with their former fellow workers.[143] An uninformed social mobility model might conclude that in the first case the people in question had 'left' their class, while in the second case they remained within it. What this also shows is that differences in skill or earnings or occupation could have different meanings in different industries. This again would rather work against any labour aristocracy idea. Crew does neglect other important differences within the Bochum labour force, namely those of religion and language as German and then Polish Catholic workers came into a town originally dominated by Protestant German workers. But attention to those features would almost certainly reduce still further the importance of any distinction between a class of skilled, better-placed workers and other workers.

All these studies consider the workplace as well as the community. There are some British studies which also do this, and generally these seem to ignore or even dismiss the labour aristocracy concept.[144] However, work which makes connections of this kind usually has the best evidence in cases where the focus of attention is upon a particular factory or a small group of employers and where there are quite close relationships between the workplace and outside work, or at least where the historian perceives close relationships. Yet it may be precisely in such situations that a labour aristocracy is unlikely to take shape – because employer paternalism, or an occupational or industrial or even factory community will reduce in importance any internal differences within the labour force. The problem is that a labour aristocracy might be more likely to take shape in a more diverse economy and in the context of a large town or city where there are plentiful opportunities for better-off workers to come together in clubs and associations, sometimes with people from other social backgrounds, and to get away from the less skilled workers of their place of employment. In these situations it is both difficult for the historian to find evidence which can connect work place to the world outside, but also it might be precisely the *lack* of such a connection which would matter for the formation of a labour aristocracy.

What this means is that connections might have to be established conceptually rather than empirically, or that the historian must recognise the relative autonomy of different (and perhaps increasingly separate) spheres of life in the experience of workers. This might mean that the concept of the labour aristocracy can be defended as one which *only* relates to the world of leisure activity, or housing, or trade union organisation. To accept this might mean limiting the more ambitious claims made for the concept, but it would also remove the force from some criticisms which argue that unless one can show that the labour aristocrat/others distinction is a significant division in *all* spheres of life, then it must be rejected.

So far as the 'cultural' history of the early working class in Germany is concerned, this has been a much neglected field of study. On the one hand there has been an interest in artisan traditions in the sense of *Handwerkkultur*, both of an older institutional kind with its focus on guild customs and of a newer sort indebted to disciplines such as social anthropology and the special German branch of study known as *Volkskunde*.[145] On the other hand there has been an interest in the culture of the industrial working class, beginning with a focus on the culture of the labour movement,[146] but now moving into the consideration of 'everyday life' and the culture of the unorganised workers.[147] However, the skilled workers of the industrial period tend to get left out, except in their capacity as those most prominent in the early labour movement.

There has been some important work on the artisan movement in Vormärz,[148] during the 1848 revolution,[149] and after the revolution.[150] However, this is usually concerned with politics. Furthermore, much of the work seeks to anticipate later developments in the labour movement, using anachronistic concepts such as reformism and revolutionary, social democratic and communist, political party and trade union.[151] Equally the attempt to interpret the artisan movements of this period in terms of 'reactionary' and 'progressive' responses to change fails to grasp the real issues involved.[152]

Some work has tried to look at the period c.1840–65 as something other than the death agonies of a reactionary *Handwerk* tradition or as the first, dim stirrings of a later working-class movement.[153] Then certain similarities with British work on the 'respectable artisan' can be discerned. This is most obvious when one looks at the workers' educational associations (*Arbeiterbildungsvereine*) and the cooperatives (*Genossenschaften*) of the period.[154] It is apparent that only skilled workers played an important role in such associations and that this frequently brought them into contact with people from higher social groups such as clerks, small employers and professionals. One can analyse the values of these workers in ways rather similar to the methods employed by Gray and Crossick.[155] One could go on to argue from this that there was the cultural and organisational basis on which a liberal labour movement could have developed.[156] Yet the argument is not very well developed, although movements of this kind continued to be of importance in some parts of Germany into the 1870s and beyond.[157] It would appear that the political failure of such a movement has meant that historians have not taken seriously enough the distinctive groupings of workers, their organisations and beliefs, which began to move to support liberalism after 1848. Alternatively, they have seen the political failure as a *symptom* of the fragility of those values and groups and have emphasised the forces of change which would undermine any accommodative labour aristocracy taking firm shape.[158] It has also meant, in my view, that German historians have neglected to interpret the culture of the early labour movement as being, in part, the product of a politically alienated labour aristocracy. Such workers expected to be treated fairly, regarded as people who could be trusted to participate politically. When such trust was not extended to them, instead of continuing to cooperate with middle-class liberals, they turned sharply against them.

d) The labour oligarchy

The rise of a mass labour movement seemed to reduce the significance of a labour aristocracy in the sense of a small minority of organised workers (whether in the workplace or outside it) separated from the great unorganised majority. Yet the very same process has been linked to the development of a new kind of labour aristocracy, based on labour organisations. The rise of a mass labour movement was associated with the development of complex organisations capable of handling the affairs of large memberships. At times it could appear that the officials involved could develop interests of their own and pursue these against their own members. This has been a central idea in German labour history for the period shortly before 1914. It has been less important in British labour history but is sometimes to be found.

A theoretical source for this approach was elite sociology. A basic assumption of this sociology was that sooner or later any large social group or institution will give rise to elites. This assumption took a particular form with regard to bureaucracies. Michels, following Weber, was highly impressed by the power of modern bureaucracies. With their hierarchy, efficient and rational methods of operation, and monopoly of information and technical capacities, bureaucracies could come to master those they were supposed to serve. The state bureaucracy could master the political democracy; the bureaucracy of large industries could master the market place; and the bureaucracy of political parties and trade unions could master their memberships. At the same time bureaucracies developed their own interests, above all in the maintenance and expansion of the organisations which supported them, which could lead to conflicts of interest with their members.[159]

These arguments have been developed a little, in particular for the SPD and some of the larger unions in the FTU, especially the metal workers' union. Their use in British labour history remains more impressionistic, the most important case being the engineering union, the ASE.[160]

First, it was necessary to show that there was a growth in organisation and bureaucracy. There can be little doubt that in Germany from the mid-1890s mass labour organisations did form.[161] Less dramatic but also very real was the expansion of trade unions and other labour organisations in Britain.[162] Second, measured by numbers of functionaries as well as range of functions, both in absolute terms and relative to the number of members, it can be shown that there was a process of 'bureaucratisation'.[163] Third, it has been argued that these officials came to be a separate stratum, even if they originally came from manual labour occupations. They became life-time officials, often with a degree of job security and a level of earnings superior to their members.[164] Finally, it has been argued that these officials developed their own interests which conflicted with those of their members. Thus the way in which the SPD and FTU leaderships handled the issue of the political or mass strike in 1905–06, or the powers of veto over strikes exercised by the metal workers' union (DMV), have been taken as indicative of the caution of these officials, anxious not to waste the resources of the organisation or endanger its existence by embarking upon radical action.[165] The point could then be reached when a critic such as Rosa Luxemburg could come to see these organisations, originally founded to assist labour in the pursuit of its interests, as one of the major obstacles to the continuance of that pursuit.[166]

To sustain a case of this sort it is necessary to show that there were differences of opinion between officials and members in which the views of officials prevailed. There are two areas in which such differences can be explored (I leave aside the issue of differences between organised and unorganised workers for the next section) – at the level of leadership and in relations between leadership and rank-and-file.

An example of the first approach is the treatment of the way in which radical and revisionist wings of the SPD were defeated between 1900 and 1914. It has been argued that both wings threatened the position of the party. The politics of the radicals could lead to repression; those of the revisionists to a loss of identity based on a resolute rejection of existing state and society. Instead, the preferred policy of intransigent passivity – justified in terms of an inevitabilist version of Marxism and a belief that the sheer growth of the SPD and its electoral support both indicated and contributed to the inevitable triumph of socialism – could be seen to express the interests of SPD officials in the maintenance and expansion of their own organisation at the expense of all other goals.[167]

There are many problems with this argument. First, it is very difficult to show that the radicals or the revisionists, or even both taken together, were more representative of the party than were the centrists. Second, one can provide better interpretations of the centrist triumph than that which sees it as the victory of the functionaries.[168] In part the two wings cancelled each other out and allowed centrism to emerge as the most effective compromise. In part the refusal of other political forces to work with the SPD rendered revisionism unrealistic, whilst the relatively peaceful, tolerated and improving position of the working class in Wilhelmine Germany undercut any support for radical actions. In part the ideology of the party functioned not so much to justify the policy of inaction, but rather to provide some consolation while people in practice got on with making small improvements.

The real test of the labour oligarchy case comes with the analysis of rank-and-file dissent. It is here that conflict between officials and members is most directly exposed. There has been some work on such dissent. Some is based on unions, especially in the engineering industry.[169] In particular, attention has focused on the way in which trade union leaders refused to support strikes or cooperated with employers to discipline workers.[170] Refusal to support strikes can be seen as unwillingness to risk harm to the union; discipline of workers as a sign of the gulf between workers and trade union officials and the desire of the officials to convince employers of their good faith and respectability. In the case of the SPD the most valuable work is that of local studies of party branches in which the activists took a different view of the matter from either the local officials or the central party leadership.[171]

There are again many difficulties with this approach. First, such dissent as is traced seems frequently to be sporadic, fragmented and the affair of a minority. One may respond that this is just another indication of how very effective the labour oligarchy was in preventing rank-and-file opposition from becoming organised and effective, but it is difficult to see how one can test such an argument. If dissent *is* important it buttresses the case; but if it is *not* important, that strengthens the case! Second, there is the problem of rank and file *consent*, not a very well-studied subject. It can be argued that the growth of bureaucracy in union and party and the granting of new powers to officials, such as the power to veto proposals to take strike action, actually reflect much rank-and-file feeling. It seems clear, for example, that there was much support for better organisation in the coal miners' union after 1890 because of strong feeling that only well-prepared and organised strikes could really benefit the miners.[172] Again, many trade union members were concerned that their subscriptions were not frittered away in the support of poorly prepared strikes with little chance of success. Very often it appears that the real disputes were between different sections of the membership, e.g. between high and low wage regions in the building industry (where strikes might seem most justifiable in low wage areas but actually had the greatest chance of success in high wage areas such as the great cities), or different occupations. It may be that the more general character of German trade unions compared to the more narrowly occupational British unions provided more scope for such sectional disagreement.

It is not easy to prove such a case. Naturally dissent leaves more trace as those who disagree with the leadership will express that disagreement by attending meetings, protesting, and acting against official policy, all the while claiming that they represent the views of the members generally. Meanwhile those who are satisfied with official policy will tend to remain silent. Nevertheless, the possibility that many members are quite happy with their leaders cannot be ignored.

There are also problems with the arguments about bureaucratisation and the power of bureaucracy. There is no doubt that the number of functionaries employed by the SPD and the larger unions did increase. Again this was mainly to provide services which were valued by the membership – welfare provision, legal advice, newspapers and periodicals, etc. But many of these functionaries can hardly be described as bureaucrats. Many SPD employees were printers, a sign of the importance of propaganda and communication for the party. However, printers were not bureaucrats and did not have any distinctive political interests or powers within the party.[173] Once these functionaries are subtracted then the number of 'bureaucrats' becomes rather small.

What is more, these bureaucrats had very few resources that freed them from pressure from below. The organisations of labour before 1914, more so in Germany than in Britain, were regarded with contempt by establishment opinion and institutions. Trade union and party officials, editors of party newspapers and SPD deputies, were exposed to vilification in the non-socialist press and harassment by police and courts.[174] To argue that these officials had in some way escaped from the working class to a secure office job is to misunderstand their situation before 1914. Trade unions and socialist parties were voluntary organisations. They were tolerated but in no way privileged. They had no official status, for example in the field of industrial relations. They could not participate in government. They were paid wholly out of their own organisation's resources – for example, parliamentary deputies were not paid. There were no 'closed shops' which gave them monopoly rights over certain groups of members. There was no state welfare apparatus in which labour institution officials could entrench themselves.[175] In this sense the comparison of SPD officialdom with state officialdom (and further analogies such as the conference as parliament and August Bebel as Emperor) is completely misplaced. State officials had a guaranteed revenue out of compulsory taxes and could back up their commands by force if necessary. By contrast the main resource of labour institution officials was their members who could always express their dissatisfaction by ceasing to be members. (One purpose of bureaucracy was to ensure that subscriptions were paid, that is to prevent at least involuntary lapses of membership.) Officials simply could not afford to alienate significant numbers of their members.

The limited number of 'real' bureaucrats and the limits on their independence from their members is often reflected in the way the organisations actually functioned. There is no sharp distinction to make between active officials and passive members. In the SPD perhaps a more important distinction is between the active and the passive member. The former often took on unpaid functions within the party. In turn they set the tone at local meetings and in the choice of delegates to the annual conference. The local full-time officials depended very much on these people.[176] What is more the 'bureaucracy' itself was hardly monolithic. The full-time official had a different position from that of the parliamentary deputy. There was also the passive member and, beyond that, the voter as other sources of pressure upon the party. Frequently conflicts turn out not to be between the 'rank-and-file' and officials, but between some activists in a city branch of the party and a broader district organisation, or between those concerned to increase the commitment of existing members and those who wanted to extend electoral support.[177]

If these points apply to Germany with its quite large labour institutions, they apply even more forcefully to Britain. It may be that the argument for a labour oligarchy has some merit after 1918, and even more so after 1945, when the improved position of trade unions and social democratic parties provide it with resources independently of its members. But for the period up to 1914, whatever the intellectual coherence and attractions of elite and organisational sociology, the idea of the labour aristocracy as labour institution officials is not only unhelpful, but can be positively misleading.

The decline of the labour aristocracy

If the politics of class accommodation in Britain, in particular the cooperation between organised labour and popular liberalism, has been linked to the emergence of a labour aristocracy, then the breakdown of that cooperation and the development of a more independent labour movement has in turn been related to the decline of a labour aristocracy. And just as arguments about the emergence of a labour aristocracy have been contested and other explanations for a liberal labour movement put forward, so the same has happened in the debate over the development of an independent labour political movement. In certain ways the arguments are the reverse of those used in relation to the emergence of a labour aristocracy, with similar variations of emphasis upon workplace, community and politics. At the same time this decline can be seen in terms of the growing power and organisation of other sections of the working class. With these points in mind the case for the decline of a labour aristocracy can be briefly surveyed.

The case begins with claims about general changes in the economy and consequently the structure of the working class. Hobsbawm, for example, argued that from around 1890 there was a growth in the importance of semi-skilled workers, of which the 'New Unionism' was but one manifestation.[178] At the same time there was a growth of the service sector and of planning, administrative and other white-collar workers in industry. This had a two-fold effect upon the labour aristocracy. The rise of semi-skilled workers undermined its exclusive and privileged position within the working class, and the rise of new white-collar groups displaced it from its secure position between the working class and the lower middle class. This process can in turn be linked to changes in the international economy, in particular the economic character of imperialism and the intensification of competition from other rapidly growing industrial capitalist economies such as Germany and the United States of America.

Some of these points are beyond dispute. The white-collar class did grow rapidly in numerical importance. Larger units of production grew particularly fast in sectors such as coal-mining and transport, in the mass production of goods such as bicycles and cars (though the latter was still in its infacy by 1914) where semi-skilled workers increased greatly, helped by the application of new engineering technology. Even in engineering and textiles the role of semi-skilled workers seems to have increased, though not so dramatically as in 'new' industries where there were no earlier patterns of investment and skill structures to overcome. The rate of unionisation within industries increased sharply between 1890 and 1914 and turned the trade unions into genuine mass institutions.[179] Most of these points apply equally to Germany, arguably even more so as there was less of a 'craft' structure of industry to stand in the way.

Other points are more contentious. A minority labour movement gave way to a mass labour movement. But should one understand this as the displacement of a labour aristocracy or simply as a matter of extension downwards of existing organisation? One approach would be to argue that the expansion of industries in which a labour aristocracy was unimportant produced a shift of power within the labour movement. Even in industries such as engineering one could argue that it was the growth of new sectors, such as bicycle and car manufacture, with a much higher proportion of semi-skilled workers, rather than changes in established sectors, which was most important.[180] In this case one would expect a relatively painless process as new organisations emerged, unless the same unions were involved. Another approach has been to emphasis the way in which managerial and technological changes undermined (whether intentionally or not) the position of labour aristocracies in established industries. Here there have been debates about the nature and extent of such changes as the importance of 'Taylorism'.[181] There have also been debates about the responses of these workers to such changes, in particular whether the effect was to produce a conservative reaction or some sort of political radicalism which would help lead broader sections of the working class.[182]

Historians who never accepted the original labour aristocracy argument but pressed instead the case of endemic sectionalism could now argue that what was happening was simply the organisation of yet further sections of the working class. There were limits to this expansion.[183] Also it is not obvious that this quantitative change would necessarily bring about changes in the nature of labour politics. The newly organised workers were as likely to take an exclusive attitude towards competing groups of workers or threats from still unorganised workers as were the members of the earlier, smaller labour movement. At best the expansion could help the emergence of an independent labour movement by increasing the power of labour institutions in relation to non-labour institutions within broad liberal movements. If the non-labour institutions failed to respond properly to this changed balance of power, then the labour interest might move to more independent organisation.

However, some historians have been impressed by the responsiveness of liberalism to new labour pressure.[184] In any case, the greater power of labour could be blunted by the growing importance of the 'new' middle class and also of organisation amongst larger and better coordinated groups of employers. In the German case the growth of large-scale industry has, if anything, been seen as bringing about a reduction in the power of organised labour.[185] So historians have looked to other reasons for a change in labour politics in Britain. Some have found this in new types of state intervention – whether in the sphere of industrial relations, welfare arrangements, franchise reform, or the regulation of production and the labour force during war.[186] Others have argued that the growing importance of international competition forced employers to try to cut labour costs. This led to more extensive industrial conflicts and that in turn stimulated the politics of class conflict.[187]

The argument which looks at workers in the community proceeds differently.

Some historians have argued that only from about 1880 onwards were the conditions established in Britain in which a working-class culture and community could take shape.[188] In part this was a matter of settling in by a generation of 'hereditary proletarians', to use Zwahr's term. Partly it was to do with the spread of industry beyond a few regions.[189] Changes in transport meant that workers no longer had to cluster around their place of work and so an urban geography of separate working-class and middle-class districts could develop.[190] The growth of real wages for a wider section of the working class stimulated consumer industries and helped provide the material basis of a working-class culture.[191] Education and steady work helped eliminate some of the worst aspects of poverty and illiteracy and helped close up the divisions within the working class. All this could be argued to have promoted a sense of working-class identity on which a new, class-based labour movement could build.

Again, one can emphasise how this eroded the position of labour aristocrats – by leading to penetration of their associations and activities by less skilled workers, by undermining their attempts at residential segregation and a distinct life style. But it has tended to be the 'displacement' rather than the 'conflict' aspect which has been stressed. The growth of cultural activity, of education, of consumer influence on the part of 'intermediate' sectors of the working class simply made the position of the labour aristocracy less important. Once more this can be interpreted in terms of an extension downwards of minority benefits rather than of the decline of a labour aristocracy. There also remains the question of the political implications of such changes. Divisions within the working class remained important. I have already mentioned the argument that a responsive liberalism removed one reason for the shift to independent class politics.

To conclude for the British case – although there can be little dispute that the period 1890–1914 saw the emergence of a mass labour movement, it remains debatable how far that should be correlated with the decline of a labour aristocracy. There is also considerable debate on the relationship between the rise of that mass labour movement and of an independent working class politics. Finally, even where it is argued that the decline of the labour aristocracy was a central feature of the period, the manner of that decline and its political implications still remain matters of dispute.

The arguments are very different in the German case. Here there was *already* an independent labour movement, and if anything the major pressures were towards greater integration with state and society, not more independence and a more radical stance. Only where this is seen as the work of a labour oligarchy, as discussed in the previous section, is a type of labour aristocracy argument introduced.

The one exception to this in German historiography has been associated with arguments about the *andere Arbeiterbewegung*. Here it has been argued that the growing importance of semi- and unskilled workers (*Massenarbeiter*) threatens the position of an exclusive and reformist organised minority.[192] The radical historians associated with this approach argue that the onset of monopoly capitalism in an increasingly competitive capitalist world economy led to many changes in technology and methods of management which undermined the position of skilled workers. The size of factories and employers' federations increased in both scale and range of functions. Established organisations of labour, representing minorities of skilled workers, tried to adjust to such changes but many of their policies were irrelevant to the new mass working class that was being formed. The new workers responded more directly to the new situation, through unofficial strikes, sabotage, riots, and an increased interest in syndicalism.[193]

The approach has been subjected to various criticisms. First, it is often associated with a set of values which sees organisation itself as inherently reformist and only unorganised militancy as potentially revolutionary, rather recalling Bakunin's differences with Marx. Even historians who sympathise with aspects of the approach point out the need to look seriously at 'organised' radicalism.[194] The treatment of 'unorganised' radicalism is often unbalanced, wrenching such actions as 'sabotage' or 'theft' out of context in order to see them all as manifestations of the *andere Arbeiterbewegung*.[195] The extent of technological and managerial change has also been exaggerated, tending to confuse declarations of intent with achievements, and to generalise from highly a-typical firms.[196] It is clear that a 'respectable' (organised) and 'rough' (unorganised) distinction for the purpose of the cultural and political analysis of the German working class leaves much to be desired, especially when the latter category is coloured by radical romanticism. This work has drawn attention to some problems of re-ordering within the working class and the inadequacies of the existing organised labour movement in the face of that re-ordering, but does not go very far towards describing and explaining what was taking place. Incidentally, one can note that at the level of community or cultural studies, there has been little German work of the kind summarised earlier in this section for Britain. The study of working-class culture has tended to be either the study of the labour movement or of 'everyday' life. The notion of the growth of a mass culture which undermines the old minority labour institutions but which is itself increasingly organised and linked to an enlarged labour movement does not seem to have been taken very far.

More important than the case put forward by the advocates of the *andere Arbeiterbewegung* school are arguments about what happened *within* the expanding labour organisations. The parties with working-class support and trade unions were changed very much between 1890 and 1914. They were much larger, with broader worker support and often facing better organised employers and governments, as well as improved and mass organisation amongst middle-class groups. They had to confront new problems – though from very different initial positions in the two countries. Any fruitful account must look at the disputes between different groups of labour within these movements – and leave aside the relatively unimportant questions concerning differences between officials and members or between the organised and the unorganised. In the German case, there was pressure for greater involvement in the broader world, but this divided into radical and reformist options, placing the new mass institutions in an increasingly immobile position. Whether they were becoming more 'integrated' is itself a matter of debate. But unless one sees the earlier *radicalism* of the SPD as the product of a politically alienated labour aristocracy, the labour aristocracy argument seems to have no role at all to play in understanding what is happening.

Conclusion

It is clear that the concept of the labour aristocracy has had a quite different role to play in British and German labour history. It seems to me that the differences are greater than can be explained by the differences between the social and economic and cultural developments of the working classes of the two countries. In many ways such differences are assumed rather than demonstrated, although that is not to deny that there are considerable differences. When one appreciates that the original purpose of the concept of the labour aristocracy was to explain certain patterns of labour *politics*, then the differences in the ways in which the concept has been used become much clearer. The concept of the labour aristocracy is, in its origins, a way of retaining a belief in the reality of the working class as something other than a heuristic device, yet being able to explain why, in certain situations, that working class failed to understand itself and act as a class. Particular kinds of social, cultural, economic or organisational differences generated powerful minorities within the working class whose function, conscious or unconscious, was to suppress or inhibit the development of genuine working-class politics. Only, therefore, when the pattern of labour politics appeared in some sense unsatisfactory as class politics was the concept of a labour aristocracy introduced.

Once introduced, particularly when used by historians of ability and integrity, it took on a life of its own. Once one has argued that the basis of labour politics must be found in the sociology of the working class or in the economic relationships between different groups of workers or in the way in which labour organisations function, there is naturally a move to study these matters in their own right. In this way the concept becomes increasingly elaborate, detached from its original starting point, and contested in different ways according to the various emphases it can be given. It is this process which makes the subject a complicated one and which means that it is not possible simply to accept or reject the concept.

It does seem to me that in its original form as a way of linking labour politics to a certain kind of division within the working class, the concept is untenable. There are too many other divisions of importance and in any case working-class politics is shaped by much more than the internal composition of the working class. Perhaps this is why the labour oligarchy variant of the idea is particularly unsatisfactory: it retains a direct political relevance and yet it is clear that the division to which it draws attention provides hardly any guide to that politics. In its other forms the concept of a labour aristocracy retains a value, but only in the limited sense of describing certain patterns of social or economic differentiation within the working class in a particular community or industry at a particular time. That means it will have only a very limited role to play in explaining the pattern of labour politics. This also implies that the great differences in German and British labour politics between 1850 and 1914 cannot be taken as direct expressions of great differences in the social and economic characteristics of the German and British working classes. To explore the similarities and differences at those levels remains a task for a properly organised comparative approach. That in turn might help us to understand more about the relationship between the working class and the labour movement.

The essays which follow seek in some respects to advance such comparisons in the social, economic and cultural fields, but that is not the main emphasis. The discarding of the labour aristocracy concept as a useful way of explaining political differences means that comparison in this field has to proceed in very different ways. The essays which follow seek to develop such comparisons, placing an especial emphasis on the autonomy of labour politics, whether in the artisan movements of the mid-century or in the minority labour movements of the period c.1850–80. It also seeks to take liberalism seriously as a component *within* those early labour movements rather than as something which socially and ideologically is external to artisan and labour movements.

Notes

1 For accounts of contemporary usages of the terms 'labour aristocracy' and *Arbeiteraristokratie* see Shepherd, 1978; Beier 1981a and 1981b; and Müller, 1976.

2 Book printers in particular have been singled out for this treatment, partly because of their early development of occupational organisation. See Musson, 1954, Chauvet, 1956, and Beier, 1966.

3 For examples of protests and petitions on these lines see Bergmann, 1971; Noyes, 1966; and Breuilly & Sachse, 1984, especially chapter 4.

4 See Wissell, 1971 for such terminology.

5 Wright, 1867, 1868 and 1873. I follow the interpretation of Wright offered by Reid, 1983.

6 Mayhew, 1971; Mayhew, 1968, vol. 3, pp. 221–367 and vol. 4, pp. 1–22. For further examples of the idea of 'respectability' which is central to Mayhew's treatment see Place, 1972; Vincent, 1981; and Prothero, 1979, especially pp. 26f, 36f, 67ff and 328–40.

7 Müller, 1976.

8 Gagel, 1958.

9 Quoted in Leventhal, 1971, pp. 56–7. See Breuilly, Niedhart & Taylor (eds), forthcoming.

10 See the essay 'Liberalism or social democracy'.

11 For the role of popular politics as part of the background to the passing of the 1867 Reform Act see Vincent, 1972; and Leventhal, 1971.

12 See especially Smith, 1966 who, in his first chapter entitled 'The emergence of the labour aristocracy', virtually accepts the claims made for such a group in the debate.

13 One area of disagreement has concerned how far it was calculation of party advantage rather than pressure from below which led to reform in 1867. Cowling, 1967, placed much emphasis on high politics. Whether Disraeli expected to win many workers' votes is difficult to determine, but he did not grant more representation to the urban constituencies in which such workers would be an important new element in the electorate and which were generally already held by Liberals.

14 Bismarck had analyses of elections under the Prussian three-class franchise prepared. These showed that during the so-called 'New Era', from 1858 to 1862, as well as in further elections up to 1866, Conservatives frequently only performed better than Liberals in the third-class category in rural areas.

15 The exception proves the rule. The same problem applied to Ireland. Then 1867 did not make too great a difference because the major extensions of the franchise were in boroughs. However, it did contribute to the rise of a separate Irish National Party, and the Third Reform Act of 1884 provided that party with a rural mass base in almost all of Ireland.

16 On party organisation see the old but still valuable study of Hanham, 1959.

17 See the essay 'Liberalism or social democracy?'. On conservative voting see Mckenzie & Silver, 1969; Joyce, 1982, especially chapter 8. Lancashire had a reputation of working-class conservatism: see Vincent, 1968.

18 Leventhal, 1971; Harrison, 1960, 1961 and 1965.

19 Harrison, 1965 argues this case. Smith, 1966 assembles some testimony from contemporaries about savings. On the significance of trade union testimony see Hanson, 1975, the criticisms of Musson, and Thane, and Hanson's reply (Hanson *et al.*, 1976).

20 Müller, 1976 and Harrison, 1960 and 1961 look more closely at Engel's views. A report Engels wrote in 1874 on the General Election campaign of 1874 for the German social democratic newspaper *Der Volksstaat* and which raises some of these points is reprinted in English in Marx & Engels, 1954, pp. 464–70.

21 See the essay 'Liberalism or social democracy?'.

22 On organisational growth in Germany see Guttsman, 1981 and Schönhoven, 1980. On Britain see Hunt, 1981, chapter 9, and Hinton, 1982.

23 See Guttsman, 1981 for a survey of these arguments.

24 See Domansky–Davidsohn, n.d.

25 See the survey by Hinton, 1983, chapter 4.

26 See generally Gore, 1982.

27 Lenin, *What is to be done?* 1902, in numerous subsequent editions.

28 Michels, 1962. First published in German in 1911 (second edition 1925) with an English translation in 1913.

29 On Britain and syndicalism see Holton, 1976, especially his section on the most famous 'syndicalist' document of the pre-war period, *The Miners' Next Step*. In Germany the main interest, both at the time and later, focused on the mass strike debate. See Grüneberg (ed), 1970. For syndicalism at the popular level see Tenfelde, 1979. See also Schöttler, 1986.

30 For Lenin's arguments in relation to Britain, see Lenin, 1969, especially Part III: 'The working class of imperialist Britain'.

31 See Beetham, 1983.

32 See Kolakowski, 1978.

33 See Beier, 1981b.

34 Gramsci, 1971.

35 See Schönhoven, 1980, Introduction, especially pp. 19ff, where the character of 'in-house history' is described.

36 See Weber, 1924.

37 Rowntree, 1901; Booth, 1893; and Oberschall, 1965 for the work of the *Verein für Sozialpolitik*.

38 Mommsen, 1987; Beetham, 1981 and 1985.

39 Breuilly, 1986.

40 The title of one book on the period: see Burns, 1964.

41 Harrison, 1965, pp. 6–7.

42 See Moorhouse, 1978.

43 Beier, 1981a. I have altered the way these categories are used.

44 Hobsbawm, 1968, pp. 272–315. The essay was originally published in 1954.

45 *Ibid,*, p. 272.

46 Hobsbawm, 1984, especially pp. 214–72.

47 This was particularly the force of Pelling's criticism: see Pelling, 1968.

48 Reid, 1980, pp. 48–61 criticises forcefully dependence on the Wages Census of 1906 because this gives only the picture for the fully employed on full time at a relatively good point in the trade cycle.

49 For coalmining, with its demand for strength and its illnesses and accidents, see Tenfelde, 1981 and Harrison, 1978, especially the introduction by the editor. For the building trades see Renzsch, 1980, chapter 2; Burgess, 1975, chapter 2; and Price, 1980. Admittedly Hobsbawm does not include coalmining amongst the aristocratic occupations.

50 See note 11 for references to building. For tailoring see Renzsch, 1980, chapter 3; and for shoemaking, Schröder, 1978, pp. 162–92. For such trades in London see Jones, 1971 which pays close attention to seasonal unemployment.

51 See Mayhew, 1971.

52 Hunt, 1973; Bry, 1960, pp. 101–9.

53 Schomerus, 1977, especially chapter III. 2.

54 See Dasey, 1981.

55 Schofer, 1975, especially pp. 54–9; Harrison (ed), 1978.

56 Hobsbawm, 1984a, especially pp. 234–5; and Gray, 1981, especially pp. 15–19.

57 Pelling, 1968.

58 Reid, 1978 presents the case most clearly.

59 See the essay on 'Liberals or social democracy?' for some evidence about wages in Germany compared to Britain. It is a problem that lack of interest in the idea of a labour aristocracy does mean that research into wage differentials and other forms of differentiation within the working class has not been pursued to anything like the same extent.

60 Musson, 1972 and 1976.

61 Turner, 1962. Other work, such as that of Harrison, 1965 simply used the idea as a background assumption. For the development of historical writing since Hobsbawm's early essays see Gray, 1981.

62 A survey up to 1979 is contained in *The Cambridge Journal of Economics*, 1979.

63 Braverman, 1974.

64 For a criticism of this starting point see Littler, 1982 which brings out the various meanings of the concept of 'job control' and relates this to different patterns of development in early twentieth- century Britain, Japan and the USA. See also the critical review of Zeitlin, 1983.

65 For an analysis of these terms see Jones, 1975, an extended critique of Foster, 1974. Examples of work on Britain which argues a case of this kind are: Price, 1980 (for building workers), Behagg, 1979 (on changes in small workshops in Birmingham), and Melling, 1980 (on the emergence of the foreman).

66 I follow Littler, 1982 in distinguishing these three different aspects of job control.

67 See references given in note 27.

68 See Burgess, 1980, especially pp. 12–16.

69 Samuel, 1977 and also the essay on artisans in this book.

70 More, 1980.

71 See Hunt, 1981, especially pp. 25–31 for figures.

72 See Joyce 1982; Turner 1962; Foster 1974; Lazonick, 1979, and Penn, 1983.

73 Burgess, 1975.

74 *Ibid.*; Price, 1980.

75 See, for example, Crossick, 1978.

76 Price, 1980.

77 Price, 1975.

78 See Humphry, 1913

79 Foster, 1974; Jones, 1975.

80 For example, Alexander McDonald, who went on to become a Lib–Lab MP. See Wilson, 1982.

81 Jones, 1975 argues this case particularly strongly.

82 On exclusive unions see Turner, 1962 who developed the useful distinction between open and closed unions. More generally one can link this to the argument that social class differences arise out of the way in which 'closure' is organised. See Parkin, 1979 especially pp. 44–73. A rather different way of looking at the matter is in terms of a distinction between primary and secondary labour markets, that is one labour market where job recruitment and conditions are relatively secure and another one where it is not. This in turn has been linked to the idea of employers having a 'core' labour force and then a another class of employees with much higher turnover and insecurity. See Littler, 1982.

83 More, 1980, and Littler, 1982.

84 Musson, 1972 and 1976.

85 Littler, 1982 deals with the continuity of worker control over the employment relationship; Reid, 1980 provides a very detailed account of craft controls in the shipbuilding industry.

86 Penn brings this out clearly.

87 See Reid for examples.

88 See Conze & Engelhardt (eds), 1979; Polh (ed), 1978; Zwahr, 1978; Crew, 1979; Ditt, 1982; and further references in Tenfelde, 1980.

89 Geary, 1986.

90 Kocka, 1983 and 1986.

91 For a general review of the subject see Kaufhold, 1979.

92 See below, the essay on artisans. This continuity approach is best expressed in various of the essays of Wolfram Fischer in Fischer, 1971.

93 See Schröder, 1978.

94 Fischer, 1971.

95 In addition to Schomerus, 1977; Ditt, 1982; and Zwahr, 1978 already cited, see Assmann & Stavhagen, 1969; and data in Fischer *et al.*, 1982.

96 For engineering see Schomerus, 1977; Schröter & Becker, 1962. For mining see Tenfelde, 1981. For iron and steel see Crew, 1979. For building see Renzsch, 1980.

97 See Albrecht, 1982 for a study focused on unions as organisations.

98 Tenfelde, 1981; and taken to excessive lengths so far as the role of tradition is concerned, Moore, 1978.

99 Schofer, 1975 reveals a very different situation in the coal mines of Lower Silesia compared to those of the Ruhr. For yet another regional pattern in mining see Mallmann, 1981. For an interesting example of how employers' controls could be turned against them see Steffens, 1981.

100 Renzsch, 1980.

101 *Ibid.*

102 *Ibid*; Crew, 1979 and Schröder, 1978.

103 See Schomerus, 1977 and Ditt, 1982 on social and regional origins. On the German/Polish distinction in mine areas see Klessmann, 1978 for the Ruhr and Machtan, 1983, chapter 3, for Upper Silesia.

104 On the importance of teamwork in mining see Crew, 1979. Job mobility has not been so extensively examined but it is clear from Schofer, 1975 that it was high.

105 On the issue of paternalism see Schulz, 1978 and Schomerus, 1977 who show its apparent effectiveness. This aligns their work with that of Joyce, 1982 for Britain. For the way paternalism could backfire see Steffens, 1981. Either way, however, the importance of workforce differences are played down.

106 See Littler, 1982 for the distinction between primary and second labour markets which relates closely to these different employer practices.

107 See Zwahr, 1978 for examples of increasingly similar treatment of workers in terms of labour contracts.

108 Eisenberg, 1986 is especially interesting on this, arguing for a more integrated workplace culture amongst skilled British workers compared to Germans, which in turn would benefit trade union strength and place the focus of activity upon economic rather than political organisation.

109 See Cattaruzza, 1984.

110 Kaelble, 1983.

111 Goldthorpe *et al.*, 1968/69.

112 Gramsci, 1971.

113 Johnson, 1985.

114 Tenfelde, 1988; Breuilly, 1989a.

115 Breuilly, 1989a. See Hobsbawm, 1984b and 1984c, and Hoggart, 1957.

116 For Germany see the studies in Evans (ed.), 1982. Hoggart, 1957 was subject to sharp criticism from this direction in Roberts, 1978. The failure of Hobsbawm to properly appreciate the role of poverty in shaping working-class culture in England is argued by Davies, 1988.

117 Gray, 1976; Crossick, 1978; Foster, 1974.

118 Other relevant work includes: Hopkins, 1975; Harrison (ed), 1978; Masumura, 1983. For relevant works in French and American labour history which also cannot be considered here see Moss, 1976; Scott, 1974; and Mackenzie, 1973.

119 Crew, 1979; Zwarh, 1978; Schomerus, 1977; Ditt, 1982.

120 Gray, 1976, chapter 3; Crossick, 1978, more diffusely in chapters 3–5.

121 Foster, 1974, chapter 6.

122 Foster, 1974, chapter 7.

123 Calhoun, 1982, pp. 29–32.

124 Gray, 1976, pp. 95–9.

125 Crossick, 1978, especially p. 119.

126 Gray, 1976, especially p. 116.

127 Gray, 1976, pp. 100–11; Crossick, 1978, chapters 8–9.

128 For the idea of 'the triumph of the entrepreneurial ideal' see Perkin, 1969, chapter 8.

129 See also Tholfsen, 1976, a more nationally oriented and purely intellectual study. He sketched out some of these arguments in Tholfsen, 1971.

130 Apart from his book, see also Crossick, 1976 for a briefer statement of these arguments.

131 Gray, 1976, p. 6. See also Gray, 1977.

132 For a critique of Gray see Morris, 1977; and of Crossick, see Reid, 1979. Two important critiques of Foster are Jones, 1975; and Musson, 1976.

133 I distinguish 'instrumental' (or first-order) statements, that is language which is part of some routine social action, from 'reflective' (or second-order) statements, that is language which presents a view about social action. For example, the testimony of trade union officials to the Royal Commission on Trade Unions presented a view about trade union action. Whether those officials used the same kind of language when actually engaged in trade union disputes is another matter. For the problems this particular case presents the historian see Hanson, 1975 and Hanson *et al.*, 1976. Obviously this testimony in turn can be seen as first-order language in the context of public inquiries.

134 Most British criticisms of Gray, unable to cope with his theoretical sophistication, have focused on 'empirical' questions, but that is where Gray is very strong. Thompson attacked Nairn and Anderson for using a concept of 'true class-consciousness', in this case dressed up in the form of 'Other Countries' (Thompson, 1965), though he seemed to think that it was the 'vulgarisation' of the concept rather than its very nature which created problems.

135 Zwahr, 1978; and more broadly, Zwahr (ed), 1981. For a general review of Zwahr's work in English see Breuilly, 1987.

136 Zwahr, 1978, pp. 129–55, where his evidence on social mobility rates does not seem to fit his argument that it was becoming more difficult for workers to move out of the working class. Apart from my critique in Breuilly, 1987a see reviews by Kocka, 1980 and Pollard, 1980.

137 Schomerus, 1977; Ditt, 1982.

138 Breuilly, 1987a, pp. 534–5 provides more detail as well as references to the work of this school and its critics. Tenfelde, 1980 makes some critical comments in relation to Schomerus's book about the lack of concern with conflict in such forms as strikes and politics.

139 Ditt, 1982, especially chapter 2. He contrasts his approach and findings on social mobility with Zwahr, 1978.

140 Crew, 1979. I have not had a chance to consider in detail Kocka, 1990a and 1990b which will be the definitive synthesis of work on the making of a German working class for a long time. However, as Kocka follows the lines he sketched out in Kocka, 1983 and 1986 (for a critical review of this see Breuilly, 1987a), then the distinction between skilled and unskilled labour will be rather less important than that between various sectors and types of wage labour, and will not in any case be linked to a notion of an aristocracy of labour.

141 An example of the American approach is Thernstrom, 1964.

142 The focus on work and strike patterns can also be found in Moore, 1978 though the two writers seem to have arrived fairly independently at their conclusions. The interest in illiberalism on Crew's part owed much to the arguments of Eley. See Blackbourn & Eley, 1984.

143 The argument was earlier developed in Crew, 1973/74. See also Crew, 1986.

144 For an earlier period see Calhoun, 1982 who asserts rather than demonstrates the community base of popular politics. Above all see Joyce, 1982. Other relevant studies are much more concerned with urban social or family history in which workers figure as just one element. See, for example, Armstrong, 1974 and Anderson, 1971.

145 For examples of the institutional approach see Wissell, 1971. An important pioneering work was Stadelmann & Fischer, 1955. For examples of more recent work see Engelhardt (ed), 1984. Outstanding, and owing much to anthropological approaches is Griessinger, 1981.

146 A pioneering work was Roth, 1963, subjected to strong criticism by Evans in his introduction to Evans, 1982. A more balanced introduction to the subject can be found in Guttsman, 1981, chapter 5. The major English-language work is Lidtke, 1985.

147 Evans, 1982 includes studies of this kind, which it interestingly tries to relate back to the world of conflict and politics. See also Huck (ed), 1982 and Reulecke & Weber (eds), 1978.

148 See Schieder, 1963.

149 Noyes, 1966. For more recent work see Langewiesche, 1981, especially pp. 471–8.

150 Balser, 1962; Offermann, 1979.

151 Thus Balser, 1962 stresses the reformist, social democratic nature of the Brotherhood of German Workers, whereas von Berg, 1981 focuses on a revolutionary and communist element.

152 See the essay on artisans below.

153 Offermann, 1979; above all the work of Lenger, 1986 and 1988. The work on liberalism and the Mittelstand can be mentioned here: see the essay below on liberalism. Also important is the unique work of Na'aman (see for example, Na'aman, 1969: a brief but richly suggestive study) which takes seriously the notion of a democratic political culture as a constant element in the labour movement of this period.

154 On *Arbeiterbildungsvereine*, apart from work cited in the last couple of notes, see Birker, 1973. On cooperatives see Offermann, 1979 and Aldenhoff, 1984.

155 For an example see Breuilly & Sachse, 1984, especially chapter 8. I make the comparisons more explicit in the essay below: 'Liberalism or social democracy?'.

156 An argument first sketched out in Conze, 1965 and now more fully considered in Offermann, 1979 and Aldenhoff, 1984.

157 For the example of Württemberg, see Schmierer, 1970.

158 I think this is the case with Offermann, 1979 as I argued in a review in *Social History* 7 (1982), though this still remains one of the best studies of the labour movement of the 1850s and early 1860s.

159 Michels, 1962.

160 *Ibid.*, for the SPD, and for an up-to-date survey, Guttsman, 1981. On the metalworkers' union see Domansky–Davidsohn, n.d. On the ASE see Hinton, 1973.

161 Ritter & Tenfelde, 1975 and Schönhoven, 1980 clearly demonstrate membership growth.

162 Hunt, 1981, chapter 9; Hinton, 1982.

163 Again, more clearly for Germany: Guttsman, 1981; Schönhoven, 1980.

164 Schröder, 1976.

165 Domanksy–Davidsohn, n.d.

166 See Nettl, 1969.

167 On the function of 'Kautskyism' as an ideology of integration within the SPD see Matthias, 1957.

168 See Groh, 1975 and Schorske, 1983 for examples.

169 Domansky–Davidsohn, n.d.; Hinton, 1973; Gore, 1982; Geary, 1978.

170 Domansky–Davidsohn; Grüttner, 1982.

171 Lützenkirchen, 1970; Nolan, 1981.

172 Schönhoven, 1980; Hickey, 1978 and 1985.

173 Much of the following argument draws upon Guttsman, 1981.

174 Saul, 1974; Hall, 1977.

175 The panels set up to administer the state sickness insurance system was the nearest thing to this but does not really fit the bill of a compulsory state institution with privileged access for labour officials.

176 Guttsman, 1981 nicely refers to the SPD as a 'functionary's democracy' (p. 244), meaning by functionary the activist member.

177 Well-known tensions are those between the south German state parties and the SPD leadership in Berlin; and between the city party in Stuttgart and the state-wide party. See Schorske, 1983.

178 Hobsbawm, 1968.

179 Hinton, 1982; Ritter & Tenfelde, 1975.

180 Mann, forthcoming.

181 Littler, 1982; and the various studies in Litler & Gospel (eds), 1983.

182 Hinton, 1973.

183 Hinton, 1982.

184 Clarke, 1971.

185 Eduard Bernstein, who thought such growth would improve the position of labour, eventually came to recognise the falsity of this idea. See Breuilly, 1987c.

186 Reid, 1978.

187 Mann, forthcoming.

188 Jones, 1973/74; Meacham, 1977.

189 Mann, forthcoming.

190 Jones, 1973/74; Joyce, 1982.

191 Jones, 1973/74; Meacham, 1977.
192 Roth, 1974.
193 Roth, 1974 and Brockhaus, 1975.
194 Lucas, 1976. See also Lucas, *et al.*, 1977: a collection debating this approach.
195 For a corrective to this see Grüttner, 1982 and Crew, 1982.
196 Wickham, in Lucas *et al.*, 1977; Homburg, 1978 and 1983.

3

Artisan economy, ideology and politics: the artisan contribution to the mid-nineteenth-century European labour movement

Introduction

Artisans are increasingly seen as central in the nineteenth-century labour movement as well as various other forms of popular politics. Revisions in economic history have also suggested a more central role for small workshop production in the economic development of the period than older views of industrialisation had allowed for. It is time that connections were made between these political and economic reevaluations. Comparison across national boundaries can also help us to understand to what extent such revisions and connections point to a common, underlying artisan experience and a response to change which has been obscured for so long by national frameworks in historical analysis.

The term artisan is taken to mean a skilled craftsman working in sectors of the economy dominated by production in small workshops. This craftsman may be the owner of that workshop or an employee. He will have served a formal apprenticeship, or at least have had to complete a term of training before being fully accepted into the trade. 'He' will be a man. By the term labour movement, I mean associations which bring together people from a range of occupations and which stress their common interest as people who work.

Clearly there are difficulties about the use of such broad terms. What is a 'small' workshop? What is 'skilled'? What is 'training'? What about craftsmen who move between small workshops and larger factories? What about associations which are largely based on a particular occupation (such as trade unions) or which have a high proportion of workers in their membership but do not define themselves in those terms (such as certain religious sectarian groups)? However, these terms are simply intended to provide a departure point for this essay. As will become clear, one cannot separate sharply an 'artisan' sector or labour movement from other sectors and movements. The small workshop underwent changes both internal and in relation to other units of production which had a major impact on artisan politics and ideology. Pressure on the artisan also affected the content and value of apprenticeship and other kinds of training and the skill and control that craftsmen could bring to bear on their work. So many of the problems raised by the use of these terms will be taken up in the course of the essay.

I will focus upon artisans in Britain, France and Germany in the period c.1830–70. I limit attention to these three cases out of practical considerations of knowledge. The choice of the period 1830 to 1870 has been made for a number of reasons. The major one has to do with the development of the labour movement. In the German case a labour movement only began to take shape in the form of journeymen's clubs and workers' educational associations from the 1830s.[1] Clearly in the British case there was a labour movement prior to the 1830s but it developed on a new scale following the disillusionment with the Reform Act of 1832, reaction to the New Poor Law of 1834, and then the rise of Chartism.[2] In France it was under the July Monarchy that there was first formed a labour movement with interests in politics, labour questions and socialism.[3] The foundation of the German Second Empire between 1866 and 1871 heralded a new phase in the history of the labour movement, bringing with it the establishment of independent labour parties contesting elections to a national parliament based on universal manhood suffrage.[4] There was also a change, if not so sharp, in the character of the British labour movement with the passing of the Second Reform Act in 1867, the formation of the Trades Union Congress in 1868, and the passing of new labour legislation in 1871 and 1875.[5] The Paris Commune, its repression, and the formation of the Third Republic with a sovereign parliament elected by universal manhood suffrage likewise ushered in a new period in the French labour movement.[6]

One can also make out a case in economic terms for this choice of period. It is increasingly recognised that the industrial development of the period before 1870 – by which is meant a shift of production to large enterprises with rational divisions of relatively unskilled labour using new types of machinery powered from inanimate sources – had had only a limited impact on the whole economy, even in Britain.[7] The appearance of much of what we associate with industrial society was in its infancy, such as separate working-class areas in industrial townships or suburbs, the numerical dominance of industrial wage-labour within the whole labour force, the economic dominance of manufacturing industry, especially that concentrated in factory production. Whether, indeed, 'industrialisation' in these terms ever did come to pass outside the imaginations of those responding to large-scale and unprecedented change is another matter,[8] but certainly the period up to 1870 – apart from specific branches of production – was not dominated by such a development. Once this point is firmly grasped, and the consequent revision of the interpretation of economic development for the period undertaken, then certain aspects of labour politics and ideology which are often regarded as 'backward' and 'reactionary' will be seen in a new light. In the rest of this essay I hope to sketch out such a reinterpretation as it applies to artisans in the labour movement.

I shall begin by setting out the problems I wish to consider. Then I shall examine the typical economic changes to which artisans were subjected. Next I shall look at how such changes could push artisans into taking up ideas and forms of action which transcended occupational boundaries. Finally, I shall consider the nature of artisan politics. In a short essay it will only be possible to make some general points and to illustrate these with some examples with no pretension to a detailed or exhaustive treatment of the subject.

The problem

I begin with three quotations which say something about the similarity of artisan values in the three countries.

(a) . . . let all the useful and valuable members of every trade who wish to appear respectable, unite with each other, and be in friendship with all other trades, and you will render yourselves worthy members of society, at once respectable and respected. (John Gast, 1826.)[9]

(b) *Article 1.* The Brotherhood of Workers is intended to create a strong organisation covering workers of all occupations, and organisation based on mutuality and brotherliness in which the rights and desires of the individual shall be reconciled with the whole, and work linked to pleasure.

Article 18. The local association shall meet at least once a week. Its tasks are: to investigate the needs and difficulties of workers both in specific occupations and generally, and to help in these matters; to advise and to guide workers on their working and economic conditions; to promote mutuality and brotherliness amongst workers through labour exchanges and the establishement and democratic management of voluntary funds for sickness, death, invalidity and other purposes; to spread knowledge and education amongst workers by means of instruction, libraries, model workshops, etc.; and thereby to realise the purposes laid down in Article 1. (From the Statutes of the Brotherhood of German Workers, 1850. My translation.)[10]

(c) We wish to conquer our dignity as men and our rights as citizens . . . we are determined to educate ourselves, constantly to seek moral improvement, to practise union and fraternity. We are determined to force the bourgeoisie and the rich to respect us and to listen to our claims. (From *'Des ouvrier, a leurs camarades'*, 1842. My translation.)[11]

John Gast was a shipwright and leading activist in the London labour and radical movement in the first decades of the century. He participated in trade union, educational, agitational, cooperative, and many other collective ventures. In Prothero's study centring on John Gast we are presented with a rich and detailed account of the artisan world of London.

The Brotherhood of German Workers was the most important labour organisation established in Germany before the 1860s. It drew its membership overwhelmingly from artisans. The 'other purposes' mentioned in the statutes included, in practice, the establishment of a national newspaper and of producer and consumer cooperatives.

The final quotation is taken from a petition of communist workers which had been drawn up by twenty men on 6 December 1841. It was published in the artisan journal *Populaire*, by which time it had attracted some 1, 150 signatures in Paris alone, and about another 500 signatures from Lyon and other places.

Against this background one can make some general points about the passages quoted and the contexts in which they were written. First, they all express a common set of values concerning respectability, security, and solidarity. The interlocking of these three concerns underpins artisan actions and values throughout this period. Second, they point to the very great variety of associational activity. In many cases – whether within, between, or beyond specific occupations – these activities were not expressed through single-purpose associations. An institutional approach to labour history which separates trade unionism, benefit societies, educational associations, cooperatives, and political associations from one another can easily overlook this essential feature of the artisan labour movement.[12] Furthermore, much of this was informally organised, or the ostensible purpose of a formal association was constrained by the law, and the association was also involved in other activities. However, it would be wrong in turn to argue that some 'ulterior' purpose was the 'real' goal of activity. Rather, formal association needs to be understood in relation to a culture of solidarity which resisted narrowly functional organisation.

Third, a closer look at these associations, especially when one moves beyond those concerning particular occupations, suggests that certain trades predominate. These are above all tailors, shoemakers, cabinet-makers, and skilled building workers – what are known as the *Massenhandwerk* trades in Germany. Partly this may be due to the numerical weight of these trades within the whole artisan sector. However, I will argue that there are other reasons.

One should also note differences. The English quotation suggests a more stable tradition of informal association. The German quotation indicates a desire for very formal organisation. The French quotation includes a clear attack on other classes. It would be too simplistic to tie these differences directly to general contrasts so often made between the three countries – the empirical, the bureaucratic, and the revolutionary. Much depends on the particular situation and other quotations could be selected with quite different implications. But this does point to the need for comparison to draw attention to differences as much as to similarities.

These observations suggest a number of tasks. First, it would seem useful to identify, by means of systematic description, the similarities and differences between these artisan organisations across national boundaries. One narrow front on which this can be carried out is in relation to the labour internationalism of the period as expressed in organisations such as the Fraternal Democrats and the International Working Men's Association (IWMA).[13] The connections between artisans from various countries and their common concerns point to a common set of experiences. Labour internationalism in this period is not intrinsically significant – it had only a very limited membership and no power – but it is interesting as one point of entry into such cross-national comparisons.

The next step beyond some comparative description of artisan associations is an investigation into the reasons artisans acted together in these ways. The obvious starting point would be a consideration of the economic difficulties faced by artisans. In general terms it is not too difficult to do this and the plight of various crafts is, in some respects at least, well-documented. However, this would not directly address the question of the general significance of such difficulties. It would also omit the problem of understanding how connections could be made between artisans across occupational boundaries. A general framework which considers the artisan trades as more than a collection of particular trades is needed.

The most common form such a framework has taken has involved the use of the contrasting concepts of 'pre-industrial' and 'industrial' society, along with the concept of 'industrialisation' as the transformation which leads from one type of society to the other. It is commonly recognised that artisans played a prominent role in the labour movement which formed in the early phase of industrialisation. Two basic reasons are given for this, one negative and one positive. The negative reason is that these artisans were resisting the threat which industrialisation posed to them. Industrialisation threatened their chances of independence by under-mining the viability of small units of production. It also threatened their status as skilled workers through the introduction of machinery which could use less-skilled labour. The positive reason is that these artisans possessed certain resources – organisations, traditions, literacy, expectations – which enabled them to put up a spirited and collective resistance to industrialisation. One could treat these workers sympathetically. One could argue that this early phase of the labour movement had important positive influences upon later phases, for example with its attachment to socialist critiques of industrial capitalism, and with its emphasis upon organisation and democracy. But the sympathy is frequently tinged with a sense of regret that the battle was doomed to failure, and the sense of any continuity is qualified by the view that there had to take place eventually a fundamental shift towards a labour movement based upon industrial workers who accepted the fact of industrialisation and who operated on the basis of that acceptance.[14]

The one argument of importance which rejected this view removed any sense of major discontinuity. This stressed that the 'artisans' of the early and mid-nineteenth century were best understood as skilled workers protecting as best they could their sectional interests. In this way they were no different from skilled workers later in the century. Clearly there had been changes in the occupational structure, the political and economic context within which skilled workers combi-ned to protect their interests, and in the consequent scale, methods and degree of success of the organisations which those workers established. But these were changes of degree rather than kind.[15] More recent work focusing on the continuity of craft trades and controls after 1850/70 carries with it similar implications.[16] This continuity argument has been pressed most effectively for Britain, where the transition from pre-industrial to industrial is often assumed to have occurred most completely and smoothly.

The problem with the first approach is that it neglects important continuities and is based upon dubious assumptions about pre-industrial and industrial society and the forms taken by the transition from one to the other.The second approach makes too much of continuity and neglects the point that the changes in context which it acknowledges amount to a fundamental disruption of the world in which an artisan labour movement was formed. The challenge is to find another, more satisfactory framework within which to place the artisan labour movement, one which both accounts for continuity and discontinuity and which also relates economic, political and ideological elements to one another without resorting to any form of reductionism.

The first step to take in constructing such a framework involves questioning the assumption about the centrality of factory production to the economic change of the period. This assumption underlies some of the most influential interpretations of the course of the labour movement. For example, the argument that reformist and 'Lib–Lab' politics in Britain was based upon the emergence of a labour aristocracy involves distinguishing this group from both an earlier class of pre-industrial artisans and a later class of less-skilled industrial wage-earners. In the German case the absence of such a phase in the labour movement has been attributed to the more abrupt transition from a pre-industrial to an industrial society dominated by a relatively unskilled and concentrated labour force. The lack of such a clear trend in the case of France has been related to the slow, uncertain, even 'laggard' pace of French industrial development and the continued importance, therefore, of pre-industrial artisans in the labour movement. From this one can go on to make the well-worn contrasts between the 'mature' industrial society of Britain (with its correspondingly mature and pragmatic labour movement), a new and vigorous industrial society in Germany (with its correspondingly militant and class-conscious labour movement), and a rather backward, handicraft dominated French economy (with its correspondingly artisan dominated labour movement attracted to such ideas as anarcho-syndicalism).[17]

There has been no shortage of criticisms of this approach. The general economic perspective was already placed in question by Clapham (1932, 1968). Recent studies have stressed the 'survival' and even expansion of artisan trades.[18] Historians have been compelled to question an approach which places 'industrialisation' at the centre of attention, by such factors as the present de-industrialisation of Britain, the growth of advanced branches of technology which do not need to be concentrated into factories, the development of twentieth-century versions of the 'putting-out' system controlled by multi-national companies on a global scale, the absolute and relative decline of the industrial labour force within the total labour force well before it had constituted the best part of that labour force, and the sheer impossibility of generalising the experience of industrial growth throughout the world.[19]

More specifically, in German labour history for the period up to 1870 there has been new work emphasising continuities in the labour movement before, during and after 1848.[20] Work on the period after 1870 has shown how artisan concerns frequently underlay 'modern' Marxist ideas in the socialist party (SPD) or the 'industrial' trade union movement.[21] In France economic historians have questioned the conventional wisdom of backwardness, and labour historians have burrowed beneath the level of leaders and programmes to reveal complex continuities within the labour movement.[22] In England there has been similar work.[23] There are still defects. For example, German historians have not related this work on the labour movement sufficiently to general economic change. English historians of the politics and ideology of labour tend not to cross the 1850 divide but to study either the Chartist or the post-Chartist period. Nevertheless, all this work puts this idea of discontinuiy into question.

I think this work could benefit by being brought into a comparative framework. To do this requires from the outset the establishment of an explicitly general framework.[24] This is what I shall try to provide. First, I will develop an argument which stresses the centrality of small workshop production and craft labour in the economic development of the period. That means that the response of the artisan labour movement to economic development was of central importance and should not be seen as backward or increasingly peripheral. Second, I will try to show how the participation of these artisan trades in the economic growth and development of the period led to a crisis which stimulated organisational and ideological innovation, especially at a supra-occupational level. However, these responses did vary from one case to another, especially because of the varying political contexts. In this way I hope to bring out differences as well as similarities in the cases considered.

Economy

I shall begin by rather crudely equating the economic sector in which artisans are of central importance with small workshops producing articles for consumption. Any detailed investigation cannot operate for long with so crude an equation, but it is a useful starting point.[25]

We can begin with some interesting statistics assembled by Wolfram Fischer for Germany.[26] In the Federal Republic of Germany (excluding West Berlin and the Saarland) there were, in 1962, about 700,000 small workshops employing some 3.5 million people. This was about 12.5 times the number of industrial enterprises, and the labour force was about one-half the size of those employed in factories. The average number of employees in a small workshop was just over five, and these units of production accounted for about 11 per cent of GNP. Measured by all of these criteria, craft-shop production had increased in importance between 1936 and 1962.

One can look at trends over a longer period of time, although statistics can furnish only the roughest of indications of what was taking place. Around 1816 official Prussian calculations suggest that those engaged in small workshop production accounted for about 4 per cent of the total population. (Obviously this indicates a much larger proportion of the labour force, but in an economy dominated by agriculture it is impossible to provide a figure for those 'in employment'. I shall therefore measure only the artisan labour force – as well as estimates of its dependents – in relation to total population.) By 1843 the figure had risen to about 4.3 per cent, and by 1858 to around 6 per cent. The figure for Germany as a whole in 1895 was about 4.5 per cent. Regional investigations suggest that the artisan labour force did decline relatively between 1875 and 1890, years of falling or stagnant price and profit levels. However, they also suggest that the decline was sharpest in the less industrialised or industrialising areas, and that the small workshop labour force expanded both absolutely and relatively in more industrial or rapidly industrialising areas.[27] Figures also suggest that there was a resumption in the general upward trend of the artisan labour force in the decade or so after 1895, years of rapid industrial development and rising prices and profits. Very generally, over the whole period 1815–1962 the artisan labour force and its dependents may have increased from about 15 per cent of the total population to about 25 per cent.

It must be emphasised that these are very crude figures. Their meaning changes over time with alterations in census definitions, practices, and precision. They measure a very arbitrary thing: the number of manufacturing units and of those employed in those units above and below a certain level. Expansion of the units below that level tell us nothing about the character of artisan production; about the sorts of goods and services produced; the skill structures, technologies, and divisions of labour within workshops; the relationship between owner and employees; the relationship with other sectors of the economy; the role of credit in the operation of these workshops; and the nature and extent of the markets for the products of small workshops. There were significant changes in all these areas so that the nature of the 'artisan' sector and its relationship to other sectors was quite different by the end of the period from what it had been at the beginning. Those who try to use these figures to argue that they prove that the artisan sector did not undergo crisis, that it prospered and demonstrated steady continuity, are going beyond what the figures can support. Above all, there was during this period a general shift of economic activity away from the primary to the secondary and tertiary sectors. Craft-shop production ceased to dominate the manufacturing sector and the urban economy. Nevertheless, the figures do suggest that there is something wrong with the assumption that industrialisation entailed the destruction, or at least the contraction of small workshop production. Statistics on skilled workers in these workshops should also give pause to those who would argue that industrialisation involves the decline of such occupations in the face of an increasing number of unskilled and semi-skilled workers.[28] One can argue about the definitions of occupation and the measurement of skill, but such figures do pose a problem for the view that industrialisation involved the growth of factories at the expense of small workshops, and of less skilled workers using machines and more elaborate divisions of labour at the expense of skilled craftsmen.

This trend in the expansion of small workshops is clearly documented for Prussia and for other German states for the period 1830–1870. It is a trend which exists irrespective of whether laws encouraged the free practice of trades or recognised and favoured restrictions by corporations.[29] It is something which Clapham recognised some time ago for Britain and for which Raphael Samuel more recently provided a mass of detail which breathed life into the dry statistics.[30] In a different way, the point has been made for France where the dominance of an artisan economy in the manufacturing sector has long been recognised. Now French economic historians argue that rates of growth in the French economy are not especially slower than those of neighbouring economies, so that one cannot equate an artisanal economy with a slow-growth economy.[31] Even here there is a danger that this revisionist work will actually understate the role of artisan production in the cases with which France is compared.[32]

Clearly in the case of France a great deal of this economic growth was concentrated in domestic and rural production, which raises very different issues from the ones considered in this essay. But the rapid economic and demographic growth of cities such as Paris and Lyon was marked by the rapid expansion of small workshops. This has led some historians to assume that these cities remained 'pre-industrial' centres, and to conclude that the labour movements of these cities were in large measure 'pre-industrial'. That in turn has shaped the interpretation of events such as the June insurrection in Paris in 1848. For example, it has been questioned whether it should be seen as the last great pre-industrial protest or the first example of modern working-class struggle.[33] But once the image of industrial development as the dominance of the factory and the unskilled or semi-skilled worker is questioned, so is the necessity of choosing one or other of these interpretations.

The same point can be made for cases further afield which are not considered in this essay. Olga Crisp, for example, has pointed to the expansion and significance of craft-shop and domestic manufacturing in the Russian economy of the later nineteenth and early twentieth centuries, though it does appear to be domestic, 'cottage' (*kustar*) production which is of especial importance. The focus in the Russian case upon the role of the state and the forced development of large factory production within a few centres such as St. Petersburg may have led to an unbalanced account of Russian economic development.[34]

We should not be surprised by any of this. The economies of nineteenth-century Europe had a plentiful supply of labour for manufacturing purposes. This available labour force was not very well organised and did not have high expectations about wage levels. Large sections of it could be trained quite easily beyond the level of unskilled work because, at least in western and parts of central Europe, there were high literacy rates and no great obstacles to 'acculturation'. The craft-workshop was the most important institution for the provision of such training (and also for the supply of skilled workers to the whole labour force) and could be expanded quite rapidly by means of the establishment of more workshops and the recruitment of extra workers at the lower end of the age and wage scales.[35] What needs to be explained is rather why capital should be diverted into large-fixed investments in factory buildings and machinery which could not be flexibly reduced or expanded in line with levels of demand and profit.

One can identify a number of specific reasons. In some cases there were technical imperatives, such as those involved in opening up deeper mines or using chemical processes. In some cases there was a very rapid increase in demand, perhaps due to the capture of certain export markets, which could only be met quickly by means of a shift to new technology and/or larger units of production, and where anticipated profits justified investments into production innovation. In some cases there might have been very specific labour supply problems (due perhaps to the scarcity of particular types of skilled labour or the organisational strength of workers with those specific skills) which would make it advantageous to invest in machines or ways of re-organising production which could ease the problem of labour supply. But in many cases, capital was more rationally invested in the re-organisation of marketing and credit, or in intensifying the use of labour and elaborating the division of labour. None of these changes necessarily reduced the quantitative role of the small workshop, indeed it could actually make them more productive. A small increase in the average size of workshops in a specific sphere of production might be due to the introduction of more fixed and elaborate divisions of labour, which in turn might bring to an end the capacity of a single worker to see a job through from beginning to end. It might also be associated with the withdrawal of the employer from any productive role and his shift into a more purely managerial one. It might involve the production of a larger number of standardised items, possibly for fewer (maybe only one) customers, instead of a smaller but more heterogeneous output for a larger range of customers. It might have been associated, from about 1900, with the introduction of electrical power. All this could involve a transformation of the character of many small workshops although the crude industrial censuses would not show this.[36] Furthermore, this might mean that these statistics actually underestimate the growing significance of small workshop production within the total economy, if productivity gains in those workshops were higher than for the economy as a whole.

There are also specific reasons why there should be an increase in the number of small workshops in some sectors which could more than compensate for their contraction in other sectors. Factories demanded certain goods and services (components, servicing, maintenance, etc.) which might best be supplied by small workshops.[37] The decline of various production and service functions within the household could provide growth opportunities for some types of small business. The growth of domestic piped water supply and water closets gives us the plumber; the later electrification of the household, the electrician – two major new occupations which sustain a large number of small firms.

One can see, therefore, that small workshop production was of continued, indeed expanding importance within an industrialising economy, although this did not rule out major internal changes within that sector. One can also see there were perfectly good economic reasons why this should be the case. However, this argument has been pitched at a very general level. To connect economic changes to transformations in artisan politics and ideology it is necessary to differentiate between various branches of small workshop production.

Broadly one can distinguish between four kinds of development. First there are the skilled occupations which were either created by industrialisation or were incorporated into large-scale industrial production. Engineering is perhaps the best example – the general occupational label comes to be replaced by a wide range of specialised occupations. Sometimes these occupations are still practised in small workshops – e.g. supplying components to larger producers using or making complex machines. Sometimes the work was carried out in virtually autonomous workshops within factories. In the case of printing, occupational skills were transferred increasingly into larger units of production. Workers moved from small to large firms and back, and traditional apprenticeship arrangements could be effectively modified to take account of new technologies and larger scales of production. It is not coincidental that these tend to be the trades selected by historians stressing the continuity between pre-industrial and industrial skilled workers.[38] Others, arguing a labour aristocracy case, stress the change produced by a growth of dependency upon the larger employer rather than any technological change.[39]

A second type of occupation is one which was destroyed by either domestic and/or factory production. Textile crafts offer the best example. They are taken to illustrate the radical discontinuity between the pre-industrial artisan and the industrial wage-earner. The rapid shift of cotton spinning into factories is the best known example. The rather more complex story of the struggle of handloom weavers against both the expansion and increased exploitation of domestic rural production and then the shift into factory production is often taken as typical of the doomed fight against the imperatives of economic development.[40]

A third type of trade is one which hardly changes during the period. This may be due to the type of product. An expensive, luxury item such as jewellery, or a service embodying an intensive input of skilled labour such as barbering, do not lend themselves to displacement by machines, diffusion into domestic production, or concentration into factories. Another reason may be that the market is too static or restricted to merit investment in new forms of production. Until the rise of large retailing establishments, which only became significant after 1870 with the growth of large urban consumer markets, these points apply to a large part of the labour force preparing and selling food in towns. So butchers, bakers, jewellers and barbers were not in trades which change markedly during this period.[41]

It is upon the fourth type of occupation that I wish to focus because I consider it to be the type which is central to the emergence of an artisanal labour movement. These are trades which supply the basic 'consumer durable' (the term is anachronistic but apposite) demands of the domestic population. There is a large and fairly stable level of demand which means that there are many people working in these trades (they are known as the *Massenhandwerk* in German). It is possible, unlike those food trades dealing in perishable goods, to separate production and distribution (e.g. by storing the output in warehouses prior to either direct sale or supply to separate retailing establishments). There is some scope for de-skilling, but more through the introduction of complex divisions of labour than of machinery. The major trades in question are shoemaking, tailoring, furniture-making, and the rather special case of building.

The separation of production and distribution means that one can establish large-scale storage and distribution arrangements without any corresponding concentration of production into large-scale units. The continued importance of skill means that the production unit still tends to be the small workshop (or building site) rather than the household, though in the case of tailoring the urban household can start to play a significant role. Limited technical innovation means that the start-up costs for new firms are not very high, so there is a high entry (and exit) rate of new enterprises into these trades. The diffuse, large, and fairly fixed market for bulky, site-produced, or inexpensive objects is largely impenetrable to foreign competition. This rules out either sharp contraction due to import-penetration or expansion due to export growth. That, along with the steady but undramatic rise in home consumer demand, means there is no incentive to invest in new technology or forms of production in order to meet extra demand. There may, however, be shifts in the concentration of production within certain regions. Unlike capital goods production, there tend not to be sharp cycles of economic activity, although there are seasonal fluctuations (e.g. due to bad weather as in the building trade). There are fluctuations related to food prices but these are greater for less 'basic' consumer goods with higher elasticities of demand. The level of real wages basically determines that of demand for these goods (only expenditures on food and rent tend to vary less with variations in real wages). The general expansion of population and increases in per capita wealth over the period ensured long-term growth in demand for these goods. Generally, therefore, one observes an expansion of output, much of which largely takes the form of a multiplication of small production units with only low-cost, and therefore limited, technical innovations. These are not trades either created or destroyed by industrialisation, but equally there are significant changes in patterns of distribution, credit, divisions of labour, and capital investment, as well as limited technical innovation which mean they are not totally untouched by industrialisation.

Perhaps the most important area of change involves large-scale capitalist control of distribution which in turn led to credit dependency on the part of small producers and could eventually lead to effective control of production by merchant capital. The expansion and concentration of demand in towns could encourage such developments which could then be extended to a region, even perhaps in a limited way to a national economy. Clothing production was especially vulnerable to this process. Tailoring in large cities such as Paris, London, Berlin, Vienna and Hamburg was increasingly concentrated into a type of putting-out industry in which women played a prominent role, although with a significant element of the market continuing to be supplied by male tailors in small workshops.[42] In fact, small workshops became just one element in a complex system of production controlled by merchant capital which included women working at home and large numbers of people concentrated into one place sewing together garments. Sweated production came early to the London shoemaking trade, and some operations had already ceased to be located in workshops by 1830. Instead, domestic manufacture increased in importance, as in the Northampton area from about this time.[43]

In some cases, such developments could lead to a centre of production being established which virtually supplied a national market. Certain types of Parisian tailoring seem to have been moving in this direction by the 1830s.[44] At times this trend could end up with very marked regional concentration and even with a single firm acquiring a large share of the market, as was the case in English felt-hat manufacture.[45] In the development of sweated production, which often blurs the line between household, small workshop, and factory production, the central figure is a type of merchant who sells directly to the final consumer, or at least controls the link between producer and retailer. This merchant could then determine the orders made to a particular producer. This could in turn lead to supplying some of the raw materials or working capital for the producer, and even extend to renting out the tools and machinery used. Gradually, but not irreversibly and by very different routes, the independent producer could be reduced to de facto wage-earner dependency. But that was the final point which was by no means reached in these occupations in many areas. But even at intermediate positions, it could place a great deal of pressure upon those working in small workshops.[46]

Furniture production displays the same general pattern of development to that of shoemaking and tailoring, but in a more limited form, perhaps because the scope for a division of labour and technical innovation was more limited. On the other hand, at the top end of the market, the expense of products could cover transport costs and allow centres of international production to develop.[47] In various towns there did grow up central warehouses through which cabinet-makers and other craftsmen could sell their products, and there was a noticeable amount of hawking of home-made articles. The building trade was distinctive because production shifted from site to site. There was, in this period, little in the way of the production of specialised components for supply to the site, so the range of trades used on the site and their skills changed little. But the award of large building contracts, both for non-domestic building such as railway stations, factories, town halls, etc., and for blocks of housing, as well as large-scale speculative building (where production was not geared to individual consumer orders) all contributed to the rise of the 'general contractor'. As a consequence the role of the small employer diminished more rapidly in building than in the other trades dealt with here (although the average size of building firms had always been somewhat larger). However, there was a marked continuity of skilled labour with considerable control over the work on site.[48]

Examples of this kind of development could be multiplied indefinitely. What is important is that these trades were expanding and were of central importance in the economy. They were not forced into contraction or extinction, so their problems cannot be seen simply as a doomed fight for survival. They were not completely transformed or created by industrial growth, so existing organisations and ideas could be used constructively to respond to their new problems. They were sufficiently numerous and of sufficient economic importance for their responses to have significance for the development of the labour movement as a whole. They have been neglected in economic history because they do not represent dramatic growth or decline, and there are no easy measures of the sorts of changes which did take place in these trades. They have been accorded much more attention in labour movement history simply because they are at the centre of so much of the labour movement of this period. But there is a danger that if the basic economic context is misunderstood, so too will be the role they played within the labour movement. The next step is to see how new collective responses to the problems I have outlined could be generated within these trades.

Occupational action and the move beyond occupation

Much of the response to these new problems took place within occupational boundaries. The traditions of these artisans were occupational ones. The struggles over control of recruitment, the redefinition of work tasks, the general control of work, and wages and conditions, were largely conducted on an occupational as well as local level. The organisations which were developed were rather different from later craft unions. Workers often owned their own tools, fixed levels of output at the same time as negotiating on the price of their work, and carried out many 'managerial' tasks concerned with the pacing of work and the sequence of operations. An owner might often possess more influence as a fellow skilled worker than as an employer. There were widespread expectations about treatment at work which could often be enforced, for example by 'boycotting' a workshop. Artisans had built up a rich variety of funds to deal with such problems as temporary unemployment, sickness, injury, and death. These were almost always occupational. They tended to have short lives as they were often based on unsound actuarial principles, but the notion of cooperation for these purposes was deeply entrenched. One effect of such funds was to reduce competition in the labour market and that in turn could be linked to wage negotiations and even to strikes. The same function was served by resistance to changes in recognised work practices.

Sometimes occupations could build up organised connections between a number of localities. Unemployment benefit would often be paid to artisans who had come from another area. To sustain this practice it was necessary to have a system for equalising the income and expenditure of the different local branches. Closely linked to this were the support funds set up for the tramping artisan (*wandernden Gesellen*, *compagnon*). Workers often maintained 'houses of call' (*Herbergen*, *bureaux d' emplacement*), often a pub (hence the trade names attached to many English pubs) to which newly arrived craftsmen reported. Often the workers running these houses sought to control the procedure of hiring, and there was constant conflict between employers and workers on this matter. In some cases trades would also use particular hostels to put up newly arrived workers. Both the houses of call and the hostels could become centres of occupational organisation and the places which sustained the rituals and ceremonies of the trade. From this could be built up a network of contacts between different towns. In this way a supra-local solidarity could be developed, though still confined largely to the occupational level.[49]

These occupational actions cannot be seen in terms of class conflict or simple worker/employer conflict. Resistance to attempts to dilute apprenticeship and expand recruitment by compelling an employer to observe certain apprenticeship rules might often receive the tacit support of other employers who felt threatened by possible 'undercutting'. Frequently the same functions, such as running hostels and benefit funds, might be organised by employers or workers or by a combination of the two. However, there was often a tension within such organisations as to where ultimate control lay. Disputes frequently cut across master/men lines, especially when the independence of the 'independent' producer had been severely undermined by the penetration of merchant capital.

At times of general political crisis this could frequently lead to forms of populist organisation and language which had only indirect links to any notion of a wage-labour movement. The lack of class-consciousness and conflict in these trades had little to do with the size of the unit of production or the likelihood of skilled workers becoming masters.[50] Class attitudes appear to have been no more marked on large building sites than in small workshops. The social psychological explanation which centres on the artisan expectation of becoming a master does not seem very useful. In many cases, for example by looking at master to men ratios and the rate at which new masterships were created, one can show that there had for long been no objective grounds for believing independence could be achieved by most.[51] Of course, this does not rule out the possibility that such a belief neverthe-less played an important role in shaping artisan expectations, but if it is supposed to help account for the growth of more class-based forms of action one would expect this to have developed at a time when such occupational expectations were being frustrated on a large scale. This is, for many occupations, rather earlier than the period when more 'class-like' action began to develop.[52]

Such organisations as did develop were neither very specialised nor formally constituted. Benefit funds were not rigorously devoted to specific purposes, a fact which could lead to financial difficulties and provide grounds for government intervention. The use of funds to pay benefits had close connections to the ability to withdraw labour in a dispute. The house of call could act as a focal point for collective activity of all sorts, including a kind of labour exchange under the control of artisans. Many of the early labour movement organisations inherited this unspecialised character, as the passage quoted earlier from the *Arbeiter-Verbrüderung* demonstrated.

In turn this lack of specialisation, especially when artisans acted together only on an occupational and local level, meant that such collective action was frequently not formally organised. Persecution by the state also encouraged informality of organisation. In some cases it could mean that an association ostensibly devoted to one purpose could secretly pursue other objectives. Overlapping interests, legal intervention, and uncertain finances often meant that particular formal organisa-tions were only short-lived. But one must not equate formal organisation with collective action. Rather one should see a continual tradition of collective action, much of it submerged and beyond the reach of the historian, which occasionally and partially surfaced through formal organisation about which historians can often find out more.[53]

There were limits to what occupationally-bounded collective action could achieve in the face of growth, increased competition, a more elaborate division of labour, and the penetration of merchant capital. One response, especially marked in the building trade, was the development of more clear-cut trade union type resistance at the occupational level. I shall not consider that response here. Rather, I shall look at the way artisans from different occupations came together to resist such developments.

This could take a number of forms. Government interference into occupational organisation could lead to inter-trade cooperation opposed to such interference. Craftsmen from different trades could also cooperate in pursuit of improvements in the legislation concerning trade union or other kinds of organisation. Examples of this were the campaigns in the late 1820s in England to prevent alterations to the law regulating Friendly Societies, resistance to the new Master and Servant Bill of

1844, and trade union political action at the 1874 general election due to disappointment with the Liberal legislation on trades unions passed in 1871.[54] In France, George Duchene, a printer, helped organise an inter-trade campaign against an 1846 law on *livrets* (pass books) and a Paris ordinance of 1846 setting up new *conseils des Prud'hommes* which gave workers no vote in their elections.[55] In Hamburg guilds had worked successfully together in the 1830s for a favourable renewal of their privileges. In 1846 a number of journeymen from different trades cooperated to write a booklet criticising these guild arrangements, and in 1847 this led to the setting up of an association, the *Verein zur Hebung des Gewerbestandes*, which brought together journeymen and small masters from a number of trades to demand reform. In 1848 an association such as this could join up with the *Arbeiterverbrüderung* to work for national reform, just as local guilds could send representatives to an artisan 'parliament' in Frankfurt.[56] Clearly the extent and type of such collective action varied enormously. German artisans tended to ask for systematic legal reform whereas English artisans focused on particular bills or Acts in which they had some special interest. Generally the political conditions were more favourable in England to open campaigning of this kind than they were in France and Germany. The abruptness with which French and German artisans acquired freedom of action in 1848 meant that they used it in very different ways from English artisans.[57] Cooperation between separately organised occupational groups was usually undertaken for specific purposes at certain times and it was difficult for it to generate more continuous forms of collective action. It is when workers turn to more general and political goals that such forms of action are developed.

It is sometimes argued that workers turned to politics when economic action proved ineffective. This idea is not very useful for an understanding of the artisan labour movement. First, it implies a deliberate choice of action which seems unlikely. Second, it tends to conflate a number of different phenomena under the heading of 'politics' such as food riots, strikes, and demonstrations, which are all labelled as 'hunger politics'. Yet these are very disparate kinds of action, some based on organisation and some not, and which are difficult to categorise with terms such as 'economic' or 'political'. So far as artisans are concerned, more important is whether there is any tradition of collective action, which can then take a variety of forms almost simultaneously. For example, for various reasons artisan organisation was very weak in Cologne in 1848–49. Some determined leadership under favourable conditions could quickly establish an association with a paper membership of thousands. But the association did little practical work and once that leadership was removed the association quickly faded away. This is very different from the type of artisan cooperation which sustained London Chartism in the 1840s, or the work of the Luxembourg Commission in Paris in 1848, or the urban centres of the *Arbeiterverbrüderung* in Berlin, Hamburg, and Leipzig.[58] It was not so much short-term crises giving rise to 'hunger politics' which underpinned these movements, but rather a collective response to longer-term problems.

To explain how this happened one could combine the 'inter-trade cooperation' and 'hunger politics' approaches. The types of changes already mentioned – overcrowding, increased competition for jobs, limited de-skilling, penetration of merchant capital – all weakened existing occupational activity without destroying it. Such changes also frequently reduced living standards. The problem was one which developed over a period of time rather than taking the form of a sudden and terminal crisis. It presented itself to a number of occupations at the same time. This provided the basis for cooperation amongst members of these various trades seeking to buttress occupational resistance with a more broad-based resistance.

This did not necessarily lead to overt political action. There might be cooperation through support of a number of trades for a strike or a boycott. This kind of support seems to have grown in importance in London in the 1820s and 1830s and contributed to the formation of general unions.[59] This in turn could promote certain types of class consciousness and language, though only of an intermittent kind. A comparison of strikes in late eighteenth-century Germany with those of the 1860s suggests that support for strikes from other trades, as well as reduced involvement of small masters on the side of the strikers, were the most important changes, though there were some impressive examples in the earlier period of multi-trade action.[60] This could easily be accompanied by an increased class perception of conflict.

Which comes first – class-consciousness or class politics? Clearly there is no simple answer, and one cannot crudely separate ideas and language from actions. Yet some kind of analytical separation is needed in order to proceed. Here I will ask how far the changes I have already outlined could be linked to a transformation of artisan ideas in ways that could promote a perception of their situation in a manner which transcended the earlier corporate and occupational perceptions. Then I will try to relate that in turn to the development of new sorts of political activity.

Ideology

Economic situations and changes can be described in fairly general terms which apply across national frontiers. It is much more difficult to do this when writing intellectual history. Ideas are expressed in language and it is not easy to find obvious equivalents in different languages. Ideas, and I treat ideology primarily as ideas, are generated in an intellectual and political context which makes comparison difficult. In order to avoid being too abstract I will illustrate my general argument with examples from Germany in order to show how certain basic concerns were expressed through specific ideas. I shall then relate these concerns more briefly to England and France. By ideology I mean ideas which interpreted social reality to artisans and suggested how they should act.

Everyone needs to have certain ideas about their society, their place within that society, and how to behave. In many cases these are rather implicit and practical and difficult to disengage from social practice. In the case of at least a minority of the artisans with whom I am concerned, it is important to note from the outset that there was an interest in more explicit and reflective ideas. Owen and Owenism, certain early theories of labour value, an interest in various religious and scientific ideas, and a tradition of radical thought generally were important within artisan circles in London and various provincial towns.[61] Utopian and other kinds of socialist thought had a great influence within artisan clubs in Paris and Lyon in the 1830s.[62] These ideas in turn were communicated to German emigré artisan groups in Paris, and found their way back into Germany.[63] For example, the phrase about a harmonious relationship between rights and desires, the individual and the whole, and work and pleasure quoted earlier from the statutes of the *Arbeiter-verbrüderung*, stands in a line of thought which can be traced back via Wilhelm Weitling, the communist tailor, to the French utopian socialist writer Fourier.[64]

These ideas can be related more specifically to artisans and their concerns. Thus the notion of the 'organisation of work' was not just a popular slogan associated with Louis Blanc, but was closely related to elaborate schemes and demands worked out in the Luxemburg Commission which in turn were linked to the activity of artisanal associations.[65] Owenism and the involvement of committed Owenites in the London tailors' strike of 1834 was closely connected to the establishment of producer cooperatives which helped reduce pressure upon strike funds.[66] The German emigre artisans established support for journals and books, and practical collective arrangements for such things as meals, which directly reflected some of the ideas about enlightenment and cooperation which became very popular in those circles.[67] People like Owen, Cabet, Weitling, Blanc, Marx and Engels who elaborated theories of society which some artisans appropriated for their own purposes, also played an active role in the artisan labour movement of this period.

In part, one can account for this in ways which have little to do with the specific concerns of artisans. This was a period when such ideas first began to be formulated, publicised, and received by people from various social backgrounds. It was a time of general uncertainty and anxiety about the nature and direction of social change. A system of capitalist production was only just breaking through and the character of this new economy and society was only dimly understood. General ideas both helped provide some intellectual bearings in this confusing situation and furnished a standpoint from which to criticise. Even middle-class groups closely associated with the transformation which was taking place were attracted to such ideas. This may account for the temporary popularity of men like Owen and Marx in such circles. As the new principles of production stabilised themselves after 1850, so this generalised anxiety tended to fade away, and with it an interest in systematic yet critical social theory.

However, there was a particular intensity and character to the reception of such ideas within artisan circles. Such a reception was not passive, but actively selected and emphasised particular themes for specific artisan concerns, often in a way which was at variance with the intentions of would-be intellectual mentors. For example, Marx and Engels were compelled to take up themes of justice and the ideal future society in order to retain influence within the artisanal League of the Communists in 1847, although this ran counter to their own views. In turn, the Communist Manifesto which they were commissioned to write by the League of the Communists, in eliminating those themes, reduced its attractiveness to artisans.

However, one should not underestimate the genuinely intellectual character of this reception. It is not a case of looking to ideas as a solace, a desperate escape into a world of fantasy when confronted with intractable reality. This is a common way of interpreting 'utopian' socialism in particular. Neither should one interpret such ideas as simply providing legitimacy and help in the pursuit of practical ends such as the establishment of producers' cooperatives and soup kitchens. Rather, there is a close relationship between the problems artisans confronted, the ideas to which they were attracted, and the actions they took in response to both those problems and those ideas. Some examples will demonstrate this point.

During the tailors' strike of 1834 in London, low start-up costs and the dominance of small units of production made temporary cooperative production a possibility which could in turn help the strike. This could be true of other trades with similar features. The idea of producers' cooperatives was attractive because it seemed to be within the bounds of possibility. Where start-up costs were higher and the idea seemed less attainable, there is less interest in the social theories which build upon the producer cooperative as a fundamental feature of a future society.[68]

The sense that the objective was realisable could then take artisans on to asking the question of why this had not happened. Given that production was possible under the control of the skilled workforce, why did capitalists play such a large part in these trades? The image of the capitalist as intermediary, monopolist of links to the market, able to control producers through exploiting this monopoly, and earning his income by underpaying the producer and overcharging the customer, could appear very plausible in these circumstances.[69] Certain thinkers went further by recognising that the new, extensive forms of production and distribution were here to stay and one could not hope simply to return to petty commodity production on a local basis. These thinkers offered new solutions of a general kind by envisaging much more organised forms of production and distribution, even if the small workshop often figured as the central unit of production.[70] As the pressure of growth and capitalist transformation bore down upon the artisan, so ideas of this sort which were also a response to more general trends proved insistently attractive. Clearly such ideas were not derived from a simple 'experience' of the problems as they presented themselves in everyday life. They need to be related to certain intellectual traditions and to the strenuous attempts by particular thinkers to master puzzles with which they were confronted by unprecedented social change. From that it is necessary to go on to analyse the ways in which such ideas were creatively appropriated by some artisans. From the outset one should note that the basic condition for this reception was that these thinkers faced as problems of understanding the same questions which faced artisans as problems of living. The clearest examples of this can be found in 'utopian' socialism which went beyond traditional radical criticisms of 'parasites' and the notion of a simple return to an old world of petty commodity production (or even more superficially, the vague idea that attaining political power would suffice to secure the position of the 'people'). Utopian ideas also suggested new identities and policies to artisans which helped the formation of the early artisan labour movement. To put flesh on these ideas I will focus on one particular German example, namely the role of Wilhelm Weitling in the early German labour movement.

Wilhelm Weitling (1808–71) was the most important utopian socialist thinker within the early German labour movement.[71] This movement developed abroad amongst artisans in Paris, London, and towns in the German-speaking cantons of Switzerland. A major reason for the growth of the German artisan communities in which this movement took shape was a crisis induced by expansion, overcrowding, and merchant capitalist transformation of the kind already outlined.[72] Exile favoured a move towards supra-occupational organisation. Artisans from different occupations came together in clubs and soon discovered that they suffered from similar problems.They were further exposed to the exhilirating experience of living in relatively free political systems. They came into contact with German political exiles, with Parisian artisans, radicals and early socialist groups, with the mass and radical politics of London in the late 1830s and early 1840s, and with the political tensions in the Swiss cantons and the concerns with making a reality of various forms of direct as well as representative democracy. A number of them moved from one centre to another so that there were communications between centres and attempts to synthesise the conclusions drawn from different experiences. Weitling was a typical figure in that he was a tailor and spent some time in all three centres as well as within Germany. He had experience of working for commercial tailoring establishments and of extensive wandering, and thus had encountered at first hand the problems of underemployment and capitalist penetration in his trade.[73]

His work as an editor of journals and as a writer of various socialist tracts was sustained through the artisan readership of the clubs to which he belonged and through more direct financial support. Police files containing confiscated papers of artisans reveal that Weitling's works were, from the late 1830s until well into the 1850s and beyond, amongst the most popular reading matter of members of the artisan labour movement. Library collections of artisan associations show the same thing.[74]

Weitling was a utopian socialist. By this I mean that his central concern as a thinker was to describe in detail an ideal socialist society. This description took priority over a consideration of action in the present which was seen simply as a means of reaching the ideal goal. But one had to have a destination before one could start on a journey. He was a socialist in that the ideal society he envisaged was one in which the means of production were in social ownership, and production and exchange were socially planned. His response to criticism exemplified the utopian mode of thought. He tried to eliminate any apparent inconsistencies within the blueprint and accumulated further details of how the future society would work. His utopian system, like all such mental constructs, was closed to external criticism. One either found the general vision attractive or not, the detailed arrangements plausible or not. The question is how and why such a mental world attracted artisans.

A closer examination of Weitling's ideas shows them to be based completely upon a vision of craft production in small workshops. Large-scale manufacturing, domestic production and farming hardly figure.[75] Utopian ideas could take many other forms. American utopianism often implied a world dominated by small independent farmers. Saint Simonian utopianism gave pride of place to science, technology, and highly efficient, large-scale production. Fourier's ideas tended to treat work as a necessary evil which should be kept to a minimum. By contrast, Weitling's ideal world is one dominated by work which is carried out in a regulated fashion mainly in small workshops.

The manner in which production is carried out and regulated bears an uncanny resemblance to the procedures of guilds. In Weitling's hands what had been local and occupational corporations controlled by masters are transformed into general and democratic institutions. For example, Weitling recognised that it would be necessary to plan the supply of labour to different branches of production. To do this he recommended that the standards of examination used to establish people's qualifications to carry out certain types of work should be varied in accordance to the number of people required. Guilds had themselves used examinations as one means of regulating labour supply. Journeymen's associations both before and during 1848 had demanded that this be done to prevent overcrowding, although the power to do so should reside either with the state or a democratised guild. Weitling's utopianism can be interpreted as a generalised transformation of ideas and practices well understood in a more partial way amongst artisans. This both helps explain how Weitling can come to incorporate such an idea into his utopia, and why that idea should appear to be relevant and attractive to his artisan audience. Furthermore, by taking a general form it could appeal simultaneously to a range of occupations.

One cannot reduce Weitling's utopia simply to such artisan terms. He was also influenced by ideas remote from artisans. Nineteenth-century utopian thought owed much to an Enlightenment tradition of the perfectibility of man and associated notions of progress, equality, and the capacity to use reason to organise society rationally. Utopianism represents the most literal application of such notions. It helped popularise enlightenment ideas, but did so in ways which could also cultivate quasi-religious enthusiasms. Weitling was also subjected to more specific influences. He took his idea about man having basic appetites which need to be satisfied in a balanced way from Fourier. He was indebted to other French socialist writers for his views about the close relationship between private property and inequality. His idea of a revolution of the 'proletariat', seen as the great mass of the population, has echoes of the way in which Blanqui thought of political and social conflict. A crude theory of the labour theory of value underpinned his violent hostility to money and his elaborate system of labour notes which were needed in the absence of money to facilitate the equitable exchange of products over and beyond socially necessary levels of output. Furthermore, his enlightenment orientation also found expression in other matters, for example the idea of constructing a universal language.

Nevertheless, one can relate many of Weitling's ideas back to artisan concerns. The artisan who experienced capitalism as control through credit, access to the market, and manipulation of competition amongst direct producers, was likely to share Weitling's hostility to money and the power it seemed to confer upon its unproductive holders. Socialisation of the kind outlined by Weitling could be seen as enabling the actual producers to enter once more into direct relations with one another. It would cut out the intermediaries and the manipulations and mystifications which accompanied their mediations. However, it would not involve any simple restoration of guilds. Given the way the guilds were seen by many artisans as corrupt and discriminatory institutions, such a restoration could hardly prove attractive.[76] So in a number of ways one can make connections between Weitling's utopianism, the situation of many artisans, and the shift of artisanal ideology beyond occupational boundaries. Because of these connections, Weitling was able to flavour his speculations about the future (or his criticisms of the present) with details about the humiliations of the tramping artisan, the egotistical character of guilds, the cold-shouldering received from local communities and the harassment at the hands of state officials to which journeymen and other wanderers were exposed, as well as the exploitation of parasitic merchants. This writing increased the sense of indignation amongst his readers and the feeling that some general solution was needed. This in turn made the audience more receptive to the utopian recommendations. In this way Weitling helped provide artisans who were joining supra-occupational associations with a range of supra-occupational identities and objectives. These could then inform practical activity in artisan associations in such areas as consumer cooperation, education, and personal relationships, even if these were only diluted expressions of the values commended by Weitling.

From the early 1840s artisans were able to set up general associations in a number of German states. Although modelled in many ways upon the experiences of the exiles, these associations had to confine themselves, at least publicly, to non-political matters. Most of these associations called themselves workers' or artisans' educational associations (*Arbeiter – or Handwerker-Bildungsvereine*).[77] Although utopian socialist and radical democratic ideas circulated within these associations, both the pressures from the authorities and the real, if very limited, practical improvements which the associations could promote, led to a stress upon peaceful change, above all through education. The 'true' socialist idea of locating the 'true' inner man and bringing him out into the social world by means of education could appear attractive in these circumstances.[78] These ideas, though more abstract than those of utopian socialism, could be connected to an image of the artisan as a truly respectable, independent, dignified person, degraded by external circumstances. The artisanal rather than the class basis of this idea was revealed, for example, in the declaration of a Hamburg worker in Vormärz that, 'The proletariat will start to vanish from the time when the self-knowledge of the worker begins to grow.'[79] It was expressed in the idea that education in this spirit could preserve the integrity of the *goldene Mittelstand*. The pressure of the economic crisis of the years 1845–47 encouraged a range of *petit bourgeois* groups, extending beyond artisans, to express interest in such true socialist ideas. The political implications of the true socialist idea of educating individuals towards a better society and the utopian socialist idea of constructing an ideal society which would transform individuals were very different. True socialism could preach harmony between classes and assert that the rich were as alienated from their true human nature as were the poor.[80] Weitling, by contrast, flirted with ideas of violent change bought about by the proletariat. This reduced his *political* significance amongst artisans, although not the appeal of his social theories.[81] But both sets of theories appealed to a class of small producers and retailers; both condemned capitalist perceived in mercantile terms; both contributed to a populist politics which was central to the revolution of 1848.

The stress of true socialism and workers' educational associations on education also shifted attention away from politics to the acquisition of knowledge. This is a frequent response of those without power. It conferred a special significance upon the efforts at self-improvement made by autodidactic artisans and the propaganda work of intellectuals and middle-class patrons of such associations. It was accompanied by quite practical concerns with vocational education (another charge against the guilds was their failure in this regard) and with repairing the deficiencies of elementary schooling. It could be used to mediate the culture of the 'educated classes' to artisans, although it is not very meaningful for this period to employ concepts such as bourgeois hegemony.[82]

These ideas continued, in different forms and contexts, to exert influence. In 1848 it was possible to move from discussion to action; many educational associations turned themselves into the centres for political organisation amongst artisans. But those actions, as for example in the objectives expressed in the statute of the *Arbeiterverbrüderung* quoted earlier, were informed by ideas elaborated before 1848. In the brief era of the 'liberal labour movement' of the late 1850s and early 1860s, self-help projects were heavily impregnated with ideas about cooperatives and education that can be traced back to utopian and true socialist views. Schulze-Delitzsch, the 'Robert Owen' of Germany, was popular amongst artisans less because of the liberal economic doctrines with which he justified his support for associational 'self-help', but more because of the practical manner in which that support was expressed. Those he helped often had little sympathy for that broader economic philosophy. In any case, liberalism of this period still had many attributes of a *Mittelstand* creed, rather than being an ideology favouring the rapid expansion of competitive capitalism.[83] In turn, the appeal of Lassalle rested both upon his exposure of the reluctance of liberals to commit themselves to democracy, and upon his programme of state-assisted producer cooperation.[84] Even later, in the development of social democracy as an almost self-sufficient sub-culture organised around a network of associations, one can trace the continuation of artisan pre-occupations, even when attached to the creed of class and an official obeisance to Marxism.

Thus, throughout the period 1830 to 1870, and even beyond, the ideas which attracted that minority of artisans who organised in supra-occupational associations were those that related to the problems of expansion, overcrowding, and merchant capitalist penetration. Utopian socialism, true socialism, liberalism and Lassalleanism were all linked to these central concerns which looked to general association and regulation as the solution. Ironically, even the ideas of Marx and Engels, who so trenchantly attacked these other ideologies (and also shaped the way they were understood by posterity) were often appropriated by artisans in ways which subverted their original class thrust. The history of the League of the Communists, for example, could be written in terms of the relationship of mutual exploitation and incomprehension between Marx and Engels on the one hand and the artisan membership on the other. Marx and Engels were often compelled to compromise with the attitudes of their potential followers, for example in the drawing up of a catechism for the League of the Communists in 1847 by Engels and the composition of the Inaugural Address of the International Working Men's Association in 1864 by Marx.[85] Even their own understanding of the nature of the working-class was in part shaped by those artisans with whom they dealt.[86] It would be quite wrong to see this simply as the independent genius of Marx, converting workers to his ideas. Central instead is the continuity of artisan concern which appropriates different ideas according to circumstances, a continuity based upon the centrality of certain tendencies in the economic transformation of artisanal production.

I have tried to illustrate this general argument about the development of supra-occupational organisation and ideology with material from the German case. Clearly a full argument would have to expand on that case and also introduce detail on the other countries. I can do no more than make some suggestive points. Some work on England and France provides support for the kind of argument I have advanced. The ideas of Stedman-Jones concerning the language of Chartism, for example, can be connected to the artisan experience of capitalism as an external pressure rather than one located within the system of production.[87] Behagg has shown how an apparently 'traditional' small workshop economy could be transformed by forms of capitalist development, and how this in turn can be linked to the emergence of new types of associative activity amongst artisans.[88] Prothero has demonstrated in detail the connections between the problems of London artisans in the first half of the nineteenth-century, and a range of ideas about cooperation, politics, respectability and socialism.[89] Tholfsen, Crossick and Gray have shown – admittedly in very different ways – how an artisan tradition rather than the values of other social groups informed so much of the effort and ideology of the mid-century labour movement in Britain.[90] The links between the attractions of Owenism and the practical problems confronting London tailors in 1834, or the way in which artisan problems underpinned the move to supra-occupational organisation in London in the form of the National Charter Association in the early 1840s, can be, and have been, analysed in broadly similar terms to those I have outlined for the German case.[91] Again, the work of Johnson on Cabet and the appeals of his utopianism in France, of Moss on the continuity of craft concerns in the French labour movement up to and beyond 1900, and of Hanagan on the centrality of artisans in both the political and industrial wings of the labour movement in late nineteenth-century France, can support this kind of analysis.[92]

One must not overstate the similarities. The weight of such trades within each national economy varied considerably. The time-lags between comparable problems arising in different trades could be large enough to inhibit a general response from a number of trades at the same time, and thus the possibility of supra-occupational action. The general social context varied. Thus artisan movements had a different character and importance in the city, the small town and the countryside. The arguments developed here are especially applicable to cities with a high degree of capitalist penetration and quite large numbers of artisans living and working close to one another. The institutional context was also very different. For example, guilds continued to have some importance in many German states. Trade brotherhoods had some significance in France where guilds had only been formally abolished within living memory. In England the significance of such formal organisations had been largely destroyed well before the nineteenth century. Yet I would argue, within these differences there are certain common concerns about restoring the dignity, independence and respectability of the craftsman. German craftsmen might demand a restored guild system; French artisans might press for radical political change; and skilled English workers might petition parliament for redress of specific grievances – but underlying these different languages there are common objectives. However, these differences, especially in the field of political action, matter a great deal and need to be considered.

Politics

If by politics is meant organised activity aimed at altering the structure or policies of the state, then artisan politics in this period was an intermittent activity. Bodies such as the National Charter Association, the Brotherhood of German Workers, or the Democratic-Socialist Party in the Second Republic were temporary organisations. Later, there emerged organisations which saw themselves as having a permanent political role, such as the Political Committee of the Trades Union Congress, the General German Workers' Association (ADAV) in Germany and socialist parties under the Third Republic.

The intermittent character of artisan political action was closely bound up with how artisans understood politics. Politics was not seen in terms of continuous bargaining between various interests. Rather it was seen as a temporary intervention to deal with an injustice which, once removed, would also remove the need for further political activity. The injustice might be a very specific one, such as the Combination Acts. A political campaign was launched to remove this injustice, in this case by repeal of those Acts. Once that had been achieved, as it was in 1824, the campaign could be brought to a close and the organisations which had been formed could be dissolved. Of course, such problems were never finally solved (after all, the new laws of 1825 restored some of the features removed by the repeal of 1824) and organised action at one time had its influence on shaping subsequent organisation. But the *attitude* was of being engaged in a campaign to redress grievances rather than one moment in an enduring political process. I will return to the question of how far this was a general attitude towards politics rather than one peculiar to artisans.

Rather more extensive than the view of politics as the redress of specific grievances, there was a broader but rather negative idea of political action as a means of eliminating state inteference. In part the popular politics of England in the 1830s was a reaction against new forms of state intervention in such areas as poor relief and policing.[93] This in part was the basis of Tory radicalism; of an 'old constitutionalist' rhetoric which sought by populist means to defend local communities and appealed to traditions of social justice. In part the demand for the Charter had a similar meaning: once there was a mass electorate it would not be possible for the state to act against the wishes of the people. Chartists do not seem to have worked out a positive view of a new political process in which the democratic state could acquire even greater power than the present state. The legacy of radicalism which they inherited had precisely the opposite implications.[94] This absence of a vision of a political process built upon the democratised state is less applicable to France where a Jacobin tradition continued to play a role. But even Jacobinism was about the final implementation of justice rather than the construction of an institutional environment which would promote continuous political conflict on a peaceful and democratic basis. Furthermore, within the labour and radical movement there were many strong reactions against the Jacobin tradition with a stress instead upon federalism, community control, and distrust of a powerful state. In Germany there was hardly any positive conception of a democratised political process as artisans reacted against the restrictive bureaucracies of the period, even, indeed especially, if these pursued economically liberal policies.[95] Interestingly, in Switzerland where some cantons did permit a broad level of political participation, often in various forms of direct and not simply representative democracy (e.g. rights of recall, petitioning for plebiscites, very wide range of elective posts), one can also observe the cultivation of a tradition of sustained and practical democratic political thought which appealed to artisans.[96]

Closely linked to the two conceptions of politics already mentioned, is one which sees it as being about the implementation of justice. Justice has to be understood in terms of the artisan ideals that have already been discussed. Once political action had achieved social justice – by abolishing the placemen, the parasites, the jobbers, etc. and by restoring to the direct producer his proper position – then politics would be replaced by the organised activity of those direct producers who would have no serious conflicts amongst themselves. The pure political radicals seemed to envisage that a limited process of political purification would suffice to create this happy state. Social-democratic thinkers did see that some changes in the 'organisation of work' would also be required.[97]

There are two ways in which one can explain such attitudes towards politics. The first focuses upon popular politics generally and sees artisan politics as just one component. What matters here is the context within which popular politics develops. If the existing political system does not provide for continuous, legitimate, and extensive political participation and if there are no institutions such as enduring political parties which contest frequent elections held on a broad franchise and a broad-based structure of public opinion formed through meetings, associations, newsapers, periodicals, and pamphlets, then it is difficult for such ideas about politics to take shape. Equally, changes which permit a continuous popular presence to be registered within the political system will be the major reason for the broad acceptance of a view of politics as a normal part of life which enables conflicting interests to negotiate with one another. Attitudes about politics are seen largely as a function of political action, and artisan attitudes as simply part of a broader spectrum of popular political thought.

A second approach would be to focus on the particular social experiences of artisans. Artisans acted within occupational communities in which various issues – political, social, economic – overlapped. Artisans did not find it easy to accept a clear division of these questions from one another and this inhibited the acceptance of the view that politics was a distinct and specialised form of action. The multi-purpose and often informal associations of artisans would shift from one type of activity to another. Thus the *Arbeiterverbrüderung* tried to influence elections during the 1848–49 revolution. Many of its local branches were engaged in forming political alliances with middle-class radicals and liberals. However, these branches also continued to act as educational associations, cooperatives, benefit clubs, trade unions, and places to relax. Usually, like the Luxemburg Commission or the National Charter Association, they also were organised on an occupational basis. People joined as members of the occupation rather than simply as individuals. However, this was not like the modern practice in the Labour Party where membership of a trade union is virtually a condition of party membership. There, at least, there is a strong sense of division of functions between trade union and political party. There is no such sense of specialised economic function for occupational organisations and political functions for general organisations. This compared sharply with various bourgeois political associations where people joined as individuals and where the language of occupation and interests was notable by its absence.

This understanding of artisan politics has certain implications. First, the emphasis upon one rather than another activity that one often finds amongst artisans, should be seen less as a switch from one clearly defined form of action to another, but rather as a matter of what was appropriate in a given context. For example, the *Arbeiterverbrüderung* became increasingly 'non-political' in 1850 and 1851, stressing the need for self-help rather than state reform and intervention, and concentrating its own energies upon cooperatives, benefits, etc. Certain West German historians have interpreted this as a move towards reformism.[98] The argument is that these artisans now abandoned illusions about radical transformation by means of revolution and instead turned to focus on practical and realistic tasks. Men like Stefan Born who had, at an early stage in 1848, stressed the need for organisation and realism, now came to take a leading role. By contrast, East German historians have seen this shift as no more than a public pose adopted in the face of a hostile counter-revolution.[99] For them, the League of Communists, now forced underground, continued to cultivate a revolutionary political attitude and remained of great importance within the labour movement.

Both approaches share the same anachronistic assumptions. They project back on to the artisan labour movement of this period sets of contrasting terms such as reform or revolution, political and trade union action, which only come to be perceived as distinct choices or forms of action in a later period. Clearly the *Arbeiterverbrüderung* toned down its political concerns because of the dangers that became apparent from 1850. Equally clearly, it had always been concerned with cooperation and education and occupational reform, and its emphasis upon these matters from 1850 was not simply intended as cosmetic or deceptive. Rather, a shift within the balance of activities undertaken within this multi-purpose organisation took place because of changes in the situation in which the organisation found itself.

If one understands the political attitudes of artisans in this way, it would not be so much specific political reforms which would undermine those attitudes as the more general break-up of the artisan world. There are a number of ways in which this could happen. The kinds of economic change I have already discussed served to divorce many direct producers from their customers, even if the size and tech- nology of production did not change dramatically. Overcrowding could produce rapid job turnover, de-skilling and the breakdown of occupational organisation. Geographical and job mobility could have similar effects. The increased tendency for dependent workers to live apart from their employer, to marry and form families, to travel longer distances to work all served to separate home from work. This could encourage artisans to take a more narrow view of their work and to turn more of their emotional energies to a more purely domestic role [100]

But one should not exaggerate this process. In many places artisans continued to live close to their work; to spend much of their leisure time with fellow artisans; to be attracted to social visions which made their work the centre of a community of solidarity. An example of this can be seen in the response to Lassalle both within and outside the ADAV. Lassalle was concerned to establish a pure political organisation which would not be diverted by the many other objectives artisan associations pursued.[101] A number of artisans followed him but not quite in the spirit he intended. They were attracted by his courage, his refusal to compromise with the existing authorities, and his unequivocal commitment to universal manhood suffrage, in marked contrast to most liberals.[102] However, many even of those who came into the ADAV, could not bear to renounce their passion for multi-purpose association.[103] They smuggled back other functions into the ADAV. Furthermore, the other plank of Lassalle's two-plan programme, state aid for producer coop- eratives, appealed directly to a well-established artisan tradition.

The ambivalence of Lassalle's appeal – on the one hand a 'modern' concern with political agitation on behalf of a class, on the other hand, artisan dominance of less specialised organisations and the attraction of producer cooperatives – can be discerned in other political movements. For example, the class perception of politics offered by Marx could be adapted to artisan needs. Class was not seen as a permanent feature of modern society, the basis of an endless political process of negotiation, but as indicating the division between the just and the unjust and 'scientifically' predicting the victory of the just. With that victory, conflict would end and the direct producer, the worker, would dominate a world in which politics had been replaced by the 'administration of things'. This utopian view of the abolition of the state, even the very notion of the 'administration of things' can be traced directly to pre-Marxist socialist views such as those of the Saint Simonians. Such an understanding was less possible with regard to ethnic or liberal political appeals. The way in which Catholic artisans could, to some extent, sustain such an understanding within a popular Catholic politics would repay investigation.

These points do little more than sketch out some questions which could be raised by students of artisan politics. The two approaches mentioned are not mutually exclusive. The development of a specialised and participatory political sphere is part of a general process of modernisation which also includes clearer separation of work and home, education and religion. Nevertheless, modernisation does not proceed smoothly, and at equal speed in different areas. It is worthwhile seeing how far the earlier development of routine, participatory politics in England helped undermine a specifically artisan politics rather ahead of France and Germany, or how far middle-class groups or other kinds of workers failed to share artisan political attitudes. It is also worth seeing how far apparently 'modern' political movements such as the Marxian socialist parties formed in late nineteenth-century Germany and France continued to appeal to long-standing artisan values.

Some other general points should be made about artisan politics. First, it was often imitative. The oaths and cell structure of artisan associations under the July Monarchy and in the German exile associations owed something to the ritual of journeymen associations but much more to the secret societies of radical republicans.[104] Much recent literature has focused on the debts Chartism owed, for example to the use of the mass platform and the oratory of gentlemen leaders.[105] Contemporaries made direct comparisons, for example, between Ernest Jones and Ferdinand Lassalle.[106] The educational associations established in Germany in the 1840s followed on closely from the setting-up of similar organisations amongst other social groups.[107] Partly, of course, this was dependent on how far artisan organisations were penetrated by members of other social groups. A tradition of middle-class 'philanthropy' which aimed to steer rather than undermine artisans' organisation inevitably brought with it aims and methods distinct from those of artisans.

Artisan political organisation often arose in the aftermath of crises which artisans themselves had done little to bring about. The reform crisis of 1830–31 and its disappointing culmination in the Reform Act of 1832 had stimulated many more artisans to organise than hitherto. Arguably the governmental reforms of the mid-1830s created the conditions for the first phase of the Chartist movement. In France and Germany, of course, the breakdown of authority in the spring of 1848 gave rise to the conditions on which very extensive artisan organisation could build. Again, it was the crisis over the constitution in Prussia from 1862 and then the wars involving Prussia in 1864, 1866, and 1870–71 which led on directly to the formation of the first two independent labour parties in Germany.[108]

Finally, the extent of constructive political activity between artisans and others influenced the degree to which specifically artisan concerns and attitudes were expressed in political activity involving artisans. This is why it is perhaps harder to distinguish a specifically artisan mode in English politics of this period compared to France or Germany. The political circumstances were very different and that in turn affected the relationship between artisans and others.

In the English case one needs to make a distinction between the period from about 1830 to 1850 and from 1850 to 1870. The first period is marked by a tightening-up of the political system and a number of innovations which threatened artisan interests. In many ways the political system was less open to artisan influence after 1832 than before. The Reform Act standardised an exclusive franchise.[109] Reform of urban government diminished the importance of older institutions such as vestries which had been susceptible to popular pressure. Changes in methods of poor relief and policing threatened labour interests.[110] In many ways Chartism, especially in its first phase of mass activity in 1838–39, can be understood as much as a response to this political transformation as to a major economic crisis or the early stages of industrialisation. This general political change affected others apart from artisans and the Chartist movement had a more general appeal, even if the language of Chartism owed much to artisan perceptions of the divide between the useful people, who produced with their hands and the parasites, who did not. In the later phase of the movement, in the early 1840s, it did acquire a more specific working-class character as many middle class sympathisers were discarded and as more explicit social and economic concerns were expressed. But even then, the range of groups involved extended well beyond artisans, although in some areas, such as London, artisan preponderance was marked. Some of the groups involved, such as outworkers in the hosiery or handloom weaving trades, did cease to act collectively after the mid-century. By then, however, a measure of reform (though not in the field of constitutional politics) and greater prosperity meant that other occupations outside of the artisan trades, such as in cotton-spinning and engineering, came to play a prominent role in the more moderate political movements that followed Chartism. An artisan presence is still important, and in part it is responsible for the continuation of radical and populist tones in the popular liberalism of the period.[111] However, it is sometimes difficult to disentangle from other strands of a broad-based movement. That is not just an analytical difficulty; it meant that artisans themselves had a range of other political identities and this in turn indicates the extent to which they had left behind the corporate artisan world. There is a need for further study of the specifically political aspects of this process, for example the impact of much more extensive newspaper and periodical circulation upon political attitudes. The preoccupation with social and economic history (above all expressed in the labour aristocracy debate) or with intellectual history (for example, in trying to determine which were the 'ruling' ideas), along with the tendency to either begin or end in 1850, has led to a neglect of political circumstances and responses.

In the French case one is dealing with a much more restrictive political system. From 1834 until the later 1840s these restrictions were intensified, although there was a little relaxation just before 1848. However, a revolutionary tradition kept alive by periodic political collapse, the latest being the July Revolution, and the continued existence of underground radical republican organisations meant that there were specialised political movements which sought to appeal to artisans. Nevertheless, by comparison with England, the labour movement itself was a much more narrowly artisan one and those broader forms of politics, when seeking to mobilise artisan support, did take up specifically artisan concerns more obviously. Men like Louis Blanc and Etienne Cabet were much more clearly operating within the artisan world than, for example, Feargus O'Connor or Ernest Jones. Blanc's political power base in the Second Republic, for example, was clearly based upon the artisan labour movement of the Paris region, and was expressed institutionally through the Luxemburg Commission.[112] In the 1850s and 1860s the appeal of Proudhon again had a clear artisan basis, although one should be sceptical about the influence of his 'non-political' strategy in the same way as I have earlier expressed doubts about the turning away from politics by the *Arbeiterverbrüderung*. As political opportunities widened in the 1860s, it was followers of Proudhon who turned back to politics. Furthermore, they clearly found in political activists in the London artisan labour movement people with whom they shared many values. That contact led on directly to the formation of the International Working Men's Association.[113]

Other essays in this book explore the comparison between German and English labour politics in more detail than is possible here. Rather I shall draw together a number of points about Germany in summary form. I have already pointed to a continuity of artisan concern underlying the interest in such various ideas as utopian and true socialism, Marxism, liberal self-help cooperatives, and Lassalleanism. One can relate the apparent shifts in ideological concern in part to shifts of emphasis within multi-purpose associations as they responded to broader changes. Thus the interest in liberalism in the late 1850s and early 1860s had a lot to do with the need to be cautious about open political activity and the merits of operating under the umbrella of a broad liberal movement which furnished political leadership and respectability. At the same time artisan associations could concentrate upon other activities such as cooperation and trade unionism. The shift of support to Lassalle (though only on the part of a small minority of activists in the artisan labour movement), as well as the rise of a conservative artisan movement amongst masters (again, only a minority), arose out of a sense of frustration at the limited role offered to artisans within the broad liberal movement.[114] But even within the Lassallean movement there was, at least among the artisans involved, a constant pressure to widen the scope of the association beyond political agitation. The more general moves of artisans towards specialised political action came with three fundamental developments. First, the breakdown of the broad liberal movement in the face of the crisis precipitated by war and annexation in 1866–67 meant that cooperation with liberals suddenly lost much of its appeal. Second, unification was associated with the construction of political institutions such as a national parliament elected on the basis of universal manhood suffrage which directly encouraged specialised political activity and an appeal to a broad range of working-class groups hitherto excluded from politics. Third, a series of economic changes, above all liberalisation of the economy and rapid growth, pushed dependent artisans into a wave of strikes and the formation of trade unions which liberals found difficult to support. This encouraged both the use of class language and the making of clearer distinctions between economic and political action. On the basis of these changes the traditional forms of artisan politics rapidly declined, although many of the broader artisan concerns continued to exercise influence.

Concluding remarks

It is possible, therefore, to discern a set of political attitudes and forms of political action in this period which might be regarded as typically artisan. One can also identify what kinds of political as well as broader changes could undermine those attitudes and actions. Finally, one can relate those general points to the different and changing political circumstances of the three countries in order to grasp both differences and similarities in the political conduct of artisans. Once these comparisons are related back in turn to the economic situation of artisans and the values to which artisans typically subscribe, it is possible to develop a framework within which characteristically artisan concerns and actions can be compared and contrasted across national boundaries. I have tried to do that in this essay and, even if particular arguments are contested, I hope this can be seen as a way forward towards placing the early labour movements of western Europe into a broad comparative context.

Notes

1 For the journeymen's clubs formed outside Germany see Schieder 1963. For the workers' educational associations formed within Germany see Birker 1973.

2 The classic account of the first phase of this development, though presented as the culmination of earlier events, is Thompson, 1963. See also Thompson, 1984. For a general survey see Hunt, 1981.

3 For a recent short survey see Sewell, 1986.

4 For general surveys see Wachenheim, 1967; and in English, Grebing, 1966.

5 These matters are dealt with in my essay 'Liberalism or social democracy?'. See also Royden Harrison's collection of essays (Harrison, 1965).

6 For a recent survey see Perrot, 1986.

7 This is not a new insight. See Clapham, 1932 and 1968.

8 Kumar, 1978.

9 Quoted in Prothero, 1979, p. 332.

10 *Grundstatuten der deutschen Arbeiter-Verbrüderung* (Leipzig, 1850). Reprinted in Balser, 1962,

vol. 2, pp. 507–23. Also now reprinted in Dowe & Offermann (eds), 1983, pp. 271–95.

11 From the workers' paper *Populaire*, 30 January 1842. I am indebted to Iori Prothero for drawing my attention to this document.

12 This is a problem, for example, in the treatment of John Doherty's activity in Kirby & Musson, 1975. The value of bringing these activities together and also seeing the formal associational activity as just the tip of the iceberg is well brought out by Behagg, 1979. See also Behagg, 1990.

13 Schieder, 1963; Weisser, 1975; Braunthal, 1967, for examples of studies of these subjects.

14 For a recent example of this approach see Moore, 1978.

15 For Britain, where the continuity argument is easier to mount than for Germany or France, see Musson, 1972 for this general view. His attacks on the concept of the 'labour aristocracy' stress that skilled workers after 1850 were no less 'militant' than their counterparts in the first half of the century, who in turn were no more 'revolutionary' than their descendants. See Musson, 1976.

16 See Reid, 1978; Penn, 1983; Price, 1983; Zeitlin, 1979.

17 For Britain and Germany see the essays on the labour aristocracy and on liberalism and social democracy printed in this book. For France this critical point has been made recently by Hanagan, 1980, though still accompanied by the assumption that France is especially backward compared to Britain and Germany. A critique of the pre-industrial – industrialisation – industrial sequence is also developed in Koch, 1986.

18 Samuel, 1977; Cottereau, 1986; the set of essays entitled 'Das deutsche Handwerk im Zeitalter der Industrialisierung' in Fischer, 1971.

19 This takes one well beyond the subject of this essay. For a set of essays clearly influenced by these points see Berg (ed), 1983.

20 Balser, 1962; Offermann, 1979; Engelhardt, 1977; Renzsch, 1980.

21 Domansky–Davidsohn, n.d.; Nolan, 1981; Schonhöven, 1980.

22 Cottereau, 1986; Markovitch, 1970; Price, 1981. For labour history, in addition to works already cited see Moss, 1976; and more specifically, Moss, 1975a and Johnson, 1975.

23 Chartism has benefited from recent work on its cultural and ideological character which has reinforced an earlier attention to its local variations. See Epstein & Thompson (eds), 1982. For some stress on political continuity across the 1850 divide see Hollis & Harrison, 1967 and Lowery 1979.

24 See introduction on why this is a necessary element in any proper comparative history.

25 The problem of definition is most explicitly handled in the German literature concerned with Handwerk. See Conze's general introduction and Kaufhold's historiographical introduction in Engelhardt, 1984; and most recently Lenger, 1988.

26 Fischer, 1971, 'Das deutsche Handwerk'.

27 The major case study was by a student of Fischer's, Noll, (1975).

28 For example, a recent monograph argues that in the city of Brunswick the period of industrial growth *reversed* the increase of unskilled and semi-skilled workers within the labour force. Admittedly, metalworking was the central industrial sector in this economy and that sector requires many skilled workers. See Schildt, 1986, section F.

29 The most convenient recent presentation of the statistical case is Kaufhold, 1976.

30 See Clapham, 1932 and Samuel, 1977.

31 Markovitch, 1970. More recently see Roehl, 1976; and O'Brien & Keyder, 1978.

32 For example, Kaeble, 1983 has recently argued that German industrialisation was neither so rapid nor so focused on heavy industry as has often been assumed.

33 Price, 1972 tends to put the 'pre-industrial' case against the contemporary observations of De Tocqueville and Marx. An article which suggests a different approach is Tilly & Lees, 1974.

34 Crisp, 1978.

35 A pioneering study of how English workers acquired skill was Musson & Robinson, 1969. On the continuing importance of skill and apprenticeship as a means of acquiring it see More, 1980. In Germany workshops in 1900 still supplied far more skilled workers to larger enterprises than did the technical institutes. See Schröder, 1978.

36 As many of the contemporary statisticians realised. Those drawing up an industrial census in mid-century Paris, for example, included 'qualitative' sections designed to convey something of these complexities which statistics alone masked. Scott, 1986.

37 Even today in Britain, part of the 'decline' of the manufacturing sector, the increased productivity of firms in that sector, and the boom in the small business service sector can be seen as a statistical illusion, all the product of one basic reorganisation. Large firms contract out a number of their 'peripheral' activities such as catering, cleaning, and security to small, specialised firms. There may well be an overall productivity gain, but the crude statistics can tell us nothing about this, and instead can be used to draw quite misleading conclusions about what is really happening.

38 Thus Musson, who strongly argues this case (see note 15 above), is an historian of the printers (Musson, 1954); as is Gerhard Beier, the leading advocate of the labour aristocracy notion in Germany (Beier, 1966 and 1981a).

39 See the extended review of Foster by Jones (1975).

40 See Bythell, 1969. Cottereau, 1986, points out, however, how economic historians can ignore the survival capacity of artisan weavers, precisely because of the assumption of inevitable extinction. Contemporary Germans, as well as historians, were exercised by the fate of the Silesian weavers, partly because of their 'uprising' in 1844 but also because of their status as apparent victims of industrial progress.

41 Lenger's study of Düsseldorf (Lenger, 1986) demonstrates the continuity and prosperity of the butchery and bakery trades.

42 For tailoring in both Germany and England, see Eisenberg, 1986. Further detail on Germany in Renzsch, 1980; on France in Johnson, 1975; and for England Parssinen & Prothero, 1971.

43 See Schröder, 1978, for Germany; and for a wide-ranging essay, Hobsbawm & Scott, 1980, reprinted in Hobsbawm, 1984a.

44 See Johnson, 1975, and Moss, 1975b; as well as Gossez, 1967, esp. pp. 160–6.

45 Production was concentrated in Lancashire and Cheshire, and Christys of Stockport acquired a dominant position, all without any marked technological innovation. See Giles, 1959.

46 Much of this is discussed in the literature on 'proto-industrialisation', although this focuses on rural production. See Kriedte et al., 1981; Berg, 1983. Specifically for Germany see Zwahr, 1985.

47 In Hamburg by the mid-century domestic furniture production could not cope with domestic demand, and there was a steady increase in the proportion of imported articles.

48 The small-scale nature of some domestic house-building in England is brought out in Crossick, 1978; and the rise of the 'general contractor' along with continued craft control in Price, 1980. For German building see Renzsch, 1984 and Müller, 1984.

49 On Germany see Elkar, 1984. For Britain see Hobsbawm, 'The tramping artisan', in Hobsbawm, 1968; Gosden, 1961; and Leeson, 1979. For France see Briquet, 1955.

50 This point had been made well for Birmingham by Behagg, 1979, where the preponderance of small workshops was also taken to mean a high level of agreement between masters and men. For the older view see Briggs, 1950.

51 Official *Handwerk* statistics bear this out for Germany, as is shown in Breuilly & Sachse, 1984, especially chapter 2.

52 One should also note that the development of merchant capital could *increase* the numbers of nominally independent producers. At the same time the move from dependent to independent producer became a fluid one, rather than a permanent change of social position. See, for example, Crossick, 1978, for the way building workers could become a small employer for a particular job, and then revert back to working for someone else.

53 Behagg, 1979, develops this point well. Focusing on the formal and specialised features of artisan collective action is easier for the historian, but the problems it can create can be seen in Kirby & Musson, 1975. As the title itself indicates, Docherty's career is divided into the different organisations with which he was connected. But it is how they connected to each other and to Docherty himself that is the most important issue, and this is in danger of being lost. See also now Behagg, 1990.

54 Prothero, 1979, for the 1820s; Goodway, 1982, pp. 54–5 for the 1840s; McCready, 1954, for the 1874 election.

55 Georges Duchêne, *Actualité, Livret et Prud'hommes* Paris, 1847. I am grateful to Iori Prothero for drawing my attention to this pamphlet and the campaign of which it was a part.

56 On Hamburg see Breuilly & Sachse, 1984. For national organisation betwen 1848 and 1851 see Balser, 1962, and Noyes, 1966.

57 For a consideration of some of these problems see my essay 'Civil Society and Class Relations'.

58 For Germany see the ideas about different 'political landscapes' developed by Na'aman, 1969. For Paris see Gossez, 1967. For London see Prothero, 1969 and 1971; and Goodway, 1982.

59 Prothero, 1979; Kirby & Musson, 1975.

60 See Kocka, 1986. For an impressive example of multi-trade action in the late eighteenth century see Herzig & Sachs, 1987.

61 On Owen see Harrison, 1969; on phrenology, Cooter, 1984; on spiritualism, Barrow, 1988.

62 See Johnson, 1970; and Moss, 1975a.

63 Schieder, 1963.

64 For Weitling, see below.

65 Gossez, 1967.

66 Parssinen & Prothero, 1971.

67 Schieder, 1963; Kowalski, 1962.

68 Thus, for example, there is far less interest in such ideas amongst metal-working artisans than amongst those in tailoring and shoemaking. There were numerous small metalworking establishments and an extension of production for the market. However, initial capital outlay was higher and this made it much more difficult for workers with little capital to set up, and hence to imagine setting up, producer cooperatives. Only where this general rule did not apply, for example in the cutlery business, does not find some receptiveness to utopian ideas.
For an example of the higher costs of setting up in metal-working compared to tailoring and shoemaking, see Lenger, 1988. For an example of the exception, amongst the metal-workers of Solingen, see Boch, 1985.

69 For England see Jones, 1984a, and Prothero, 1974. For France see Johnson, 1970 and Sewell, 1980. For Germany see Breuilly & Sachse, 1984, especially chapter 2.

70 Marx, of course, argued that the 'solutions' of the utopian thinkers frequently smuggled back the ideals of petty commodity production although in arguments which were self-contradictory. The idea of exchange on the basis of the labour embodied in a product, for example, may superficially have done away with money but not with the idea of commodity exchange based on the labour value contributed by *individuals*, that is, the basis of the system of production for the market. Further to this see Breuilly & Sachse, 1984, pp. 54–5 and Marsiske, 1986, pp. 73–4. But Marx's attacks on this idea are in part testimony to its influence amongst the craftsmen for whose support he was striving. See Marx, 1973, especially 'The Chapter on Money', pp. 115–238; and Marx, 1956.

71 For a much more elaborate development of the arguments which follow, see Breuilly, 1989b. The book in which this essay appears (Knatz & Marsiske, 1988) and the conference which gave rise to this book are indications of the revival of interest in Weitling amongst German scholars. The most scholarly biography remains at present Seidel-Höppner, 1961, but there is a lot of current research and also plans (see Marsiske, 1989) to bring out an edition of Weitling's complete works.

72 Breuilly & Sachse, 1984, chapter 2.

73 Marsiske, 1986, p. 44 cites Weitling's experience of working for a *Damenschneider* employing fourteen workers in Leipzig. His wanderings and underemployment are documented in Seidel-Höppner, 1961.

74 The least important of his three major books is translated into English as *The Poor Sinner's Gospel* (Weitling, 1969). For the German version of that as well as his popular pamphlet of 1838, *Die Menschheit, wie sie ist und wie sie sein sollte*, with a useful introduction by Schafer, see Weitling, 1971. The major work, the first edition of which was published in 1842 is *Garantien der Harmonie und Freiheit* (Weitling, 1974). Various journals Weitling edited have been reprinted and other work of his has been published. For further details on his writings see Marsiske, 1989. *The Poor Sinner's Gospel* raises one issue of major importance in artisan ideology which I have had to omit for reasons of space – the abiding interest in a radical form of Christianity.

75 I would qualify this in the light of the work Hans-Arthur Marsiske has recently carried out on Weitling's American career following his exile from Germany after the failure of the 1848 revolution. Weitling was then attracted by other currents of utopianism, for example those associated with currency fads. This can be linked back to his long-running antipathy to money but is now subject to the more commercial American context. However, by this time Weitling was no longer an influential figure within artisan circles. So qualification supports rather than undermines my general argument.

76 For a traumatic break between guilds (often an instrument of government in territorial states after 1800) and journeymen around 1800 see Griessinger, 1981. For details of anti-guild feeling in one particular case see Breuilly & Sachse, 1984.

77 For a general survey see Birker, 1973.

78 The labelling and critique of other forms of socialism was a major concern of Marx and Engels in *The Communist Manifesto* and *The German Ideology*. Engels singled out 'true socialism' for attack in 'The True Socialists'. (Engels, 1976, pp. 248–90). The attack, of course, testified to how seriously Marx and Engels took the influence of this current of thought amongst artisans at this time.

79 See Breuilly & Sachse, 1984, p. 192.

80 These points are explored in some detail for Hamburg in Breuilly & Sachse, 1984, especially chapter 5.

81 This is the case I argue in Breuilly, 1989a against the arguments of Seidel-Höppner & Rokitjanski, 1985.

82 Whether it is ever meaningful is a broader question. The idea is developed, rather ineffectively in my view, in Vierhaus, 1986.

83 For this general approach to early German liberalism see Gall, 1975. For its detailed application, with some modifications, to the work and influence of Schulze-Delitzsch, see Aldenhoff, 1984.

84 Renzsch, 1980; Stephan, 1977.

85 For 1847 see Struik, 1971. For 1864 see Marx, 1974, pp. 73–82 (the Inaugural Address of the IWMA) and Marx's letter of 4 November 1864 to Engels on the drafting of this address. (Marx, 1987, pp. 11–19.

86 So far as I know the way in which a variety of experiences (the social question in Germany, Engels' work in Manchester, Marx's contacts with artisans in Paris, Cologne and elsewhere) shaped Marx's complex, even contradictory idea of the proletariat, combining poverty, respectability and factory work, has not yet been accorded the attention it merits. An interesting step in that direction is Draper, 1972.

87 Jones, 1984a.

88 Behagg, 1979.

89 See especially, Prothero, 1979.

90 Crossick, 1978; Tholfsen, 1976; Gray, 1976. Much of this kind of work is summarised and evaluated in Gray, 1981.

91 Parssinen & Prothero, 1971; Prothero, 1969 and 1971.

92 Johnson, 1970; Moss, 1976; Hanagan 1980.

93 Corrigan & Sayer, 1985; Rose, 1970; Storch, 1975.

94 Jones, 1984a.

95 See below, the essay on law, for further consideration of these contrasting political attitudes.

96 Wirth, 1981.

97 Jones, 1984a; Breuilly, 1987c; Schieder, 1963; Loubère, 1961 for various meanings of radical democracy and social democracy. The division between a Jacobin like Blanqui and a 'social democrat' such as Louis Blanc makes the distinction clear.

98 Balser, 1962.

99 Von Berg, 1981.

100 See Lenger, 1986, especially chapters 6 and 7; and Lenger, 1988, especially pp. 58–63.

101 Na'aman, 1970.

102 See the essay 'Liberalism or social democracy?' for more details.

103 For the example of the Hamburg branch (*Gemeinde*) of the ADAV, the largest branch in the 1860s, see Breuilly & Sachse, 1984.

104 Schieder, 1963.

105 Epstein, 1982; Belchem, 1985.

106 Breuilly, Niedhart & Taylor (eds), forthcoming, especially the general introduction.

107 Breuilly & Sachse, 1984; Birker, 1973.

108 This is discussed more fully in 'Liberalism or social democracy?'.

109 Frank O'Gorman has also argued recently that the electorate was by no means enlarged as much, if at all, as is claimed by many historians. O'Gorman, 1989, especially pp. 178ff.

110 See references in note 92 and my essay 'Civil society and the labour movement'. Chartism, along with the Irish problem, in turn promoted a stronger state action. See Saville, 1987.

111 On these continuities see Breuilly, Niedhart & Taylor (eds), forthcoming.

112 Gossez, 1967; Loubère, 1961.

113 See Breuilly, Niedhart & Taylor (eds), forthcoming, introduction to chapters 4 to 7 and chapters 6 and 7.

114 Na'aman with Harstick, 1975

4

Liberalism or social democracy?
Britain and Germany, 1850–1875

Introduction

In the period between 1850 and 1875 labour politics in Britain and Germany moved in very different directions. In Britain the decline of Chartism was followed by a shift on the part of politically active working men from independent action to the pursuit of franchise and other reforms in cooperation with elements in established political parties. The co-operation between the Reform League, the most important working-class political organisation in the 1860s, and members of the Liberal Party in the campaign for franchise reform and in the General Election of 1868 (the first held on the new franchise) marked a step towards the Lib–Lab alliance which dominated labour politics up to 1914 at least. In Germany, by contrast, the partnership between liberalism and the labour movement was brief and of limited importance. The small labour movement which began to re-emerge in the late 1850s and early 1860s after the period of counter-revolution following the failure of the 1848 revolution was patronised by prominent liberals. This trend was first seriously challenged with the formation of the *Allgemeiner Deutscher Arbeiter Verein* (ADAV) in May 1863. Most of the organised labour movement continued to remain close to liberalism, especially in the loose organisation, the *Verband der deutschen Arbeiter (bildungs)vereine* (VDAV) founded in June 1863 in response to the ADAV. However, in 1868 most of the associations within the VDAV voted to affiliate to the First International or International Working Men's Association (IWMA). In the following year this group, along with breakaway elements from the ADAV, established an independent political party, the *Sozial Demokratische Arbeiter Partei* (SDAP). The amalgamation of the ADAV with the SDAP in 1875 through the formation of the *Sozialistische Arbeiter Partei* (SAP) set the seal upon the creation of a single, independent political party claiming to speak for the working class as a whole.

One should not exaggerate the differences. In Britain there were always tendencies towards more independent political action than that practised in association with the Liberal Party.[1] In some urban constituencies there were no autonomous labour organisations which could make any choice between cooperating with or opposing one of the main parties and so those parties mobilised directly whatever working-class support they received.[2] The Conservative Party was always able to command a substantial working-class vote.[3] In Germany liberal and democratic parties retained a strong influence over workers in many areas, especially in south Germany, well into the 1870s and even later.[4] There were also instances of practical cooperation between the social democratic parties, especially the SDAP, and other parties drawing support mainly from non-working, class groups. Strong central organisation and separation from, indeed hostility towards, all other parties was very much the product of the anti-socialist law period.[5] In both countries a significant element of the working class supported regional, ethnic, or confessional parties.[6]

Nevertheless, it is clear that by 1875 the dominant trends in organised labour politics in the two countries moved in opposing directions between the choice of popular multi-class liberalism or exclusive, working-class socialism. In this essay I look at how historians have explained these different trends and how arguments used in the one case can be related to what happened in the other. I confine my attention to the period of relative prosperity up to about 1875 as the period of depression which followed raised many new issues.[7] Also I focus upon the question of the relationship between liberalism and the labour movement. A fuller comparison would also look at the relationship between industry and agriculture and the impact of religion on popular politics as well as much else.[8]

The next section outlines the historiography of the subject, concentrating on the ways in which historians have explained the opposing trends, comparing the approaches historians have taken in the two cases, and suggesting reasons for differences of approach. The following section considers how interpretations offered in one case can be brought to bear upon the other case. This both enables one to provide a limited test of the general validity of certain kinds of argument and to bring out clearly certain assumptions about what might 'normally' be expected to be the pattern of development of working-class politics. Some historians of Britain regard the absence of independent working-class politics as something requiring special explanation.[9] Some German historians have the same attitude towards the failure of a broad-based liberalism.[10] Comparisons could pinpoint problems with such assumptions.

Historiography

The historiography of the two cases is very different. The British literature is particularly strong on such matters as trade union organisation, occupations, and working-class culture. The German literature pays more attention to formal political organisation, ideology, and individual leaders. In part this is an expression of more general differences between British and German historians. However, it is also to do with the rather different problems the labour history of this period poses for the historian.

In the British case the issue which for a long time preoccupied historians was the demise of Chartism. The third quarter of the century appears as an interlude between two periods in which class conflict was directly expressed in political form. Chartism was seen as a major working-class challenge to state and society. Its demise cannot be explained simply in terms of repression. The amount of repression was small in comparison to the size of the Chartist movement at its height, to earlier repression of radical and labour movements, and to the treatment meted out to such movements in continental Europe.[11] Yet at a political level Chartism collapsed dramatically after 1848, even if recent studies have traced continuities in the attitudes of ex-Chartists active in labour politics afterwards.[12] Furthermore, there was no obvious shift in the making of political concessions at this time which might have undermined the appeal of Chartism.[13] This has suggested to historians that one should look 'below' the political level for an explanation.[14] The decline of Chartism has therefore been explained in terms of changes in the economy, in the composition of the working class and its values, and in the relationship between working-class groups and others. In addition, for those historians who implicitly or explicitly assume that independent working-class politics is what one can normally assume in industrial, capitalist societies, the explanation for the demise of Chartism can also serve to account for the relative unimportance of such a politics in the post-Chartist period.

The social approach has been dominated by the labour aristocracy debate which focuses upon the internal composition of the working class.[15] The economistic approach has stressed above all prosperity after 1850 and the real material gains made by important groups of workers.[16] The cultural approach has drawn attention in a variety of ways to the ideological subordination of workers.[17] The stress on social relationships with middle-class groups has used ideas of paternalism and of social control.[18]

One could reintroduce a more explicitly political approach to the subject. It tended to be non-British historians working in the inter-war period who focused more on the actual politics of labour after 1850.[19] There is some indication of a renewal of interest, although this focuses upon political language and ideas rather than action and institutions, and tends to be more interested in continuities than discontinuities.[20] An approach of this latter kind (which I would favour) might treat Chartism less as a social and economic response to various problems or as one form of political radicalism, but rather as a reaction to a political crisis arising out of the institutional revolution of the 1829–1835 period.[21] If one took this approach, the decline of Chartism could be seen as arising out of a combination of adaptation and successful resistance to such institutional changes. Chartism drew support from trade union demands, resistance to the New Poor Law, and reactions against changes in the structure and elective basis of parliamentary and urban government and in the system of policing.[22] Some successes were registered, for example in the way in which the New Poor Law was enforced.[23] In other areas, above all the franchise question, there were no concessions and the local political activists who had become involved in Chartism often sought to adapt to the new middle-class dominance of many urban governments. One could go on to interpret the labour politics of the post-1850 period as the pragmatic acceptance of new political realities after a period of upheaval. The study of post-1850 labour politics could then explore more precisely what those realities were and the ways in which labour politicians sought to use or alter them.

The problems facing German labour historians are very different. There is nothing like the British pattern of an apparent development of mass-based class politics followed by a shift to popular non-class liberalism. Instead, the first emergence of labour organisations with some political concerns in the 1840s, especially during the 1848 revolution, was followed fairly quickly in the 1860s by the setting up of independent political parties. The delay in moving from the popular politics of 1848 (there were artisan dominated organisations but there was very little idea of pursuing at a political level a distinct class interest) to the class politics of the 1860s can be explained by drawing attention to the very new and emergent character of the working class at this time.[24] Political repression, especially following the 1848 revolution, would suffice to explain the inhibition of any kind of labour politics, independent or not.[25] As the formation of independent labour parties followed on very quickly from the period of political relaxation beginning in about 1858, it was often assumed that this was the political expression of working-class formation in the first period of sustained industrial growth in Germany.[26] This assumption, in conjunction with the general historiographical bent towards political and intellectual history, meant that German historians saw little point in engaging in economic, social, and cultural investigations to explain labour politics. Rather, their concern was to account for the various and conflicting programmes and organisations to which labour activists were attached. The questions that were raised included the extent to which the ADAV broke with the traditions of the labour movement, [27] the reasons for the affiliation of the VDAV to the IWMA in 1868 and the setting up of a second workers' party in 1869, [28] and the influence of Marx and his ideas upon the programmes of the various socialist parties for the whole period.[29]

These emphases were reinforced by the post-war division of Germany. There was a strong and understandable preoccupation with the differences between reformist social democracy and Marxist socialism. West German historians were concerned to locate the roots of a democratic commitment in the labour movement and to intepret the appeal of Marxism as the product of insufficient political and social reform rather than as the inevitable consequence of class exploitation under capitalism.[30] By contrast East German historians interpreted the development towards a single working-class party which adopted a Marxist programme in terms of the journey of the working class towards true self-knowledge, though a difficult journey constantly beset by false turnings.[31] One might think that East German historians who regarded themselves as Marxists would have paid attention to the social and economic basis of class, but with a few important exceptions their work was even more focused upon politics and ideology (and that in the very narrow form of official programmes) than the work of West German historians.[32] How historical treatments of the labour movement might change now that East and West Germany have been reunified on western terms remains to be seen. Certainly some of the more objectionable features of DDR historiography have been brought to an end.[33]

Even those who question whether labour politics had to be class politics and stress the potential of a liberal labour movement have tended to concentrate upon ideological, organisational and personal failings within liberalism in order to explain why this potential remained unfulfilled.[34] Engelhardt's massive study of liberalism and trade unions does point in a different direction.[35] Nevertheless, even in some of the best and most recent work there is a tendency to asume that social and economic developments favoured some sort of class politics or that liberalism was in some sense flawed and unable to relate positively to the interests of labour.[36] In this way a general bias in German labour history towards organisations, pro- grammes, and leading individuals has been reinforced by the type of problem presented by the actual development of the German labour movement during this period.

This brief account and comparison of the historiography suggests a way of proceeding. One can see how the explanations offered for the absence of class politics in Britain might apply to Germany where such a class politics clearly did develop. In turn one can explore how the explanations for the failure of liberalism to secure broad labour support in Germany might apply to Britain where liberalism in this sense clearly did succeed. This should make it possible to test to some extent the validity of the various kinds of explanations that have been proposed. In the concluding section of the essay I will argue that historians in the future must pay much more attention to the specifically political factors which shaped the direction and character of labour politics in this period.

Comparisons

Economic growth, wages, and the labour force

Generally the period between 1850 and 1875 in Britain was one of economic growth and prosperity, although some of the more optimistic accounts of the period need to be qualified.[37] Some estimates put the rise in real wages on average between 70 and 80 per cent over the longer period 1850–1900.[38] Another estimate is that average real wages rose by about 91 per cent in the whole period 1860–1913 and that the rate of increase in the earlier period 1860–1895 was higher than in the later period.[39] The real wage index constructed by G. H. Wood indicates the following:[40]

Table 1 *Real wages in Britain, 1850–1874* (1850=100)

1850	100
1855	94
1860	105
1865	120
1870	118
1874	136

Notes A major reason for the upward trend in real wages was a shift within the labour force from lower to higher earning occupations.[41]

Between 1850 and 1881 the basic structure of the labour force altered as follows:[42]

Table 2 *Structure of the labour force 1851 and 1881*

	Agriculture, fishing, forestry	Manufacture, mining	Trade, transport	Domestic, personal	Public, professional, & other
1851	21.7	42.9	15.8	13.0	6.7
1881	12.6	43.5	21.3	15.4	7.3

Unemployment was low in this period (and certainly not rising sharply), so taking that into account would not markedly alter the trend revealed by incomes of those in employment. Unemployment averaged about 4.5 per cent for those trade union members for whom figures are available.[43] As for the length of the average working week and day, this went down. In the engineering, building and cotton industries the average working week went down from about sixty to sixty-one hours in 1850 to fifty-four to fifty-seven hours in 1875. However, much of this reduction was concentrated in the period 1870–1875.[44]

It was skilled workers who did particularly well. There is some evidence that in textiles, building and engineering, differentials between skilled and unskilled workers increased.[45] There was marked prosperity in certain industries such as cotton (except for the period of the American Civil War) and engineering. It was amongst skilled workers in such industries that union membership grew fastest and that there were movements towards national and more tightly organised unions.[46] It might then be argued that it was the prosperity and organisation experienced by these workers in particular that was responsible for the accommodating attitudes within the labour movement at this time. Furthermore, this prosperity was based upon liberal economic and financial policies (with which Gladstone was especially associated[47]) and the rapid expansion of exports of manufactured articles. All this would seem likely to entrench pro-liberal attitudes amongst such workers. As this period of expansion did not involve marked technological changes of the kind which would undermine the position of such skilled workers, one possible radicalising influence was not present.[48] One could conclude that the basic reason for the decline of independent working-class politics was the prosperity after 1850 and in particular its impact upon key groups of skilled workers. Furthermore, one could argue that variations within this general upward economic trend would also account for variations in the strength of pro-liberal attitudes. The point is put forcibly by Vincent:

The movement of prices throws much light on the popular lack of enthusiasm for Reform in 1861–66, and the ardour and activity of 1866–67; and the continued high level of prices in 1867–68 similarly corresponded to a spell of political militancy extending well after the passage of the Reform Bill. Gladstonian Liberalism began in a series of lean years when it became almost twice as difficult for the breadwinner to earn the main article of his diet, bread – if he had a job at all.[49]

How does this compare with the situation in Germany? Figures on such matters as wages and prices are less reliable and generalisation is more difficult than is the case for Britain. This reflects the much greater regional diversity of the German economy as well as the quality of the sources and the research effort. Different compilations of statistics reveal varying patterns.[50] Money wages certainly increased substantially over the period but so did prices.[51] The best general guess to date gives real wage trends as follows:[52]

Table 3 *Real wages in Germany 1850–1873* (1913=100)

1850	64
1855	43
1860	60
1865	63
1870	65
1873	69

Notes In general the pattern is one of stagnation, even decline, in the 1850s (though there are considerable variations from year to year) and then a steady improvement during the 1860s up to 1873.

Changes in the structure of the labour force should also be noted:

Table 4 *The labour force in Germany in 1849 and 1871*[53]

	Agriculure	Industry/craft trades (Handwerk)	Services, etc.
1849	56.0	23.6	20.4
1871	49.3	28.9	21.8

The industrial sector was much smaller within the German economy. But from a smaller initial base the rate of growth of employment was more rapid than in the British industrial sector.

Table 5 *The growth of the industrial labour force in Germany, 1861–1875*[54]

	1861	1875	Increase(%)
Total population (millions)	35.5	40.0	13
Employment outside agriculture (millions)	4.7	5.9	26
Chemical industry (1861=100)	100	160	60
Machine & tool production (1860=100)	100	172	72

As in Britain this occupational shift assisted the rise in real wages. Also, it was in the growth industries, especially amongst the more skilled occupations, that real wages did well and that an organised labour movement was concentrated.[55] The increasing market power of such workers is shown in the increase in strike activity, especially in boom periods, with an increased success rate; with the development of larger and more stable trade unions than had hitherto existed.[56] Although, therefore, there was less prosperity than in Britain, both in absolute terms and in terms of the rate of growth of real wages, there were similarities in the trends.

But there was one major difference. The very rapid rate of growth of the industrial labour force in Germany was supplied out of an agricultural sector. This declined proportionally slower than the British agricultural sector but as it was much larger to begin with, both in absolute terms and as a proportion of the total economy, the German agricultural sector could still release far larger numbers of workers. This labour force had few skills and qualifications to bring to industrial employment. One would expect, therefore, that German employers would have to invest more heavily in technology and organisation in order to be able to substitute this cheaper, less qualified labour for more expensive and skilled labour. Although the speed and character of German industrialisation compared with that of Britain has sometimes been exaggerated, there does appear to have been an important contrast in this respect.[57]

It is difficult actually to measure such a difference in terms of the levels and types of capital investment and changes in the skill levels of the industrial labour force. It is nevertheless possible to look for certain indicators of such trends. One would be an erosion of differentials in the earnings of skilled and unskilled workers. It is very hard to obtain reliable information even for this indicator, although there is some evidence to suggest, for example, that a narrowing took place in the building trade.[58] Differentials frequently appeared to have been very wide in the first half of the nineteenth century and to have offered little scope for further increase.[59] But no really definite statement on this matter can be made. In any case, in general economic terms it is not the differentials between those employed so much as the proportion of the total wages bill for more skilled and less skilled workers which one would expect to move in favour of the less skilled. This would be even more difficult to calculate.

One would also expect some of the economic growth to be furnished by a greater degree of labour utilisation. It does appear that average hours of work in industry increased over the period 1850–1875, including sharp increases in major growth sectors such as mining.[60]

Tentatively all these comparisons would lead one to expect a less accommodating attitude on the part of more skilled workers who were doing both relatively and absolutely less well than their British counterparts. Yet their living standards were probably rising quite satisfactorily,[61] and they were able to organise increasingly effectively in the labour market. In other words, the simple fact of prosperity itself has several dimensions and tells us little about how the nature of economic development will affect the ways in which labour can organise and, once organised, what goals it will pursue. The figures can tell us that workers in Germany (especially more skilled workers) were less numerous, powerful and prosperous than in Britain.

The concept of a labour aristocracy

I deal with this concept in detail in another essay in this book and there is no need to repeat those points here. I would only note that the concept has been used in this period above all to show how the formation of an aristocracy of labour in Britain – whether in terms of position in the workplace, amongst income earners, and within the community – inhibited the emergence of independent working-class politics. Instead, I will simply ask whether these different ideas of an aristocracy of labour have any application to the German case, where such a politics did develop.

If we ask whether a labour aristocracy can be identified at the workplace in Germany, there are a number of occupations in which this might plausibly be argued. The printers have long been taken as an 'aristocratic' occupation.[62] The engineering industry which grew rapidly after 1850 created a well-paid occupational group with considerable control over their jobs.[63] Generally it appears that these particular occupations were not in the forefront of independent labour politics and that engineering workers in Berlin, for example, were amongst the strongest supporters of a liberal labour movement.[64] Lassalle, for example, made little initial impact in the capital and Berlin engineering workers were staunch supporters of Schulze-Delitzsch.[65] This might suggest that the kinds of workers active in the more independently inclined labour movement would not possess these 'aristocratic' characteristics. As such an independent orientation came to be the dominant trend that in turn might suggest that such an aristocracy of labour was much less important in Germany than in Britain.

Both points appear to have some validity. The Lassallean movement and even the increasingly independent Eisenacher movement appear to have drawn their support from less industrialised trades such as building, shoemaking, tailoring, and weaving in urban workshop, sweated domestic, and rural industrial production.[66] Even in more industrialised sectors it appears that skilled workers were often less able than their British counterparts to adapt themselves in order to create a privileged position at work. For example in the British shipbuilding industry, shipwrights managed to preserve a good position for themselves in the change from wood to steel, whereas shipwrights in German yards were quickly swept aside in the course of this change.[67] One could fit this into more general arguments of the kind advanced earlier about the availability of less skilled labour who could be used by employers in Germany more easily to substitute for more skilled labour, although there are other factors such as the rate of expansion and the type of product market which need to be taken into account.[68]

However, this contrast between Britain with a more important aristocracy of labour and Germany where skilled workers in both traditional and new forms of production were under greater pressure does need to be qualified. The material cited for Germany is very impressionistic. The comparisons appear to work well for such sectors as cotton, engineering and shipbuilding, but they work less well for other sectors such as mining, building, and clothing.[69] The building trade in particular seems to display many similar characteristics of fast growth, continued dependency on skilled labour, movement towards more clear-cut market relations, especially in large towns, and a rapid expansion of union organisation and strike activity.[70] Yet in Britain the leaders of building unions displayed 'pro-liberal' attitudes and were a major prop of Lib–Lab politics,[71] whereas in cities such as Berlin and Hamburg the leaders and members of such unions were important sources of support for an increasingly independent social democratic movement.[72] Clearly an explanation of these differences needs to be sought elsewhere – in the relative importance of such trades within the labour movement, in the pattern of industrial relations, in the political sphere.

Little has been done in Germany to indicate the presence of an aristocracy of labour within the community.[73] Generally the impression is that the more rapid industrial growth in Germany, based on sectors in which it was possible to use a large amount of unqualified labour, would not provide conditions as conducive in the British case to the formation of a labour aristocracy, and that this in turn would remove one of the principal sources of support for a popular liberal movement. However, this *is* no more than an impression in the absence of much good research. Furthermore, one should remember that recently the idea of explaining pro-liberal labour politics in Britain in terms of a labour aristocracy has come in for very severe criticism.[74]

The role of ideology

One particular area in which comparison can be made more effectively, concerns the degree to which certain groups of workers accepted liberal ideology. This argument, insofar as it sees labour aristocrats as particularly receptive to liberalism, forms part of the case for emphasising the role of a labour aristocracy. One can see a fairly direct and simple way in which the acceptance of liberalism comes about. Employers and other middle-class figures advocate the merits of free competition, a society open to talent and encouraging self-help, a minimalist government subject to accountability through a representative assembly in which skilled workers at least have a part in electing. Skilled workers, able to use the labour market to secure good contracts, hopeful of advancement in their trade, and grateful for legal equality and the vote, accept these liberal values and throw their support behind liberal parties.[75]

A more subtle and plausible approach outlines the acceptance of liberal 'hegemony'.[76] In this account workers do not simply accept the whole liberal package as preached by middle-class liberals. Rather, they accept some of the basic liberal assumptions which serve to shape and limit the way in which specific labour interests are ideologically represented. This distinction between basic assumptions and limits of an ideology and its actual content is brought out well by Tholfsen:

> The channelling of militancy into forms that did not remotely threaten radical change but yet conveyed the impression that something big was in the wind was a powerful self-stabilising mechanism. The symbolic and ritual forms of militant protest fell neatly into place in this latitudinarian liberal – all-embracing culture. Thus, even when workingmen rejected political economy and denounced employer cant and avarice, they were in effect confirming one of the central values of the official ethos: a man should think for himself, refuse to accept the dogmas handed down from above, and come to rational conclusions based on the evidence. If workingmen erred in the short run they would see the light eventually.[77]

The advantage of this approach is that it deals with the self-evident fact that there was a different content to the kind of liberalism espoused by 'respectable' workers and the liberalism of classical political economy and Smilesian self-help. Very few trade unionists, for example, could accept the arguments about collective bargaining being in restraint of trade.[78] The disadvantage is that it can, by accommodating just about every idea which does not explicitly challenge liberal assumptions, become so flexible as to lose all shape. For example, if working men had rejected this 'official ethos' by refusing to think for themselves and instead accepting dogmas imposed from above (or rather by not employing a rhetoric to that effect), would this have made them more or less liable to containment within the existing value system? If opposite causes can produce the same effect, it is difficult to know what counts as a verifiable explanation of that effect. There is a danger that the argument begins with the 'fact' of liberal success in capturing labour support and then accounts for that support, *no matter what interests and values are involved*, in terms of liberal 'hegemony'.

One possible objection to either of these approaches is that they misunderstand the function of 'ideas' in politics. Rather than seeing ideas as the primary forces which shape political perceptions, one should rather treat them as a rhetoric which is used to justify prior objectives. For example, at the Royal Commission on Trade Unions of 1867–68, trade union leaders presented a respectable, 'liberal' image of the practice and values of trade unions.[79] Yet we know that this image frequently diverged from reality. Trade unions did use threats and sometimes actual violence to deal with the problem of blacklegs during strikes.[80] Sometimes the trade union leaders who argued the liberal case for unions before the Royal Commission were directly implicated in such unliberal actions. This is not to say that they were being hypocritical and simply trying to make the most favourable impression upon the Royal Commission. It may be that trade union leaders had a different attitude from that of many of their members,[81] though that is difficult to establish. It could simply mean that in the setting of an inquiry in which it did appear that men of good will were seeking, by rational and peaceful methods, to find reasonable answers to the problems of industrial conflict, the sentiments expressed by those testifying to the Royal Commission were genuine. In other words, it was the particular context which, largely reflecting liberal ideals about legislative progress, made such values appear so appropriate. Change the context and the appropriateness of those values could be quickly called into question. One danger in the fashionable concern about 'language' and 'discourse' shaping attitudes is that it does not take into account sufficiently the exact contexts in which that language is used. A language used about strikes in the context of an inquiry into strikes is different from the language that might be used in the context of running a strike. Most of the language that has survived for the scrutiny of historians is what I would call 'second order' or 'reflective' language, that is it is language *about* social actions rather than the language *of* those actions. Historians then assume an identity between the two languages and imagine this reflective language actually tells us about how people understood themselves and their situation when engaged in that action. That is not acceptable.

Both the direct and the indirect versions of the acceptance of liberalism by workingmen see the initial ideological source originating from outside the ranks of labour. A third approach, one with which I have rather more sympathy, points to how working-class liberalism also arises out of certain labour intellectual traditions. For example, the suspicion of government intervention and paternalism is an integral part of the radical tradition, owing little to the arguments of classical political economy. The same is true of the demands for legal and political equality. Respectability and protection of the rights of property (especially if a man's skills are regarded as a form of property) were values with strong roots amongst the artisan trades from which so much of the early labour movement sprang.[82] From this perspective, Gladstonian Liberalism could be seen as a new way of pursuing goals which Chartism, craft unions, and radicals had pursued by other means at other times.[83] This can help explain why some autobiographies of working men who had been active both in the Chartist movement and later in popular liberalism stress the continuity between the two rather than the differences.[84]

There are also problems with this approach. E.P.Thompson has argued that the notions of respectability and self-improvement can be used so flexibly as to lose all meaning.[85] The same core values can be related equally well to various anti-liberal ideas such as restrictions on entry into a trade or threatening, if not violent, action to achieve legal and political equality.[86] The argument then can only be sustained by identifying clearly the conditions which will promote an independent, class-collective attempt to realise these values and those which favour acknowledgement of liberal leadership. Linked to this argument is the assumption that one can identify a core set of material or moral interests. These interests sometimes are better pursued in alliance with the interests of others. If that is the case, it becomes necessary to create both practical and ideological coalitions of interests. Popular liberalism could be understood as such a coalition. Clearly there are dangers in assuming a 'set of interests', each with its own values, and neglecting the way in which these interests change over time and can mutually influence and alter one another. There is also a general problem of explaining shifts from one political strategy or ideology to another in terms of some kind of rational judgement that a change of situation dictates a change in the methods by which a fairly constant final goal is pursued. Nevertheless, I do think that this approach offers rather more to the historian than that which stresses the acceptance of the values of others, whether directly or indirectly.

One reason is that the idea of the acceptance of the values of 'others' implies that there is an alternative, namely to construct one's 'own' values. This is the silent assumption accompanying much of the work on 'hegemony', 'incorporation', and the working-class 'acceptance' of middle-class liberalism. Just as there is the assumption that workers could have constructed an independent class politics and that the task of the historian is to explain why they failed to do so; so there is the assumption that workers could have constructed an independent class ideology and the task of the historian is to explain this failure. If this possibility is merely an abstract one, with no indication as to what this ideology might be like or some empirical evidence as to attempts at least to formulate such an ideology, then this is a matter of faith, best debated amongst the faithful rather than by critical his-torians. But frequently it is assumed that there was a real, concrete ideology that was available to workers and which some, at least, moved towards. This is Marxism. In Germany there was an early reception of Marxism within the labour movement. Could this, as well as the rejection of liberalism by the labour movement, be explained in terms of the failure of liberalism to achieve hegemony? If it could, then it might help us identify the particular British conditions in which liberalism becomes much more ideologically acceptable and thereby prevents the diffusion of a more class-specific ideology within the labour movement.

There are many variants of Marxism. Some historians, for a slightly later period, have argued that certain kinds of Marxism actually helped to 'integrate' the German labour movement into the wider society and the state.[87] In this way even Marxism becomes 'incorporated', ceasing to possess hegemony. There is a danger that a 'hegemonic' Marxism in turn becomes no more than an abstract possibility, that the failure of such a creed to penetrate the working class becomes the pre-occupation of historians. This is sometimes combined with the identification of one 'true' form of Marxism, possibly that associated with the positions taken by Marx and Engels. The history of the labour movement then becomes the history of how far this true Marxism was accepted. The danger of this approach is that, once again, 'true class-consciousness' is turned into a function of a particular faith on the part of the historian.

I would suggest a different approach to the ideology of the early German labour movement. First, it is important to recognise the fairly marginal part Marx and Engels played in that movement. The League of the Communists was a small, sectarian organisation. Marx and Engels played a limited role in it before 1848; ignored it during the period of revolution; and came to lead one branch of it, after the revolution and that the less important in terms of following within Germany. Preoccupation with theoretical matters in the counter-revolutionary period of the 1850s reduced that marginal role still further. Marx came once more into prominence in the early 1860s with the IWMA and by virtue of his personal and intellectual influence on such men as Wilhelm Liebknecht, August Bebel, and Ferdinand Lassalle.[88]

In terms of the comparison being pursued in this essay, this influence is best seen as a form of *anti-liberalism*. The concern will be to try to explain why ideas so opposed to those of liberalism managed to secure a much stronger hold over the early German labour movement than that of England. In this context, the ideas of Marx will be treated as just one kind of anti-liberalism. In the 1850s the anti-liberalism of the radical republicans had more appeal within the exile radical and labour community than did the ideas of Marx.[89] Arguably, in the 1860s it was the anti-liberalism of Lassalle which was more important. Lassalle certainly derived some of his key ideas from Marx but in certain respects was even more anti-liberal in that he saw the liberal movement as the immediate enemy and was prepared to cooperate with conservatives in the fight against liberalism.[90] Lassalle's own anti-liberalism has been very well studied. What is less clear is what were the attitudes of those who followed or opposed Lassalle within the labour movement. Here I want to pursue two arguments – that those who followed Lassalle did not share all his anti-liberal values and that those who opposed him, often remaining within a popular liberal alliance, did not accept many of the ideas of middle-class liberalism. On the basis of these arguments I will then suggest a rather different way of explaining the reception of particular political creeds within the labour movement than that which focuses on ideological persuasion.

It would be best to develop these arguments with reference to particular examples. I will draw upon my own research into the Hamburg labour movement, although there are problems about typicality. Throughout the 1850s there had been attempts to persuade members of the Workers' Educational Association, the most important labour organisation in the city at this time, to accept liberal values and to abandon any interest in the various radical and socialist ideas which had surfaced in the association since its formation in 1844–55. Lectures were given on political economy and a local newspaper declared that 'Clear views on profits, wages, etc. will prove a better antidote to communism than police action against the diffusion of ideas which careful consideration shows to be meaningless'.[91] This was typical of the kinds of efforts liberals made in both German and English working men's associations in the 1850s.[92] What is more difficult to establish is how members of these associations responded to such efforts. A survey of the library holdings of the Hamburg association shows that some works of economic or political liberalism were included. However, the publications of the best-represented of these writers, Schulze-Delitzsch, consisted primarily of reports and guides on cooperatives of various kinds. Their presence on the shelves of the library are better explained in terms of the practical help they offered to those wishing to set up such cooperatives rather than of the political values they commended. As we shall see later, such cooperatives could be understood in anti-liberal ways. However, the most popular non-fictional author was Pastor Dulon, the radical preacher of Bremen. There were numerous socialist and radical works by writers such as Etienne Cabet, his German follower Allhusen, Wilhelm Weitling, Proudhon, Engels, and Thomas Paine. It is an eclectic collection. We do not know how popular were individual books or authors or what was donated rather than purchased. It does suggest, however, that there was no great preoccupation with literature that preached liberal values and there was an interest in many ideas which opposed liberalism.[93] I have argued elsewhere that underneath this apparent eclecticism there are consistent and enduring preoccupations of the type of artisan who dominated the association throughout this period.[94]

Of particular interest is a piece of evidence concerning the response of one member of the association, the tailor Fritz Appel. Appel deeply resented the lectures on political economy that were given to the association. He found them patronising. He wanted the association to take a bolder political line (this was in 1853), thought it wrong that the association should fall under the influence of members of the respectable middle class, and believed that liberals laid far too much stress on such matters as individual savings. Workers could achieve little in that direction given their low incomes. Appel also disliked an approach to education and cooperation which stressed their usefulness to individuals. Instead he valued these as ways of raising men up spiritually and of inculcating an ethos of fraternity and solidarity. Appel does not appear to have accepted the individualist ethic at the heart of bourgeois liberalism.[95]

What is of particular interest, however, is that Appel went on to become a leading *proponent* of a liberal labour movement in the 1860s and a founding member of the local branch of the Progressive Party. In the decade since 1853 Appel had advanced from being a journeyman to being a master who employed others. One might therefore seek to explain his liberalism in terms of his change of social position. However, I think that over-simplifies. It is more important to identify a certain consistency in Appel's views.

In the early 1850s Appel opposed any idea of independent political action on the part of the labour movement. Above all, it was too dangerous. The association had, fairly uniquely for Germany, managed to survive the counter-revolution but had been compelled to turn away from politics and to seek protection from middle-class patrons. There had been a history of cooperation with liberals since the formation of the association in 1844–45, even though this was as much a matter of necessity as of shared values. Artisans like Appel shared with liberals an antipathy to privileges conferred by restricted citizenship and guild membership which both survived in Hamburg until a period of reform between 1859 and 1867.[96] There was a feeling that there was a community of interests amongst the 'productive' classes. (Appel's resentment of lectures in classical political economy was partly to do with the fact that it was a lawyer, a member of an unproductive occupation, who gave them.) Apart from the danger of abandoning cooperation with liberals – cooperation which was to achieve a great deal in the decade after 1858 – there was also the problem that a politically isolated labour movement would lack influence.

One can understand Appel's 'liberalism' in terms similar to those used in the British case. There were points of contact between the values of the artisan labour movement and bourgeois liberalism – although the artisan view of cooperation, education, 'self-help' differed in important respects from that of the individualist liberal.[97] At the same time there were social tensions and aspects of that artisan view which could clash with liberalism. In Appel's case, and that of the Workers' Educational Association, the survival of the association, the practical benefits of cooperating with liberals, and the danger and impotence which threatened to accompany independent political action all pointed to the continuation of an alliance with middle-class liberals. All this suggests that we should analyse the relationship between labour and liberalism not in terms of the influence of an aristocracy of labour or of the persuasive power of liberalideas but rather in terms of the specific balance of costs and benefits attached to maintaining that relationship.

Nevertheless, it was the case that the largest single branch of the ADAV was set up in Hamburg. The specifically political reasons for the establishment of the ADAV are discussed in the next section. Here I will consider again the role of ideology in the process. If people like Appel could cooperate with liberals without sharing their values; could others follow Lassalle without being Lassallean? The short answer is that they could. The most prominent activists within the Hamburg ADAV had been members of the Workers' Educational Association and enthusiasts for such liberal causes as self-help cooperation. Against Lassalle's own views and wishes, the Hamburg activists reintroduced many of the non-political activities associated with the traditions of an artisan labour movement. The dispute about 'self-help' as opposed to 'state-help' turned out to be less an argument between laissez-faire and socialist economics and more an argument about whether one should cooperate with states controlled by other groups. The stress on *producer* cooperatives was common between artisan liberals and artisan Lassalleans. In secret many artisan Lassalleans were unhappy about the call for immediate universal manhood suffrage and many artisan liberals about the elitism of their middle-class patrons. Ultimately it was specifically *political* differences which mattered in Hamburg – above all attitudes towards the vote and strikes. I emphasise *political* differences because, for example, on the matter of strikes, liberals actually had a more positive view of their economic rationality than did Lassalleans. But for political reasons Lassalleans were more fully committed to supporting strikes and this could earn them labour support.

This is not to discount completely ideological differences as a basis for political differences. The Hamburg example, with a continuity of organisation since before 1848 and with the same kinds of occupations supporting the ADAV as had supported the Workers' Educational Association, might exaggerate the lack of a strong conflict of basic values. However, it is clear that in other regions there were artisans and domestic workers who were drawn to the ADAV out of desperation. Liberalism with its stress on gradual change, the free market, and economic progress had little appeal to such workers. Lassalle's simple two-point programme which reduced democracy to the vote and socialism to producer cooperatives appealed much more. Nevertheless, in many cases it was specific political conditions which determined whether the labour movement worked with or against middle-class liberalism. Ideology in the form of official 'programmes' often then *followed* and justified particular political choices.

Before looking in more detail at those choices and the political situations which gave rise to them, it is necessary to refer briefly to two other ways in which ideology has been accorded a role in explaining the politics of the British labour movement. Until now the accounts I have discussed focused upon particular groups of workers – labour aristocrats, skilled craftsmen, respectable artisans. The mass of the working class was implicitly seen as less important, incapable of political initiative and either following the elite of workers or not acting politically at all. In some essays published in the early 1960s Perry Anderson and Tom Nairn tried instead to argue that the whole British working class was subject to ideological containment.[98] The argument proceeded by assertion rather than demonstration, operating at a very high level of generality. Underpinning it was the assumption, already criticised, that there was some alternative possibility of a fundamental rejection of existing arrangements in the name of a set of values which were wholly those of the working class. Actual differences and conflicts between workers and those above them were ignored in favour of meditating upon the absence of this set of values. There was an assumption that elsewhere, in 'other countries', the labour movement made more progress towards elaborating an independent ideology because this process of containment worked less effectively.[99] No evidence about the specific mechanisms of ideological containment, persuasion and repression was offered. The whole purpose of the argument was to attack 'labourism' and the accommodating position reached by the Labour Party on the eve of its election to government in 1964. Until the proponents of this argument produce methods and evidence that deal with actual historical problems, it is one that can be left aside.

A more persuasive argument is one that also focuses on the 'whole' labour force but in terms of paternalism rather than ideological containment. Here the stress is upon the way in which employers manage to persuade workers to accept notions of consensus and community. Patrick Joyce presented an important case of this kind in his study of the successful practice of employer paternalism in some cotton towns in Lancashire.[100] There are, however, problems. First, even if the argument is true in some areas it is the case that the conditions for this kind of employer paternalism are very special. Workers have to be concentrated around certain factories and there have to be sufficient resources to fund provision of housing, welfare, pension and other benefits. Second, such paternalism might explain workers being either politically indifferent or following the political lead of their employers. Unless those employers were liberals, this would not explain labour support for liberalism. Lancashire was noted for the strength of working-class support for the Conservative Party and this might be related to employer influence. Cotton spinner union leaders supported Conservative candidates in the 1868 General Election.[101] In Germany it took a long time for independent labour politics to penetrate the mining and metal industries of the Ruhr where the conditions for the effective practice of employer paternalism were favourable, and even then much of this labour activity went into Catholic or ethnic rather than social democratic politics.[102] But in both cases this goes against the general trend which is under consideration in this essay. In any case, it would be misleading to portray all working-class political behaviour in Lancashire as conservative; there was much more diversity and a tradition of working-class liberalism and radicalism which a simple summary of election results misses.[103]

If one accepts that the argument about paternalism has some application to particular regions and industries, it can indirectly contribute to an explanation of national differences. Political indifference or conservatism amongst groups of working men could reduce the ability of those active in the labour movement to generate a broad base of support. This could influence the political choices made by those activists. For example, after the Second Reform Act of 1867 the Reform League considered the possibility of putting up its own candidates in the General Election of the following year. The response from many provincial trade unions, including that of the cotton spinning operatives, was largely negative. This negative response was one reason that leaders of the Reform League gave for having to work closely with the Liberal Party in the election.[104]

But such an argument has its limitations. So far as the English case is concerned, it is clear that men like George Howell had no wish to turn the Reform League into an independent political organisation and they used evidence about lack of working-class support for such a strategy to strengthen their case.[105] It is also clear that employer paternalism and political acquiescence within the labour force as a whole were much stronger in Germany, yet this does not appear to have inhibited the early move on the part of the labour movement to independent political action. If anything, it was the much more powerful and organised labour movement which in Britain did not choose to act independently. I would argue that this is best explained in terms of the political balances of power both within the labour movement and between that movement and external political forces.

The role of politics

One argument used to account for the absence of direct class-based politics in Britain stresses the opportunities given to working men to participate in the existing political system, which led them to accept that system as legitimate and to follow the lead provided by others with greater political influence. The franchise reforms of 1867 and of 1884, along with the introduction of the secret ballot in 1872 were the major political reforms which enabled this to happen. Trade union reform, above all in measures passed in 1871 and 1875, also removed major grievances which could have stimulated more independent political action. I will argue that these points do not clearly lead to any explanation of support for liberalism.

An argument actually employed during the debate on franchise reform which preceded the Second Reform Act of 1867 was that 'respectable' working men had proved their fitness to have the vote and that there was a danger that such workers, a natural source of leadership within the working class as a whole, would move in a more radical direction if they continued to be denied this privilege. The Reform Act can be understood as one of a series of piecemeal reforms which enabled the British political system to adapt to popular politics without undergoing radical, violent, or rapid change.

There are difficulties with this view.[106] It does not account for the very limited moves towards independent political action before 1867. It presupposes that the sociological and political assumptions behind such a view were broadly correct and that these assumptions guided the legislative provisions. However, one could argue that the idea of the 'respectable' working class was a piece of political rhetoric used to justify or motivate reform and that the Reform Act itself was the unintended consequence of a series of amendments and sudden impulses. Above all, given that the Act was passed by a Conservative government which sought popularity in various ways, it does not by itself account for labour support for liberalism. Furthermore, it does not explain the character of that support, for example the very genuine enthusiasm for Gladstone amongst many politically active working men. Finally, it ignores the many real controls which continued to be enforced upon working men throughout this period. I will return to these points when considering the reasons historians give for the success of liberalism in Britain. At this point I will examine the arguments about political reforms as they might be applied to Germany.

In one sense reform was more radical, innovative, and offered greater opportunities in Germany. The introduction, in 1867, of the secret ballot and of universal manhood suffrage as the basis of elections to the Reichstag swept away many of the limitations upon working-class participation in politics. It was, on these criteria alone, far more of a risk than Disraeli's 'leap in the dark'. Yet it was hedged around with constraints. The Reichstag was not a sovereign parliament; restrictions on rights of association, assembly, speech and publication continued and, at times, were reinforced; many important powers were vested in state and communal institutions which had exclusive or weighted franchises; and in any case these institutions had limited powers in relation to their respective executives.

This had a two-fold effect. The restrictions on political participation as well as the smaller number of organised workers meant that labour politics was the affair of a much smaller group than in Britain. On the other hand, to this small group new opportunities were suddenly opened up at the level of the national parliament. The restricted size of the group involved and its very limited influence meant that it had little to gain by compromising its principles in order to enter a broader political coalition because it would gain little in return. However, the new opportunities at national level required a sharp break with the existing patterns of political action which had developed mainly at local and state level. The price to be paid for independent organisation and programmes at that national level was, however, impotence for the foreseeable future. Such isolation and impotence inclined the labour movement to select ideologies which turned those qualities into virtues. To carry this argument through it is necessary first to look at the reasons liberalism failed to sustain its hold over the labour movement and then to consider the consequences of more independent political action.

GDR historians offered a fairly straightforward explanation for the failure of liberalism to secure working-class support. Liberalism was the ideology of the emergent capitalist class. Given that it made sense for that class to compromise with elements of the existing order and that the interests of capitalists conflicted with those of workers, then it was inevitable that German liberalism would have little appeal to workers, would acquire an authoritarian character, and would founder on the basic fact of class conflict.[107] West German historians by contrast, have seen the problem as less to do with the development of class society than with the particular circumstances which disabled liberalism. Particular attention then has been drawn to the liberal distrust of democratic politics, an enduring sympathy for the 'strong' state, a lack of interest in or hostility towards specific labour interests, and an unwillingness to challenge a still strongly entrenched conservative state and society. In principle there existed the basis for a liberal labour movement, but these qualities of German liberalism prevented the realisation of that potential.[108]

The implicit assumption must be that, where liberalism *did* retain labour support, it did not exhibit these qualities. With that in mind we can turn to look at British liberalism in the 1860s. Clearly liberalism here did not face the formidable problems which confronted German liberals at that time. A liberal party in Britain could hope to dominate a parliament elected on a still quite narrow franchise and did not have the immense task of liberalising state, society, and economy, which confronted German liberals. But that in itself hardly explains the lack of liberal influence in Germany. If anything it might be thought that, faced with such tasks which working men as well as liberals would generally wish to see tackled, there would have been an even greater incentive for cooperation between them. Certainly, when the events leading up to the Reform Act of 1867 and the General Election of 1868, as well as the record of the Liberal Government from 1868 to 1874 are examined, what is interesting is how *little* liberalism offered to specific labour interests. This is particularly true with regard to franchise reform and the laws affecting trade unions and strikes.

One 'advanced' element within the Whig–Liberal parliamentary grouping had advocated extensive franchise reform from the 1850s onwards. A number of reform bills had been introduced before 1867 but had all been fairly easily defeated. However, there were many Whigs in particular who were opposed to extensive reform and they had been instrumental in undoing such attempts.[109] They were less powerful in the 1860s perhaps than a a decade earlier, but certainly could prevent reform when acting with Conservatives. Even reformers were, for the most part, opposed to simple universal manhood suffrage.[110] Old Chartists and radicals were well aware of these inhibitions and continued to insist on the fundamental division between those who wanted 'one man, one vote' and everyone else. These divisions do not seem very different from those within the Progressive Party in Prussia and the German liberal movement generally, at least so far as elections to a national parliament were concerned.[111] What is more, German inhibitions on the subject could be shared by radicals within the labour movement. In Britain the hostility to franchise reform was purely to do with doubts about the fitness of the working class and more generally about democracy. In Germany there was a fear that the rural population could be manipulated in a conservative manner under a system of universal manhood suffrage. This was a fear that many politically active working men shared, even within the ADAV.[112] Nevertheless, by the end of 1862 the National Verein had demanded the implementation of the Imperial Constitution of 1849 for a future German nation–state. This constitution included universal manhood suffrage and parliamentary sovereignity in its provisions. Prussian liberals were less positive in demanding a democratic reform of the Prussian electoral system for town councils and the Landtag. However, in other states, especially in southern Germany, liberals were more committed to democratisation.[113]

In both cases, of course, franchise reform was undertaken by conservatives. Bismarck hoped to manipulate a mass electorate in just the way liberals and radicals feared. He had closely analysed liberal successes in the three-class system of voting to the Prussian Landtag and had noted that often it was only in the third-class of voters in rural districts that conservatives were returned. That category of voters, the poorer majority of the rural population, would be the largest section of the mass electorate created by the granting of universal manhood suffrage. To some extent this was all intended not so much to undermine liberalism as to push it in a conservative direction, but the point is that from 1848 onwards Bismarck had belonged to those conservatives who saw their way forward in terms of adaptation to and exploitation of constitutional and popular politics, rather than resisting such change.[114] Ironically, English radicals, either indifferent to or unaware of Bismarck's motives, hailed his reform and contrasted it with British backwardness. For a brief period pictures of Bismarck appeared at radical meetings alongside those of Garibaldi. The Reform League even wrote to Bismarck to congratulate him on his democratic conduct. They received back a reply in which Bismarck, presumably tongue in cheek, expressed his democratic sentiments.[115] In both cases one cannot argue that the measure was purely a conservative one. Disraeli was forced to or prepared to take amendments, many from Liberals, which transformed his original bill. Equally Bismarck was constrained by liberals to accept the secret ballot, although he did resist other important proposals such as making ministers responsible to parliament. Generally for both cases one can argue that some liberals played a part in introducing franchise reform, but they were not alone, most of them were not democrats, and they could hardly be regarded as the key force behind such reform. On this subject at least it is not obvious that liberalism had any more claim to labour support in Britain than in Germany.

Similar arguments can be made concerning trade unions and the right to strike.[116] By the time the Royal Commission on Trade Unions had finished its work in 1868, trade union leaders were fairly clear as to what reforms they wanted.[117] The Liberal Government proposed extending recognition to trade unions which could be registered and this was carried out in the Trade Union Act of 1871. At the same time, however, the Criminal Law Amendment Act of 1871 maintained, and indeed arguably increased, restrictions upon effective union action, especially in the conduct of strikes. These restrictions, as well as liability to prosecution under the common law of conspiracy and continuing inequalities between worker and employer in the Masters and Servants law, rankled with trade unionists. The prosecution and imprisonment of gas stokers who had taken strike action in 1872 crystallised this dissatisfaction. Some trade unions refused to register under the terms of the Trade Union Act. Much has been made of the pro-labour leanings of the Gladstone Administration of 1868–74 and there has been a good deal of attention paid to those liberals such as Mundella and Morley who took a progressive liberal view of industrial relations. However, one should not forget that there were many employers who supported the government who did not share these views. Further-more, the effective strike action of the period, especially when associated with certain well-publicised incidents of violence and intimidation, turned much middle-class opinion against trade unions. This helps explain the very restrictive features of the law on picketing, molesting and intimidation. It also helps explain the 'respectable' image that trade union leaders sought to project. In a way they had been hoist with their own petard. If trade unions did not need or wish to act coercively, they would not be damaged by tight legal restrictions on such action.

By 1873–74 the issue was poisoning the relationship between the government and trade unions, now at an unprecedented peak of some 1,200,000 members. A recent investigation has persuasively shown that this worried government ministers and that steps were in hand to introduce further reforms to the labour laws.[118] However, not many were aware of this, and the snap election called by Gladstone in 1874 made it impossible for the government to claim any credit on this matter. In a number of key English boroughs which the Liberals lost, there is strong evidence that the issue of the labour laws was crucial.[119] The incoming Conservative Government, aware of the importance of this issue to its victory, established another Royal Commission about which the trade union leaders were suspicious. However, the Government introduced bills in 1875 which went a long way to meeting trade union grievances. The Conspiracy and Protection of Property Act provided some legal protection for picketing, and the Employers and Workmen Act removed workers' criminal liability for breach of contract. The Masters and Servants legislation now ceased to operate and the new Act established full equality before the law for employers and workers. Other measures restricted the use of the common law of conspiracy and ended the situation where the punishment for conspiracy could be greater than for the offence intended.

On these grounds alone, one might suppose that the logical conclusion to be drawn by trade unionists was either that they should act as an independent political pressure group, especially at times of elections, or even that they should shift their support to the Conservative Party which had done the most for their interests. This needs to be qualified in that the legislation of 1875 had a bi-partisan quality about it, as had the Reform Act of 1867. Nevertheless, as with franchise reform, it is not obvious that Liberals earned labour support because of the distinctive position they took on labour laws. To establish the basis of labour support for liberalism one has to look elsewhere.[120]

In Germany most liberals were also hostile to trade unionism and especially strikes. With the onset of counter-revolution such collective activity had been outlawed and either repressed or driven underground. This was as much subject to general restrictions on freedom of association and assembly as to any specific labour laws. German workers started off in a much worse legal position than their English contemporaries. It is against that less favourable point of departure that one has to measure liberal attitudes and actions. As in England there were progressive liberals such as Wirth, Schulze-Delitzsch, Hirsch and Duncker who supported permissive trade union action on both political and economic grounds.[121] Prussian liberals in 1865 supported reforms designed to remove legal restraints upon trade union organisation.[122] In 1869 a liberal-dominated Reichstag removed many of the constraints upon trade unions. The Gewerbordnung for the North German Confederation recognised the right of workers to form coalitions in order to pursue demands concerning wages, hours and conditions of work. Admittedly the next clause of the law placed very tight restrictions upon how to pursue those goals, but this is comparable with the British case.[123] Amongst the rapidly expanding trade union movement of the time, which had reached perhaps 50,000 members by 1877, were unions supported by leading liberals.[124] Liberal unions even led the way in some of the largest strikes of the period, for example in the coal mines of Waldenberg in Lower Silesia in 1868.[125] Admittedly these pro-union liberals were in a minority. The strike alienated many liberals. Generally the strike wave of the period hardened middle-class opinion against collective bargaining, and these sentiments were intensified by a hostile reaction to the Paris Commune.[126] Nevertheless, German liberals do not compare so badly with their British counterparts in terms of their response to the labour interests in trade unionism and the right to strike, especially if one takes into account the initially worse position of German workers.

Furthermore, liberal reforms were enacted in Germany in many other areas of life which greatly improved workers' conditions, areas in which British workers already held a secure position. In 1862 Ferdinand Lassalle condemned the proposed agenda for a labour congress which included such matters as freedom of movement throughout Germany or the right to practise any trade (subject only to restrictions in the interests of public safety). He did so on the grounds that these were secondary matters which distracted workers from the key question of political power.[127] But however valid that view might be, it did reveal Lassalle's distance from the concerns of most organised workers. These matters had preoccupied members of the artisan labour movement for at least a couple of decades. Illiberal restraints on movement, settlement and freedom of occupational choice, as well as many other such rights were still widespread in Germany in the early 1860s and voices were still raised in defence of the continuation of such restraints. However, by the end of the decade massive institutional and legislative change had removed many of these restrictions.[128] There is a good case to be made for the argument that the decade of the 1860s in Germany saw the most dramatic victories won by a clear and coherent liberalism at any time in nineteenth-century Europe.[129] Workers benefitted from these victories. Given their weakness and their debts to liberals, one would have imagined that this would strengthen rather than undermine labour support for liberalism. The argument that liberalism succeeds directly in relation to the extent to which it concedes specific labour interests does not appear to be well-founded.

More convincing explanations of the differences between Britain and Germany should be sought on policy questions which are not specifically about labour interests and on the different ways in which effective political action can be taken.

The artisan dominated labour movement of this period did not instinctively think in class terms. Only Lassalleans made class the touchstone of political interest and identity, and even within the ADAV it is debatable how well such a view was understood, let alone accepted and practised.[130] People were as inclined to refer to other identities, the productive and the parasites, the people and the aristocracy. Even class terms often were used in a political rather than a socio-economic sense – the class with political rights against the class without. Demands for trade union reform, the right to strike, and the vote were often justified on the basis of the simple radical creed that every man was equal, not on class terms.[131] The fact that labour movement organisations tended to act as pressure groups encouraged them to think of specifically labour issues as simply one part of politics rather than the basis of all political values. Where such single-issue pressure group politics was well-developed, as in Britain, one could find people who combined with other workers to pursue labour law reform equally easily associating with other Non-conformists, or temperance reformers, or advocates of universal manhood suffrage to demand their particular objectives. One finds this constant involvement in political life present even before 1867, for example in the radical and worker deputations who waited upon government ministers to make their views known on issues of foreign policy or civil rights.[132] What then became important was the way in which a loose Whig-Liberal Party could become the political focus or umbrella for a range of such pressure groups.

In Britain a combination of policy and power helped this come about. On policy questions, what brought working-class and middle-class reformers together was less the acceptance of a specifically liberal set of values, than an enduring *radical* tradition. John Bright, by far the most popular figure within the political labour movement in the 1860s, embodied this radical tradition. In the mid-1860s he took up the cause of franchise reform, having been an opponent of Chartism. The radical image of the gentleman leader clearly plays a role in Bright's central position in the popular politics of the period, as it did with Ernest Jones and Ferdinand Lassalle. Bright's position on the radical wing of the Whig-Liberal Party served to link politically active working men to mainstream politics. His non-conformity (Bright was a Quaker), his support for educational reform, his advocacy of land and political reform in Ireland, and his later support for changes in the labour laws were all aspects of an enduring radical tradition which secured Bright's position amongst working-class radicals. His employment of the mass platform, of demagogic eloquence, and his assiduous use of his own personal image (for example, playing upon his earlier nervous breakdown as the product of political persecution) all contributed to his unique standing amongst working-class circles.

What is equally important is that the issues on which Bright campaigned on his return to public life in the 1860s were precisely those on which liberals and conservatives divided. Not only that, but they were closely inter-related issues. The Irish question raised matters of church and land reform. Educational matters touched upon the role of religion in schools. The Conservative Party, defender of the Church of England, found itself opposed to major reform in all these areas.

Nevertheless, there were many Whigs who were unhappy about land reform, extending the vote, disestablishing the Church. They were prepared to support some reforms, above all in church matters and issues of equality before the law – the subjects which traditionally had distinguished Whig political values. The final ingredient in fusing these disparate elements together into a fragile coalition was Gladstone. Already his policies as Chancellor of the Exchequer had endeared him to radicals.[133] His conversion to the need for franchise reform in 1865 secured him a more popular backing. Even when he backtracked during the passage of the Second Reform Act, his position was now too strong to be undermined amongst radical and labour circles, though how far this was a pragmatic choice on their part is difficult to judge. Gladstone's policy of church and land reform in Ireland, as well as church disestablishment in Wales, had at least a unifying effect in 1868–69.[134]

One could perhaps sum this up by pointing to liberalism in the sense of commitment to civic and religious equality as a fragile thread which tied Whigs and radicals together. There were very few 'liberals' in the sense in which someone like Cobden and the ACLL had defined this position. Rather there were radicals, many concentrating their energies into single-issue pressure group politics; there was the mass of much more moderate people who filled the Liberal backbenches, and there were the great Whig families who still dominated the front bench.[135] Issues which touched directly upon labour interests – the vote, labour laws – were not so much carried through by one party against the other, but rather were a product of bi-partisan action as was opposition to such reform. But on other policy issues in which a common radical tradition brought together politically active people from a variety of social backgrounds there was the basis for cooperation on party lines.

When we consider politics in terms of preoccupations with policy rather than in terms of class or interests or values, then one can immediately see the great difference between Germany and Britain. By 1862 in Germany the dominant issue was the national question. In the case of Prussia this was also closely related to the matter of constitutional reform and increasing the power of parliament. At first sight this would appear to offer a firm basis for cooperation between the labour movement and middle-class liberalism. The commitment to national unity on a constitutional basis was one they shared and which placed them against state bureaucracies and those privileged groups whose interests were bound up with the continued existence of the various states. Liberal nationalists assumed that they would lead a broad coalition, including the labour movement, in pursuit of a satisfactory solution to this national question. They argued that specific interests should not be allowed to break up this coalition. For a number of years this argument was accepted. A few liberal figures did acquire a genuine following within the labour movement, above all Schulze-Delitzsch. However, the political fragmentation of the Germany and the much more limited importance of popular politics meant that no figure comparable to Bright or Gladstone emerged. What is more, there was no radical tradition which could act as a unifying idea across a range of policy questions. Revolution in 1848 had discredited much of the radical ideology in the eyes of many middle-class liberals. Religious issues tended to divide people on social and regional lines rather than cutting across such divisions as they did in Britain.[136]

Nevertheless, the inter-related issues of national and constitutional reform appeared to provide a broad agenda on which middle-class liberals and working-class radicals had much in common. However, the national question posed a different *kind* of problem from all those so far discussed. The policy questions that shaped political allegiances in Britain involved either adjustments to the existing political structure or could be obtained within that structure. A reform of the labour laws could be pursued by pressure for a bill to be introduced into Parliament, cooperation with sympathetic MPs to obtain suitable amendments, and organising in such a way as to influence public opinion and the government of the day accordingly. The conduct of political affairs remained stably defined over time. Political contacts equally remained stably defined. Political compromises can be made within such a framework because there is a confidence that a concession made today will be paid back tomorrow in order to maintain effective political coalitions. However, the national question in Germany raised the prospect of a transformation of the basic political structure itself. A new state was to be made. That very transformation would call into question every existing political alignment. If the national question could have been 'solved' in a gradualist and peaceful manner perhaps it would not have had this unsettling effect. However, that is not what happened.

Instead the national question was solved by means of war and annexation, the forcible destruction of shared (or alternatively non-existent) sovereignity within the German lands. This came in two phases: 1866–67 and 1870–71. In terms of its impact on the German political structure 1866–67 was the more radical upheaval. Austria was expelled from having any interest in northern Germany; the Confederation was destroyed; most other north German states were annexed to Prussia. It was in the years that followed that the institutional basis for a German state was created. By contrast, in certain respects 1870–71 was a conservative moment internally. War was against a foreign enemy; annexation was justified in terms of nationality and security; the identity of the German states south of the River Main was respected in a constitution which took the form of a treaty. It is not surprising, therefore, that the major political realignments came in 1866–67 and the years immediately following and that these laid down the pattern of political allegiance which remained remarkably stable up to at least 1914 and arguably to about 1928.[137]

Until 1866 the bulk of the labour movement had remained within the liberal camp, accepting the point about a community of interest on national and constitutional issues and the danger of fragmentation. The ADAV was a sectarian and divided organisation, concentrated into particular areas and types of support which seemed to offer little prospect of much further expansion. So long as issues remained as they had been defined up to 1866 the ADAV would have little attraction for politically active working men. It broke with too many labour movement traditions; its radicalism had more in common with the sectarian left of 1848 than any broader tradition.[138] ADAV success was based upon tapping certain social constituencies for the first time (above all in home industries), in gaining support from radical intellectuals, often in areas where the labour movement was very weak so that there was no challenge from the established leadership of such a movement, and sometimes to the outbreak of factional conflict within existing labour organisations.[139]

However, the events of 1866–67 shattered existing political alignments, although sometimes it took a year or so before the consequences became clear. Above all, liberalism divided on the issue of whether to accept what Bismarck had created as the basis for future political action or to reject that because of the manner of its creation and the many illiberal features of the new state. That division itself took on a different character in different regions. In pre-1867 Prussia it was above all a question of forgiving Bismarck for his conduct in the constitutional crisis. In the annexed north German states it was a question of having access to a larger and more progressive state. In the south German states it was a question of how to respond to the prospect of further steps towards unity. As liberalism divided so it posed questions about the future political allegiance of subordinate interests within the liberal movement such as those of labour. At the same time the introduction of universal manhood suffrage made the class agitation of the ADAV an appropriate political style.

In these circumstances the ADAV flourished. The liberal wing of the labour movement, the VDAV, also had to respond to this new situation. An alliance with a fragmented liberal movement had less attraction than before. Democratic liberalism in south Germany tended to be bound up with the individual states. It had been generally the pro-Prussian liberals who had managed to construct something on wider lines. It had also been the pro-Prussian elements within the labour movement that had organised more extensively, but it was impossible for them to continue to cooperate with those liberals who rallied to Bismarck. Even within individual states the democratic movement frequently failed to mobilise much of the new mass electorate which turned instead to Catholic, ethnic or particularist politics.

The labour movement was, under these circumstances, almost compelled to take a more independent political stance. To do that it required an independent political image which had some chance of mobilising support from elements of the new electorate. Relations with the ADAV made it impossible for anti-Prussian, usually south German, labour groups to adopt the Lassallean programme. However, some combination of democratic principle and class appeal was the obvious direction. The affiliation of the majority within the VDAV to the IWMA provided a programme which contained these elements. It was also by this route that Marxism, or rather the personal influence of Marx, came to have institutional access to the German labour movement.[140] The radicalisation of the IWMA programme, above all the commitment to land nationalisation, completed the gulf between democratic populism and the VDAV and led directly to the formation of an independent political party in 1869. The members of the new SDAP had concluded, as had Lassalle prematurely in 1862, that an appeal to class offered a new basis for constructing a national movement and finding a mass base within the electorate. This was an *effect* rather than a *cause* of the breakdown of a broad liberal movement. It was a matter of political realignment in the context of the re-making of states. It could be described as a separation between 'bourgeois' and 'proletarian' democracy, provided this is understood in terms of political values and styles, not as the political expression of clear social divisions and conflicts.[141]

The liberal movement in Germany fragmented immediately in the face of the political transformation of 1866–67. But it also faltered in the longer term in its response to the new mass electorate.[142] Usually this is attributed to the disinclination of liberals to learn the methods of mass politics, preferring to use informal and oligarchic forms of influence nationally and to rely upon continued restrictions on popular politics at state and communal level. It is also linked to the idea of a shift in liberalism from a populist to a more bourgeois character.[143] Clearly there is something in these arguments but I think they can be exaggerated. First, just as 'proletarian' politics can be seen as an effect of political transformation rather than a direct expression of emergent class realities, so can 'bourgeois' politics. Second, one should not neglect the sheer organisational problems posed by the political transformations which accompanied unification.

Even the much more limited opening out to a large electorate brought about by the 1867 Reform Act in Britain posed organisational problems for the two major parties. It helped stimulate the creation of party machines with more professional and central leadership, although a good deal of initiative still remained at the local level.[144] A larger electorate had to be mobilised in a more professional and impersonal way. It was possible to adapt existing party organisation to take account of this because electoral boundaries remained the same and the pre-1867 electorate formed a very large part of the new electorate. Electioneering became more difficult and expensive than before (especially due to the need to locate and register voters). This made it difficult for new parties to enter the fray, and in any case the more limited extension of the electorate compared to that of Germany meant that the rewards for such independent activity did not appear very great.

Furthermore, the labour movement, especially the Reform League, had worked closely with prominent figures in the Liberal Party to obtain franchise reform. In the election of 1868 the issue was not one of registering a political presence but of helping to win a majority which would form the next government. It made sense to bargain with others in the Liberal Party to maximise influence within that potential government. This is what the Reform League did in 1868 although it was criticised by both contemporaries and some historians for not striking hard enough bargain.[145] One particular example of this bargaining which I deal with in more detail elsewhere concerned the adoption of the former Chartist Ernest Jones as a Liberal candidate for Manchester.[146] Here it was clear that the alliance was a pragmatic one although there were common views on a variety of non-class issues. Precisely because Jones was thought to have a standing amongst the new voters and because Jones thought he needed support from many of the old voters, a firm basis was provided for agreement. Both policy and power considerations pointed to the construction of Lib–Lab agreements.

None of these points apply to Germany. The Progessive Party in Prussia, for example, was a party of notables even though its electoral support in the period 1858–66 was socially quite varied.[147] Discipline within the party was minimal. The three-class system of voting both reduced the need to gain popular support and eliminated the need to register voters. The low polls associated with this loaded franchise further reduced the need to influence voters en masse. Restrictions on the franchise for elections to many other state parliaments as well as to communal institutions such as town councils had the same effect elsewhere. The extension of the Prussian franchise into the newly annexed territories meant that pro-Prussian liberals in those areas were not compelled to move in a more democratic direction. Finally, there simply was no rival for the votes of urban working men, the only alternative being conservatives opposed to most labour values and demands.

Furthermore, the introduction of universal manhood suffrage was much more radical than Disraeli's measure. It was simply beyond the capacity of existing parties to respond effectively. There were no special problems about voter registration which might confer an advantage upon existing parties. Influence on the new electorate could best be achieved in ways which broke with existing party practice. Instead of an appeal to members of a movement, the appeal had to be made more impersonally to a large category of people identified by religion, ethnicity, region, or class. It was an adjustment which the labour movement itself had to make and which was resisted by some activists.[148] Liberalism was ideologically disabled in the face of such a challenge because its whole style had been opposed to appealing to 'interests'. Liberals drew back from competing in this way but rather relied upon their existing influence and prestige at national level and their continued ability to dominate undemocratic political arrangements at local and state level.[149]

Finally, even if liberals could dominate state or national parliaments, this did not mean control of government, unlike in Britain. The reward for occupying a subordinate position within a broad liberal party did not, therefore, offer immediate access to power and influence. Neither did it have any organisational advantages; indeed, by inhibiting the type of appeal that such a broad notion as that of class justice might have to large categories of the new electorate it could actually prove a liability in this respect. The compromises and restrictions imposed by maintaining a link with liberals simply did not bring with it a prospect of sufficient reward to make the price worth paying. As a vehicle for the creation of mass support and/or the shaping of government policy, therefore, German liberalism became rapidly less attractive after 1867. This applied not only to the labour movement but other 'interests' within the broad liberal spectrum. For example, a separate movement to press artisan interests developed. This process also created a momentum of its own: as liberal support waned, so there was less to be gained by hitching one's wagon to that particular star.

Given this, it was the *differences* between liberals and organised labour which came to be more salient than before. The hostility of most middle-class supporters of liberalism to trade unionism and industrial action, especially strikes, in the absence of any countervailing tendency to cooperation, provided a good reason for anti-liberal sentiments to take hold amongst workers who did unionise and go on strike. Ironically, the legalisation of unions in 1869, as well as other liberal legislation which had removed restraints on geographical movement and on occupational choice, promoted unionisation and strikes and thereby led to greater dissatisfaction with liberals when they failed to support these actions. This dissatisfaction could then be turned to good account by the anti-liberal minority within the labour movement. The Lassalleans, although preaching the futility of unions and strikes as a means of raising the standard of living of workers, were prepared to provide support for strikes in their meetings and publications, precisely because they regarded strikes as instances of class conflict rather than market disputes. On the other hand, even those liberals who supported strike action did so on the grounds that it was a last resort and that the point of such action was to help workers to arrive at a reasonable, negotiated agreement with their employers.[150] Furthermore, because unions had fewer members and less influence and strikes were less successful than in Britain, the tendency to blame liberals for lack of support was greater.[151] Conversely, this lack of strength meant that liberals had less incentive to make concessions to organised labour than they did in Britain. Again, it was less a matter of fundamental values which explains cooperation or conflict, but rather one of relative strength.

Nevertheless, the question of what ideological alternatives to liberalism were available does need to be considered. Was it the case that fewer such alternatives were available in Britain? In looking at this we should not think of ideologies as intellectual packages which people deliberately choose in order to justify a course of action already determined upon. Ideology is not a simple rationalisation or reflection of a pre-existing interest.[152] To have an 'interest' implies preferences which are themselves culturally shaped, as are the perceptions of how such an interest is to be pursued. However, the level at which that takes place can only be explored through the study of language, of upbringing, of work experience and much else which goes far beyond the scope of this essay. If we confine the notion of ideology to more formal political languages and the values those languages convey, the question becomes rather one of the variety of such languages available and the conditions which influence the receptiveness of people to them. I have already tried to show both in this and other essays in this book that in principle there were many points on which the values of liberalism could find a resonance within the ranks of organised labour. However, this is only the first step in an argument about the reception of political ideologies. Next one has to show that people tend to be most receptive to those ideologies which best describe their situation and which support policies designed to protect or promote their interests. This cannot be seen just in passive terms. An ideology can, by seeming to provide a key to understanding one's situation, have a revelatory effect and this will in turn suggest new ways of acting. In this sense the language and ideas employed by political movements can prove very creative. I have outlined ways in which this creativity can be understood in other essays in this book.[153] Here I want to move on to the next step in the argument, which is the 'availability' of ideologies.

It is simply not the case that middle-class liberal values crowded out other alternatives in Britain at this time. Within the labour movement there continued to be a strong radical tradition which only shared some common positions with middle-class liberals. The memory of Chartism was preserved. A man such as Ernest Jones derived tremendous prestige from his involvement in the Chartist movement and continued to preach the need for independent working-class action in pursuit of universal manhood suffrage and the other points in the Charter. In London, but also elsewhere, radical associations kept this tradition alive and continually organised conferences in an attempt to revive a broader movement for radical political reform. This radical tradition has not received the attention it deserves, but without it, it is difficult to make sense of much of the labour response to foreign policy matters such as the American Civil War, the Polish insurrection of 1863, and Garibaldi's visit in 1864 or to understand fully the emergence of the Reform League in the mid-1860s.[154] Elements of this radical creed were expressed in mass circulation publications such as Reynold's Weekly, as well as in more specialised periodicals and newspapers.[155] Fragments of the creed, rendered partial and somewhat irrational because of the lack of any powerful political movement which could integrate various radical values, can also be seen in such apparently bizarre affairs as the Tichborn Case.[156] The problem was not so much that radical ideas were not readily available, but that they were available in too many separate and often mutually isolated varieties.

There were also other ideas on offer. John Stuart Mill and his followers offered a 'left-wing' version of liberalism, hinting at the merits of state intervention to deal with social problems at a time when radicals tended to espouse causes such as land reform, church disestablishment, and retrenchment, which all implied a very restricted role for the state once the reforms had been carried through. Even on franchise reform Mill himself added the question of votes for women. Another possible set of ideas which went beyond the liberalism of the day were those of positivists like Frederic Harrison, a follower of August Comte and a man who had the ear of leading trade unionists.[157] Finally, Marx was in close contact with leading trade unionists and working-class radicals, above all after the establishment in 1864 of the IWMA.[158]

It was not, therefore, a question of organised labour not having access to other political values than those of liberalism which might explain liberal success. Rather it was that so far as radicalism is concerned none of these ideas could be made to appear *relevant* to labour except in partial ways. In some ways this was because certain liberal values actually helped prevent workers from 'seeing' their situation in a way which would make them open to other values. It is interesting that the strands of radicalism which continued to attract, shared with middle-class liberalism an antipathy to state intervention. State intervention was 'continental'; it was what a Bonapartist ruler might do. Where radicalism parted company with liberalism was in its assertion that there was still much to do before real liberty existed. Some churches remained privileged; some groups such as employers and landowners continued to enjoy legal advantages over workers and people whose property was not in land. Above all, only some had the vote. In this sense radicalism blurred into 'advanced liberalism' rather than pushing workers to positivist or Marxist ideas which envisaged a free society and a weak state as simply one historical stage. What mattered in this period was that liberal politics, both because of shared values and because of the need to incorporate labour into a political coalition, prevented any coherent radical alternative from being offered to workers. As long as politicians such as John Bright could operate within that coalition, and as long as Gladstone's political language, with its moralism and its (final and painfully arrived at) commitment to religious liberty could mobilise political enthusiasm, then the labour movement saw no need to associate itself with any principled challenge to liberalism.

In the German case the values and concerns of politically active working men were no less compatible with aspects of liberalism – above all in the construction of a constitutional political order and the reform of institutions which entrenched privilege. At the same time there were also present elements of a radical tradition which was impatient of the timidity of liberals and suspicious of their commitment to democracy. As in Britain the differences were primarily about the speed and extent of political reform, rather than about different visions of the social and economic order. There were also available ideas which did take up social and economic themes. There was a stronger tradition of the state as the instrument of social and economic reform. Partly this can be explained in terms of the greater strength of the bureaucratic and interventionist state as well as of powers of regulation held by corporations.[159] Above all, I would argue, it can be explained in terms of the lack of opportunities on the part of organised workers to act as a pressure group to secure piecemeal legislative redress of grievances. Instead, therefore, of regarding the state as a political institution which could be pressured into altering the context of the generally liberal social and economic order within which labour operated, German workers were encouraged to see the state as the principal regulator of that order. Naturally, when that state failed to act as they wished, ideologies which envisaged how a *future* state could act in that way became attractive.

However, one should not exaggerate this point. For so long as most organised workers obtained benefits from working within a loose liberal coalition (as they did up until 1866) there was little incentive to take up ideas which centrally challenged liberal values. It was the organisational break with liberalism which tended to stimulate the move towards an ideological challenge rather than the other way around. Lassalle's arbitrary and opportunist programme of 1863 offered one such challenge.[160] The programme of the IWMA offered another.[161] It is interesting that in both cases it was a matter of an element within the labour movement deciding it needed a different 'programme', rather than a more gradualist shift of emphasis. Again, this suggests that it is rapid changes at the political level which explain formal ideological shifts. In the case of the SDAP programme of 1869, one can interpret its provisions in terms of connecting the pre-existing concerns of VDAV activists with political democracy and social reform to the commitments of dissidents from the ADAV. It was necessary to construct a party with a distinct image and organisation which could mobilise voter support. The idea of a 'progamme' is much more important to a party seeking votes from a mass electorate than it is to a pressure group within a broader political coalition. In turn, in the merger between the SDAP and the ADAV in 1875, it was the organisational motive which is the primary one. Indeed, the relatively casual treatment of the drafting of a programme to provide an ideological justification for the new organisation explains in part the eclecticism which Marx attacked.[162]

This stress on political situation and organisation rather than on ideology can be further supported by comparing individuals active within the labour movement. August Bebel and George Howell occupied comparable political positions in the early 1860s.[163] Bebel acted at the local level in Leipzig as a go-between for liberal and labour groups. He was a skilled worker with a strong desire for respectability. He opposed the independent, class-based and agitational politics of Lassalle. His political role and commitment widened with the formation of the VDAV which provided him with a national stage, working as a subordinate part of the liberal movement. His concern with liberal reform and with national unification on democratic lines were too important to permit him to allow concerns with specific labour interests to lead him out of that movement.

George Howell also was a skilled worker in the London building trade who moved from local and occupational activity to national prominence with the setting up of the Reform League. He also acted as a go-between at times of strikes, seeing it as his job to maintain the unity of a broad liberal movement whilst trying to ensure that the sectional interests of labour were recognised within that movement. At the same time, just as Bebel did, Howell genuinely shared radical views which put him on to the left of that liberal movement.[164]

The liberal failure on the national question forced Bebel into new forms of political action. By 1867, as a man whose political base lay in Saxony and a fairly democratic liberal tradition, he recognised the need to break with pro-Prussian liberalism. He tried to continue with non-class democratic politics both in Saxony and more generally in southern and central Germany. But at the same time the VDAV needed to be strengthened and to do this it needed a clearer and more positive image. This was achieved by means of affiliation to the IWMA. By this route Bebel came into contact with Marx's writings, some of which he first read properly in prison. Imprisonment itself predisposed him to a more complete rejection of the status quo and of those liberals who supported it. The failure of a broad democratic movement in the years following 1867 as well as the challenge posed by the ADAV led on to the new party of 1869 and the need for new principles to underpin it. Later the experiences of the Second Empire, especially those of persecution under the anti-socialist laws of 1878–90, would confirm in Bebel's mind the ideas of Marx about the class nature of society and state. It also provided him with some kind of guarantee of a path out of the present situation of isolation and impotence.

Howell, on the other hand, was never forced into this kind of political and ideological re-evaluation. The Reform League and the Parliamentary Committee of the TUC largely succeeded in their objectives of franchise and trade union reform, even if this was not always and only through the work of Liberal administrations. The ties with other liberals on a series of non-class issues were not therefore seriously threatened. Howell consequently became hardened in his popular liberal attitudes, later denouncing socialists and others who preached a separate politics against the mainstream of liberalism. It was not so much the strength of liberal values in Howell's attitudes and their weakness in Bebel's which explains this great divergence, but rather the appropiateness of those values to their activities as labour politicians.

Conclusion

From this review and comparison of the historiography of labour politics in Britain and Germany between 1850 and 1875 various points emerge. First, the simple assumption that German liberalism was weaker than British liberalism in terms of its sympathy towards specific labour interests or its capacity to impose directly or indirectly liberal values upon the labour movement appears very dubious. Second, the simple assumption that the German working class was less sectionalised and therefore more likely to move towards independent class politics also appears debatable.[165]

Labour politics in this period, in both countries, was a minority affair involving certain types of skilled workers. Those active in the labour movement shared certain objectives and attitudes with some middle-class liberals but also came into conflict with them, especially over matters touching their particular group interests. The principal task is to establish which factors would push this mixture of conflict and agreement towards pro-liberal or independent labour politics.

At an economic level one particular contrast seems to be important. Skilled workers in Britain at this time were a more prosperous, numerous and powerfully organised group than their German counterparts. That is not to say that skilled workers in Germany were any more closely tied to the less qualified labour streaming in from rural areas (be this from agriculture or rural industry) and it is not to be taken to mean that in Britain these workers formed a cohesive group in the manner suggested by the labour aristocracy concept. The greater power in the hands of these British workers was based primarily upon the nature of economic development: the demand for certain types of skilled labour and the lack of large injections of capital to substitute for that labour.[166] It was this economic power which led to accommodation in some measure between working men and employers rather than any independently-formed social, cultural or political relationships. It was this power which also led both major political parties to accommodate organised labour demands. In other words, it was not the *attitudes* of working men and employers towards industrial relations which mattered so much as the actual balance of power in the labour market.[167] Accommodation based on this power relationship was clearly not so obtainable in Germany. One must not push the argument too far. Key occupational groups such as skilled building workers did seem to share many common characteristics, and engineers could occupy an elite position in Germany. But overall, just looking at unionisation and strike patterns and success rates makes clear the different degrees of labour power.

That meant in turn that these economically more powerful workers played a more prominent role in the political labour movement in Britain. The Reform League began to acquire a real mass base when the London Trades Council and its trade societies decided to move away from their 'no politics' rules. By contrast, although Engelhardt has demonstrated that early German trade unionism was not the creation of political groups, it is equally clear that the political groups took a more distanced and instrumental attitude towards unionising workers than was the case in Britain.[168] Linked to this, employers who recognised the need for stable industrial relations with organised workers had more political influence in Britain than in Germany. Morley and Mundella, for example, patronised the Reform League and advocated trade union reform. German liberalism was less directly connected to and informed about labour movement attitudes, and this could lead to needless anxiety and over-reaction to strikes and other collective labour actions.

However, the accommodation in the British case came from the political elites of *both* parties, and the lack of understanding about labour demands was stronger amongst conservative than amongst liberal political groups in Germany. To understand the particular way relationships between labour and liberalism developed, we must turn to the sphere of politics.

The first point to make is that the major political concern in Germany in this period – the national issue – raised questions about the very nature of the state whereas the major issues in British politics were less fundamental. In the manner in which the national question was posed up to 1866 it made a good deal of sense for the limited German labour movement, operating in a very illiberal political world and largely favouring unity along liberal lines, to remain a subordinate element within a broad, national and liberal movement. However, the breakdown of that liberal movement in 1866–67 in the face of a revolution from above, a breakdown both in terms of principles and organisational effectiveness, meant that the rapidly growing labour movement of the late 1860s was suddenly compelled to construct a new political identity for itself. To enable itself to achieve this it turned to various illiberal ideas. These had been 'available' before (just as many of them were 'available' though ignored in Britain) but had not been influential because politically inappropriate. These ideas could be linked to a style of agitational politics designed to exploit the new provision of universal manhood suffrage. When Lassalle first unveiled his programme and insisted on appealing to a whole class rather than to the members of labour institutions, the established labour leadership condemned this as demagogy. For them 'democratic' politics was the properly debated and collectively determined politics of associations. The appeal to 'class' was seen as anti-democratic because class was a rhetorical construct rather than a real group which could express its will at meetings. But the new electoral style, coupled with the breakdown of relations with a broader political movement to which labour associations could bring their particular concerns, meant that labour needed its own independent programme and a way of presenting that programme to a mass electorate which was not involved in present labour associations. The idea of class became irresistible.[169]

This rhetoric, coupled with a strike wave and a sense of political crisis (especially with the Paris Commune) could lead to middle class panic and also encourage a repressive response from the state. Given the relative weakness of the labour movement compared to that in Britain, such repression could quite quickly undermine established labour organisation, especially with the depression which set in from 1873–74. This served to 'confirm' the new class language being developed by the leaders of the emergent labour parties. Liberalism did now seem to be a middle-class affair and liberals had surrendered the more genuinely universalist components of that creed to form an alliance with an authoritarian state. All these components of a working-class party opposed to both the militarist, authoritarian state and to the liberal middle class were therefore being assembled by 1875, before there was either a numerous industrial working class or mass support for that party. The growth of such a working class under the conditions of depression and political repression between 1873 and 1890 then hardened and strengthened the political option taken between 1867 and 1875.

In Britain, by contrast, there was no revolution from above. Association with liberalism on the basis of issues which transcended social and interest group differences, as well as more vigorous and independent action designed to secure recognition of sectional interests on trade union matters, sufficed to enable the labour movement to achieve practical objectives. Never being compelled to act alone and to construct a new political identity as a consequence, the labour movement in Britain never felt constrained to repudiate openly the values of liberalism. Rather, it quietly pursued its own independent values within a broad liberal umbrella – tending to present its differences with liberals in empirical, specific ways rather than generalising these into an alternative set of values. A different balance of power, a different set of opportunities for political action provide the key to the 'choice' of political ideologies.

These are provisional conclusions. There are many areas which still need to be researched to provide stronger support for the arguments of this essay. For Germany it would be useful to analyse more closely the social and economic characteristics of those occupations whose members were particularly closely involved in the labour movement and it would be helpful to consider the relationship of such occupations to other elements of the working class as well as with social groups above them. This would enable one to test, to some extent, whether the shift in the politics of class really was based upon the emergence of new class formations.[170] In the British case it is necessary to turn to the close analysis of political language and ideas, to try to identify the continuing influence of radical and Chartist traditions within the 'liberal' labour movement and to ask how far these traditions limited and shaped political choices.[171] It would also help to analyse more closely the ways in which the costs and benefits of cooperation with liberals were weighed by politically active workers. An analysis of the divisions within the Reform League, and the radical and labour movement more generally, about how to act in the 1868 General Election and whether to maintain independent organisation afterward, are examples of the kind of work that is needed.[172]

In both cases the most important work will need to be undertaken at a local level, though not in isolation from the broader political context. The researcher would need to begin by analysing closely the values and interests of politically active workers, and then establish what political choices were available for the realisation of those interests and values. It may be that the case for choosing a pro- or anti-liberal course of action was overwhelming. If so, further investigations of these groups of workers – primarily in occupational and community terms – will serve only to explain why they were politically active at all. However, in some instances there will appear to be a quite fine balance of advantages associated with the choices, usually accompanied by disputes amongst labour activists about which road to follow. At this point it will become necessary to explore particular hypotheses about social and economic distinctions within the ranks of politically active workers. For example, workers in more fragile situations (rural industry, declining craft trades) might be more alienated from the economic creed of liberals than those in stronger positions (skilled factory work, the building trades). If these fail to account for the political divisions which develop (e.g. when one finds members of the same occupational groups in a branch of the ADAV and in a labour association which remains attached to the liberal camp), it will become necessary to consider matters like factional conflict and varying political experiences such as those related to generational and regional differences. Finally, it may be necessary to resort to explanation in terms of particular individuals. There is no doubt, for example, that a movement like the ADAV could not originally have got off the ground without the presence of the extraordinary personality of Lassalle. However not only the organisation and programme which he founded must be related back to the values and interests of early ADAV supporters, but also the cult of personality which surrounded him.

A general procedure of this kind, constantly controlled by the use of comparisons, both between and within the two countries, could provide fuller answers to the question of why labour politics in Britain and Germany moved in opposing directions between 1850 and 1875. At the moment, my answer to this question would stress above all differing levels of power in the labour market of skilled workers and differing kinds of political issues and changes in political structures which affected labour groups as well as all other political groups. By contrast I place ideas about class structures and conflicts in the background. It remains to be seen whether the research agenda I have sketched out would strengthen or challenge this view.

Notes

1 For the 1860s see Coltham, 1964–65; for the 1870s, McCready, 1954; and for the later moves towards socialism focused on London, Thompson, 1967. Generally see Gillespie, 1927; Rothstein, 1983; and Breuilly, Niedhart & Taylor (eds), forthcoming.

2 For the case of Salford see Garrard, 1977.

3 McKenzie & Silver, 1969 pioneered the study of 'working-class Toryism'.

4 Schmierer, 1970; Schadt, 1971.

5 Lidtke, 1966.

6 For examples see Gibbon, 1975; Blackbourn, 1980.

7 For a comparative treatment of that later period see Schmidt, 1974.

8 Such comparisons are suggested in Schmidt, 1974; see also White, 1976.

9 See the essay on the labour aristocracy.

10 See the essay on liberalism and the essays in section II. of Langewiesche (ed), 1988, 'Liberalismus im britisch-deutschen Vergleich'.

11 For the relationship between the state and Chartism see Mather, 1959 and 1965; and Saville, 1987. For the repression of radicalism in the 1790s see Emsley, 1979; and in the period 1810–40 Prothero, 1979. For political repression in France see Merriman, 1978; in Germany Offermann, 1979, chapter 1.

12 See Hollis & Harrison, 1967 for one example. Joyce, 1991 and Biagini & Reid (eds), 1991 also treat the problem of continuity.

13 See Jones, 1984a for the idea of a reformist current emerging with Chartism already in the early to mid-1840s in the face of the reforms introduced by Peel's Tory government. However, these did not include specifically *political* reforms and cannot be invoked to explain the Chartist collapse after 1848.

14 One approach which insists that political controls and lack of power lie at the heart of the explanation is Moorhouse, 1973. This is a stimulating contribution to the debate, but has the problem of explaining how Chartism or the German labour movement took a more independent line whilst suffering under similar political constraints.

15 See the essay on the labour aristocracy.

16 See Musson, 1972.

17 For early and rather general approaches of this kind see Anderson, 1964 and 1965; and Nairn, 1964a, 1964b and 1964c. More focused on workers during this period is Tholfsen, 1976; and Gray, 1977.

18 On paternalism see Joyce, 1982. The idea of social control is developed in a variety of ways in the essays in Donajgrudzki (ed), 1977. It is criticised in Jones, 1984b.

19 Gillespie, (1927) was Canadian; Rothstein, (1983) was German; as was Gustav Mayer, whose research remained largely unpublished by the time of his death. See the introduction to Breuilly, Niedhart & Taylor (eds), forthcoming.

20 Indications of a renewed interest in political language are to be found in Jones, 1984a and Joyce, 1991.

21 See Corrigan & Sayer, 1985; McDonagh, 1977; Brundage, 1988. A book which controversially insists on the survival of an *ancien-régime* Britain up to 1829 is Clark, 1985. An interesting study in cultural history which draws attention to how much of a watershed this period appeared to be to contemporaries is Houghton, 1985.

22 On the trade union and poor law aspects see various essays in Ward (ed), 1970. A study which draws attention to protest against local government change is Garrard, 1976. On policing see Davies, 1985; and Storch, 1975.

23 See Rose, 1970.

24 See Kocka, 1986 for a sketch of working-class formation over this period. That sketch is now superseded by Kocka, 1990a and 1990b.

25 The major study of labour during this period of repression is Offermann, 1979 which seeks to connect what happened then to the later period of the liberal labour movement.

26 Before the study of Offerman, 1979 the overwhelming tendency was to treat the period before 1860 as a kind of 'pre-history' of the labour movement. Balser, 1962 did stress some continuities, though largely of individuals, but there was little apart from this.

27 The outstanding historian most recently to deal with this question is Na'aman, 1969, 1970, and Na'aman with Harstick, 1975. For an evaluation of his work see Ritter, 1983.

28 Na'aman, 1976, Introduction; Morgan, 1965; Dominick, 1982.

29 Emig & Zimmermann (1977) cite twenty dissertations on this subject alone. Most issues of the German periodical *Beiträge zur Geschichte der Arbeiterbewegung* contain references to work of this kind.

30 On democratic and reformist roots see Balser, 1962; on alienation from an illiberal state see Conze & Groh, 1977 and Lidtke, 1966.

31 A typical East German work is the collectively authored publication, *Der Kampf von Marx und Engels* (1977).

32 See Breuilly, 1987a for some further discussion of the historiography as well as the essays in Tenfelde (ed), 1986. A general evaluation of social history in West Germany is provided by Ritter (1989) and for East Germany by Handke (1989).

33 Just to offer one trivial but symbolic change, the East German labour history periodical *Beiträge zur Geschichte der deutschen Arbeiterbewegung* contains a bibliography in each monthly issue. Until the end of the DDR the section on German labour history was entitled 'The history of the SED', the ruling party in the DDR. As from the first issue of 1991 the section is simply entitled 'History of the German labour movement'.

34 A pioneering biographical approach was Conze, 1965, now superseded by Aldenhoff, 1984. Organisational and ideological shortcomings were analysed in Sheehan, 1978. See also Langewiesche (ed), 1988, and Langewiesche, 1988, section III.

35 Engelhardt, 1977; see also my extended review of this in *Social History* 4/3 (1979).

36 This seems to me to be the case with Offermann, 1979, as I considered extensively in a review of that book in *Social History*, 7/1 (1982) and Aldenhoff, 1984 as I also argued in a review of her book in *European History Quarterly*, 17 (1987).

37 Church, 1975.

38 Hunt, 1981, p. 73.

39 Phelps Brown & Browne, 1968, p. 161.

40 Wood, 1909, cited in Church, 1975, p. 72.

41 Hunt, 1981, especially pp. 74–75.

42 Hunt, 1981 p. 26.

43 Hunt, 1981 p. 74.

44 Hunt, 1981 p. 78.

45 Burgess, 1980, p. 16.

46 As argued in Webb & Webb, 1920, chapters 4 to 6. For a criticism of this argument see Musson, 1972, especially pp. 49–63.

47 Biagini, 1991 and Matthews, 1979.

48 For a sustained argument along these lines see Burgess, 1975 which considers the four industries of engineering, building, mining and cotton. See also the essay on artisans.

49 Vincent, 1972, p. 301.

50 Phelps Brown & Browne, 1968, pp. 159–61; Mitchell, 1978, pp. 71–2, 78–9, 389.

51 Fischer, *et al.*, 1982, pp. 155–7; Kuczynski, 1962, II, p. 152.

52 Gömmel, 1979, pp. 27ff., cited in Fischer *et al.*, 1982, pp. 155–6.

53 Fischer, *et al.*, 1982, p. 52.

54 Kuczynski, 1962, p. 130.

55 See Fischer, *et al.*, 1982, pp. 147–53 for details on money wages in a range of occupations.

56 Engelhardt, 1977; Machtan, 1978.

57 Kaeble, 1983.

58 Kuczynski, 1962, pp. 222–8.

59 See also Fischer, 1972, pp 258–84.

60 Fischer, *et al.*, 1982, pp. 139–42.

61 As indicated, for example, by statistics on food consumption, Fischer *et al.*, pp. 173–8.

62 See Beier, 1966 and 1981a.

63 Renzsch, 1980, chapter 5.

64 Engelhardt, 1977.

65 Na'aman, 1970 and Na'aman with Harstick, 1975; Aldenhoff, 1984.

66 For Hamburg, where the Lassallean movement have its greatest initial success, see Laufenberg, 1911. For Berlin see Renzsch, 1980. For the importance of rural industry in the support Bebel received in his Saxon constituency, see Benser, 1956. See also Boch, 1989; Zwahr, 1989; and Dowe, 1989.

67 See Reid, 1980 for Britain; and Cattaruzza, 1984 for Germany. However, these studies only consider certain regions and how far one can generalise from them is another matter. For a general argument which points to a similar contrast see Goodman & Honeyman, 1988, chapter 8.

68 Some of these points are developed a little more in the essay on the labour aristocracy.

69 For shipbuilding see Reid, 1980 and Cattaruzza, 1984. For engineering see Renzsch, 1980 and Burgess, 1975. For mining see rimlinger, 1967. For the clothing trades see the artisan essay, and specifically on tailoring, Eisenberg, 1986.

70 Compare Renzsch, 1980 with Burgess, 1975 and Price, 1980.

71 See Burgess, 1975, especially pp. 102–5, as well as the biographies of two men who started out as trade unionists in the building industry and ended up as prominent liberal figures: Humphrey, 1913 and Leventhal, 1971.

72 Laufenberg, 1911; Renzsch, 1980.

73 See the essay on the labour aristocracy. Works of particular importance in this respect are Beier, 1966 and 1981a; Crew, 1979; and Zwahr, 1978 whose particular contribution is further analysed in Breuilly, 1987a. Kocka, 1986 refers to work on the cultural and social aspects of different occupations or working-class areas, but there is little that supports any idea of an aristocracy of labour.

74 See the essay on this subject. Even Gray, 1981 in his short book reviewing the idea, an idea he himself used in his own research (Gray, 1976) seems a little defensive about it.

75 For the idea of the 'triumph of the entrepreneurial ideal', at least for the period in question, see Perkin, 1969. For his more recent work on the subsequent emergence of ideals associated with the professions rather than with industry, see Perkin, 1989.

76 For a general account of what this means see Gray, 1977.

77 Tholfsen, 1971, pp. 69–70. For a fuller development of his ideas see Tholfsen, 1976.

78 See below for the trade union question. Of course, 'liberalism' even amongst middle-class groups had different, often conflicting meanings, some of which I dealt with in the essays on liberalism in this book. Furthermore, some historians have argued that the 'triumph of the entrepreneurial ideal' was short-lived and half-hearted, even within the commercial middle classes. See Wiener, 1981 although there is much that is problematical about the argument of this book.

79 See Hanson, 1975; and then the criticisms of Hanson by Thane and Musson, as well as Hanson's responses (Hanson, 1976).

80 See, for example, Price, 1975.

81 Burgess, 1975 is inclined to argue this, taking up an idea of a 'functional' or 'organisational' labour aristocracy which I deal with in the essay on labour aristocracy.

82 For the artisan roots of liberal values see Prothero, 1979; Crossick, 1976 and 1978; and Palmer, 1978. On continuities of radical ideas see Joyce, 1991; Biagini & Reid (eds), 1991; Jones, 1984a.

83 An interesting account of how, for example, Gladstone's finance policy as Chancellor of the Exchequer was seen to be in a radical tradition is provided by Baigini, 1991. A similar analysis of Gladstone's policies on Ireland, land, church establishment, and the franchise could be provided, though obviously one would also have to draw attention to the aspects of these policies which did not satisfy radicals.

84 For one particular example see Hollis & Harrison, 1967; and Lowery, 1979. More generally see Vincent, 1981.

85 In his review of Prothero, 1979 in *New Society*.

86 As both Crossick, 1976 and Prothero, 1979 recognise.

87 Matthias, 1957.

88 On Marx as an active political figure see Nicolaevsky & Maenchen-Helfen, 1973.

89 Lattek, 1991.

90 Na'aman, 1970.

91 *Freischutz*, 14 December 1851.

92 On Britain see Tholfsen, 1976; Offermann, 1979; Aldenhoff, 1984.

93 I base these remarks on a catalogue of the library of the *Hamburg Bildungsverein für Arbeiter* of 1855 as well as police files. See Breuilly & Sachse, 1984, especially pp. 368–70.

94 Specifically for the Hamburg case see Breuilly, 1983. More generally see the essay on artisans.

95 Breuilly & Sachse, 1984, pp. 370ff.

96 See the essay on Hamburg and Manchester as well as Breuilly & Sachse, 1984.

97 This argument can also be connected to the literature concerning the relationship between the *Mittelstand* and early German liberalism which is considered in more detail in the essay comparing British and German liberalism.

98 Anderson, 1964 and 1965; Nairn, 1964a, 1964b, and 1964c.

99 For the reference to 'other countries' see the critique of Anderson and Nairn by Thompson (1965).

100 Joyce, 1982.

101 Hanham, 1959; Vincent, 1968.

102 Crew, 1979; Moore, 1978; Schönhoven, 1980 on 'under-unionisation'.

103 See Taylor, forthcoming.

104 Harrison, 1960, 1961, and 1965.

105 See Breuilly, Niedhart & Taylor (eds), forthcoming.

106 Moorhouse, 1973.

107 Fesser, 1976.

108 Conze, 1965; Conze & Groh, 1977.

109 Vincent, 1972; Breuilly, Niedhart & Taylor (eds), forthcoming.

110 Breuilly, Niedhart & Taylor (eds), 1991.

111 Gagel, 1958.

112 See Na'aman with Harstick, 1975, document 70 (p. 284).

113 Schmierer, 1970; Schadt, 1971; Langewiesche, 1974.

114 Gall, 1986 argues this case very persuasively.

115 See documents 10 and 11, chapter 11 in Breuilly, Niedhart & Taylor (eds), forthcoming.

116 More detail on these matters is provided in the essay on law.

117 Webb & Webb, 1920, pp. 270–2.

118 Spain, 1991.

119 *Ibid.*; Brown, 1982; McCready, 1954.

120 One place one could look would be in the work of liberal town councils which might have pursued policies that labour organisations could support. I have not had the opportunity to take this further because there were clearly differences between councils whose 'liberalism' consisted of spending as little as possible and others which were prepared to carry through programmes of social improvement which needs fuller consideration. I am indebted to Frank O'Gorman for making this suggestion to me.

121 Engelhardt, 1977; Aldenhoff, 1984.

122 Fesser, 1976, pp. 77–87.

123 For further details see the essay below on civil society and the labour movement.

124 Fricke, 1964, pp. 366–7 fn. 103; Engelhardt, 1977.

125 Engelhardt, 1977, for a detailed consideration of this strike.

126 See Machtan 1981a on middle-class hostility to strikes.

127 See Lassalle, 1970.

128 Hamerow, 1969 and 1972, especially 1972.

129 See Sheehan, 1990, chapter 14, which only takes the story up to 1866; and more generally Sheehan, 1978 and Langewiesche, 1988.

130 For examples supporting this from Hamburg see Breuilly & Sachse, 1984, chapter 9.

131 Opposition to the Master and Servants Laws was intensified because the liberal ethos of equality before the law was not observed: employers were treated differently from employees. For Germany see Engelhardt, 19786 for a treatment of trade union demands as demands for human rights.

132 See Breuilly, Niedhart & Taylor (Eds), forthcoming for examples; and arguments which develop this point in the introduction to chapters 8–10 and chapters 11–12 in that book.

133 Biagini, 1991; Matthew, 1979.

134 Parry, 1986.

135 For the political sociology of the Liberal Party, something still very imperfectly understood, see the very stimulating but rather speculative points made in Vincent, 1972.

136 See the essay on liberalism.

137 On the national question see Breuilly, 1990. On the establishment of political alignments or 'milieus' for the sixty years after 1867 see Ritter, 1985.

138 Na'aman with Harstick, 1975.

139 On social bases see Dowe, 1989 and Boch, 1989; on the role of radical intellectuals see Na'aman with Harstick, 1975; on factional divisions see Breuilly & Sachse, 1984, chapter 9.

140 The other route was through the ADAV, partly because Lassalle used some of Marx's ideas, partly because after his death influential figures within the ADAV such as Bracke drew even more upon Marx. Thus the 1869 and 1875 convergences served to increase the role of Marx's ideas, even if he was unhappy at the terms of the 1875 agreement.

141 This refers to the seminal article, first published in 1912, by Gustav Mayer, 'Die Trennung der proletarischen von der bürgerlichen Demokratie in Deutschland, 1863–1870' (Mayer, 1969). It is interesting that over twenty years later Mayer researched into labour radicalism in Britain in this period but never sought to provide any sociological reasons for the different political consequences. See Breuilly, Niedhart & Taylor (eds), forthcoming.

142 Hamerow, 1973 and more generally on Liberal failure in the face of a mass electorate see Sheehan, 1978 and Langewiesche, 1988.

143 Gall, 1975; Langewiesche, 1988 who offers some powerful criticisms of the usual arguments about the 'decline' of liberalism.

144 Hanham, 1959; Fraser, 1979; Moore, 1975.

145 Harrison, 1965; Breuilly, Niedhart & Taylor (eds), forthcoming.

146 See the essay below comparing Hamburg and Manchester.

147 For an analysis of Prussian liberalism as a parliamentary organisation and its electoral base see Hess, 1964. On organisation see Eisfeld, 1969. On the social characteristics of the leadership see Gugel, 1975.

148 Breuilly & Sachse, 1984 document the criticisms of demagogy directed at the new political style. Na'aman, 1963 does much to uncover the different notions of democracy that were involved.

149 Sheehan, 1978, especially pp. 141–58; Langewiesche, 1988. A case study in which this is a central point is White, 1976.

150 Engelhardt, 1977 provides a very full account of the way in which the ADAV and the SDAP sought to exploit the growth of trade unions. For examples of how liberals and Lassalleans responded to particular strikes, see Machtan, 1983 and Breuilly & Sachse, 1984, chapter 9.

151 To substantiate this point, however, one would need a more systematic comparison of strikes in both countries. At the moment only German labour historians have sought to anslyse strikes as a whole for this period, as in Machtan, ref, and Machtan 1978, 1983. See Kocka, 1986, pp. 322–4 for a brief summary of this work.

152 For a fuller statement of this position see Breuilly, 1982, pp. 334–5, 365–73.

153 Above all the essays on artisans and on law.

154 See Breuilly, Niedhart & Taylor (eds), for a fuller treatment of this, as well as Biagini & Reid (eds), 1991.

155 Breuilly, Niedhart & Taylor (eds), forthcoming. On *Reynold's Weekly* see Berridge, 1976 and 1978.

156 McWilliam, 1991.

157 Vogeler, 1984.

158 Collins & Abramsky, 1965.

159 The essay on law deals with the first of these matters; the comparison between Manchester and Hamburg explores the second.

160 Lassalle himself was well aware of the arbitrary character of this programme as is made clear in a letter he wrote to Rodbertus on 22 April 1863. See Lassalle, 1921–25, vol. 6, p. 325.

161 On the affiliation to the IWMA see Morgan, 1965.

162 See Dominick, 1982, on the adoptions of the programmes of 1869 and 1875. For Marx's response see, Marx, 1968.

163 For Bebel see Bebel, n.d. and Maehl, 1980. For Howell, see Howell, 1902 and Leventhal, 1971.

164 For example, he took up a radical position on certain foreign affair problems. He also was a great admirer of Ernest Jones and wrote a biographical study of him. He was hostile to the monarchy. See Breuilly, Niedhart & Taylor (eds), forthcoming as well as Leventhal, 1971.

165 More interesting is the idea developed by Eisenberg that social ties amongst skilled workers in Britain were stronger than amongst their counterparts in Germany, and this made for both more stable relations with employers and more powerful organisation. However, there are problems in that Eisenberg focused upon crafts such as tailoring rather than the 'new' skilled trades as in textiles and engineering (Eisenberg, 1986). Comparison along these lines could prove fruitful but will need much more basic research and will also need to pay attention to leisure (where Eisenberg has now turned her attention) and to the family for which see now Ehmer, 1991.

166 Burgess, 1975. The economic explanation of this in terms of such matters as the demand for certain skills, the nature of markets, and the divisions amongst employers are brought out variously in More, 1980; Lazonick, 1979; Zeitlin, 1979. The continued importance of skilled craftsmen is richly illustrated in Samuel, 1977.

167 A point which I also argued in my review of Engelhardt, 1977 *Social History*, 4/3 (1979) but which needs to be tested further.

168 Engelhardt, 1977; but criticised for going too far against the previous arguments about political domination by Eisenberg, 1986.

169 A detailed attempt to understand the development of the political language of class in this way, as well as in terms of generational conflict amongst labour leaders, is presented in Breuilly & Sachse, 1984, chapter 9.

170 For example, in Breuilly & Sachse, 1984, I was compelled to recognise that the arguments about class language being the product of new political circumstances and labour leaders remained provisional until one had properly researched the types of social and economic changes taking place in Hamburg. Only in this way could one test the (so far purely assertive) arguments that class language reflected the emergence of new classes and class conflicts.

171 There is a move in this direction. Most of the work focuses on the Chartist period (Jones, 1984; Prothero, 1974) but some considers the post-1850 period (Joyce, 1991; some of the studies in Biagini & Reid (eds), 1991) and there is some interesting research in train which uses comparisons within Britain as well to gauge more precisely the role of political language and traditions (Vernon, 1991; Taylor, forthcoming).

172 I mention the case of Ernest Jones and his adoption as a liberal candidate for Manchester in 1868 in the essay comparing liberalism in Manchester and Hamburg.

5

Civil society and the labour movement, class relations and the law: a comparison between Germany and England

Introduction

Law is too important a subject to be left to legal historians. The study of law can tell us much about how people thought about the ways in which their society was arranged; how their attitudes could influence relations between different groups; and how law could shape the way in which various groups behaved. The form and content of laws, as well as the institutions through which law was produced and put into effect, can also provide an important route into the study of the political culture of a society.

I will focus on laws concerned with certain political rights, above all the right to vote in elections, and certain economic rights, above all the right to strike and the right to organise in trade unions. I will compare and contrast the legal provisions on these matters in Germany (mainly Prussia) and Britain (mainly England). I will consider how existing law and the demands for legal reform influenced the relationship between politically organised middle-class and working-class groups, what this tells us about the attitudes of those groups and how they were organised, and what clues this offers us as to the different kinds of political culture which existed in the two countries.

These are large and difficult subjects and in a short essay all I can do is to offer some ideas on what comparison can tell us.

Law and society: some general points

There is an assumption that the development of an industrial capitalist society based on free market principles tends to be associated with certain kinds of legal arrangements. First, there are the relationships within the market. The sanctity of private property and of contracts made between property owners requires and is expressed through a system of civil law.[1] The definition of what belongs to the sphere of civil law takes priority over defining what belongs to the spheres of criminal and public law. The purpose of the state so far as civil law is concerned is to guarantee the proper enforcement of legal procedures and judgements, although the initiative for setting such procedures in motion lies with private individuals. All individuals are formally equal within the sphere of civil laws. People possess rights and acquire obligations by virtue of the property they own and the contracts into which they enter, and not by virtue of any quality appertaining to them as persons. As a consequence civil law exhibits a highly abstract and formally rational character and can be systematised into a set of high-level principles which can then be applied to a very wide range of actual cases.

It is of course possible to argue that such a legal system provides a misleading picture by masking the real inequalities and irrationalities in the distribution and types of property and the capacities of individuals to acquire property. Conservative critics might argue that certain types of property (such as land) should be treated in a special way because they are associated with certain kinds of social relations. Marxists and other radical critics might argue that formal equality between owners of capital or land and those who own only their labour power masks a real relationship of inequality and exploitation. But both criticisms frequently concede that capitalism tends to be associated with a certain type of formal legal structure relating to the definition of property and its accompanying rights and obligations. One might then use this formal legal structure as an ideal type, both for descriptive purposes but also as an outline of the state of affairs to which the legal structure of a competitive capitalist economy will 'naturally' tend. To the extent that this state of affairs is not realised, one might look for particular factors to account for this 'unnatural' situation. One might also argue that such a situation will give rise to certain kinds of problems and tensions.

The concept of 'private' property rights and contracts implies a contrast with some other set of relationships and activities which are defined as public. There is a different character to the legal definition of the public sphere. Rather than the relationship between the individual and property being central, now it is the relationship between the individual and participation in public affairs. Constitutional law needs to define those rights of participation and the way in which such participation is institutionally related to the state (above all through the franchise and the powers of parliament).[2]

One can argue that the same kinds of historical changes bring about these developments in private and public law: that it is not just a matter of the logical arguments of a particular school of jurisprudence. First, one might argue that the growth of an industrial capitalist economy involved the decline in the power of pre-capitalist elites, above all a landed aristocracy, that had been expressed through a legal structure which formalised civil inequality between different classes of men. An attack on that power also involved an attack on that system of formal inequality. The catalogues of the rights of men drawn up from the late eighteenth-century testify to this attack. Second, the fluidity of social movement in a free market economy makes it difficult, if not impossible, to maintain formal inequality amongst men. Changes in the occupational structure, as well as growth in population and production, make the corporate system of guilds difficult to sustain. Third, the large and changing composition of those groups with some property and claims to influence makes it necessary to establish some system of representation if these groups are to express any sort of political will. Fourth, in order to formulate such a political will it is necessary for the groups to have the capacity to articulate their views and to transmit these views in a politically organised way to state institutions. All this, it could be argued, favours the development of civil equality, a structure of participation in which 'public opinion' can be formed, the construction of representative institutions and the accompanying rise of electoral politics, and pressure for political reform. Again, it might be argued that this state of affairs develops naturally out of general changes towards a free market society, and that failure to move in this direction is unnatural and creates particular conflicts.

These arguments have a clear link to the *Sonderweg* debate. It is sometimes argued that it was the failure of Germany to proceed very far in this direction in the field of public, constitutional affairs while at the same time doing so in the field of market relationships and civil law, which accounts for certain problems in modern German history. Of course, if this is simply a value judgement this is not something which can give rise to any useful historical argument. It is quite clear that the Third Reich 'failed' to be a liberal democracy, but equally Roosevelt's America 'failed' to be a fascist state. The key issue is whether one can sustain the argument that competitive capitalism is closely bound up with formal equality between various kinds of property holders in the private sphere of civil law which largely regulates economic activities, and with civil and political equality in the public sphere in which an elected parliament, political parties and a developed system of public opinion play a central role, and whether any 'lag' in the development in one sphere in relation to the other sphere requires special explanation and creates special problems.

Relationships between middle-class and working-class groups

One argument that can be formulated following on from the previous section is that socio-economic groups that are the product of industrial capitalist development will favour the construction of legal arrangements conducive to that economic development. Movements for rights of assembly, expression and publication, the establishment of representative institutions with powers defined in a constitution, and the removal of social and economic privileges – one would expect these to be dominated by the various middle and working-class groups most closely associated with modernity.

However, one would also expect differences, even conflicts, between the demands of these various groups. These differences, above all, relate to different positions in the systems of property and politics. Owners of land and capital, while subscribing to equality before the law, would often be suspicious about the idea of giving equal rights of political participation to those who owned only their labour. In the private sphere there were problems about how far working people could act collectively to negotiate the terms on which they sold their labour, and what actions would be permissible in the course of such negotiations. Clearly the different kinds of property, the extent to which various classes of property holders might act collectively rather than individually, and the extent to which such actions might be regarded as coercive over others complicated the abstract notions of individuality and equality that underpinned the classical liberal view of law.

This difference between those with property in land, capital, or office (the professional middle class) and those who owned only their labour was the most important one between modern groups. Clearly there could be differences between landowners and capitalists, between capitalists and state officials, between skilled workers and unskilled workers, as well as between members of different occupations or economic sectors. Also there were differences other than socio-economic ones, such as those based on religion or nationality. But here I wish to focus on this broad middle-class and working-class relationship. In looking at this one can see that the extent to which workers pressed for the rights to vote, to form trade unions, and to withdraw their labour, and the extent to which the middle classes supported that pressure, would have a crucial influence on that relationship. In turn, the degree of cooperation or conflict could also help explain the legal changes which actually came about.

Organisation and attitudes

A legal structure does not only express the power and interests of various social groups and the social structure within which those groups are located. It can also shape the way in which groups organise, as well as their attitudes. The inability to pursue an interest by legal means on the part of a group can have far-reaching consequences if and when that group turns to illegal forms of action. It can also affect how members of that group perceive law and the state that both produces and is defined by that law. Equally, law can encourage certain forms of action which will deeply influence the group in question and its attitude towards the law. Part of the effectiveness of law is based upon it being perceived as legitimate by the various, often unequally placed parties to which it is applied. In turn, to preserve that legitimacy, law must be seen as being actually, or at least potentially, above any of the parties involved. It is considerations of this kind which can lead even those who regard the state as functional for socio-economic purposes to concede that it must possess at least some 'autonomy' from society and economy.

These introductory points condition the form of the rest of this essay. I will examine certain economic and political rights which could lead to conflict or cooperation between workers and the middle classes. These are the rights to vote, to form trade unions, and to strike. After a brief background section which sketches out how far these rights were realised in Britain (mainly England) and Germany (mainly Prussia) I will deal with the following questions:

(i) What were middle-class attitudes towards these rights and to possible changes which could be made to them?

(ii) What effect did the legal state of affairs have upon the organisation and attitudes of workers, and how did it influence the relationship between the labour movement and the middle classes?

(iii) According to how we answer these questions, what light do those answers throw upon the *Sonderweg* debate?

I will look briefly at the situation in England from about 1832 to 1848 and in Germany a little before and after the revolutions of 1848. This will be mainly to establish the background to the main focus of the essay upon the period from the mid-century to about 1875. In this period, especially in the last fifteen years, significant progress was made in both countries in the realisation of these legal rights. But progress took rather different forms and was associated with different relationships between the labour movement and middle-class politics.[3]

By singling out the legal aspect of these issues I hope to show the degree to which law is about much more than the expression of certain social interests or structures, but can actually shape these. I will argue that one has to see law as having an influence in its own right and not just as a function of social change, economic interest or political power. I will particularly highlight the contrast between the centrality of common and statute law in England compared to that of administrative orders and legal codes in Germany, and how this was related to the different ways in which the labour movement in the two countries could actually participate in the law-making process.

The legal background

The mere existence of a decree, a legal code, a statute, or an established body of case law does not automatically tell us what practical importance a particular law might have. Laws are complex, diffuse, ambiguous and often conflicting. Police and court practice cannot be deduced from the letter of the law. A specific law also has to be placed within its legal – let alone any broader – context. For example, one can only understand the significance of the right to vote if one also knows what power the elected institution enjoys.

The right to vote

I will consider the right to vote in the election of state parliaments, provincial and urban institutions. Part of the argument of this essay is that working and middle-class relationships were affected in important ways by institutions of local, especially urban, government and the franchises for elections to those institutions.

a) Germany

Before 1848 no state institutions were elected in Germany on the basis of an extensive franchise which might involve working-class participation. Most state or provincial institutions were elected on the basis of fairly exclusive franchises involving distinctions between social estates. Only the lower chamber in Baden was based on a non-estate franchise, although this was still exclusive. In addition, these assemblies were largely consultative, although some had rights over the approval of taxes and even limited rights to scrutinise budgets.[4]

In Prussia there were also elected town councils. The nature of these varied according to whether they were regulated under the 1808 or 1831 ordinance or, as in the Rhinelands, under separate arrangements. Only the 1808 ordinance allowed for an extensive franchise (leaving aside some exceptional occurrences such as certain urban elections in the Rhinelands in the 1820s). This involved making a distinction between citizens and residents, with only those regarded as economically independent amongst the citizens having the right to vote. This did mean that some of the kind of artisans found in the early German labour movement did have a vote. The elected city assembly had only limited powers. Executive powers were vested in a mayor and councillors whose appointment by the assembly had to be approved by the central government and who tended to be professional bureaucrats. Important powers such as the administration of law and the control of the police remained in the hands of central government, although in practice the city government might have a good deal of control over routine policing.[5] The franchise under the 1831 franchise was more 'modern' in that it removed the citizen/resident distinction but the financial conditions for having the vote were made more restrictive. Eventually in the 1840s the Rhenish cities settled upon a franchise. This was inclusive but biased in favour of the better-off, as it divided taxpayers into three descending classes which each paid one-third of the tax involved. Each class had an equal number of votes. Interestingly, each franchise was progressively more modern in that both those of 1831 and the Rhinelands eliminated any status distinctions, and in the latter case legal distinctions between urban and rural. At the same time, each franchise grew progressively more oligarchic.[6]

There was a dramatic extension of voting rights following the outbreak of revolution in March 1848. During the following six months constituent assemblies were elected throughout the German states as well as a German National Assembly.

The franchises varied though they were generally more extensive than anything earlier. Here I will focus on the German and Prussian parliaments. These were elected in two-stages on the same two days in May 1848 and on the same franchise. In theory this was one of universal manhood suffrage although restrictions concerning residence and the definition of independence, coupled with the discretion given to state officials, the public character of voting, and the indirect form of the elections all served to limit the democratic nature of the elections.[7]

The imposed Prussian constitution of December 1848 and the proposed German constitution of May 1849 both envisaged a broad adult male franchise. The Prussian franchise was used just once in an election in early 1849. A coup by the monarchy led to the dissolution of this parliament and the proclamation of a new franchise modelled on the Rhenish three-class system, although with a more extensive electorate. Voting was to be public and in two-stages, with the original voters electing a college which in turn elected the deputy for the constituency. This franchise remained in force until 1918. It did mean that most Prussian men had the vote from 1849 but it was of little weight. Furthermore, other changes to the 1848 constitution reduced the already limited powers of the Prussian lower house (Landtag).[8] The Imperial constitution never came into operation, and elections to the parliament called into being in 1850 by Prussia during the period of her *Unionpolitik* were based on a more restrictive franchise.

The last significant change came in 1867 with the establishment of the constitution of the North German Confederation. The lower house (Reichstag) of the parliament of this Confederation had only limited powers, but it was elected on the basis of universal manhood suffrage exercised by means of the secret ballot in single-member constituences. This was taken over into the Reichstag of the German Empire established in 1871.[9]

b) England

The First Reform Act of 1832 established for the first time a uniform franchise for elections to the House of Commons. The franchise was different only between the counties and the boroughs. A fairly high property requirement based on the freehold or rental value of land in the counties, and on the rental value of the place of residence in the boroughs excluded workers.[10] The electorate was about 0.8 million, perhaps one in six or seven of the adult males in the population. This expanded to perhaps 1.35 million by 1865, due to registration practice as well as increases in the numbers of those with the required qualifications. The Second Reform Act extended the vote in borough constituencies to all householders as well as certain types of lodgers, and this nearly doubled the electorate to around 2.5 million in 1868. In 1872 the secret ballot was introduced. Voting could be for one, two or three-member constituencies and voters might have two votes. Thus in Manchester there were three seats and each voter had two votes. He could give one vote to each of two candidates or, if he wished, just one vote to one candidate. The

House of Commons was more powerful than any German electoral body, because it had more authority *vis-à-vis* both the upper chamber of the Parliament and the monarch. Furthermore, unlike German constitutional practice, there was no executive separate from Parliament.[11]

Until 1835 urban areas could be divided into those with and those without corporations. The corporations varied greatly in the level of participation and power. Parish and borough institutions of other sorts – vestries, special Improvement Commissions, Police Commissions – were often elected, sometimes on fairly extensive franchises. In 1819 and 1820 Acts established a weighted franchise which gave anything from one to six votes to ratepayers according to the amount of rates paid. This was used in some urban institutions and for elections to the Boards of Guardians established under the Poor Law Amendment Act of 1834.[12]

The Municipal Corporations Act of 1835 swept aside the existing structure of urban corporations, although it was only permissive in character and towns had to apply and demonstrate support for the granting of a charter under the terms of the Act. In the place of the old system of 'closed' corporations there was created a system of elected councils with police and judicial powers. The franchise was in theory broader than that for parliament as it included all rate-payers, although in practice it was often more restricted than this. Many unincorporated towns soon turned themselves into corporations, such as Manchester and Birmingham. Generally the new councils extended their authority over other urban institutions such as Improvement Commissions, and also expanded their functions into new fields such as sanitation and water supply. The franchise was also extended in the 1850s by allowing tenants whose rents included a rate charge ('compound rate payers') to vote. By the end of the period many working men could vote for powerful institutions of urban government.[14]

c) General points

At the level of parliament after 1848, many Prussian workers had the formal right to vote, but it did not mean much. That this was realised can be seen in the very low turn-outs of the third class of voters. Most German male workers had the vote once they reached the age of twenty-five for elections to the Reichstag, and this meant rather more numerically and also politically as the Reichstag had significant, if largely negative powers. But urban workers remained a minority of the electorate because the vote had also been extended to all adult males in the countryside. No English workers had the right to vote until 1867. From then on a significant section of better-off workers did have the vote. This was important because the parliament elected had real powers, because urban workers were a larger part of the total population, and this was further increased by the franchise being broader for boroughs than counties until 1884.

So far as urban government was concerned, most Prussian workers did not have the vote. Many English workers did have a vote in elections to town councils. In both cases town councils became increasingly important as the functions of urban government were expanded, so this was a significant power for English workers and a significant exclusion for Prussian workers.

The rights to form trade unions and to strike

a) England

A complex variety of laws affected these matters. Under common law workers could be prosecuted for taking part in illegal conspiracies acting in restraint of trade. This remained in force until 1875. A number of laws, collectively known as the Masters and Servants laws, concerned breach of contract. The origins of these laws can be traced back to the thirteen century, although a number of provisions had fallen away in the meantime. The Elizabethan Statute of Artificers (1563) laid down punishments for leaving work unfinished. A number of statutes in the eighteenth century specified the offences and punishments for breach of contract in particular industries. These applied to outworkers as much as wage-labourers directly employed by masters. The major statute used in prosecutions in the nineteenth century was 4.Geo.IV.c34 (1823). Employers could be proceeded against under civil law for unfair dismissals or the failure to pay wages, although the obstacles in the way of workers who wished to pursue this course meant that it had little practical importance. Employees could be proceeded against under criminal law for leaving work before the time agreed or failing to produce goods which had been contracted for. The notion of what was an agreement or contract and, therefore, what was in breach of that, was interpreted broadly by many Justices of the Peace who could take summary action, often sitting alone in their private houses. Between 1858 and 1875 there was on average some 10, 000 prosecutions every year under these laws. The laws were amended in minor ways in the 1850s and finally removed from the statute book in 1875.[14]

Another set of laws are those known as the Combination Acts. In 1799, and in a moderated form in 1800, a whole host of specific statutes directed against combinations of workers in various industries were brought together under a single statute directed against workers' combinations only. The importance of these Acts is a matter of dispute. Some historians have argued that prosecutions under the specific statutes remained more important than those under the Combination Act of 1800. In 1824 the Combination Acts were repealed and trade unionists were excluded from prosecutions for conspiracy under either common or statute law. This Act was repealed in 1825 and replaced with a law rather less favourable to workers. Workers retained rights of combination and collective bargaining in respect of wages and hours, but trade societies were again made subject to the common law of conspiracy in order to prevent criminal acts of intimidation and coercion. Trade unions were permitted but their practical powers were hedged about with many restrictions. In practice the treatment of combinations and strikes varied very much from one trade to another.[15]

Workers could be prosecuted under other laws, such as the law concerning the administration of oaths which was used against the 'Tolpuddle Martyrs' in 1834. Workers could also (and still can) be prosecuted under laws concerning such acts as behaviour likely to cause a breach of the peace or the uttering of threats.[16]

Further major legal changes came between 1867 and 1875. In 1867 the Masters and Servants laws were amended to establish greater equality between employers and employees. In 1871 the Trade Union Act recognised trade unions and, overturning the legal situation since a court decision of 1867 (Hornby v.Close) concerning the Friendly Societies Act of 1855, provided protection for the funds of registered unions. Also in 1871 the Criminal Law Amendment Act '. . . effectively endorsed existing law which made strikes liable to prosecution for intimidation, molestation and obstruction.[17] Prosecutions of gas workers following a strike of 1872 also made it clear that the common law of conspiracy could be used against workers. The Act of 1871 was repealed in 1875 and replaced with the Conspiracy and Protection of Property Act which legalised peaceful picketing and removed the threat to prosecute actions taken in 'restraint of trade' under the common law of conspiracy. Now workers could only be prosecuted for intimidation and coercion, although this could be interpreted by police and courts in a very restrictive way. Also in 1875 the Employers and Workmens Act removed the remaining inequalities of the Masters and Servants law (as well as establishing a more acceptable terminology) and made breach of contact a matter purely of civil law.[18]

b) Germany

An Imperial Law of 1731 provides us with an example from the eighteenth century of a very comprehensive law aimed at journeyman combinations, though this was of limited effectiveness.[19] More effective action was taken around 1800 by state governments. The Prussian *Allgemeine Landes Recht* (ALR) of 1794 made worker combinations illegal, though in rather general terms. A more specific ban on such combinations was contained in a law of 1798 and this was reiterated in a law of 1816. The German Confederation (Bund) passed a law in 1835 aimed against the movement of journeymen to foreign countries where workers' leagues had been established. A further law of 1840 was directed against all journeyman combinations. Combinations in the form of guilds had also been legally ended with the abolition of guilds in Prussia. The Prussian *Gewerbeordnung* (GO) of 1845, in clauses 181–184, forbade combinations amongst employers or employees, as well as discussing, threatening or engaging in strike action. This was briefly set aside both in law and practice in 1848, but workers were already being prosecuted again under this law by 1849.[20]

Equally, if not more important than laws dealing specifically with workers' combinations and strikes, were more general laws restricting freedom of assembly, organisation and expression. The Bund had passed laws of this kind in 1819 and the early 1830s.[21] In 1850 the Prussian government had passed a law on associations which imposed tight restrictions upon and supervision over organisations concerned with public affairs.This was used by police and courts against workers' combinations, especially after 1869 when the law on trade unions and strikes was relaxed.[22]

This relaxation came with the *Gewerbeordnung* of 1869 which was valid for the whole of the North German Confederation. This code expressed a liberal economic philosophy which was applied to workers' combinations. Under clause 152 all legal bans on combining to present wage demands were removed. Clause 153 placed severe restrictions on the means which could be used legally in furtherance of a trade dispute.[23]

These were only the major laws. The legal situation was different in states other than Prussia. Some Confederal laws after 1850 were concerned with banning particular organisations. Local regulations could be used by the police. For example, 'foreign' workers who were involved in strikes could be expelled under laws concerning residence and employment.[24]

c) General points

In Britain by 1825 and north Germany by 1869 trade unions were legally tolerated. However, severe restrictions were placed upon strike action, both under the laws relating specifically to workers' combinations, and under more general laws. However, these laws tended to be public laws concerned with political associations in Germany, whereas they tended to be common law concerned with conspiracy or the Masters and Servants laws concerned with breach of contract in England. By 1875 British trade unions had advanced to the position of being recognised as bodies with legal rights, whereas in Germany they merely remained tolerated.

Middle-class politics, the labour movement and the franchise

England

Worker and middle-class political alliances clearly played a major role in the extension of the franchise in Britain. Part of the pressure leading to the Reform Act of 1832 came from popular movements in towns such as London and Birmingham in which middle-class radicals and politically active workers cooperated with one another.[25] But clearly many middle-class groups did not want anything as extensive as univeral adult male suffrage or even a more restricted franchise such as household suffrage. The Birmingham Political Union, for example, which played an important part in the reform agitation, largely lapsed in the few years after 1832, as much of its middle-class leadership was satisfied with what had already been obtained.[26] The middle-class radicals pressing for futher reform were only a minority amongst the MPs who formed the Whig-Radical majority in the House of Commons between 1832 and 1841. Furthermore, that radical minority was itself divided. Some elements looked to 'modernisation' through measures of administrative centralisation such as that embodied in the Poor Law Act of 1834.[27] In some areas, such measures of centralisation, coupled with disillusionment with the 1832 Reform Act and the bourgeois gains made through measures such as the Municipal Corporations Act, led in fact to working-class Radical/Tory alliances.[28] This helps to explain some of the paradoxical features of the Chartist movement, especially in its earlier phases. One strand of Chartist values was that of a long-standing political radical tradition. Another strand may be called 'old constitutionalism' which objected to new-fangled interference with local autonomy through municipal reform, poor law reform, and the introduction of police forces.[29] In part the new measures actually narrowed working-class access to the political system.[30] By the mid-1830s the political effectiveness of the right to petition parliament had been severely eroded.[31] The acts of 1819 and 1820 weighting ratepayers' votes was extended to elections to the Board of Guardians charged with administering the New Poor Law. In certain ways defence of old institutions such as the vestry was a rational working-class strategy.[32] In part Chartism was politically an archaic, working-class reaction against the restructuring of both local and central government by middle-class forces.[33]

However, there were many variations. In some places, for example Manchester, the shift of authority to the manufacturing interest led to a decline in interest in further political reform and a growing separation between the major middle-class groups and working-class groups (expressed, for example, during the campaign to incorporate the town). Nor could this separation be bridged by middle-class radicals interested in further extensions of the franchise. On the other hand, in Leeds some Chartists were actually elected to the new council and were in a position to play a more positive role in local politics.[34]

Another element in the Chartist movement was, of course, the increasing 'social radicalism' that from 1839 accompanied its political radicalism, old constitutionalism and response to the institutional changes of the 1830s. It was this which as much as anything accounted for middle-class hostility to further franchise reform.[35]

The opportunities for middle- and working-class involvement in the reformed political system, both at national and urban levels, and the factors which led to the rise of the Chartist movement, also made possible mass political mobilisation amongst both classes in the late 1830s and 1840s. The parliamentary parties played a part in this – especially as they realised the importance of registration under the new parliamentary franchise. However, a more important role was played by extra-parliamentary groups such as the Anti-Corn Law League [ACLL] and the

Chartist movement. Much of this organisation was structured through the legal-political framework created by Parliament. The mass platform, the petitioning of Parliament, the application of pressure during elections were all responses to the opportunities that were provided.[36] In some constituencies the unenfranchised could exert pressure by, for example, the practice of 'exclusive dealing', that is buying from enfranchised shopkeepers only if they voted for the favoured candidate.[37] The Convention of 1838 organised by the Chartists, the idea of 'People's Attorneys', the use of popular traditions and symbols in elections all point to ways in which, though formally excluded from the political process, working-class groups could find legally tolerated ways of informally participating.[38] In the case of the ACLL it was more a question of maximising electoral power, for example by purchasing 40s freeholds in order to acquire votes in the counties. Both movements could exploit improved transport and communications (railways, the Penny Post). However, it was clear, perhaps most obviously in the struggle of the unstamped press, that Chartism operated on the edge or the other side of legality, whereas the ACLL was seeking to exploit as effectively as possible the points of middle-class penetration into the political system.[39]

Also of importance was the linkage between urban and national politics. Most of the laws which extended the authority of urban governments took the form of private bills passed by Parliament in response to pressure from particular interests. Labour groups were often important elements in the pressure for such measures and their operation once passed.[40] Linked to this was the importance of continuing tensions between Whigs and Radicals which never led to the breakdown of the loose two-party system, but placed these Radicals in a key position between the majority of the Whig-Liberal party and the labour groups which remained organised. Of course these groups also had other common interests such as those that held Nonconformity together.[41] Finally, measures of centralisation and uniformity helped the local movements that made up Chartism to form into a national, if loose, politics.

What is central to all this is that there were local/national and Whig/Radical/labour movement linkages which allowed continuous participation of locally active workers even when formally excluded from the political system. Of course, especially after the dying down of the mass political mobilisation that occurred during the high points of Chartism, the workers involved were overwhelmingly adult, skilled and male.

There were all sorts of initiatives for further franchise reform between 1848 and the early 1860s. For various reasons, only one of which is that it might be true, a view was more widespread by the early 1860s that many workers of the kind who could not be trusted with the vote in the 1840s could now be. The decline of Chartism itself contributed to this view: in other words, workers could only be trusted with the vote when it was granted from above rather than demanded from below. There was a continuity of radical and Chartist traditions into the 1860s which were expressed, for example, in the Reform League, but largely detached from the 'social radicalism' of the Chartist period and also lacking some of the 'old constitutionalist' aversion to new political institutions in which the middle classes were entrenched. Rather better organised trade societies were able and willing to get involved in politics by 1865. Issues concerning foreign affairs (e.g. the American Civil War or the Polish rising of 1863) also helped unify the radical movement. What is more, through links to parliamentary radicals, through deputations of working men who periodically waited upon leading politicians, through the more extensive periodical press which grew in the 1860s, and other ways, organised working men could already play some positive part in the existing political system. These changes, allied to competition between the two main parties, all form the background to the reform agitation of 1865–67 and then the introduction and passing of the Second Reform Act.[42]

The Act also promoted the further development of the political labour movement. In the General Election of 1868 the Reform League acted in effect as a component of the Liberal Party. That cooperation was partly based on pragmatic views of the best way to advance labour interests (although the Reform League had little success in getting working-class candidates elected as liberals in 1868), partly was due to shared objectives in such matters as church reform[43], education[44], and Ireland.[45] Labour groups could take an independent or even anti-Liberal stance (as to some extent happened in the General Election of 1874 on the part of trade unionists dissatisfied with the trade union reform of the Liberal government), but the general tendency was to the 'lib-lab' pattern.[46]

What all this means is that in the post-Chartist period, the franchise came to be seen as an issue which was closely linked to other political concerns, taken up by labour organisations which were already partially integrated into the life of the political nation, and in alliance with some middle-class reformers. The continued resistance to reform, along with the better organisation of trade societies, did mean that a language of class played some role in the labour movement of this period, but in practice the stress was upon working in conjunction with middle-class reformers and playing down the implications for social change by giving at least some working men the vote.

Germany

The situation was rather different in Germany. Before 1848 there was very little in the way of an organised labour movement and very little pressure for an extension of the franchise for elections to parliaments or other elective institutions. Where discussions took place on the franchise issue, for example in various meetings of the provincial Diet of the Rhinelands, one can note two things. First, they generally envisaged a very restrictive or unequally weighted franchise established on the basis of a high property or income qualification. Second, much of the debate was theoretical, for example with proposals for corporation-based franchises which were seen as more appropriate to modern conditions than the old social estate distinctions.[47] This is hardly surprising. Given the lack of lower class organisation and indeed the fears associated with the 'social question', one could hardly expect middle-class liberals or even radicals to concern themselves much with the issue of mass voting. Given the impotence of elected institutions it was far more important for these groups to create the basic means which would enable them to act politically (freedom of expression, organisation, and assembly), to alter the rules governing access to institutions such as town councils in their own favour, and to increase the power of such institutions against the princes and their officials.

The brief experience of popular elections in 1848 was not the result of organised and focused pressure from below. Rather it stemmed from the fear and uncertainty created by the rapid breakdown of order in 1848, a breakdown due as much to the incompetence and panic of governments as to the actual strength, commitment or extent of popular movements. It was the extensive franchise and the holding of elections which contributed to the creation of more organised, popular politics rather than the other way around. Even then, it was not so much electoral activity focused on the new parliaments that was important, but the way in which the new freedoms of organisation, assembly and expression allowed a whole range of extra-parliamentary movements with a popular following to develop. These built as much upon earlier traditions of trade societies and educational associations as they did upon any idea of a modern pressure group or party oriented to parliament.[48] The parliaments tended to be regarded as 'once and for all' affairs, and people organised to influence the present assembly by means of petitions and demonstrations rather than to build organisations that could fight future elections. There was no real sense, therefore, of parliament being an institution around which political participation should be shaped, but rather of it being a means of reforming the state.[49]

The reasons for the swift and relatively easy success of counter-revolution cannot be dealt with here.[50] What is important to note is that there was little defence of elected parliaments or democratic franchises as such, but rather of the paper constitutions of which these might form a part. This was most clear in the 'second revolution' of May–June 1849, ostensibly in support of the Imperial constitution.[51] The democratic franchise in the Imperial constitution was the work of a radical minority, a price it exacted for its support for the *kleindeutsch* line. The pro-Prussian liberals never regarded it as sacrosanct, imagining it could always be bargained away in dealings with the Prussian monarchy.[52] Prussian, especially Rhenish liberals, supported the franchise change from a democratic to the three-class system for elections to the Prussian Landtag. This franchise broke decisively with conservative traditions by abolishing social estate or landownership as specific criteria determing political rights. It was a highly artificial franchise which had little positive meaning – rather it was a combination of negative motives (getting rid of the awkward lower chamber elected in early 1849) and symbolic gestures of goodwill to bourgeois interests.[53] Only by the late 1850s did it start to have significant political consequences, as liberals began to win elections to the Landtag. This is fairly typical of the pattern of franchise reform in Germany: they were a cause rather than an effect of new forms of political participation and pressure.

By the early 1860s this had become important and the three-class system underpinned the liberal majority. Furthermore, it did create an extensive electorate, even if those at the lower end had little weight. The claim to popularity was an important part of the liberal self-image.[54] Given that, the movement was open to pressure to take a more radical position on the franchise. But again this was more theoretical and symbolic than practical. When the Progressive Party adopted the Imperial Constitition as its official objective it was not doing anything of great practical significance. It would be a long time before anything like a German parliament would be set up and one could adjust to political 'reality' by that time.[55] More to the point was that the party did not energetically pursue franchise reform for elections to the parliament which did exist, namely the Prussian Landtag.[56]

Equally, however, it is not clear that the franchise was of major concern to the emergent labour movement. The bulk of the labour movement remained tied to the liberals into the late 1860s despite their rather half-hearted and theoretical commitment to any sort of radical franchise reform. The demand for the vote was, of course, made a central element of the Lassallean programme. But it is important to note that Lassalle resisted organising the ADAV on the lines of representative democracy, but insofar as he had any democratic view it was of himself as the direct and authentic voice of the fourth estate.[57] The demand was taken up for agitational purposes. Even then it was not so much seen as having agitational significance because it spoke to a long-standing tradition or central concern within the labour movement, but rather because it combined the virtue of simplicity with the idea of transformation. Lassalle's main concern was to find a demagogic or populist platform which would break decisively with liberalism and at the same time attract masses of hitherto unorganised and inactive workers into a political organisation. The franchise demand alone would not achieve this, so it had to be coupled with a socially radical demand (state aided producers' cooperatives) which, rather like the social radicalism associated with Chartism, served to repel even the more democratically inclined middle-class liberals.[58]

In fact the platform also repelled many workers who wished to work with the liberals rather than against them, wished to stress the importance of non-political activity in labour organisations, and were in any case worried about the potential conservative exploitation of the mass electorate concentrated in rural areas.[59] So franchise reform in Britain was more closely related to the pressure and interests of the labour movement than it was in Germany.

Bismarck, therefore, did not introduce universal manhood suffrage in response to great pressure from below, but rather as one of a number of experiments (any of which he imagined could be reversed if they failed). This one was designed to limit liberal strength and possibly to build up that of the conservatives. Bismarck had analysed the Prussian Landtag elections and seen, for example, how in some of them conservatives had done best in the lowest class of the rural voters. One should also note that Bismarck only introduced this measure for a totally new assembly which had few powers and as yet little standing. He never seems to have contemplated any tampering with the franchise for the Prussian Landtag, at that time a more significant institution than the Reichstag.

Once again the franchise was more important for stimulating certain kinds of popular politics than for being the objective of popular politics. As it was, the mass electorate, with a secret ballot, became the basis of political parties which both challenged the liberals and the conservatives, building instead on nationality, religion and class. Liberals began to lose ground in national elections, even if the extent of this has been exaggerated.[60] At first, liberals were able to capitalise upon their close association with the new nation-state and the creed of nationalism, and they dominated the early elections. However, the 'normalisation' of the nation-state would undermine this dominance as other groups adjusted to the new situation. Furthermore, liberals never really adjusted their political methods adequately to a mass-based electoral politics. Thus as electoral participation increased, as other parties did organise more effectively to mobilise mass support, and as the glories of unification began to dim, so the liberals lost ground in the national parliament. In response they tended to retreat to urban and state institutions in which there were more restrictive or weighted franchises, and where local notability counted for more. These institutions continued to retain very important powers. It was the *separation* of electoral politics at the national and lower levels which was important. For liberals the connections to the nation-state were increasingly made through pressure groups and informal links with the administration rather than through parliamentary contacts. In this way, those mass parties which did develop in the Reichstag were cut off from the 'real' political life of town councils, state parliaments and the national administration and tended to stress rather negative and principled stances; whereas the liberals appeared increasingly elitist and detached from mass politics.[61]

General points

In Britain particular groups with some access to existing political institutions pressed for franchise reforms that would serve their interests. Franchise reform in response to such pressures tended therefore to be extensions of existing trends, especially as this took place within a stable territorial and institutional framework. In Germany there was little pressure for extensive franchise reform which came about for other reasons (response to the breakdown of authority, method of creating the basis of a new state). This franchise reform could, in turn, produce marked changes in political trends. The different reasons for franchise reform were linked to quite different relationships between the labour movement and middle-class groups. The significance of these differences will be taken up in the conclusion.

The right to form trade unions and to strike

There are marked contrasts between the way in which reform in these areas came about in Germany and Britain. After providing a brief background on earlier developments I will focus on the period *c*.1860 to 1875.

Before 1860

a) England

It is well known that Francis Place played an important part in the pressure group activity which led to the repeal of the Combination Acts in 1824. Place was not a trade union leader and indeed took a severely classical political economy view of trade unions. Nevertheless, he did have contacts with trade societies and these were involved in the political process which led to reform. This shows the extent to which, even in the unreformed political system, there was room for participation to secure legislative change.[62] Attempts to change specific laws which put trade societies at a disadvantage continued to be a feature of labour activity.[63] In the 1840s, for example, there were attempts to alter the Master and Servant laws.[64] By and large these campaigns on a fairly narrow front were typical of the trade societies of skilled workers in reasonable conditions of security. More extensive political activity, such as that of Chartists, tended to be found in more depressed craft trades, factory employment and outwork such as handloom weaving.[65] Even as late as the 1860s leaders of such bodies as the London and Glasgow Trade Councils found it difficult to get much interest from their members in broad political issues such as franchise reform, but were able to press for amendments to Master and Servants laws.[66] Indeed, sometimes the best case those trade unions who wanted to engage in more extensive political movements could make to their members was to argue that Parliament would only accept the case for specific labour law reforms if workers had the vote and could place their own people in parliament.[67]

There were various middle-class groups which sympathised with these demands for improvements in labour laws. Some agreed with Place that once combinations were legalised wokers would soon learn that they had very limited powers to upset the more important laws of supply and demand. But the bulk of the organised middle class opposed substantial reform after 1825. Thus every time amendments were proposed to the Masters and Servants laws, employers' organisations argued in favour of the present laws. It has been argued that the employer groups were located in particular industries – Staffordshire potteries, mining, various sorts of outwork – and that these were of declining importance in the total economy.[68] The case is persuasive, but no powerful employers' groups actually pushed the case for reform. What one could argue is that middle-class groups within the Liberal Party who supported reform for one reason or another found that employer resistance declined so that it was easier to achieve reform by the late 1860s and early 1870s than it had been a decade or so earlier. Again, research suggests that there was little pressure to alter the laws governing strike activity, except to remove the power to prosecute under the common law of conspiracy. However this may have been because it was realised that there was little chance of achieving anything in this regard.

b) Germany

The situation was very different in Germany. Just as there was no pressure for franchise reform from labour groups before 1848, so there was little pressure to secure rights to combine or strike. There was more concern to secure the right to organise at all, and practical movements to obtain and exercise that basic right only really became significant in 1848.[69] Pressure for a secure legal position at that time took very different forms from in England. The demand was often for a sweeping *Gewerbeordnung* in which rights to combine were but one element. The state (whose legal and political structure was not necessarily specified) would, it was hoped or requested, provide a comprehensive legal code which would enable workers to organise in various ways. Some of these ways were envisaged along the lines of corporations. Workers and masters should be part of a corporate structure which would itself have legal powers and privileges. In part this could be a demand for some sort of guild restoration. However, the precise nature of those demands varied between those made by masters and those made by journeymen, and also according to the trades and regions which predominated.[70] But even where a free set of arrangements were envisaged, this took the form of state guarantees for the rights of voluntary associations and included quite elaborate schemes of arbitration courts and educational provision.[71]

Two things are important to note about these demands. First, they were directed at governments and constituent assemblies. Second, they were usually sweeping in nature. They were often drawn up by congresses which disbanded once they had completed the work of drawing up a programme. In both respects this differs from England where the demands were usually more specific (mainly for amendments to existing statutes, or statutes to reverse judicial interpretations of either statute or common law), and where they were usually associated with the formation of a pressure group which would seek to influence parliamentary opinion.

One should not exaggerate the contrast. Notions of sweeping transformation can be found in the English labour movement, suchas the appeal of Owenism in the

1830s. It has been argued that in some places Chartism constituted a counter-culture rather than a practical reform movement.[72] Conversely one can see the practical concerns which often preoccupied the Brotherhood of German Workers.[73]

Furthermore, one should in neither case separate 'utopian' from 'practical' demands and ideas too far. Producers' cooperatives, for example, which had a wide appeal to craft- and out-workers in both countries, did so as much as a means of combatting unemployment and improving the chances for successful wage-struggle as because they represented a vision of a transformed society.[74] My point is only that these rather similar types of workers with rather similar types of concerns operated within a very different political and legal context and this gave a very different character to the ways in which these concerns were organised and expressed. Basically I would make a distinction between an *empirical* and *participatory* political-legal culture in Britain, which tended to force even sweeping and radical demands into pressure group organisation and specific goals; and an *abstract* and *non-participatory* culture in Germany which often hampered even the organisation of quite limited demands and tended towards the systematisation of even fairly specific goals.

Liberal middle-class opinion in Germany was either hostile or indifferent to these labour demands in 1848. Trade protection offended liberal views, and the various parliaments barely responded to these demands.[75] At the same time, the protectionist demands of small employers were highly sectional and opposed both to the idea of 'democratic corporations' and of the state backing free associations of journeymen as well as masters.[76] The greater liberal interest in labour concerns in the late 1850s and early 1860s had little to say about trade unions and strikes, but rather focused on cooperatives and educational associations.[77]

1860–1875

a) England

The strikes in the building industry in London in 1859–60 helped rejuvenate the labour movement. Once more there was pressure for reform of the Masters and Servants laws and other legal changes. Union leaders such as George Odger tried to connect this to the broader need for franchise reform but at this time they were largely unsuccessful. (They were to have more success some five years later.) But in the Trade Councils there did exist a type of supra-occupation institution which could at least raise general labour interests.[78] There were also points of contact with middle-class radicals and reformers. Christian Socialists and Positivists were concerned to improve the labour laws and remove what they saw as unfair disadvantages to which labour was subject.[79] Beyond the domestic question of franchise reform a range of foreign policy questions aroused common concerns from 1858.

For instance the emergence of a broad reform movement by the mid-1860s was influenced by such questions as the political refugee problem raised by Orsini's attempt on the life of Napoleon III[80]; the response to the war of 1859 between France and Piedmont on the one side and Austria on the other; the support for the North during the American Civil War; the Polish rising of 1863; the visit of Garibaldi to Britain in May 1864; and the formation of the International Working Men's Association (IWMA).[81]

By the mid-1860s, this reform movement was able to play an important role in the introduction of a failed reform bill in 1866 and then in the passing of the Second Reform Act in 1867. Around the same time an unfavourable decision against trade unions (Hornby v.Close)[82], a number of violent incidents during disputes in the Sheffield cutlery trades (the 'Sheffield outrages'[83]) and in the Manchester brickmaking trade[84] aroused middle-class opinion and threatened to make things worse for labour. An inquiry was proposed to look into the events in Sheffield. The leadership of the London Trades Council (the so-called 'Junta') and their middle-class sympathisers managed to get this inquiry extended into a general investigation of trade unions. A Royal Commission was set up:

. . .to inquire into and report on the Organisation and Rules of Trades Unions and other Associations, whether of Workmen or Employers, and to inquire into and report on the effect produced by such Trades Unions on the Workmen and Employers respectively, and on the Relations between Workmen and Employers, and on the Trade and Industry of the country.[85]

A further success was to get Frederic Harrison, the positivist, on the Commission. Harrison regarded trades unions as a major civilising influence within the working class as well as an indication of the superiority of collectivism over individualism. He ensured that hostile witnesses such as spokesmen for particular employer interests were carefully cross-examined and, so far as was possible, their testimony devalued. He also helped the trade union leaders who testified to the Commission[86] to put forward the best possible image. Men such as Applegarth[87], the leader of the carpenters' union, and Allan, the leader of the engineers' union, presented a picture of unions as made up of the better men in the trade, helping to overcome the worst features of economic anarchism to the mutual benefit of the good employer and the good working man. They emphasised the benefit function of the unions rather than that concerned with wage-struggle. Strikes were presented as a last resort which unions and working men sought to avoid as much as possible.[88] The image was plausible and accepted by many contemporaries (as well as historians). Harrison succeeded in getting the majority report of the Commission modified in ways favourable to labour, for example with its proposal that the legality of workers' combinations be recognised even when these were acting in restraint of trade. But he also wrote a minority report which went even further and advocated a more positive legal treatment of trades unions including certain corporate privileges.[89]

These developments have to be taken in conjunction with the events accompanying and following the Second Reform Act of 1867. These self-same labour leaders and middle-class radicals had been involved in the pressure which preceded and accompanied the passing of the Act, and which had involved more trade society support than in an earlier phase of the reform movement.[90] The Reform League remained close to Gladstone and the Liberal Party and played a subordinate role in the General Election of 1868 which returned the Liberals to power with Gladstone as Prime Minister.[91] The relative lack of independence of the Reform League, and its disappointment at getting hardly any working men returned to Parliament, was perhaps in part due to the lack of trade society support for a more independent labour stance. However, it did help establish a receptive response within the new Liberal Government to the proposals of the Royal Commission.

However, the sympathy was tempered by a concern about strikes and violence, partly due to the middle-class and employer sentiments which were important amongst the supporters of the new ministry. Furthermore, in a way the trades unions were hoist with their own petard in the labour laws which eventually reached the statute book in 1871. The Government accepted the image that union leaders had assiduously cultivated of their organisations as benefit societies which incidentally negotiated with employers, strove always for a peaceful solution, treated strikes as a very last resort, and which sought to avoid any violence or intimidation. The laws conferred upon the trades unions the privileges of Friendly Societies but restated, indeed tightened if anything, the laws relating to the conduct of strikes. This was achieved by means of a typically liberal distinction between private and public. As a private association unions could discuss issues and handle the savings of their members. But they would be in breach of the criminal law if they interfered with the freedom of other workers to sell, and employers to buy, labour. However, the continued inequality of employers and workers in the Masters and Servants laws, and the continued power to prosecute under the common law of conspiracy for actions in restraint of trade, rather undermined this distinction between private and public and equality of legal treatment, and could lead to a liberal critique of the existing legal framework.[92]

Dissatisfaction with the Criminal Law Amendment Act of 1871 led to increased trade union pressure for its repeal. This weakened labour support for the liberals. Although by the time of the rather hastily called General Election of 1874 the government had signalled its willingness to engage in further reforms[93], the hostility was strong enough to lead to the putting up of some independent trade union candidates in the election which damaged electoral support for liberal candidates.[94] The Conservative Government came into power on the basis of a tacit understanding that it would be more sympathetic to labour concerns. After the brief delaying tactic of an inquiry, the Government soon moved to repeal the Act and to replace it with one which removed the final 'inconsistencies' in the distinction between the freedom of workers to organise themselves and bargain about the terms on which they sold their labour, and the freedom of any individual to buy or sell property (including labour).[95] Beyond that the trade unions were also granted certain corporate privileges in the form of legal protection of their funds, or so it was believed until the adverse legal decision represented by the Taff Vale judgement beyond the turn of the century.[96]

It is interesting that it was a Conservative government which proved at least as receptive as Liberals to the cause of labour laws reform. The alliance between politically active working men and the Liberal Party was based less upon the specific issue of liberal sympathy for specifically labour interests, than upon shared values on a range of broader matters such as schooling, foreign policy, the position of the Church, and Irish policy.[97] In fact this separation of broad political questions from the narrowly economic interests of labour was probably an advantage because it meant labour interests were not seen as one complete set of class concerns and could be addressed to different governments.

b) Germany

The situation was very different in Germany. As already mentioned, the liberal interest in, even patronage of, a labour movement in the late 1850s and early 1860s had little to say about trade unionism. One reason may have been because this was not yet a particularly important form of worker organisation. The mid-1860s did see an increase in the number of strikes and some liberals did seek to respond to this in a positive way.[98] But generally one can say that the great expansion in trade union organisation and strike activity followed, rather than preceded legal reform. As with the franchise question, the legal change helped stimulate organised labour activity rather than such activity pressing effectively for legal change. So far as I know there was no organised labour pressure involved in the debates and decisions of the Reichstag of the North German Confederation which led to the *Gewerbeordnung* of 1869. This can be explained as part of the liberalising of economic legislation which had been carried through at the level of individual states and inter-state agreements before 1867.[99]

There had been some demands raised by labour groups in the 1860s, but these were not very powerfully organised and often phrased in the more general terms of natural rights rather than those of labour.[100] In the discussions in the Reichstag concerning clauses 152 and 153 the views expressed had little to do with the economic interests of labour. Schweitzer, the ADAV leader who was a Reichstag deputy, was less concerned with the specific advantages accruing to workers of the right to combine than he was with the political consequences which he expected to flow from the granting of that right. That was consistent with the Lassallean view of trade unions and strikes as, in themselves, futile activities. On the other hand, the view of a liberal such as Schulze-Delitzch had little to do with any positive economic benefits he expected to follow from the legal changes. He, like the Lassalleans, tended to the view that under free market conditions the laws of supply and demand would regulate the price of labour, and labour organisation could do little to alter that. However, he was concerned to avoid the accusation that as a liberal he was not prepared to see labour entitled to the same rights under the law as other groups and to retain labour support for liberalism. His view was similar to that of Francis Place over forty years earlier. Until workers had the right to combine they would entertain grandiose illusions as to the significance of that right and that could lead them to political extremism. So again, though from a different perspective to that of the Lassalleans, it was the political perspective which predominated. Even conservatives such as Wagener, who welcomed the granting of the right to bargain, did so because they thought it might help workers organise in ways which would lead to demands for greater state intervention against the false doctrines of liberalism.[101]

All these responses, whatever their differences in terms of the political values involved, exhibit a number of similarities. They saw the right to form a trade union primarily as a political, rather than an economic question. What is more, they campaigned for that right to be included in a general legal code concerned with many other matters. No one really focused on this as an isolated legal question or considered what might be the practical economic consequences of conceding this right. This helps support the earlier distinction made between the empirical and participatory English mode and the abstract and non-participatory German mode, even when one recognises that in practice what those workers who could organise effectively wanted to do with this legal right was very similar.

In part because the legal changes in Britain were a response to pressure from existing trade societies, they did not lead to any sharp change in the pattern of industrial relations. However, the legal revolution from above in Germany, coupled with a boom in the late 1860s and early 1870s, led to a strike wave and an expansion of trade unions.[102] This required some sort of response. Some (but not many) liberals sought to ride the wave by supporting trade unions and strikes if considered legitimate. Socialists sought to build trade unionism into their political strategy. While Lassallean socialists exploited the class conflict dimension involved, Eisenacher generally tried to help support practical organisation. It has been convincingly demonstrated that the trade union schemes of this period were a political response to autonomous labour organisation, and should not be understood simply as political organisation and manipulation of unions from above.[103] More recently, from an interesting comparative perspective, Eisenberg has challenged this view and re-stated in a new way the older view of the 'primacy of politics'.[104] However, this focuses on a limited number of craft trades, so perhaps generalisation is difficult. It is clear that trade unionism was much more powerful in England than in Germany at this time, but what really matters is the growth in Germany in relation to the situation earlier and how far this preceded political involvement. Whatever the balance between political and economic activity, however, the predominant middle-class response was to observe higher wages and also to fear political radicalism. This was especially the case after the Paris Commune and in the new and uncertain conditions of the Second Empire.[105]

It was difficult to amend the GO of 1869 and impossible to repeal it. It had, after all, been passed very recently and was seen as a general and systematic enactment. However, as the strike wave and the expansion of worker organisation was feared mainly as a political phenomenon, perhaps this would not have been an appropriate course of action in any case. It suited both an authoritarian state and a fearful middle class to use police action and political laws to deal with the problem. It was after 1869 (and especially after 1874 when an economic downturn if anything made middle-class opinion even more anxious) that the Prussian Law of 1850 on political associations began to be turned increasingly against trade unions. The police, if supported by the courts, also had extensive powers under clause 153 of the GO. What is more, the very lack of trade union power made it impossible for union leaders to discipline their members (and even more, non-members who joined in strikes) and to mount the type of organised strike which did not depend upon violence or at least the threat of violence. This, along with the demagogic Lassallean tactic of treating strikes as an emanation of class struggle which would only end with the abolition of capitalism, all seemed to confirm middle-class fears. After 1874 the repressive strategy which such fears favoured enjoyed a good deal of success, especially as the economic conditions for strike action also worsened.[106]

c) General points

Once again, one must not exaggerate differences. The types of workers who organised, especially in occupations such as the skilled building trades, were similar in both countries, as were many of their values and objectives.[107] However, there were great differences in their level of organisation and the power they had relative to employers and governments. At one level one could try to explain major differences in terms of market power which in turn could help account for different middle-class responses. In the British case there was a pragmatic response to distinct but limited pressure which used arguments about the need to extend political and economic rights to 'respectable' workers. These arguments, would prove widely acceptable to middle-class opinion in mid-Victorian England.[108] especially when the workers involved *did* seem to be respectable and when there were significant levels of trade unionism which represented both power and a source of discipline over workers. In the German case, much weaker labour pressure had had little to do with the legal reforms which were more part of a general process of liberalisation. The legal reforms were fortuitously linked to a wave of strikes which, in the absence of strong trade unions, were more undisciplined and unpredictable than in England, and which consequently could be perceived, both by radical supporters and anxious middle-class opponents, as going beyond limited market disputes. There was thus both a stronger incentive to repress rather than to guide labour organisation, and easier success given labour weakness, especially when economic recession set in. That in turn would force workers to look to radical political solutions to their problems. One could go on to explain these differences in market power in terms of the different kinds of economic structures.[109] So one could connect both legal and political differences back to a more 'basic' economic level.

There is a lot to be said for this approach. However, in my opinion it does not explain everything. One also has to take into account the differences in political structures and the distribution of political power, something I have tried to do in the earlier essay 'Liberalism or social democracy?'. But in addition to these political and economic considerations, there are cultural issues to take into account. The very broadest level in which these issues can be studied – for example in relation to family life or religious beliefs – have been little studied and would take me beyond the scope of an essay.[110] Here I want to focus on the legal framework within which labour movements operated. From one angle law can be regarded as a vital component of a political culture. It is produced and enforced by state institutions and clearly bears upon the political power of different groups. At the same time, it is not merely a function of power. There are legal traditions, embodied in modes of reasoning and in the education of members of the legal profession. There is the need, even when seen in narrowly functional terms, for law to at least appear to be independent of particular interests. For many people, it was through legal institutions that they most closely experienced the world of politics and the power of the state. The character of these institutions and the type of legal reasoning they employed were, therefore, of vital importance in shaping perceptions of the state and of politics.

In British politics these elements did not foster a view of the state or law as being ideal entities above society. Statute law, above all, established very definite and visible connections between a parliamentary majority, government, and legal enactments on specific matters which left little room for manoeuvre for judges. If the state was looked at in a hostile way, this tended to be because it was seen as being in the hands of 'placemen' and 'jobbers', the 'aristocracy' and the 'parasites'. For those who wished for change, this same set of close connections offered an obvious way forward. Through parliament, above all the House of Commons, one could take control of government, produce amended or better laws, and thereby redress particular grievances. The extension of governmental intervention, above all in the increasingly important sphere of urban government, fostered that attitude. Th idea of a specific Act, often brought about by a single member introducing a private bill, meant that law tended to be seen in a very empirical way, both in terms of how it was enacted and what it covered. What prevented it from being seen as the arbitrary instrument of interests was not so much arguments about how law constrains power, but rather about how politics and tradition can do this. The arguments about politics focused primarily on the electoral base of the House of Commons. The arguments about traditions revolved around the maintenance of 'liberties' (*habeas corpus*, the irremovability of judges, etc.) and a stress upon the importance of procedure (in the interpretation of common law, in the functioning of Parliament). All this encouraged a very concrete, apparently commonsensical and empirical attitude to politics.

It was also important that labour groups, both by virtue of their power, but also of institutional opportunities such as the hustings and the right of petition, could participate in campaigns to amend and improve laws. This could help tie them to the broad features of the existing political and legal system. Even if there was hostility between labour and middle-class liberals on specific matters, such as the law on strikes, these could be compromised because broader issues in which labour could play some role encouraged a continuation of contacts and cooperation.

The situation was very different in Germany. The state did not offer opportunities for participation, except at times of breakdown and crisis as in 1848. Even if one envisaged the state as a legally bound and defined structure, rather than as an authority over society (e.g. the divine right monarchy) which in turn produced law, this was argued through the abstract (and often logically contradictory) notion of the *Rechtsstaat*. The state, as a legal structure, might guarantee freedom of association, or underwrite corporate privilege, but this was argued as something which could be embodied in an authoritative, general enactment. In turn one put these as demands *to* the state, rather than seeing them directly as the specific achievements of political movements, that is of working *through* the state.

This perception of the state as an abstract entity above specific social interests was related to distinctive forms of political action. There was the 'paternalist' form of action where workers petitioned the state for reform. This might involve strict, indeed near-servile, attention to legal forms.[111] The implication was that law was an instrument of state power which one asked to be used benevolently. It was not far from that position in thought, though apparently the opposite extreme in action, to see oppressive law as the product of an oppressive state. If, therefore, one could ignore or destroy that state, these laws would end and with them oppression. The very same groups who had petitioned a wise king to rule benevolently could move rapidly to an effectively anarchist position. This fluctuation from deference to destruction is a well known feature of peasant action, but it can also be found amongst working-class groups.

The perception of the state in more abstract terms, coupled with the greater education of workers and the growth of a collective sense of identity could lead this basic, anti-political attitude in a different direction. The reversal of hopes in the late 1860s and early 1870s, especially with the anti-socialist law in 1878, could make workers receptive to the old idea that the state was an instrument of power, but they now saw that power in terms of an oppressive class. Law now was class law. The destruction of class power would mean the ending of class law and with it oppression. A particular form of Marxism, therefore, far from being the affair of remote and small groups of intellectuals, could actually turn into a latter-day version of this anti-political attitude, only now countering its own abstract understanding of the state to that positive one which viewed it as the source of order and justice.[112]

Unlike the notion of the state as the instrument of placemen or 'Old Corruption', with the implication that a change of political power (but not of the structure of state institutions) is all that is needed, this is a rather abstract and systematic perception, even if the particular interests the state is seen to serve might appear similar. These ways of perceiving and talking about the state and politics could also make cooperation between middle-class and working-class political groups more difficult in Germany. Ideas of specific and permissive trade union law were aired in the 1880s but, given the weakness of labour, this was seen by powerful groups of employers as well as the authoritarian state as needless concession which might actually promote trade unionism.[113] Legal reform tended to be tackled in a broad way, with the growing socialist movement simply pressing its philosophy in a way which made piecemeal concessions difficult to identify, let alone offer.[114] Obviously this has to be linked to the impact of recession upon the economic conditions in which the labour movement operated. It also has to be related to the breakdown of a broad and national liberal movement following the events of 1866–67, which removed the pressure to compromise and increased the temptation to express maximalist goals as doing so did not involve sacrificing the chance of obtaining more limited objectives.[115] However, the abstract and non-participatory political-legal culture made it much easier for labour politicians to respond in this way, and to accept a particular kind of Marxist political language.

Conclusion

How does one explain the differences that have been brought out in this essay?

I have already pointed to some economic factors which could help us understand why labour developed as a specific pressure group in Britain, acting, especially from the 1860s, as one element in the party political conflict in the urban and parliamentary arenas. I have also looked at the political opportunities and issues which pushed labour into a broad, if often uneasy, cooperation with the Liberal Party. In Germany, by contrast, one could look at economic factors such as weaker market power on the part of skilled workers, to help explain the lack of bargaining influence in relation to employers. This could lead to stable, negotiated, relations which both sides would wish to embody in legally institutionalised forms. One can also point to the peripheral role of labour in broader national political movements, themselves largely excluded from direct contacts with governmental power, which would in turn inhibit the development of limited, practical objectives and cooperation with others. One could then relate this to different relationships to middle-class, especially liberal politics, and in particular to the rights to vote, to form trade unions, and to strike.

Another important consideration would be the different forms taken by the state in Germany and Britain.[116] These cannot be seen as a direct expression of social and economic structures, or even as the work of political elites currently in power. Earlier political conflicts and continuing political and legal traditions played a crucial part as well. In turn these different state forms shaped the political oppositions that developed by encouraging particular sorts of organisation and language. The basic point I would make here is a very unoriginal, even platitudinous one, though no less valid for that. The British state, especially in England (and especially *not* in Ireland) was very stable territorially and institutionally. It was also highly integrated in the sense that there were very close and positive political links between different levels of political action.For example, the connection between 'local' politics (i.e. within the counties and boroughs) and 'national' politics at Westminster and Whitehall were so close that, from at least the seventeenth century, it has been difficult to understand these levels in terms of separate and distinct political worlds.[117] The counties never achieved the importance or variety of form that one can observe in the French *départements* or the Prussian provinces. Precisely for this reason there has never been a strong emphasis in England on centralisation as an administrative process. Politics itself was so centrally focused (rather than centralised – a term which again sets centre against locality) that it did not require elaborate and deliberate initiatives from the central administration against autonomous local political spheres in order to achieve political effectiveness.

This effectiveness as well as this 'central focus' was, above all, achieved through Parliament.[118] Even before 1832 the system of representation had been flexible in responding to the development of new interests, and the electorate had increased.[119] This integration was further developed after 1832. It was not the new, arguably 'alien' forms of administrative centralisation, above all embodied in the New Poor Law, that were important. Indeed, opposition to the New Poor Law threatened to destabilise the political system. Rather it was the incorporation of middle-class interests into the political system that was vital. The 1832 Reform Act, the greater development of party structures after 1832, and the reform of urban government were the key elements of this. Although aspects of these changes, especially where it involved the destruction of older institutions which working-class groups had been able to influence, could in the short run encourage a more radical as well as national labour response in the form of Chartism, in the longer run these changes provided new points of entry for working-class politics. This process of integration also involved focusing on particular issues, such as laws on factory reform or urban improvements, often laws which arose out of local initiative and were confined to one locality. But it was always necessary to bring about such legal change by participating in broader political movements which culminated in parliamentary action.

The Prussian state had far less institutional or territorial stability. It was a highly diverse political structure, with different legal systems and institutions in each province, even in different parts of provinces. Beyond the monarch and the central bureaucracy there was nothing in the way of a common set of institutions. For example, even after the carrying through of urban government reforms in the first half of the nineteenth century, there were at least three areas with different arrangements. The 'state' therefore was at its centre something above and distinct from the legal systems and local institutions with which most people were concerned. Even if the state came to be perceived as something more than the monarch and his officials, the perception took the abstract form of a rational entity imposing systematic rules upon society in the general interest. Institutions and laws were seen, therefore, not so much as the form taken by the state, but rather as the forms sanctioned by the state in the general interest. From this perspective constitutions and representative institutions were amongst the instruments employed by the state to try to develop a more integrated political system, rather than the source of power and the major institutional expression of state power.[120] Political opposition, therefore, came to see these institutions as devices for putting demands or applying pressure to the state. Insofar as these institutions were valued in their own right it was either as areas beyond state interference or as the institutional basis of a future state. Whatever the particular concern, there was an enduring separation between the institutions in which one acted politically and the state.[121]

These different forms can clearly be related to very different historical experiences. Clearly there is not time to explore these matters here, though I mention the role of war in order to make it clear that an explanation of these differences cannot see them exclusively, or even primarily, in terms of domestic socio-economic factors. Again, one could consider those elements which enabled certain state forms and types of political activity to continue to function through the nineteenth century. The fact that the British state had evolved in a certain way up to the nineteenth century does not alone explain further evolution in that direction. The special nature of industrialisation in Britain, the benefits conferred by British Imperialism: clearly these things help account for the capacity of the political system to make concessions to working-class groups.[122] Nevertheless, that political tradition had an importance of its own and was related to the development of a specific kind of political culture.

I have tried in this essay to bring out some of the differences between English and Prussian political culture. I have suggested that one way of doing this is by using two pairs of contrasting concepts: empirical/abstract and participatory/non-participatory or exclusive.[123] (I would stress that, although I am using these paired concepts in two particular contrasting combinations, one could envisage different combinations. The French labour movement might, for example, be usefully analysed by combining the notions of empirical and participatory, which might help to explain the central role of the idea of revolution in its political language.) An empirical and participatory political culture encourages compromise over specific political objectives which are pursued through state institutions. An abstract and non-participatory political culture encourages the positing of systematic, reflective ('ideological'?) political objectives which are addressed to or against the state and which are difficult to compromise. Clearly 'concrete' political objectives were pursued in Germany, and these were often similar to those pursued in Britain, as we have seen on such matters as the vote and trade unionism. Clearly there was in Britain political languages and movements which went beyond the empirical style and the specific goal. However, the political rhetoric involved was always pressed back by the political framework back into the language of empiricism and the piecemeal.[124] Thus franchise reform in Britain, although demanded often for very general reasons to do with political rights and the radical change it was believed would follow, was always pressed into making connections with parliamentary history and traditions, with the need to represent particular interests, and was also expressed through actions directly related to Parliament (private bills, independent candidacies, exclusive dealing, hustings). In Germany franchise reform, even in the 1850s when those active in politics tried to adopt a more 'realistic' style, was discussed in much more abstract terms by conservatives who stressed almost mystical notions of corporate division and privileges; by liberals who tried to qualify notions of natural rights with contrived property qualifications; by radicals in terms of natural rights alone; and by socialists who talked of the rise of the fourth estate or the direction of change envisaged by scientific socialism or what was needed in a 'truly human' society.

Can one say that one political culture was more 'modern' than the other? I do not think one can. If one takes a 'rationalist' view of modernity one might see something more modern about an industrial ordinance which systematically regulates the rights of labour according to the liberal economic view in the manner of the GO of 1869. But equally one might argue that the cluster of specific laws concerning the rights and obligations of labour organisations that was in existence in Britain by 1875 was more flexible, more 'functional' for the development of the economy. Similar arguments can be developed in relation to civil law.[125] Anderson and Nairn when making comparisons between Britain and 'Other Countries' have found the more rational and explicitly ideological mode of politics more advanced.[126] The supporters of the idea of a peculiar German history (*Sonderweg*) have tended, by contrast, to see German politics as backward.[127] But at one level one simply confronts two sorts of political culture with roots in the pre-industrial era. It seems arbitary to characterise 'modernity' in terms taken from just one of these cultures.

On the other hand I would be loath to move towards an historicist position which simply sees each country as unique, either by virtue of different histories as a whole or because the different forms of industrial capitalism each produce different state forms or political cultures.[128] Equally, just to argue that politics is 'autonomous' tells us nothing.[129] It is clear that the growth of industrial capitalism did lead, in both cases, to the development of structures of civil law which regulated most economic dealings, that abolished most formal inequalities embodied in legal privilege, but which always found that the legal regulation of labour as property required rather different provisions than those that applied to other forms of property. Equally, it is clear that a structure of public opinion along with a system of political parties did develop and that this served, in one way or another, especially for bourgeois groups, to crystallise and transmit political views to state institutions. Some broad and rather abstract notion of this development, which involved a growing distinction between the 'public' and the 'private', and which we may as well call modernisation, is needed if we are to identify and analyse this type of change. Only then can we place both cases within a common framework which enables proper comparisons to be made.[130] One thing that should then be recognised is that the problems of how to handle the growth of a wage-labour force, and its political and economic demands, are perceived and responded to in different ways according to the kind of political culture which exists. One important component of this political culture is the way in which law is produced and enforced. Law is simultaneously an effect and a defining feature of the state. Ultimately the importance of the different legal forms lies in the way they define the state and in turn shape the perceptions and actions of those who both control the state and who are controlled by the state.

Notes

1 For arguments concerning links between law and society see Wieacker, 1974, and Blasius, 1978. On the legal distinction between public and private, see Grimm, 1987

2 On basic rights and constitutional law see Grimm, 1988a; and Grimm, 1988b

3 At the conference to which I first presented these arguments, and in the subsequent commentary published in the book in which an earlier version of this essay appeared, Gerhard A. Ritter suggested that, as Germany was lagging behind Britain it might have been more useful to compare a later period in Germany, for example, 1875–1914, with the period actually considered for Britain. As I have argued in my introduction, such a strategy of comparison depends upon a theory of common stages through which the various cases are presumed to pass. That in turn has to be related to the particular things being compared. If, for example, one was comparing the part played by a mass labour movement in an industrial society, then the later period for Germany would be more appropriate, although there would then be problems as to whether to take the same, later period for Britain or an even earlier period than the one taken here, namely that of the Chartist movement. My concerns were with certain types of legal change and the political relationships between workers and the middle classes at the time of that change, and for that purpose it made more sense to select the same period.

   Another commentator at that conference, Jürgen Kocka, noted that I did not directly address the issue of class formation and politics. The reasons were that these were not directly relevant to an essay on political-legal questions, although related points are touched upon, that it would have taken up too many new issues in a short essay, and that other essays in this book, especially 'Liberalism or Social Democracy?' and that on the labour aristocracy, take up these matters.

4 On constitutional arrangements see Huber, 1960 and Grimm, 1988b. On the various financial powers and conflicts over these see Wehler, 1987b, chapter IV

5 Haupt, 1986. By contrast, political policing was under state, even national control. See Siemann, 1985

6 On local government see Heffter, 1969. On the Prussian city ordinances see Koselleck, 1981. On the three-class franchise in the Rhenish cities see Boberach, 1959. On how oligarchic it could be see Lenger, 1990, pp. 107ff

7 See Hamerow, 1961; Eyck, 1968, chapter 3; Repgen, 1955; Mattheisen, 1976.

8 Huber, 1960, chapters 11 and 12; and documents 108, 108a, and 189–195 in Huber (ed), 1978. For the Prussian constitution of 1850 see Huber, 1963, chapter 2.

9 Huber, 1963, chapters 12 and 13. For the text of the 1871 constitution see Hucko (ed) ,1987

10 See Evans, 1983 for a brief summary of franchise qualifications under the 1832 and 1867 Reform Acts.

11 Generally see Hanham, 1969, especially chapters 3 and 4. On the practice of voter registration see Thomas, 1950.

12 A useful introduction to these complex arrangements is Fraser, 1979.

13 Fraser, 1979. On the general trend of change as well as a number of case studies, see Hennock, 1973.

14 Simon, 1954.

15 Musson, 1972, chapter 3.

16 In the miners' strike of 1984, police and courts did not use recent legislation dealing specifically with trade unions but rather provisions under the criminal law ('behaviour likely to cause a breach of the peace', 'obstructing the police', etc.) along with preventive measures such as interference with free movement along the highways and the setting of highly onerous bail conditions. See Hugo Young, 'The party of law and order that fears its own legislation', the *Guardian*, 21 May 1984 and Tony Gifford & Louise Christian, 'New sheriffs of Nottingham', *The Guardian*, 9 July 1984.

17 Hunt, 1981, p. 267.

18 For the details of these matters see Hunt, 1981, pp. 264–71; Fraser, 1974, especially chapter 8; Brown, 1982, especially pp. 116–19; and Spain, 1991.

19 Ritscher, 1917, especially part IV; Walker, 1971, especially chapter 3, and the appendix, pp. 435–51 which contains an English translation of the law. More generally on the treatment of journeymen combinations in the eighteenth century see Reininghaus, 1984.

20 On actions against journeymen around 1800 see Griessinger, 1981, especially chapter 5. For the texts of the various laws cited see Blanke (ed) *et al.* (eds), n.d., documents 1 and 2; and Huber, 1978, documents 20, 21, and 49.

21 See Huber, 1978, documents 31–3, 42–8.

22 For the law of 1850 see Blanke *et al.* (eds), n.d., document 10. On its use in 1850–1 against workers see Balser, 1962. More generally on legal repression in the 1850s see Offermann, 1979, especially pp. 39–152. For use of state law on associations against workers after 1869 see Albrecht, 1982, especially pp. 33-8.

23 For the text of these clauses see Blanke *et al.* (eds), n.d., document 21.

24 For examples, see Breuilly & Sachse, 1984, especially chapter 8.

25 Generally on the reform agitation see Brock, 1973.

26 Hennock, 1973, Book 1; Behagg, 1983 and 1990.

27 Finer, 1952; Thomas, 1979; Hamburger, 1965.

28 Driver, 1946; Rose, 1970.

29 On resistance to new police forces see Storch, 1975. On forms of action and thought in Chartism related to 'old' constitutional ideas see Parsinnen, 1973.

30 For the example of Salford, see Garrard, 1976.

31 Leys, 1955.

32 See the example of Oldham considered in Foster, 1974.

33 On the innovative features of state reform see the stimulating study by Corrigan & Sayer, 1985.

34 Hennock, 1973.

35 On Chartism generally see Thompson, 1984, and especially chapter 10 'The Chartists and the Middle Class'. On Chartist ideology see Jones, 1983.

36 On the mass platform see Belchem, 1983 and 1985.

37 Foster, 1974 provides examples.

38 Parssinen, 1973; Epstein, 1982.

39 Wiener, 1969.

40 Examples of Birmingham, Leeds and some other large towns are dealt with in Hennock, 1973. See also Fraser, 1976; Garrard, 1983.

41 See Vincent, 1972, though this is for a later period. Nonconformity was an important element in binding together groups in support of the ACLL.

42 On the Reform League, see Harrison, 1965 and Leventhal, 1971. On radical continuities see Joyce, 1991 and Biagini & Reid (eds), 1991. On the passing of the Reform Act see Smith, 1966 and Cowling, 1967. On the revival of reform agitation and its links to franchise reform see Breuilly, Niedhart & Taylor (eds), forthcoming.

43 See Parry, 1986.

44 Hennock, 1973 lays great emphasis upon this. It formed an important element in Joseph Chamberlain's early political career.

45 See Breuilly, Niedhart & Taylor (eds), forthcoming, especially chapter 13.

46 I deal with this at greater length in the essay above, 'Liberalism or social democracy?'.

47 Boberach, 1959.

48 For a convenient survey of the role of labour see Schieder, 1974.

49 Generally on parliaments and parties in 1848 see the large and comprehensive treatment of Botzenhart, 1977.

50 See Hamerow, 1967; Nipperdey, 1983, chapter 4, section 8; and Breuilly, 1981.

51 See Klessmann, 1974.

52 Nipperdey, 1983, chapter 5, section 6.

53 Boberach, 1959.

54 For elections to the Landtag see Hess, 1964. The relatively popular support received by liberals is considered in Langewiesche, 1988.

55 German liberal publicists in the 1850s and 1860s made a great deal of being 'realistic', working with rather than against powerful states, and basing their optimism upon a view of 'actual, historical development'. See Sheehan, 1990, chapters 13 and 14; and Langewiesche, 1988, chapter 3.

56 Generally see Gagel, 1958.

57 As Na'aman has persuasively argued, Na'aman, 1963.

58 Lassalle confessed to this opportunist motive in a letter of 22 April 1863 to Rodbertus. See Lassalle, 1921-5, vol. 6, p. 325.

59 See, for example, the fears expressed by Yorck, a leading figure in the ADAV in Hamburg in a letter reprinted in Na'aman & Harstick, 1975, document 70.

60 See Langewiesche, 1988, chapter 4.

61 On the events of 1866 and the institutional changes it ushered in see Nipperdey, 1983, chapter 6, sections 8 and 9. On Bismarck's motives and actions, with an especial stress upon a *rapprochement* with Liberals, see Gall, 1986, especially pp. 373-458. On liberal responses see Sheehan, 1978; and more specifically, Sheehan, 1973. For a good example of the separation between national and local levels see White, 1967.

62 Place, 1972 and the introduction by the editor, Mary Thrale.

63 For this active role in the 1820s see Prothero, 1979.

64 When a new Masters and Servants Bill was introduced into Parliament in 1844.

65 Prothero, 1971; Thompson, 1984.

66 Simon, 1954; Fraser, 1974.

67 For examples of such statements, see Fraser, 1974, p. 24. However, in 1866–7 the Reform League, and in particular the London Working Men's Association, did succeed in getting political involvement from various of these trade societies. See Breuilly, Niedhart & Taylor (eds) forthcoming, especially chapters 8 to 10 and the sectional introduction to those chapters.

68 Simon, 1954.

69 Langewiesche, 1981.

70 This is taken further in the essay on artisans published in this book.

71 A broad overview of such demands in English is provided in Noyes, 1966, although the analysis is rather static and exaggerates a basic journeyman/master division at the expense of other differences such as occupation or region. For a more recent overview from a different perspective see Lenger, 1988. For the continuation of artisan programmes and organisation into the 1850s and early 1860s see Balser, 1962 and Offermann, 1979.

72 On Owenism, see Harrison, 1969. On Chartist culture and community see Yeo, 1986; and Thompson, 1984.

73 Balser, 1962. Nevertheless, even the most pragmatic leaders such as Stefan Born stressed the construction of organisation rather than the particular aims of organisation. See Friedensburg, 1923.

74 Parssinen & Prothero, 1977; Prothero, 1971; Balser, 1962; Renzsch, 1980. I develop these points at greater length in the essay on artisans published in this book.

75 Recent work has sometimes stressed the positive links between artisanal interests and liberal values: Gall, 1975; Sedatis, 1979; Offermann, 1979 and 1984. But there is very little in 1848 in practical terms to support this view. (Langewiesche, 1981 and 1988.) I deal with this in more detail in the essay below on German and British liberalism.

76 Noyes, 1966. On the language of corporations see Zerwas, 1988. The seminal work is that on France by Sewell, 1980.

77 Offermann, 1979, especially chapter 2; Aldenhoff, 1984.

78 Fraser, 1974.

79 Vogeler, 1984.

80 Porter, 1979.

81 See Breuilly, Niedhart & Taylor (eds), forthcoming, especially chapters 4 to 7 and the sectional introduction to those chapters.

82 Fraser, 1974.

83 The best treatment of these is still Pollard, 1959.

84 Price, 1975.

85 Fraser, 1974, p. 90.

86 Vogeler, 1984.

87 Humphrey, 1913.

88 On benefits and strike functions see the debate between Hanson, 1975 and Hanson, Thane and Musson, 1976; and Musson, 1975 and Thane, 1975.

89 The subject has been well studied. Apart from works already cited, especially Fraser, 1974 and Vogeler, 1984, see the most recent study by Spain, 1991.

90 Harrison, 1965; Leventhal, 1971; Breuilly, Niedhart & Taylor (eds), forthcoming.

91 Harrison, 1960 and 1961.

92 Fraser, 1974; Spain, 1991. Still of interest is Webb & Webb, 1920.

93 Spain, 1991.

94 McCready, 1954.

95 Spain, 1991.

96 See Fraser, 1974 for a summary of the laws of 1875.

97 See above, the essay 'Liberalism or Social Democracy?'.

98 The major work is Engelhardt, 1977. For English language readers, see my lengthy review of this work in *Social History*, 4/2 (May, 1979), pp. 393–7.

99 Sheehan, 1990, chapter 14; Langewiesche, 1988, chapter 3.

100 Engelhardt, 1978.

101 See extracts from the Reichstag speeches of Schweitzer, Sculze-Deltizsch and Wagener in Blanke *et al.*, n.d., document 20.

102 Apart from Engelhardt, 1977 and 1978; see also Machtan, 1978, 1981b, and 1983.

103 Engelhardt, 1978.

104 Eisenberg, 1986.

105 See Machtan, 1983 and 1981b.

106 See the various works by Machtan cited in the previous notes for the detail of this repression as well as Albrecht,1982. On the consequences for the labour movement, especially the pressure 'from below' for the SDAP and the ADAV to unite, see Renzsch, 1980.

107 See above, the essay on artisans.

108 See the essay above on the labour aristocracy for further details on this subject.

109 I deal with some of these arguments in the essay 'Liberalism or social democracy?'. One can go on to make connections to the pattern of strike activity and in turn with long-term developments in working-class formation. See Kocka, 1983 (now translated into English as Kocka, 1986), especially pp. 154-62.

110 I make some suggestions on these matters, especially those concerning religion, in the general essay on liberalism and the essay comparing Hamburg and Manchester.

111 Tenfelde, 1982.

112 It is, of course, difficult to know much about rank-and-file responses to Marxism, but for the situation in German social democracy, especially after 1878, see Lidtke, 1966 and 1985. For a careful study of the reception of Marxism see Steinberg, 1976. For the Wilhelmine period we have better information, though the situation now allowed for more positive participation. For English language readers see the treatment of surveys of workers' attitudes in Moore, 1978. The contemporary survey by Levenstein, 1912 gives good grounds for seeing why Marxist ideas continue to have a hold amongst workers..

113 See Schröder, 1976. The anti-socialist law can also be seen, from the point of view of those in power, as an example of looking at the labour movement in an abstract way and seeking to deny it any participation.

114 See, for example, the form taken by debates on the promulgation of a civil code up to 1896. John, 1989; Kögler, 1974; Martiny, 1976.

115 See my essay 'Liberalism or social democracy?'.

116 I have focused on Prussia and England. A consideration of Baden or of Ireland would present a rather different picture.

117 Hughes, 1985.

118 For the idea of 'central focus' I am indebted to studies of colonial nationalism, especially those undertaken by the 'Cambridge School' of Indian historians. See Seal, 1973 and Low, 1977. For a treatment of European state development in the nineteenth century from the perspective of national integration see the various case studies in Grew, 1978.

119 Plumb, 1969; Hirst, 1975.

120 See Koselleck, 1981 who both reflects this idealist view of the state in his work, and analyses how that view could lead to a particular view about constitutional reform and its relationship to a more general process of reform and progress.

121 This idea in one form is a major theme of Krieger, 1957. For more specific applications of the idea to Germany, especially the notion of a 'dualism' between parliament and state, see Boldt, 1980; Langewiesche, 1981 and 1988; and Grimm, 1988a, especially pp. 138-41.

122 For an interesting attempt to analyse the relationship between state forms, the labour movement and economic development with a number of concepts which permit international comparison see Waismann, 1982. The cases taken for comparison are England and Germany in the age of Disraeli and Bismarck, and twentieth century Argentina.

123 For an interesting sketch of the views of English intellectuals around 1848 who saw the contrast between their own political culture and that of the continent (especially France) in terms of this empirical/abstract (or 'rationalist') distinction see Grainger, 1979. More generally for this as a British/ European distinction see Dyson, 1980.

124 See my comments concerning utilitarianism in the general essay on liberalism below.

125 Max Weber clearly saw the German or continental path as the 'normal' one to modern civil law, and felt it necessary to explain the peculiar but effective English evolution. Weber, 1978, chapter 8, 'Economy and Law (Sociology of Law)', esp. pp. 889–91.

126 Anderson, 1964 and 1965; Nairn, 1964a, 1964b, and 1964c. The term 'Other Countries' is used by E. P. Thompson in his critique of Anderson and Nairn: Thompson, 1965.

127 Blackbourn & Eley, 1984; Grebing, 1986. For some of the early critical response to the German version of Blackbourn & Eley see Wehler, 1981 and Kocka, 1982.

128 This new historicism has been developed at length in Nipperdey, 1983 which I criticise at length in Breuilly, 1984. The 'critical' approach is now being worked out exhaustively in Wehler, 1987and 1987b. A reading of German politics as an instrument of class is developed in Machtan & Milles, 1980. I leave aside the crude Marxist versions developed up to 1990 by East German historians.

129 That is the main problem with Blackbourn & Eley, 1984.

130 The general issues involved are dealt with more explicitly in the introduction and conclusion to this book.

6

Liberalism in mid-nineteenth-century Hamburg and Manchester

Introduction[1]

Liberalism succeeded in nineteenth-century Britain but failed in nineteenth-century Germany. If by that is meant that constitutional and parliamentary government, a free market economy, and toleration of different opinions and beliefs were further advanced in Britain, the point is beyond dispute. If, however, this is attributed to the strength of a distinct liberal movement, then this is something which can usefully be the subject of comparative study. By taking two cities I hope to give such comparison a fresh perspective.

The nature of liberalism in Germany, how it changed over the nineteenth century, and why it largely failed are matters which have been much debated by German historians.[2] In English historiography there has not been the same kind of focused debate because there has not been the same problem of 'failure', but from different perspectives liberalism as an ideology, the extent to which liberal values were realised in practice, above all the way the state functioned, and the political organisation of liberalism have all been considered.[3]

In this essay I will consider some of the issues raised in these debates by a comparison of two cities which arguably were at the forefront of mid-nineteenth-century liberalism in their respective countries. My main interest is in pin-pointing the situations in which liberalism can develop and to explain its impact. Put very broadly and non-historically one might argue that those with power and influence have little interest in increasing the scope of individual freedom, and that those without power and influence have little capacity to extend freedom and in any case generally look to authority to deal with their material problems. To understand the rise of liberalism, a movement concerned with expanding the scope of individual freedom, historians have looked to a special combination of circumstances – above all the formation of middle-class groups which believed that reduction of arbitrary and excessive state power, the extension of freedom of individual economic activity, and toleration of different beliefs were best suited to their own interests as well as being worthwhile ends in themselves. By taking two comparable cities in England and Germany I hope to show precisely what kinds of groups will support liberalism and why they will have more or less success.

There is the initial problem of what is meant by liberalism. Too tight a definition of liberalism can create an overly rigid and normative approach to the subject.[4] Too loose a definition can lead to the jumbling together of very different things.[5] My own approach is to treat liberalism as those movements or organisations which demand reforms that would, in the current situation, expand the degree of individual freedom, or which oppose measures that would diminish the degree of individual freedom. Obviously the definition varies with the challenges liberals confront. There are problems about what is meant by the individual and his freedom and how best to promote it. Finally different liberals can have different priorities. But I think this gives one a general but definite point of departure. Placed in the circumstances of mid-nineteenth-century England and Germany one can be more precise. In the political sphere liberals demanded that government be made accountable to public opinion, above all by granting powers to elected and representative institutions. Also they demanded that the government confine itself so far as possible to providing the framework within which private individuals could conduct their own affairs. In the economic sphere liberals called for the ending of restrictions upon free competition, whether this be exercised by the state, by monopolies, or by privileged corporations. Liberals also called for the toleration of beliefs and freedom to express opinions.

This is a very broad characterisation, even when it is related to the particular circumstances of mid-nineteenth-century Europe. It excludes some whom various historians have treated as liberals. Thus Lothar Gall and those who have followed him in the study of early German liberalism include people who favoured the regulation of individual economic activity for the sake of the community, although those same people also opposed arbitrary government and central state bureaucracy.[6] However, this is a very negative kind of liberalism which wishes merely to substitute illiberal government at a local level for illiberal government at the centre.[7] As the Hamburg example will make clear, non-bureaucratic government at a city level can be highly illiberal.

There is also the problem of how far these different aspects of liberal belief form part of a coherent ideology or movement. One of the features of Gall's argument was to claim that economic liberalism could and did go together with acquiescence in authoritarian government, and that those who struggled hardest for restraints upon arbitrary government did not necessarily accept the principle of unbridled individual economic freedom. Although there is something in this idea, it has been exaggerated and usually those who favoured one aspect of liberalism also favoured the other aspects. Certainly I will treat liberalism as a broad set of views.

To anticipate my main conclusions I will argue that liberalism was a genuinely strong movement in Manchester but a very weak and superficial one in Hamburg. The reasons for this were above all to do with the more favourable initial conditions which obtained in Manchester rather than with the strength of explicit support for a liberal politics. The most important of those initial conditions are to do with the differences in the economies of the cities, with the nature of urban government, and with the relationship between the city and the national political framework. In the next section I will provide a broad comparison of the two cities in the mid-nineteenth century with these three points in mind.

Liberalism has also to be analysed in terms of its social base, its ideology, and its political organisation. In the second section, I will describe the major phases of liberal activity and achievement in the two cities in relation to these three aspects. One specific issue I wish to consider more closely is how far liberalism succeeded in attracting radical and labour support, and that is the concern of the third section. In the conclusion I will offer some explanations for the differences between the two cities and how this can be connected to some of the general debates about nineteenth-century liberalism.

Manchester and Hamburg in the mid-nineteenth century

A personal connection

In October 1847 Richard Cobden was entertained at a lavish banquet in Hamburg.[8] As one of the leading figures of the Anti-Corn Law League (ACLL) Cobden had shared in the great triumph of the Repeal of the Corn Laws in 1846. In 1847 he had made a grand tour through most of Europe, being received by crowned heads of states, high officials, and members of liberal oppositions to established governments. Hamburg was the last stop on his journey.

Cobden was well received in the city because the cause with which he was identified – free trade – was one to which the city was fully committed. Hamburg was also a republican city-state which believed in cheap, even amateur government and low taxes.[9] Cobden himself had made his fortune in the Manchester area. He had first come into politics with the campaign to incorporate Manchester.[10]. Subsequently Manchester formed the headquarters of the ACLL and its political machine dominated the city from the late 1840s and 1850s and into the 1860s. Cobden and his listeners at that banquet clearly believed they had much in common with one another. Many toasts were offered, but the most interesting was that given by Cobden himself: 'To free trade, the source of all other freedoms.' The clear implication was that free trade was to be valued not merely as something good in its own right, but also as establishing the conditions which would enable other freedoms which liberals cherished to be achieved. Both cities preached and practised free trade, but how comparable were they in other respects?

The economies of Hamburg and Manchester

There are no good general economic histories of either city on which to draw so what follows is drawn from a range of more partial studies.[11]

The two cities were of comparable size. Hamburg in 1800 had a population of about 100,000 and this had increased to nearly 200,000 by 1870. Manchester (with Salford) had about 100,000 inhabitants in 1800 and this had increased to about 350,000 in 1870. In both cases the great bulk of this extra population came from net immigration.

a) Manchester

The growth of Manchester was closely linked to that of the cotton industry, and there is no doubt that it was the dramatic increase of cotton manufacturing which provided the basis of the Manchester economy. However, recently historians have insisted that this must not be exaggerated.[12] Artisan workers still outnumbered factory workers in mid-century Manchester. The city functioned in many ways as the regional financial centre for the cotton industry and the bulk of actual manufacturing was carried out in the industrial townships to the north of Manchester. Also the cotton industry generated other types of production, such as textile engineering, which diversified the economy. The city was in many ways the consumer centre for the middle classes of the surrounding townships. All these factors led to a rather complex and diverse occupational structure. This is rather at odds with the image popularised by Charles Dickens and other British as well as European contemporaries depicting the city in terms of a brutal divide between a mass of proletarians and a small class of philistine capitalists.[13] Nevertheless, it was the manufacturing base of the cotton industry which dominated the economy. The merchants who dominated the trading sector of the economy were those who specialised in textile products.

b) Hamburg

Hamburg was not a noted manufacturing centre. If anything it had declined as a manufacturing centre by mid-century in comparison with its situation towards the end of the eighteenth century. The Napoleonic period had shattered production in areas such as sugar. In the post-1815 period the city had prospered with the increase of central European trade with Britain, and with the newly independent states of North and South America. It was entrepot trade from which the city prospered, and it did little to process raw or semi-finished goods for re-export. Although its merchants had their specialisms, the city was not tied primarily to any one kind of product. Lacking political influence beyond the city, these merchants favoured the minimum of government restriction upon trading.[14]

As with Manchester, the Hamburg economy generated a very complex occupational structure. Merchants, both large and small, as well as shipowners, were clearly the economically dominant group. But they only directly employed a minority of the labour force on ships, in docks, and in the counting houses.[15] A large section of the labour force was engaged in the production of articles for daily consumption – food, clothing, furniture, housing, etc. – and in retailing. With the growth of incomes from the mid-century, as well as the development of Hamburg as a regional consumer centre, there developed a wider and more diverse range of consumer production and retailing.[16]

c) General points

Two points can be drawn from this, so far as an analysis of liberalism is concerned. The first is that the centrality of cotton production in the Manchester economy and of entrepot trade in the Hamburg economy both established a presumption in favour of free trade. However, these were very different kinds of presumptions, one based on a particular branch of production, the other on the import and export of a wide range of goods. Second, the complex social structures meant that any successful political movement had to make an appeal which went beyond identification with very specific economic interests. Liberalism could not simply be an affair of factory owners and merchants.

The government and regulation of the two cities

I stress the term 'regulation' in addition to that of government because areas of life were regulated in Hamburg which it would never have occurred to anyone in Manchester to seek to control, and because such controls were not always operated by government in the strict sense of the term.

a) Manchester

Manchester prior to 1839, when it was incorporated, did not possess a coherent set of local government institutions. As a mere township Manchester was subject to the authority of magistrates appointed by the county. Church of England affairs and a good deal of poor relief were regulated by the parish, in which ratepayers had a role in elections to the vestry. A manorial court in the nominal control of the Moseley family had policing and other rights in the town until these were bought out by the new council in 1846. From the late eighteenth century the most important institution had been the Police Commission which was founded in 1792. This was elected on a fairly broad franchise, although as political conflict intensified in the 1820s, participation in the affairs of the Commission were reduced. But the fragmentation of authority can be appreciated by the fact that daytime policing in principle fell under a different authority from night-time policing!

This situation was brought to an end with the incorporation of Manchester in 1839. The city now had its own magistrates, and an elected council. This council took over the responsibilities of the manorial court, the vestry, and the Police Commission. In principle the council could also significantly increase its own powers by special Acts of Parliament concerned with such matters as sanitation, public health and housing.

Three points should be noted which will be taken up later. First, it is impossible to understand the way in which the government of Manchester operated without reference to the national political framework. The county magistracy operated under a national framework of control. The Police Commission was established by Act of Parliament. A key element in the rise of liberalism in Manchester was the successful reform agitation leading to the Reform Act of 1832 which not only created a uniform franchise and a larger electorate but also provided Manchester with representation in the House of Commons. The campaign for incorporation could only take place on the basis of the Municipal Corporation Act and only succeed when recognised by Parliament. Further additions to local government power could be created only by statute. A local politician had to have national connections in order to exert influence.

Second, the alteration in the structure of local government was closely bound up with the rise of a liberal political movement in Manchester. That alteration in turn provided a basis for a new kind of politics to develop. Liberalism then has to be considered not as oppositional politics but, at local government level, as governmental politics after 1839. The securing of a local political base could then lead on to an extension of liberal influence regionally (e.g. by penetrating the county magistracies) and nationally.

Third, the right to participate in Manchester affairs was based purely upon property considerations. People could move freely into the city and once they achieved a certain level of property or income they were automatically entitled to take part in municipal affairs. The only significant political distinction was between those with sufficient property to participate and those without. Where precisely the line was drawn changed over time, above all with the 1832 and 1867 Reform Acts and with the setting up of the council in 1839. The franchise was rather different for parliamentary and council elections.[17]

b) Hamburg

Hamburg was a republican city-state. With the removal of French control in 1815 the old constitution was restored. This confined participation in government to Lutheran citizens. Citizenship was a legal privilege for which one had to apply and was only possessed by a minority of the residents of the city. For some time this only applied to those living in the city proper. Later the two suburbs of St.Pauli and St.Georg were integrated into the city, but it was a long time before the rest of the territory of the city-state received equal treatment. Broadly speaking the rest of the population was divided between residents, immigrants, and special groups such as Jews.[18]

The citizenry as a whole were entitled to participate in the *Bürgerschaft*, a body which needed to approve government proposals before they became law. Executive power rested with the Senate, a body made up of senators appointed for life and chosen by the existing senators as well as some more professional officials. They in turn delegated a good deal of day-to-day affairs to deputations, each headed by a Senator. The Senators were not paid, and indeed only lower-level officials worked full-time at their governmental tasks.[19]

As a state Hamburg sought to control the influx of immigration and imposed increasingly elaborate restrictions in the 1830s and 1840s. Within the city further restrictions were operated by the guilds which had also been restored in 1815. Free trade only applied to the entrepot trade. The manufacture of basic goods for the city remained under guild control and foreign competition was excluded.

This remained the situation until the end of the 1850s, although serious attempts to change it were made in 1848–49.[20] In 1859 the *Bürgerschaft* was abolished and, under a new constitution, replaced by a body partly elected by the citizenry and partly nominated by particular constituencies. In 1865 the guilds were abolished and citizenship became a purely political category which did not carry with it any social or economic privileges.

By contrast with Manchester there was little change in the formal structure of government until the very end of the period under consideration. As a city-state Hamburg was formally independent of any wider political control, although she was a member of the loose German Confederation established in 1815 and had to take into account the influence of more powerful neighbours, above all Prussia. Far more of life was regulated than in Manchester, and citizenship as a consequence carried with it a bundle of religious, social, and economic privileges as well as the right of political participation.

The relation of the city to the nation

a) Manchester

I have already mentioned that Manchester politics cannot be understood without reference to the national political framework. Although a powerful and unified system of urban government was created in conjunction with the rise of liberalism, it always operated within the limits defined and constantly supervised by Parliament. Furthermore, the city lacked any kinds of control over who or what might move in and out of city. This meant, for example, that any attempt to alter social or economic policy involved pressing for change in national policy. Not only free trade, but poor law or banking policy were subjects on which Manchester pressed particular views. It is quite artificial to distinguish between 'local' and 'national' as self-enclosed levels of political action. Clearly *issues* could be local or national, but any politician had to work within both local and national institutions if he wished to be effective.

b) Hamburg

The distinction between local and national makes much more sense for Hamburg. National institutions before 1848 were of minor importance for the city, with a few exceptions such as the German Confederation's treatment of political radicalism. Hamburg had to take account of the views of powerful neighbours such as Prussia, but this was a matter of diplomatic dealings between states. In 1848–49 it did appear as if national institutions might start to impose uniform structures upon various states, but that failed. In the later 1850s there was more uniform regulation of such matters as banking and population movement, but it was still more a matter of inter-governmental agreement than national regulation. Only with unification from 1867 was Hamburg compelled to accept such regulation, and even then she resisted for some years the rules of the North German Confederation on treatment of citizens, and had to be forced into the Customs Union by Bismarck. Despite its limited size and power in relation to territorial states in Germany, Hamburg has to be understood as a city-state, rather than simply as a city.

Liberalism

Manchester

One can distinguish three phases in the development of Manchester liberalism from the 1820s until the 1860s.[21] Until 1839 it was an oppositional politics directed against the dominant Tory/Anglican elite. It registered successes with the 1832 Reform Act, the winning of subsequent parliamentary elections, and church rate reform, but local institutions were still largely out of its control. From 1839 this was no longer the case. The period c.1839–1857 is that of ACLL dominance of local politics and Manchester liberalism. However, that was only a rather fragile dominance. This second period itself can be sub-divided. Up to 1846 the ACLL had a clear objective and rallied Liberals against the government. After 1846 it lacked a clear objective and the temporary eclipse of Toryism encouraged greater conflict within the Liberal camp. From the late 1850s the re-emergence of a two-party system encouraged different kinds of Liberals to come together, though no longer under the aegis of free trade.

In the period after 1815 the main concerns of liberals were with reform of government and of church. Although there was resentment of the corn tariffs introduced during the war years, it was not yet a central issue. Manchester affairs were dominated by a Tory and Anglican elite which controlled the Police Commission and church appointments. It was church matters which were especially controversial and also provided an outlet for opposition. The vestry, a body elected by all rate-payers, could provide a platform for those who wished to end the practice of all paying church rates, whether they were Anglicans or not. Conflict also emerged in the Police Commission which led to its reform in 1828.

Local church and governmental issues were closely tied up with national ones. In

1828 the Test and Corporation Act which disqualified Dissenters from taking part in government was finally repealed (although it had regularly been set aside every year) and in 1829 the bar on Catholics taking a seat in the House of Commons was removed. In part liberal Tories had supported some of these measures. The effect was to produce a crisis within the Tory party and to provide the opportunity for a movement for parliamentary reform to develop. Liberals led the popular movement for reform in Manchester, although it had nothing like the support (or the tensions) to be found in a city such as Birmingham.

Few people in Manchester could oppose any kind of parliamentary reform. Many Tories, although not favouring general reform, believed that Manchester itself should have some direct form of parliamentary representation. But it was naturally Liberals who could claim most success for the actual reforms carried out. On that basis they could obtain support from the new and larger electorate of the town, and they won the first elections of 1832 to the two seats which Manchester had been granted. Thereafter, however, this popular support for liberalism began to decline, as Liberals disputed the need for any further reform, and expressed some sympathy for unpopular issues such as poor law reform or opposition to factory reform. It was in the period following, c.1832–46, especially with the formation of the ACLL, that Manchester liberalism gained its reputation as a narrow middle-class creed devoted to the self-serving dogmas of classical political economy, though we need to see if this reputation was deserved.

Although the Reform Act of 1832 and subsequent election, as well as the successful campaign against church rates in 1834, signalled Liberal advances, local political control still remained out of their hands. However, the 1835 Municipal Corporations Act (itself a product of Liberal influence within the national government) created the opportunity to press for incorporation. With that success in 1839 Liberals went on to capture control from Tories. In the few years that followed, disputes that remained such as over control of policing, the rights of the vestry, and the surviving privileges of the manorial court were all settled in favour of the council. Manchester was now a Liberal stronghold.

For Cobden this achievement was simply the jumping-off point for national political action, as is made clear in the following passage from his pamphlet *Incorporate Your Borough* written as part of his agitation during the incorporation campaign.

The battle of our day is still against the aristocracy. . . The lords of Clumber, Belvoir and Woburn, although they can no longer storm your town, and ransack your stores and shops, at the head of their mailed vassals, are as effectually plundering your manufacturers and their artizans; for, by the aid of their parchment votes and tenants-at-will serfs, they are still enabled to levy their infamous bread tax upon your industry . . . imitate your forefathers by union and cooperation; amalgamate all ranks in your town, by securing to all classes a share of its government and protection; give unity force and efficiency to the intelligent and wealthy community of Manchester, and qualify it by organisation as it is already entitled by numbers to be the leader in the battle against monopoly and privilege. In a word, INCOR-PORATE YOUR BOROUGH.[22]

For Cobden the issue that enabled one to move on from local to national politics was the 'infamous bread tax', that is the Corn Laws. The instrument for effecting that move was to be the ACLL. Cobden and the major Liberal politicians of Manchester now left municipal affairs largely to others, many of them drawn from the smaller retailers and craftsmen. The ACLL was turned into the most sophisticated political pressure group of the day. It sought to build upon a sense of values which went far beyond any appeal to narrowly conceived economic interests. For Cobden and many like him, as the passage above from his pamphlet makes clear, the abolition of the bread tax was invested with almost utopian significance. It was seen in terms of an heroic class struggle in which the forces of progress and productiveness led by the new industrial cities defeated the reactionary parasites led by the landed aristocracy. Cobden believed that this would not only transform government and society in Britain; it would also transform relations between states. Free trade would remove the basis for commercial warfare, and the destruction of the aristocracy the basis of wars of prestige.[23]

The work of the ACLL has been well documented and in any case takes us beyond a specific concern with Manchester.[24] A few general remarks will suffice. First, the ACLL resolutely resisted the temptation to be drawn into the pursuit of varied goals such as franchise or currency reform. This did help give the organisation a constant and precise aim which was a source of strength in the rapidly changing political climate of the 1840s. Clearly, at a national level one cannot identify liberalism with the ACLL. This is above all the case when, after the repeal of the Corn Laws in 1846 those involved in the ACLL faced the problem of where to go now that their objective had been achieved. For those for whom the abolition was an end in itself there was no need to continue political activity. For those for whom the abolition was bound up with more general issues of political and social reform, there was the shock of realising that not as much had changed as a consequence of repeal as had been expected.

However, it is less easy to separate the ACLL from liberalism generally within Manchester. Here the ACLL had built up a political machine named after the building in which it was located, Newall's Building. From there men like George Wilson kept their finger on the local political pulse and ensured that Cobden and other national leaders were kept in touch with their political base. The machine organised the national affairs of the ACLL – the production of newspapers and other propaganda material, the fighting of parliamentary by-elections and general elections, the dealings with other political organisations. It also maintained control over local politics – selecting candidates for the two, later three, Manchester seats, registering voters, and running the campaigns. Furthermore, it exercised great influence over the politics of the whole region. Even after 1857 and the parliamentary defeats of Bright and Cobden the old ACLL organisation continued to exercise influence, recovering its position in the elections of 1859 and dominating the revived reform movement of the 1860s.[25]

On this basis it might be easy to equate Manchester liberalism with the ACLL, and to see that liberalism as clearly dominating the politics of the city. Such a successful politics could be understood in one of two ways. One way would be to treat it as representing the economic interests of the city, in particular its businessmen. The broader claims of the movement could be regarded as ideology, possibly sincerely believed by those businessmen, but effective only for so long as that selfish economic interest was satisfied. The other way would be to understand it as expressing the general value-system of a new society; a value system which extended beyond the dogmas of political economy and utilitarianism and which, therefore, could call upon far wider support than that of the business community. However, what both views have in common is the sense of a militant and dominant political movement, even if it is one which loses some of its momentum after 1846.[26]

However, a closer analysis reveals a more complex picture. The political dominance of liberalism, and in particular of the ACLL brand of liberalism, was far more fragile than first appearances might suggest. In the by-election of 1839, for example, the very year of success in the incorporation campaign, the Liberal candidate only just scraped home against the Tory. In 1857 the liberal movement in Manchester split, and two free trade candidates fought two Palmerstonian Liberals, while the Tories did not put up any candidates. The Palmerstonians won decisively. By 1868, under the new conditions of the Reform Act of 1867, there were three seats for Manchester and each voter had two votes. The votes had to be cast for two different candidates, but the voter could choose to cast only one vote, a practice known as 'plumping'. Six candidates stood – three Liberals, two Conservatives, and an independent liberal. The Conservatives came first and fourth; the official Liberals came second, third, and fifth. What is more, of the two Liberals returned to Parliament, one was a free trade liberal and the other a Palmerstonian.

This indicates a number of points. First, there remained throughout the period a significant degree of support for the Conservative Party. Second, free trade liberalism had only limited support even amongst those prepared to vote for a representative of the broad Whig/Liberal spectrum.

Gatrell's analysis of the 1839 by-election reveals that within the category of big businessmen there was more support for the Conservative candidate than for the Liberal. It was amongst shopkeepers and craftsmen that the Liberal had the greatest support and these were the groups who ensured liberal success. The crisis of the early 1840s might have induced otherwise Conservative businessmen to shift towards supporting the abolition of the Corn Laws, but in the changed economic circumstances of the 1850s and 1860s those same businessmen were more likely to look to the aggressive foreign and commercial policy of Palmerston in the Far East than to the extension of free trade agreements with other European states for a resolution of their economic problems.[27]

Partly the period of Liberal dominance concealed the continuity of splits between Liberal Dissent and Tory Anglicanism which had also informed the political conflicts of the 1820s. Partly the Liberals were able to ride on the success of the 1832 Reform Act and incorporation which both boosted the political status of the city. Partly liberalism took up a range of issues in the 1830s – cheap government, poor law reform – which appealed to the lower elements of the electorate. Partly the specific crisis of the early 1840s gave the free trade argument a particular relevance. Finally, the construction of a political machine enabled free trade Liberals to turn that fragile political pre-eminence into a more enduring form, although by the mid-1850s even such organisation could not always hold out against the pressure for more active government policy.

However, that had nothing to do with bourgeois 'acquiescence' to more aristocratic and illiberal values, but rather with a change of perception of self-interest in which imperial power rather than free trade became central. Militant dissent did decline within the Manchester bourgeoisie but this is better explained by economic success rather than by more elaborate theories of ideological subordination.[28] Such a decline in militancy and utopianism also took place in conservative and labour political ideology around mid-century. There still remained an emphasis upon self-help, hard work, very limited internal state intervention, limited and cheap government, and arguably these bourgeois values were now the dominant ones.[29] What had gone was the sense of embattled isolation against aristocratic forces, but more because it was felt these had been overcome rather than because there had been any surrender to them.[30] As this more generalised form of liberalism came to inform the basic organisation of society and government, so did liberalism cease to take so narrow and precise a political form as it had assumed earlier.

More difficult to relate to the rise and strength of liberalism is its cultural aspect. One must remember that in 1820 one is still dealing with a rather volatile, amorphous middle class. The old image of all the successful merchants and manufacturers being first-generation examples of self-made men has been questioned. Nevertheless, there were many new men. Furthermore, as we have seen, until 1839 the city lacked political institutions around which a distinct middle-class identity could focus. There was a Chamber of Commerce, but this also was a limited institution. More important for bringing middle-class men of liberal views together were a variety of voluntary institutions. Increasingly historians are realising that it is the character of these institutions which provide the key to the 'making of the middle-class'. However, as yet we lack any broad study of these various institutions for Manchester.[31] All I can do here is make some fairly speculative points.[32]

Perhaps the most important element binding middle-class groups together was religion. Liberal Anglicanism and dissenting Protestantism played a central role in shaping the values of Manchester Liberals, defining the issues on which they organised, and providing the social ties which could form the jumping-off point for political activity. The Unitarians, for example, based on two chapels in the city, played a role in liberalism out of all proportion to their numbers. These religious affiliations had two other important effects. They *divided* middle-class, especially upper-middle-class, groups in Manchester. After all, the reason the liberal cause, especially on matters such as church privilege and the role of religious instruction in elementary schools, was so active was because it faced opponents. But they also *connected* the leading political figures to various strands of lower middle-class and working-class support.

Also important were a variety of secular voluntary associations. Some had a clearly broad political function such as the Athenaeum (which was to sponsor various worthy causes), the Mechanics Institute, and the Statistical Society which gathered data on social problems. But even here one must bear in mind that these did not just express pre-existing solidarities and values, but played a vital role in creating them.

Other associations had a less obvious political import. The Royal Manchester Institute, for example, was concerned with the promotion of design and art by means of education, collection and exhibition. What is clear is that in quite a short time after its beginning in 1823 the RMI became a forum for middle-class sociability and for the cultivation and promotion of distinctly modern, bourgeois tastes in the arts. The visit of Prince Albert to the city in 1857, cited earlier, can from this angle be given a rather different significance from that of capitulation to the values of tradition. Albert had played a vital role in defining the agenda of the Royal Arts Exhibition of 1857. But when one looks at that role closely, it should be seen as a way of helping the middle-classes of Manchester to generalise their values beyond the local, and as a way of helping to establish a confident claim to cultural leadership.

In conclusion, one can see that divisions within the middle classes, the loose and diverse range of voluntary associations in which liberal values are developed, as well as the changing political and economic context could all appear to render liberalism a rather fragile movement. On the other hand, conflict gave definition to liberalism. Religious and cultural activity helped extend liberalism socially and rooted it in something more enduring than political controversy or economic interest and the loose network of associations meant that it was not overly dependent upon one particular organisation. The ACLL retained its influence not so much because of its particular organisational resources, though that was of importance in elections, but because it could build upon this diffuse commitment to liberal values.

I will return in the next section to the question of what this meant for the relationship between liberalism and the labour movement.

Hamburg

To begin with we must distinguish sharply between support for free trade and any more general form of liberalism. No-one in Hamburg disputed the need for the unhindered flow of imports and exports on which the city depended. In the immediate post-1815 period Hamburg benefitted from concluding most-favoured nation treaties with South American countries and from the flow of goods between western and eastern/central Europe. The key point is whether there was support for establishing *general* economic freedom. To do this it would be necessary to abolish the guilds and the ban on imports of major articles of consumption. It would also be necessary to divorce the right to establish a business from the political privileges of citizenship. Hamburg only extended such economic rights beyond the citizenry by means of special concessions to certain categories of people (e.g. merchants from countries with which the city had concluded trade agreements or Jewish merchants and bankers), rather than opening up such rights to all comers. Of course, such a radical move would also have destroyed the existing nature of citizenship. Additionally it would have led on to divorcing citizenship from religious belief and establishing some kind of representative government. Admittedly Hamburg did not possess a privileged patriciate, as many other large cities in Germany did. Anyone with wealth would acquire citizenship, or least quasi-citizenship rights. Nevertheless, these rights took the form of privileges for which one had to apply to the government; not as in Manchester, where rights automatically flowed from certain levels of wealth-holding.

Put very bluntly, a liberal in the Hamburg context would be someone who demanded general freedom to practise a trade, religious emancipation (especially Jewish emancipation), and representative government. Measured in that way there was no liberal movement of importance before the 1840s. Few had disagreed with the decision to restore the old constitution once the French had been removed from the city. The French had imposed a liberal system, but the occupation had been so strongly associated with catastrophe that there was strong support for sweeping away all traces of it. The overwhelming desire was to return to 'good, old Hamburg'.

In the 1820s there was some limited pressure for liberal reform but it had little influence. The city was little affected by the disturbances of 1830/31.[33] The response to increased immigration in the late 1820s and early 1830s was to try to *increase* controls: citizenship was made more exclusive and extra bureaucratic supervision of immigrants, servants, and the population as a whole was introduced. In the mid-1830s the rights of the guilds were renewed. The main objections to these measures were purely sectional. For example, some of the citizenry objected to immigration controls insofar as they also involved surveillance of their own children. Some non-guild workers objected to guild controls. But there was little objection on liberal grounds. There were a few Jews calling for emancipation, but they received little support either from within the Jewish communities or from the Christians of Hamburg.[34]

This changed in the 1840s. In Germany generally there was a relaxation of state control over freedom of expression and association. In Hamburg the crisis caused by the great fire of 1842 and its aftermath led to the formation of various associations, some demanding constitutional reform along liberal lines.[35] For the first time there were clear material interests at stake, for example over questions of the costs of rebuilding the burnt-out parts of the city. This was only part of the general need for an urban 'modernisation' programme – sewage, water supply, railway line and station, dock and harbour improvements, etc. as well as public building projects such as the Town Hall and Exchange designed to raise the prestige of the city.[36]

The reform movement did not succeed before 1848, but in the period 1842–48 a liberal opposition did take shape, a rudimentary 'public opinion' was formed, and a range of groups such as lawyers, artisans, property-owners, and Jews were able to develop some organisation. It was also at this time that a dissenting Protestant movement, based on German Catholicism and 'free communities' began to emerge, even if limited in numbers and organisation compared to Manchester.[37] This movement could draw upon a diverse lower-middle class support and had contacts with other oppositional, radical liberal groupings such as the Workers Educational Association.[38] Some of the modern studies such as those by Prelinger and Paletschek have focused on the connections to early feminism; others such as that by Eger on the theological issues involved. There still remains scope for the connections to be made to the rise and decline of a popular liberalism. How far these Hamburg endeavours paralleled or had connections with similar developments in other parts of Germany is also a matter requiring further research. Finally, there were some connections between these radical and reforming elements and the city elites. The Workers' Educational Association, for example, was able to get established only under the patronage of the long established Patriotic Society. This did, however, create tensions as well.

What this all meant was that, with the outbreak of revolution in 1848 these groups were in a position to come together, to lead the movement for reform in the city, and to dominate the work of the newly formed constitutional assembly – the Konstituante. This body did clearly outline a liberal programme: an end to the guilds, the construction of representative government, and the acceptance of the Basic Rights worked out by the liberal majority within the German National Assembly meeting in Frankfurt. Within the Konstituante the different groups – moderate liberals, more radical democrats, and some artisans in favour of government action to deal with 'social' questions – were able to cooperate broadly along the lines set out by the liberals.

However, there was opposition. The governmental and merchant elites had no particular desire to see fundamental constitutional change. Guild masters and those with secure property or business in the city were not anxious to see the removal of all restrictions on potential competitors. It was possible to appeal to such sentiments and interests. But although the Hamburg Senate deliberately sought to delay and sabotage the programme of constitutional change[39], the real cause of failure lay in the more general defeat of the revolution, especially at the hands of Prussia.

Reaction proceeded less ferociously in Hamburg than in many other parts of Germany. The Worker's Educational Association, for example, was allowed, uniquely for an organisation of its political character and importance, to continue to exist. However, it had to become a-political, and that required internal suppression of political activity in order to prevent a ban. The dissenting Protestant communities were dissolved, as well as various educational institutions connected with them.

By the late 1850s, in more favourable conditions, the coalition of forces which had sustained liberalism in 1848 began to re-emerge. However, certain ingredients, such as a dissenting Protestant tradition, were no longer of importance. In place of the rather radical liberal tendencies of the 1840s which had a good deal of lower middle-class support, there now emerged a more moderate, secular liberalism under the control of the educated bourgeoisie. This became clear in the Schiller centenary celebrations of 1859. The organisers clashed with the Lutheran conservatives of the Senate, who refused to allow celebrations on Thursday, 10 November as this was a religious holiday, the Day of Repentance (*Buß- und Betttag*). When the celebrations went on in the following three days, on a scale unseen since 1848, leadership lay in the hands of lawyers, teachers, headmasters, doctors, etc. The organisers in turn dominated the elections to the new Constituent Assembly, held on the following Monday.[40]

This emergence of a moderate, secular cultural liberalism can be linked to the political and economic developments of the period. The rapid growth of the city and the need for labour, skills and capital from immigrants had also rendered the existing constitution increasingly unworkable. Although the 1859 constitution provided some privileged protection for particular groups, it did recognise the need for a representative component to government.

However, the decisive changes came about more through pressure from outside. Economic development had rendered the guilds pointless and they were finally abolished in 1865. Hamburg still tried to control the influx of population, and only under pressure from Prussia after the setting up of the North German Confederation did Hamburg finally give up its control of immigration.[41]

So for a long period liberalism remained a very weak force within Hamburg. The merchant commitment to free trade extended no further than the entrepot trade of the city. Subordinate groups found it difficult to organise against this illiberal merchant and governmental elite except when more general conditions in Germany favoured such organisation. Insofar as a popular movement based on a variety of religious and secular associations had formed between 1842 and 1848, it was disrupted and in part repressed by the failure of 1848. The liberal movement which had developed by the mid-1860s was much more secular and upper middle-class dominated, with a programme which centred on a rather vague national programme. This movement was to prove weak in the face of popular grievances and was ready to capitulate to the first challenges it confronted. This is the subject of the next section.

Liberalism and the radical and labour movement

Manchester

In the agitation of 1831–32 liberals, radicals and working men's groups formed a broad coalition. Where the popular element appeared particularly powerful, one already finds some middle-class hesitancy and retreat, as in Birmingham, but this was less marked in Manchester. Generally there was little middle-class fear of popular politics. The only significant disturbance had been the 'Peterloo massacre' of 1819. Briefly in 1842 the spectre of mass strikes also meant that political conflict within the Manchester middle class was overshadowed by fear of working-class action, but the moment soon passed.

There are two different reasons for this middle-class indifference to working-class politics and any radical challenge. One was the confidence that causes taken up by middle-class groups could also attract working-class support. The other was that any independent working-class politics could fairly easily be kept under control.

So far as the first is concerned I have already noted that the reform agitation of 1831–32 drew upon worker support. Working men and radicals were disappointed with the limited franchise granted by the Reform Act. They were disenchanted with the way many of the middle-class reformers now declared themselves satisfied with the new franchise. Finally, the actions of the Whig Governments of the early and mid-1830s created a good deal of hostility. Nevertheless, there remained causes on which the liberal movement could draw popular support. In some Lancashire towns, for example, the issue of church rates aroused popular passion. John Bright's popularity in Rochdale had much to do with this issue, and in the 1830s vestry elections could mobilise more people than parliamentary elections.[42] Liberals supported a policy of conciliation towards Catholics in Ireland. In a city like Manchester where O'Connell's Home Rule movement could draw on the support of numerous Irish workers, this could mean substantial worker support for Liberal politics. Finally, one should remember that many activists in the ACLL stressed its radical ambitions and that this was accepted by many workers. Indeed someone like John Bright later turned to the cause of further franchise extension because he believed the middle classes had betrayed that radical cause and one needed to look to workers to continue with it.[43] What all this meant was that in Manchester, when popular politics boiled over, as in 1838–39 and in 1842, the ACLL could arguably call upon as much working-class and radical support as the Chartists. From 1846 until 1866 radicalism largely remained a detached political position which sometimes cooperated and sometimes conflicted with other strands of the liberal movement.

In fact in Manchester independent working-class organisation was fairly weak and this reduced the social base of that radical tradition. The labour force was highly diversified and conditions for effective trade unionism were poor apart from certain skilled occupations such as engineering and cotton spinning.[44] The Chartist movement in Manchester tended to be led by people from very miscellaneous backgrounds and they had something of a declassé, adventurer quality about them. Their politics was more the expression of big-city radical culture than of solidary working-class organisation. They were only effective in association with middle-class political movements. Again, it must be remembered that the middle class was itself politically split. Hostility to the New Poor Law of 1834 was shared by Tory Anglicans as well as Chartists. Chartists could condemn ACLL opposition to factory reform as proof of a selfish business interest, but the Ten Hours movement failed initially more because of the issue of denominational control of children's education at factory schools. Middle-class political splits, rather than providing greater opportunities for workers to press their own political demands, actually served instead to shape conflict amongst workers themselves, and was predicated upon the absence of any serious threat from below.

Partly this was a consequence of the very diverse structure of the Manchester population. In towns north of Manchester where particular industries dominated and manual, even factory, wage-labour was a far higher proportion of the total labour force, it was easier to generate solidary trade union and working-class political movements, even if these were not always particularly radical.[45]

After 1846/48 both the success of the ACLL and the failure of Chartism encouraged Manchester politics to revert more clearly to conflicts within the middle class between different kinds of liberalism and radicalism. I have already briefly touched on the forms this took in the mid-1850s, especially with the free trade Liberals losing the election of 1857. The greater prosperity of the post 1850 years reduced the fear of popular or radical politics even further. Changes in the nature of policing, for example, suggest that there was less fear of working-class districts and more concern to focus specifically upon crime and to elicit cooperation from working-class communities.[46] The New Poor Law was not enforced so harshly as had once been feared. There was rather more middle-class philanthropy than perhaps the image of hard-faced employers would lead one to expect.[47] In additional employer paternalism and power could create the basis for labour support for conservatives as well as liberals.

Against this background, the renewal of a movement for further franchise extension in the 1860s could serve to bring liberals closer to radicals and organised workers. There were already examples of the continued strength of popular liberalism in the late 1850s and early 1860s in the way in which elements associated with the ACLL continued to play a leading role in movements such as the anti-slavery campaign during the American Civil War.[48]

The maintenance of this liberal hold over popular politics was not an easy or smooth process. The moderate franchise extension envisaged in a proposal such as Russell's household franchise bill represented a totally different political view from that embodied in the People's Charter or in the demands for universal manhood suffrage that were still pressed in the 1850s. A good example of the way in which working-class radicalism and middle-class liberalism could come together is pro-vided by the events leading to the adoption of Ernest Jones as an official Liberal candidate for the General Election of 1868.[49]

Ernest Jones had become well-known while still a very young man as a particu-larly radical Chartist leader.[50] In 1848 and the years that followed he had become a friend of Karl Marx. The first English tranlation of *The Communist Manifesto* was actually published in a periodical edited by a close associate of Jones, G. J. Harney.[51] In the 1850s he continued to play a prominent part in radical and trade union affairs, partly through use of his skill as a lawyer. In certain ways he was a similar figure to Ferdinand Lassalle. It was a similarity which struck some contemporaries.

The great orator of the party was Ferdinand Lassalle. I always couple him in my own mind with my early friend Ernest Jones, the great Chartist leader. Lassalle was a man of essentially the same type, a great orator, a poet, a linguist and to a certain extent a statesman.[52]

The argument could be taken further. Both used their legal training to appear as 'advocate for the people'. Both suffered terms of imprisonement which enhanced their standing in the eyes of their working-class supporters. Both fit the type of the gentleman radical. It was their very distance from the working class, their aban-donment of their 'own' class in the name of social justice, their 'Robin Hood' character which in part accounted for their hold over their supporters.

But in one vital respect the last stage of their political careers diverges. Lassalle founded an independent party aimed against middle-class liberalism whereas Jones abandoned his independent stance for cooperation with middle-class liberalism. The reason for this appears basically simple – faced with a choice between con-tinuing impotent isolation or influence within a coalition that had a real chance of exercising power, Jones finally opted for compromise and influence. Already in the culmination of the franchise agitation in 1865–66 Jones had cooperated with middle-class franchise reformers like John Bright and his brother Jacob, giving up some of the demands of the People's Charter in the process. With the passing of the Reform Act in 1867 Jones and his supporters demanded their reward – adoption as a Liberal candidate.[53]

Under the terms of the Reform Act the urban electorate was considerably expanded. Furthermore, Manchester had been granted a third seat, although every voter continued to have only two votes as before. The idea behind the 'Minority

Clause' which created this situation as well as allowing voters to 'plump' (i.e. casting only one of their votes for one candidate rather than one vote for each of two candidates) was that Tories hoped that the minority of the electorate supporting them could concentrate their votes on one or two candidates, while the Liberals would seek to win all three seats with their usual electoral majorities in the urban constituencies. This could lead to one Tory being returned for such constituencies. The response of the Liberals was to try to organise the voting of their supporters in such a way as to ensure that votes were divided evenly for their three candidates so that all of them were returned. Both the Tory and the Liberal strategy called for very effective electoral management.[54]

For Manchester Liberals the adoption of Jones as the third Liberal candidate could attract new working-class voters not only to his candidacy but to those of the other two official Liberal candidates. In return Jones could hope to attract middle-class Liberal votes as well as the support of the Liberal political machine. But it was not a painless agreement. Jones had to promise to speak in support of Liberals in other consituencies even (or rather, from a Liberal standpoint, especially) where no radical Liberal was standing, but often where the Liberals were opposed by an independent radical. Thus Jones had to turn publicly against his own radical and Chartist past. Furthermore, in some of his speeches in Manchester he also sought to tone down that past in order to avoid alienating middle-class voters. He could not take this too far, because that in turn could alienate working-class voters. It required a difficult, if not impossible balancing act. On the other hand, Liberals were risking the loss of middle-class voters repelled by the association with Jones.

There was then a fine balance of costs and benefits to be calculated. A number of factors pushed these politicians towards hostile cooperation. First, both sides had votes and organisation which they could make available to the other, and the fear that without those resources they could lose the election. Second, there were shared concerns on such questions as Ireland, the Church of England, state schools, and land reform which united them against the Conservatives. I argue in a more general way in the essay 'Liberalism or Social Democracy?' that this agreement on non-class issues as well as hard-headed compromise between parties with something to offer each other was the key to the success of 'Lib-Lab' politics.[55]

That provided the basis for cooperation, but it did not guarantee success. Jones came fifth in the poll and one of the Tory candidates came first. The Liberals had not been able to manage their voters sufficiently well. Partly this was a matter of organisation. Partly it was because many middle-class liberal voters were simply not prepared to vote for Jones, whatever their leaders may have advised. In fact, Jones and his supporters argued bitterly that the Liberal leadership had actually helped to sabotage his candidacy. On the other hand, some Liberals accused Jones of losing them middle-class votes and thus allowing a Tory to head the poll. There is also some indication that Birley, the successful Tory candidate, attracted some working-class support in areas where his standing as an employer had an influence.

Finally, Jones attracted bitter attacks from labour and radical activists for betraying the Chartist tradition.[56]

The cooperation had involved risks and on this occasion the calculation had gone slightly awry. But it may have been only slightly, because there is the (unprovable) possibility that without that cooperation both Liberals and Jones would have fared even worse. Probably the majority of the new working-class voters in Manchester and other urban constituencies in Lancashire voted Liberal rather than Conservative, even if the region was generally more Conservative than other parts of the country. Popular toryism was to develop far more on the basis of the lower middle classes of suburbia. But that Lib-Lab coalition was not an easy or a one-sided relationship. If it had been easier to achieve, it would have undermined the position of conservatism far more in 1868. However, if it had been much harder to achieve, if neither side had had anything to offer to the other, then it would have stimulated a much earlier development of independent labour organisation. As it was, the process of hostile cooperation contributed to sustaining the pattern of two-party political conflict for some considerable time.

Hamburg

By the late 1850s a liberal movement was beginning to take form in Hamburg.[57] However, this rapidly declined in the mid- and late 1860s. By the time the Second Empire had been founded Hamburg politics had polarised between illiberal social democracy and oligarchic national liberalism. Popular liberalism of the kind which prospered in many English cities at this time was in Hamburg squeezed between these opposing political camps. Yet Hamburg, a trading rather than an industrial city with a large and diverse wage-labour class as well as lower middle class, would have appeared to present ideal conditions for such popular liberalism. Why did organised labour move decisively away from liberals and towards Lassallean politics and subsequently class-based social democracy? Why did bourgeois politics move so sharply into a conservative direction, leaving liberal politics in a fairly weak central position, more concerned with local than national issues?

One set of explanations can focus on the appeals of Lassalleanism and conservative politics. Lassallean politics could be taken up by a new generation of labour leaders, hostile to the entrenched position of those who had come to dominate the Workers' Educational Association, the cooperative societies, and other such institutions. The greater continuity of such institutions in Hamburg following the failure of 1848 compared to states like Prussia created greater scope for such generational conflict. These new men had no experience of the dangers of independent, radical action that was the legacy of 1848. Rather they were more conscious of the way in which middle-class liberals patronised them and sought to gain their support without committing themselves in turn to providing workers with a proper role within liberal organisations or to genuine democratic political reform. The simple Lassallean programme of universal suffrage and state-funded producer cooperatives provided an attractive alternative position. The turn to open public meetings and the appeal to the 'working class' beyond the membership of existing labour organisations could offer to these activists strategies for breaking the control of the older men who ran those organisations.

But although there is something in these arguments, it is a fairly narrow explanation which accounts only for the actions of a minority of activists. It does not explain why many workers followed those activists. At the other extreme a 'deep' explanation would involve looking for processes of working-class formation within the city which would in turn underpin the turn to class politics. However, it is difficult to see any obvious support for this argument in terms of new kinds of industrial production, or sharp increases in the size of existing firms, or marked changes in the social geography of the city. Support for Lassalleanism came from the same kinds of artisan trades which had previously dominated labour movement politics.[58]

There is a third kind of explanation which focuses on more limited institutional and conjunctural changes. One could argue that certain artisan trades had been 'proletarianised' through the penetration of merchant capital which did not express itself in any dramatic change in the crude occupational statistics.[59] This could explain the attraction of ideas of state-help and producers cooperatives, as Renzsch has argued for similar trades in Berlin at this time.[60]

This in turn could be linked to more formal institutional changes. In the decade 1859–69 liberalism had *succeeded* in transforming many important institutions both in Hamburg and more generally in Germany. In Hamburg a form of representative government had been created, citizenship narrowed down to a political category, immigration controls considerably reduced, and guilds abolished. In the North German Confederation a parliament based on universal manhood suffrage had been created and the liberal majority within that parliament had liberalised banking and currency, freedom of expression and political organisation, freedom for workers and employers to organise.

This had a marked effect upon the labour movement. In conjunction with an economic upswing which had already sparked off a wave of strikes in Hamburg, the permissive provisions of the north German *Gewerbeordnung* of 1869 encouraged a further expansion of strike activity.[61] In this situation the unconditional Lassallean support for such strikes (even if purely instrumental and in contradiction to their own economic ideas) was more attractive than the more qualified support from liberal and other labour organisations. The mass electorate for Reichstag elections provided an impetus to Lassallean methods of political agitation and shattered established patterns of politics.

One can also apply these kinds of explanations to the middle-class component of liberalism. The penetration of merchant capital and competition into craft occupations stimulated an illiberal response from self-employed artisans in some trades, although this has probably been exaggerated. Former radicals like Wilhelm Marr now turned towards more populist, anti-semitic ideas. The strike wave provoked fears of working-class action and pushed bourgeois opinion towards support for authoritarian responses.

However, I think perhaps the most fundamental bourgeois concern was to do with the sense of a loss of control. The response of the Hamburg elites to problems such as excessive immigration in earlier periods was to increase regulation of the population.[62] By the 1850s this was increasingly ineffective and pressure from states such as Prussia compelled Hamburg to give up various of these controls. The liberalisation of the 1860s had completed this process. What is more, it had done so in the context of war and the violent reorganisation of the German political system. The elites of Hamburg had never tried to build a popular political base for their rule but had depended on policing and paternalism and prosperity. Now much of those regulative powers had very suddenly been taken from their hands and they had been plunged into a situation in which mass mobilisation of workers played a prominent role.

Without any tradition of building popular support and deprived of many of its earlier controls it was natural that these middle-class groups cast about for some other response. They found it in the cooperation between Bismarck and national liberalism which blocked the growth of legitimate mass politics at state level and began to undo some of the freedoms which liberalism had achieved during the 1860s. In the same way, the lack of any popular liberal tradition also meant that the labour movement also had little interest in building the kind of consensus needed for a multi-class politics. Even the middle-class and worker politicians who tried to take this route did not have the time or the values which would allow them to work out new methods. They remain locked into postures of opposition to 'demagogy', 'unreasonable strikes', too rapid an extension of the vote, hostility to 'state-help' rather than 'self-help'. Finally, neither side had anything to gain from cooperation. Trade unions were still too weak to compel compromises from employers. The mass electorate could not be handled through careful adjustments and deals of the kind attempted in Manchester in 1868. There was no prospect of obtaining power through cooperation betwen liberals and labour after Bismarck had split the liberal movement in 1867. It made more sense for middle-class groups to look to agreements with the powers in Berlin, and for working-class groups to try to build up a new position within the mass urban electorate for the national parliament, than for the two sides to try to work together.

One should not exaggerate the polarisation. Within Hamburg there remained important differences between lower middle-class interests in cheap government and a static economy and a merchant interest in growth and development. In local politics the emergent socialist party was by no means closed off from middle-class radicalism and in turn received some lower middle-class electoral support.[63] But that lower middle-class interest could hardly connect itself to broader currents of liberalism beyond Hamburg, so it remained a very limited politics. As Hamburg did develop into a major industrial centre from the 1880s, its polarised politics were reinforced by the class divisions of industrial society. But one should always remember that Hamburg was the 'Hochburg' of social democracy long before social democracy in Hamburg became the politics of the industrial working class. Also oligarchic national liberalism was the politics of free trade merchants long before it was taken up by protectionist and anti-trade union industrial employers.

Conclusion

There are four themes I wish to consider: the context within which liberalism operated in the two cities, the social and ideological character of liberalism in the two cities, the way in which liberalism was influenced by the relationship to the broader national and international situation, and the political form taken by liberalism.

The city context

Both cities had a good deal of autonomy. From 1839 the Manchester council was a powerful institution under liberal control. Hamburg was a city-state, though its autonomy declined rather than increased during the period. In both cases the business community had a particularly powerful influence over city government. In both cases that business community largely favoured cheap government and free trade. In both cities there was a diverse 'middling' population of artisans, shopkeepers, small businessmen, and skilled craftsmen with an interest in broadening political participation and influence beyond urban elites. Yet in Hamburg the only kind of 'liberalism' to succeed was that of an oligarchic kind which depended upon narrow political participation in city government and alliance with established authority in Berlin. In Manchester, by contrast, a diverse and often conflicting coalition of forces nevertheless succeeded in maintaining local control and exercising national influence through the political mobilisation and organisation of a broad liberal movement.

Part of the reason is that initial conditions in Manchester were far more favourable to popular liberalism. The inability to regulate locally social and economic conditions prevented the development of sectional politics aiming to use such powers of regulation to benefit particular interests. Furthermore, the corporate nature of government in Hamburg inhibited the development of a politics of open debate and choice which is most congenial to liberalism. National pressure – censorship, political policing, etc. – also had this effect. Manchester was used to debate in newspapers. Elections were a part of the political process – not just to the post-1832 House of Commons and the council set up in 1839, but also to the vestry and to the Police Commission earlier. Only through the construction of broad political coalitions could one hope to have influence.

The social and ideological character of liberalism

Free trade is not the essence of liberalism. In Hamburg it was a very narrow and pragmatic position which was not even extended to the economy generally. In Manchester it was something which the business community took up only pragmatically and with particular enthusiasm in the first half of the 1840s. In economic terms it did not involve major changes in Britain which was already largely a free market economy. In Hamburg it involved radical economic change with major political and social implications. Its great significance in Manchester was as a symbol of a much broader set of concerns which had little to do with political economy and utilitarianism. In Hamburg it only became significant as a general reform demand in the early 1860s, and even then was rather pressed upon Hamburg from outside.

In Manchester liberalism divided the urban elite and that division extended downwards. It was born out of conflict between Tory/Anglican and Liberal/Nonconformist elites. Those elites had distinct social characters, for example in the education of their children and marriages between families.[64] The Tory influence was never eliminated, even during the years of apparent ACLL dominance. Liberal elites had constantly to maintain their political organisations and popular support if they wished to remain in control.

In Hamburg the only significant religious division within the merchant elite was between Lutherans and Jews. Some Jewish merchants did take up the cause of religious and political liberalism, but this was clearly a sectional position which could command little popular support even within, let alone beyond, the Jewish community. Other divisions within the elite were ones of narrow and constantly changing interest-groups, handled by informal methods and influence over the corporate institutions of government. Furthermore, in Manchester the involvement of the business elite in the major branches of production in the city tied that elite closely to other parts of the population. In Hamburg the merchant elite had far fewer ties to the bulk of the labour force, and spent more time cultivating contacts beyond the city. For these merchants the functions of guilds and other corporations was to keep that largely unknown population under control.

This made it difficult for a distinct liberal politics to penetrate downwards into the population. One can identify the same kind of *interests* amongst comparable social groups in the two cities. Small businessmen, craftsmen, and shopkeepers wanted cheap government and the maintenance of law and order. But in Manchester that could be achieved by voting Liberal in council elections; whereas in Hamburg such interests were expressed in the form of protests against government proposals. Furthermore, such groups in Hamburg often demanded specific social and economic regulations (low interest loans, maintenance of guild exclusions, immigration controls, etc.) which were inconceivable to Manchester inhabitants.

The national and international context

In Manchester the close inter-penetration of local and national politics reinforced the development of liberalism. Liberal elites and their followers in the city built up a movement on the basis of the reform agitation of 1831–32 and the incorporation campaign of 1838–39 aimed at Parliament. The 1832 Reform Act provided the basis for Liberal success subsequently in Manchester. The ACLL dominated Manchester liberalism but used this as a political base for national action. The temporary eclipse of toryism nationally after 1846 in turn increased the scope for political conflict within the broad spectrum of Manchester liberalism. The re-emergence of two-party politics in the 1860s in turn stimulated those conflicting elements to negotiate compromises with one another.

In Hamburg the separation of local and national politics largely had the opposite effect. The reactionary politics of the Confederation inhibited the prospects for liberalism within Hamburg before 1848. The counter-revolution in Prussia from 1849 was extended into Hamburg. The crisis of unification served to fragment liberalism nationally. At each point Hamburg was encouraged instead to consider its purely local interests. Arguably liberalism can only flourish in large territorial states because in small communities sectional interests and protection against the outside world predominate.[65] Even when Hamburg was finally forced into the Second Empire, it continued to treat the nation state as a resource for local interests, as the issue of its relationship to the German Customs Union amply demonstrates.

At an international level Manchester could take for granted the power of the British state and economy. Free trade liberalism could ignore or deny the problems posed by large military establishments and war between states. Even Palmerstonian liberalism did not have fully to confront these illiberal realities. In the case of Hamburg it was vital that the city was shielded from outside threats. The Confederation was supposed to provide such security, but increasingly it was to the European balance of power and Prussian protection that Hamburg had to look. The fact that Germany was unified by wars (and Hamburg had been particularly enthusiastic about the war against Denmark) also meant that Hamburg elites accepted the militarist institutions of Prussia as a necessity. It was impossible for such elites to cooperate with more radical liberals who could not accept those Prussian institutions.

Political organisation

Electoral politics requires organisation. In Manchester after 1832 it was necessary to extend party organisation beyond the immediate fighting of elections to cover such issues as voter registration. This, as well as the organisation of the incorporation campaign, created the basis of ACLL organisation after 1839. It was as much effective organisation as the appeal of its policies which enabled the ACLL to maintain its control over liberalism within Manchester through the 1840s and 1850s. That organisation weakened in the 1850s, partly because of a change of mood, partly because of resentment from other strands of liberalism, partly because the shattering of the Tory party removed the need to keep the different strands of the Liberal coalition together. However, as the episode of the 1868 Election demonstrated, it was once again necessary to develop stronger and more inclusive political organisation.

In Hamburg a liberal politics could hardly develop any organisation beyond a loose set of associations before 1848. Many liberals were suspicious of 'party' organisation as something sectional and divisive. In 1848 they were compelled to develop such organisation, mainly through cooperation between different political associations. Even then it proved impossible to extend such coalitions beyond the limits of individual states. Any chance of building up such organisation was abruptly stopped by counter-revolution. Again a weak organisation was developing in the late 1850s and early 1860s, though of a more secular and elitist kind, this time with rather better links to other states. But the unification crisis shattered that trend and instead the different components of the potential liberal coalition were encouraged to promote their sectional interests in an exclusive way. The radical transformation of national institutions in any case made it very difficult for established political organisations to adapt successfully to the new conditions. Religion, ethnicity, and class served as the rallying cries of new mass parties, and liberal elites found it difficult to respond effectively to this.[66] Furthermore, so long as they could control local institutions and work effectively with the authorities in Berlin, it did not appear necessary to extend their electoral bases of support. Rather, they could use their elite controls to reduce the electoral basis of the local parliament.[67]

Concluding remarks

What all this meant was that in Manchester there developed a political culture dominated by the idea of open and organised conflict at both national and local level in which broad ideological appeal and effective organisation were essential to success. That was, of course, a culture which was in itself liberal. It was also one in which liberalism as a political movement could flourish. Yet the fact that liberal principles underpinned this political culture often makes it difficult to pinpoint precisely what in fact was liberalism. A radical tradition of accountable government, a concern with free trade and efficient government, an antipathy to religious and political privilege, and a more general stress on hard work and self-help can all be included, though at times these different elements conflicted rather than cooperated.

In Hamburg it is much easier to identify liberalism because it was defined against a much more hostile envirnoment. A liberal wanted representative government, a free market economy, religious and political toleration. But to demand that was radical. Instead the political culture of the city was inward-looking and based on sectional pursuit of interests within a corporate and regulated society. When liberal demands did emerge it was very difficult to give them general appeal and to build up effective political organisation. When mass political organisation did become necessary from the late 1860s, therefore, liberalism was unable to respond effectively.

In these ways one can explain why liberalism 'succeeded' in Manchester but 'failed' in Hamburg.

Notes

1 I am grateful for comments made on a paper given at a conference in Hamburg in which I first developed the ideas expressed in this essay. Patrick Joyce, Frank O'Gorman, Iori Prothero, and Tony Taylor – all colleagues at Manchester – made some very searching criticisms of that conference paper and I would like to acknowledge their help.

2 The seminal piece is Gall, 1975. For the most recent general treatment of the subject see Langewiesche, 1988. Many German studies have been informed by implicit or explicit comparison with the 'success' of British liberalism. See also now Langewiesche, 1988, especially section II, 'Liberalismus im britisch-deutschen Vergleich'. I attempt national level comparison in the essay below, 'Liberalism in mid-nineteenth-century Britain and Germany'.

3 For a recent general treatment of liberalism as political thought see Gray, 1986. On the question of how far a liberal state was actually created see McDonagh, 1977. On the relationship of thought to practice see Pearson & Williams, 1984 and Eccleshall et al., 1984. On liberalism in terms of party see Bentley, 1987, though this only deals with the later part of the period under consideration.

4 The points made in this paragraph are dealt with at greater length in the general essay on liberalism below.

5 Bentley, 1987, after a very interesting consideration of other approaches to the subject, settles for British liberalism being whatever the Liberal Party does. There is a problem of being clear about liberalism before the rise of the Liberal Party. Because liberalism has a more embattled character in Germany and there is no single, dominant liberal party at any time, German historians have been rather better at defining their subject.

6 Gall, 1975. For further treatment of this 'pre-industrial liberalism' see the essays in Schieder (ed), 1983.

7 As is made abundantly clear in the study by Walker (1971, part 3).

8 *Hamburger neue Zeitung und Addreß-Comptoir-Nachrichten*, nos. 237 (6 October 1847) and 238 (7 October 1847). One of the most recent studies of Cobden (Hinde, 1987) mentions the episode on p. 180.

9 For a recent broad characterisation of this belief and how it shaped the government of Hamburg, see Evans, 1987, especially chapter 1. For the development of government up to 1830 see Lindemann, 1990.

10 In 1835 Parliament had passed the Municipal Corporations Act which enabled towns to establish a new form of elected local government to replace either 'closed corporations' or subordination to the surrounding county institutions. However, the law was only permissive and towns had to petition for the right to be 'incorporated'.

11 The work I have found most useful for Manchester is Gatrell, 1971, a copy of which the author kindly lent to me. A small part of Gatrell's arguments are published in Gatrell, 1982. An up-to-date bibliography is appended to Kidd & Roberts, 1985. Since that was compiled an interesting economic analysis for the earlier part of the period has been published: Lloyd-Jones & Lewis, 1988. For Manchester, understandably, the main focus of economic historians has been upon the cotton industry rather than a more general treatment. See Farnie, 1979.

Hamburg is very ill-served for general economic history. As a narrative of basic economic activity see Baasch, 1915. Trade and shipping naturally receive the most attention. For a general survey see Ahrens, 1982 and Böhm, 1982.

12 See Gatrell, 1971, especially Introduction and chapter 3; and Alan Kidd's introduction to Kidd & Roberts (eds), 1985.

13 Gatrell, 1971 deals with this question. Recent published works which question the image are Kidd and Roberts (eds), 1985, especially the introduction by Kidd; and Wolff & Seed (eds), 1988, especially the essays by Gunn and Seed. The 'Gradgrind' image of Manchester was popularised in Germany through the writings of Dickens, whose works were quickly translated and which sold well, and in those of German visitors. The most famous of these works was, of course, Friedrich Engels, *Die Lage der arbeitenden Klassen in England in 1844*, first published in Leipzig in 1845.

14 See Baasch, 1915.

15 In 1866 only about one-eighth of the total labour force was directly employed in the trading sector. See *Statistik des Hamburgischen Staates* (Heft II, Zusammenstellung der ortsanwesenden Bevölkerung nach Stand und Beruf . . .) (Hamburg, 1869).

16 This is borne out by the analysis of occupational listings in the *Bürgermilitär Umschreibungen* which is part of my present research for a social history of mid-nineteenth-century Hamburg. In the three years selected for analysis – 1834, 1849, and 1864 – there is a clear increase in these kinds of occupations, especially from 1849 to 1864.

17 In theory the franchise was broader for the municipal than for the parliamentary electorate, though that did not turn out to be the case in practice. See Gatrell, 1971.

18 See Lehr, 1919.

19 For details of Hamburg's constitution and government see Bolland, 1959.

20 The most recent account is Schmidt, 1983.

21 I am grateful to Frank O'Gorman for suggesting changes in the periodisation I had originally intended.

22 Quoted in Fraser, 1976, pp. 21-2.

23 For an interesting aspect of this utopian element in Cobdenite liberalism see Semmel, 1986.

24 McCord, 1968.

25 See Breuilly, Niederhart & Taylor (eds), forthcoming for this reform activity, including some detail about events in Manchester.

26 For a critical survey of the arguments about how the English bourgeoisie 'lost its nerve' and allowed itself to be subjugated to aristocratic, gentry, and imperial values see the editors' introduction to Wolff and Seed (eds), 1988.

27 Gatrell, 1982 provides an analysis of the 1839 by-election. I borrow from his arguments in Gatrell, 1971, Part 3, on the shifting position of the cotton industry towards free trade policies.

28 Seed, 1982.

29 Though for the problem of identifying dominant values in this way see Sigsworth (ed), 1988.

30 The example of Prince Albert's visit to Manchester in 1857 and his reception at Abney Hall by James Watt is very effectively used by Gunn, 1988, pp. 38–9 to support this kind of argument.

31 For Leeds see Morris, 1990; and for Bradford see Koditschek, 1990.

32 In part I can draw upon work already done in a collaborative research project with Patrick Joyce and Iori Prothero to compare the cultural history of mid-nineteenth-century Hamburg, Lyon and Manchester. Much of this work has been undertaken by our research assistant Dr Sally Taylor.

33 See Husung, 1983.

34 Zimmermann, 1979; Krohn, 1967 and 1974.

35 On the various associations see Freudenthal, 1968, chapter 3. On the way in which a 'public opinion' developed after 1842 see Levy, 1929.

36 Unfortunately this cluster of projects have generally been considered in isolation from one another or it has been their technical and aesthetic aspects upon which historians have concentrated. Examples are Faulwasser, 1892 and Schuhmacher, 1920. The water and sewage projects have most recently been considered by Evans, 1987, but from the angle of public health. What is needed is an attempt to see these as a cluster of projects which became a source of conflict within Hamburg.

37 Eger, 1973; Prelinger, 1976 and 1987; Paletschek, 1990.

38 Breuilly & Sachse, 1984. The social composition can be gauged from the baptism and marriage registers for the German Catholic congregation which were kept from 1847–53 and 1848–52 respectively.

39 As is made clear in Bavendammn, 1969.

40 The Schiller centenary has not been the subject of much research. For a consideration of one aspect see Jaeger, 1980. Endrulat, 1860 provides a full contemporary account. There is a considerable amount of contemporary material which could be investigated.

41 These are provisional conclusions based upon research into the archival material in Hamburg concerning control of immigration and relations with Prussia in the North German Confederation.

42 See Robbins, 1979.

43 See Vincent, 1972; and Breuilly, Niedhart & Taylor (eds), forthcoming.

44 Gatrell, 1971 analyses the reasons for weak labour organisation. See also Sykes, 1982.

45 For this see Foster, 1974, even if he exaggerates the extent of such working-class radicalism in Oldham. See also Joyce, 1982 for cases of rather conservative forms of working-class organisation based on paternalism. Lancashire displayed examples of conservative trade unions and conservative working-class voting patterns in 1868.

46 Davis, 1985.

47 Rose, 1985.

48 Breuilly, Niedhart & Taylor (eds), forthcoming.

49 Much of what follows is based upon Taylor, 1984.

50 In addition to Taylor, 1984 see Saville, 1952.

51 This translation was published in the last four issues of *The Red Republican* (nos. 21–4) in November 1850 (reprint, Merlin Press, London, 1966). The introduction to the 1966 reprint by John Saville provides details of the close links between Harney and Jones.

52 Edward Owen Greening, *Memories of Robert Owen and the Co-operative Pioneers* (pamphlet, Manchester, 1925). My thanks to Tony Taylor for drawing this passage to my attention.

53 For the generally disappointing results of such demands from labour and radical leaders see Breuilly, Niedhart & Taylor (eds), forthcoming, especially the sectional introduction to chapters 13 to 16 and the documents in chapters 14 and 15.

54 For details on this see the rather old but still valuable study of Hanham, 1959. For a more detailed study of liberal political organisation in Manchester see Whittaker, 1956.

55 There were other considerations as well, such as the quality of liberal leadership, as Vincent, 1972 emphasises.

56 See, for example, the articles in *The Democrat*, 10 and 24 October 1867. This was a radical paper published in Carlisle. I am grateful to Tony Taylor for drawing this to my attention. He in turn was alerted to this source by Dorothy Thompson.

57 I have dealt with this phase and the breakdown of labour support for liberalism in Hamburg in the

1860s in Breuilly & Sachse, 1984, chapters 8 and 9. Some of these points are briefly outlined for Hamburg in Breuilly, 1983. The essays in Herzig *et al.*, 1983 by Na'aman, Offermann and Trautmann are also relevant and provide references to other works, including their own important studies of aspects of the subject. However, all these studies consider the matter from the point of view of the labour movement. We lack any study that focuses on the nature of Hamburg liberalism and middle-class attitudes.

58 For the ways in which working-class formation at these 'deeper' levels can be linked to the emergence of independent working-class politics see Breuilly, 1987a.

59 For a general argument of this kind see the essay above on artisans.

60 Renzsch, 1980.

61 The general significance of this strike wave has been considered, from very different perspectives, by Engelhardt, 1977, and Machtan, 1983.

62 For suggestive material in the Staatsarchiv Hamburg on this issue see Bestand III–1. Cl.VII. Lit Bc. *Bürgerschaft, Bürger und Heimatsrecht*; and Bestand 332–8, *Meldewesen*, especially A1, A11, B8–14, 16, 17, 24–6, 29, 36, 37, 48, and 55.

63 Kutz-Bauer, 1988.

64 Gatrell, 1971.

65 This point would take me beyond the subject of the essay, but it could be developed to explain why Prussian liberalism was far more advanced than Hamburg liberalism, despite the apparently less promising economic and governmental context.

66 Though Langewiesche, 1988, especially chapter 4, argues convincingly against the general exaggeration of liberal failure. In the course of that argument he makes points about how splits amongst liberals and loose organisation could actually be strengths for a political current which did not appeal to a particular 'milieu'.

67 Evans, 1979.

7

Liberalism in mid-nineteenth-century Britain and Germany

Introduction

The preceding essays indicate a shift away from a fairly narrowly defined labour history towards artisans in a broader framework, relations between workers and the middle classes, and finally a focus on liberalism in two particular cities. To complete this shift it is necessary to look more generally at the subject of liberalism and from a perspective wider than its relationship with the labour movement.

I will begin with some definitions of liberalism and the problems these present. I will then go on to consider the major challenges which confronted liberals in the two countries over this period and how they responded to those challenges. That will lead me on to draw some conclusions about the major differences and similarities between liberalism in Britain and Germany.

Definitions and their problems

The key value associated with liberalism is that of individualism. Broadly speaking socialist, nationalist and conservative creeds are more concerned with the preservation or construction of a certain kind of social order which is seen in terms of its capacity to achieve goals such as the maintenance of tradition, law and order, social justice, or national independence. Religious creeds are principally concerned with creating ways of life in accordance with whatever they envisage their god or gods require of them. By contrast, for liberalism social arrangements are evaluated principally in terms of their capacity to enhance the freedom of the individual.

This is necessarily a broad starting point. Clearly there are certain kinds of socialists, conservatives, nationalists and religious believers who are not indifferent to freedom of individual choice. Some of them, indeed, would argue that their values take more account of that value than do liberals, in that they recognise the frailty of the individual and the need to shape or define freedom. There were also many we now call liberals who were preoccupied with religious questions, or who were prepared to see individual liberties curtailed in various ways, or who tended to raise a particular set of social arrangements virtually to the status of an end in itself (for example, a competitive free market economy).

However, it is necessary to begin with definitions and they must be broad ones. The only alternatives to this starting point are either to begin with no definitions at all or to adopt rather more precise ones. The problem with the first approach is that it is difficult to establish what is being considered. Many single-case studies of liberalism have this character.[1] It is easy to see why historians prefer this course. Historians are suspicious of definitions as strait-jackets and are sensitive to the complex and varied character of ideas and political movements.[2] But the refusal to identify explicitly the subject of one's study means either that the historian simply accepts contemporary self-definition or works with his own implicit characterisation of his subject without providing the reader with a clear sense of what that is. Neither is satisfactory.

The problem with an over-precise definition is that it leads one into the problems of which the historian is only too aware. For example, the recent revival of neo-liberal thought associated with such thinkers as Hayek has led to a renewed emphasis upon what might be called 'classical' liberalism, that is, a set of ideas which places the competitive free-market economy at its centre. Gray's recent study adopts this view of liberalism, comparing classical liberalism with what he calls 'revisionary' liberalism which is really seen as a retreat from the classical position.[3] The problem with such a definition is that it is liable to become normative. The writer will frequently point out the extent to which 'actual, historical' liberalism does not live up to the normative definition; just, of course, as late nineteenth-century defenders of the laissez-faire economy and minimal state powers such as Dicey, Spencer and Belloc accused others of 'collectivism', of embarking on the era of the 'nanny-state'.

Any comparative approach has to confront these problems quite squarely. Clearly German 'liberalism' is very different from British 'liberalism'. The differences may inhere in the very nature of liberalism in the two cases or it may be a product of different historiographic traditions and implicit ways of identifying the subject. Without some initial identification of subject the choice of material for comparison will be arbitrary. On the other hand, a comparative approach makes it clear from the outset that a precise definition such as that of 'classical' liberalism tends not only to make the definition a normative one, but also relates it more closely to one particular case (that is, the British one) than to any other case.

Therefore, there has to be a definition of subject and it has to be a broad one. Furthermore, it has to be a definition in terms of the ideas to which liberals subscribe. Obviously any political orientation is about much more than the commitment to certain principles, but it is difficult to see how one can *define* any political ideology except in terms of ideas. What is important is not to confuse definitions with theories or evaluations of importance. Having defined liberalism in terms of a commitment to the principle of individuality one may well conclude that issues of social character, economic interest, or political organisation and style tell us more about liberals than does that principle.

There are certain difficulties, however, with this broad definition in terms of the principle of individuality as the necessary starting point of any study of liberalism. The difficulties relate to the very different conceptions of what is meant by individuality.

First, there is the distinction to be made between liberalism as a methodological principle and as a moral goal. For example, Bentham and the utilitarian school in England assumed that social arrangements and institutions could only be evaluated in relation to their capacity to satisfy the needs of individuals. However, they sought to construct an a-historical concept of the individual based on assumptions about human psychology. This enabled them to make comparisons between individuals, above all in terms of the amount of satisfaction they derived from various social arrangements. On this basis one could measure the extent to which one set of arrangements created more satisfaction than another. Utilitarians believed that, armed with such measurements, they could then determine which arrangements created 'the greatest happiness of the greatest number'. In principle there was no reason, unless happiness was identified with freedom, why the actual arrangements deemed most propitious should not be the highly centralised and coercive ones. Bentham and many of his followers accepted for a long time that the free market was the best way in which the economy could be arranged in order to provide goods and services most efficiently and thereby to contribute to an optimal level of happiness. James Mill argued a similar case for representative government, based mainly on the principle that other forms of government would increase the amount of human misery. However, this was quite unlike the justification for the market in terms of its contribution to freedom and individuality because of the way in which it extended property rights, seen by many liberals as an essential component of individuality, and blocked the excessive accumulation of economic, and subsequently political power which would undermine freedom. Again, James Mill's defence of representative government was quite different from that of either a natural rights liberal who might argue from the basis of the right to participate in political affairs or from the view that government was based on a contract to which all individuals were parties. Neither was it like that of a Whig such as Macaulay who could argue the case for the extension of the franchise and for a greater role for an elected parliament in terms of historical progress and the need to adjust the constitution to take account of the gradual extension of human liberty. One could argue these kinds of cases for free markets and parliamentary governments even if it could be shown that these were not the most efficient means of satisfying many human needs or even of creating the greatest amount of happiness, at least happiness in the sense that it was understood by utilitarians.[4]

Just as methodological individualists such as utilitarians might not be liberals, liberals might not be methodological individualists. Individualism might instead be considered a moral goal rather than a psychological or social reality. Indeed, one might take the view that this was a moral goal which present social arrangements made it difficult, even impossible, to achieve. This judgement could be struck at a more superficial and at a deeper level. At a more superficial level one might see present social arrangements as external constraints upon individual freedom. Privileges of the kind enjoyed by guilds, nobles and established churches prevented large numbers of people exercising their individual freedoms to practise a trade, buy and sell land, and profess particular religious beliefs. Remove the constraints and the individual could enter into the kingdom of liberty. There might need to be an initial phase of strong state intervention in order to overcome the resistance of the privileged groups, but once that had been negotiated one could expect the state to retreat from extensive intervention and to leave a liberal order to function primarily through the rational exercise of individual freedom.

The deeper analysis saw the notion of 'constraint' as a much more fundamental problem. People were not merely prevented from doing or believing various things by existing social arrangements; their conceptions of their material and moral interests were also shaped by those arrangements. An established church did not simply prevent people from believing anything contrary to its own doctrines; it determined the positive beliefs of its adherents. One might grant people freedoms and then find that they used those freedoms to oppress others and themselves. This was not only a matter of interest. After all, any liberal should recognise that an individual might quite rationally perceive that constraints on the freedom of others could increase his own capacity to maximise his interests. That could be dealt with by ensuring a diffusion of power such that no individual could abuse liberty and would instead recognise that his interests were best pursued through a liberal order. More problematic was that people might hold views of their interests which were either irrational or anti-individualist. Liberals could only explain this in terms of upbringing because, if it were deemed 'natural' for human beings to act irrationally or to wish to submerge their individuality into some greater cause, then the liberal project had little chance of success.

But the problem of upbringing presented its own very thorny difficulties. A good example of the move from the superficial to the deeper assessment of the obstacles facing liberals can be seen in the career of Edwin Chadwick. Chadwick played a key role in drafting the report which led to the passing of the New Poor Law Amendment Act in 1834. The central notion of 'less eligibility' was that the labour market must be so organised that it would be irrational for those who could find employment to choose instead to take poor relief. This would ensure that the rational pursuit of individual interest would be through the free operation of the labour market which in turn would produce optimal economic benefits. However, Chadwick soon began to have doubts about this point of view. Disease, bad housing and inadequate education made it impossible for many poor people to develop the minimal capacities of reasoning and decision-making in order to function properly in a free market. Chadwick now turned his attention to the ways in which the state could intervene to raise standards of public health. This construction of the concept of individuality in terms of capacities which needed to be positively promoted, often by measures of state intervention, could lead to completely different policy conclusions from one in which individuality simply needed to be set free from external constraints.[5]

A further problem is that such a move to justify collective measures could involve disputes between different kinds of liberals and could bring adherents of other values on to the side of the 'positive' liberals. In Germany a tradition of state building, of 'reform from above', and generally of a tendency to idealise the state as an autonomous agency above a factious society could easily graft itself upon this positive liberal position. In Britain the shift from one kind of liberalism to another was accompanied by a shift of utilitarian analysis from a preference for free market arrangements to more positive institutional interventions. The relationship of idealism to German liberalism and utilitarianism to British liberalism is something to which I will return in the conclusion of this essay.

Apart from these very basic difficulties of defining liberalism, there are also the problems that liberals will disagree amongst themselves as to priorities and prospects, as well as that specific liberal goals might be taken up by particular interests for reasons which have nothing to do with an acceptance of general liberal values.

On the matter of disagreement amongst liberals there were great differences as to the extent to which certain categories of people, such as the poor or women, were regarded as sufficiently possessed of the attributes of individuality as to be entrusted with a fair share of political power. One liberal might support the need to maintain for the moment a strong, non-constitutional state in order to pursue liberalising policies in social, economic religious and legal affairs; whilst another might consider the extension of individual freedom in the political sphere as having first priority, even if this might slow down the rate at which liberal policies generally could be pursued. Liberalism, after all, had a diverse set of historic roots arising out of religious conflicts, clashes with arbitrary monarchy and noble privilege, the pursuit of economic liberty and much else. It is therefore hardly surprising that these diverse concerns should divide liberals from one another at times, even while at the same time providing the idea of liberalism with an all-round character.

As for alliances of convenience under a liberal banner, these were manifold. In both Britain and some parts of Germany, Catholics could ally with liberals against a state which was both authoritarian and which supported a Protestant church establishment. Economic interests which felt they were shut off from lucrative export markets or hampered in their treatment of labour or choice of occupation would take up the cause of laissez-faire, but then drop it as soon as their economic circumstances changed.

One could argue that all political ideologies obtain a broad base of support and influence only if such interests are engaged and that it is pointless to distinguish between a core of true believers and collections of interest groups which treat the ideology in a pragmatic manner. There is much truth in this argument but it can be pushed too far. If liberalism (or any other political idea) only acquired support on the basis of pragmatic calculation or in relation to fairly narrowly defined interests or concerns, it would be an erratic, fluctuating and ultimately weak political force. If, on the other hand, the same groups of people found themselves supporting liberal values in a variety of spheres, for a variety of reasons, and if liberal concerns created cross-cutting bases of support, then liberalism could begin to develop as a way of life, as a culture in its own right. Such a political idea might be more difficult to define and its constituencies harder to identify but it would also be a more enduring and influential idea. I shall argue in this essay that this is precisely one way of distinguishing British from German liberalism, and that it makes comparison both difficult and necessary.

In practical terms a political movement is often shaped in direct relation to the (self-perceived) challenges it confronts. Challenges impose choices of priorities. Not all goals can be pursued at once and it is those that are taken as the most pressing challenges which shape the key ideological concerns and practical actions of a political movement. So, having made these broad definitional points and having raised some large problems of identifying liberalism, it is necessary to turn to the practices of liberalism in relation to the challenges it confronted.

Challenges to liberalism

I will begin by distinguishing between different spheres in which liberalism can find itself confronted by practices which appear to restrict or deform the possibilities for the individual to exercise his freedom. These concern the organisation of the state, relations between states, economic arrangements, the profession of beliefs, the nature of the legal system, and the treatment of social problems such as poverty. These are necessarily rather crude distinctions. Clearly there are many areas of overlap and interconnection. For example, if one argues that the freedom of occupational choice is a basic human right that should be enshrined in law, this has implications both for the arrangement of the economy and the character of the legal system. Again, some liberals argued that giving rights of political participation to poor people had to wait until certain social problems had been satisfactorily treated. Nevertheless, these do provide us with a framework for a preliminary analysis.

The organisation of the state

a) England

For English liberals after 1815 the main problems concerning the organisation of the central state were: continuing restrictions upon the rights of those outside the

Church of England to participate in politics; the continuing influence of non-representative institutions such as the Crown and the House of Lords compared to the House of Commons; and defects in the system of voting for the House of Commons.

Each of these features can be seen to offend the basic liberal concern with increasing individual freedom. However, as I have already argued in general terms, different 'liberals' had different priorities, opposition was based on different versions of liberalism, and there were also non-liberal opponents of some of these arrangements.

At a national level the major religious handicaps concerned Catholics and Nonconformists. Naturally these confessions opposed these political disadvantages. Every year Nonconformists had to be granted special dispensation by Parliament from the Test and Corporation Acts passed in the late seventeenth century. In the 1820s Daniel O'Connell led a mass movement in Ireland against political discrimination against Catholics which meant that he could not take his seat in the House of Commons if and when he was elected. To some extent one can explain the legal changes which removed these handicaps in 1828 (repeal of the Test and Corporation Acts) and 1829 (Catholic Emancipation) in terms of a pragmatic retreat by the Tory Government in the face of growing opposition from these confessional groups.

There was, however, also a liberal dimension to these measures. Whigs had long campaigned on a platform of civil and religious liberty and regularly voted for repeal of many continuing religious discriminations. In part it was this issue which sharply distinguished them from the Tory defence of the privileges of the Anglican confession. It was also a more liberal faction within the Tory Party, led by Canning until his death in 1827, which pressed for more liberal religious policies. The repeal of the Test and Corporation Acts was based on this cross-party alliance between different kinds of liberals. It did not raise the same passions as the Catholic question because this was a measure for fellow Protestants and because it really only regularised the situation created by the annual indemnity. Catholic Emancipation, on the other hand, was due to a combination of Catholic pressure, the breakdown of Tory unity following Canning's death, the common opposition to the Government from both liberal Tories and the Whigs, and the pragmatic decision by Wellington and Peel in favour of concession.[6]

The crisis occasioned by Catholic Emancipation led on directly to the issue of franchise reform. The Government had already undermined the case that the 'old constitution' should not be subjected to any systematic alteration by raising the Irish country franchise qualification when granting Catholic Emancipation, in order to reduce the political impact of the measure. Some Tory opponents of Emancipation believed that the Government had got its measure through by means of its control of patronage of rotten boroughs and office-holding, and were also prepared to consider reform in order to reduce the influence of such patronage. Above all, general economic crisis coincided with the breakdown of Tory unity to enable a Whig ministry to come into office on a programme of reform. Liberal pressure formed only a small part of the background to the moves towards reform in 1830–31.[7]

What is more, there were different kinds of liberal arguments which were employed to justify reform and to suggest the kind of reform which should be carried through. Very broadly one can distinguish between the utilitarian, the Whig and natural right positions. The utilitarian position, expressed most cogently in James Mill's *Essay on Government* deduced the case for universal manhood suffrage and representative government from utilitarian principles. All men seek their own interests; if government only represents a minority within a society, that minority will use its control of government for its own interest against the interests of the majority. The only way to prevent this happening was to ensure that all had some control over government. Mill's argument has many problems, and was subject to acute attack in 1829 by Macaulay, but it is liberal in the sense that it makes the individual, acting as a rational egoist, the foundation of the political system.[8]

This kind of radical liberalism was, however, in a minority even within radical ranks. For Mill government was a means to an end, and the organisation of the state likewise was seen in instrumental terms. He had no time for the other kind of radical who argued that all men should have the vote as a natural right. That position was often associated with forms of argument which also argued that the whole social system denied most men their natural rights and that obtaining political power would enable those men to alter the social system in order to enter into their whole inheritance. Mill indeed had to argue that poor people would not insist on seizing the property of the rich (because in anything other than the short term it would not be in their own interests) in order to avoid the accusation from Macaulay that universal suffrage would undermine society. Again, the natural rights argument was individualist, though in an ethical rather than a methodological manner. It really seems to have been the least important argument used to justify the case for reform or to motivate those seeking reform.

Although these two kinds of radical liberalism played their part in the events which led to the Reform Act of 1832, and could have some appeal to elements of the unenfranchised, it was what might be called the Whig position which was of most importance. The Whig position, most eloquently presented by Macaulay in speeches in the House of Commons during the reform crisis, envisaged reform as a process of adjustment to historical change. New forms of property were developing but had not yet been provided with political representation. In order to prevent a crisis developing in which property as a whole might be endangered, those forms of property which already had political rights (above all land) should concede a political voice to new forms of property (above all the new manufacturing interests). The assumption was that representation was of interests or groups rather than of individuals, and that the case for alteration had to be made on the basis of prior alterations in the balance of such interests.

This way of thinking about political representation was not unique to Whigs. Tories also argued in this way, only they did not believe franchise reforms were necessary to enable new forms of property to acquire a political voice. A rich manufacturer could buy his way into parliamentary representation under the unreformed system. It is a position some historians such as Namier have developed, arguing that 'real' interests acquire political influence under any franchise system. It seems to accord no autonomy at all to political arrangements. At most some Tories of this kind were prepared to concede piecemeal alterations, transferring a parliamentary seat from a particularly small or corrupt borough to a growing but unrepresented town. But the real difference was not over whether representation was of interests rather than individuals, but instead about the merits of such piecemeal reform compared to a systematic reform designed to incorporate new interests once and for all. Many conservatives not only contested the efficacy of systematic reform; they feared it would open the way for further demands for reform because of the admission that the old reformed *system* was at fault. Nevertheless, even those who demanded the vote for the propertyless often justified this in terms of giving a voice to an unrepresented interest, rather than on the basis of individual right or utility.

However, this position was indirectly a liberal one. It was linked to a notion of progress, whether this be understood as specifically British or whether Britain merely led the way. Progress was seen in terms of the development of a more complex division of labour and the growth of new forms of economic activity. In turn, this was only possible under conditions of individual liberty. Macaulay, for example, looked to the Scottish Enlightenment and writers such as Adam Smith for support for this view. This commercial (but note, not necessarily an industrial-urban) society was seen as one in which individual mobility and its counterpart, equality before the law, were essential characteristics. It was because of the general and complex nature of this change that Whigs like Macaulay could not be satisfied with piecemeal changes such as the abolition of the occasional rotten borough and the award of its seat to an unrepresented manufacturing town. A more systematic reform of the franchise which made it reflect property in a rather general sense (measured by income or the value of land) was needed. This was the view that prevailed and the Reform Act swept aside the diverse franchises of pre-reform parliament and replaced them with a uniform franchise awarded on the basis of impersonal criteria of property, while at the same time giving representation to new, growing urban centres such as Manchester and reducing the importance of small boroughs.

Part of the argument for reform had been to curb the influence of the aristocracy who, it was often argued, controlled many of the seats in the Commons and who lived off the offices and incomes fed by the national debt. It is a moot point whether the reform really did reduce aristocratic influence on the composition of the Commons.[9]

The actual crisis did involve a confrontation with the House of Lords and its defeat. It also served to reduce the influence of the Crown. On only one more occasion, in 1834, was a monarch able to call a general election at his own pleasure. The post-1832 Reform Parliament did make a determined attempt at 'retrenchment', and later administrative reform, which were also designed to reduce the patronage powers of the executive. In all these ways, different kinds of liberal critiques underpinned and promoted reform of state organisation in the 1830s.

There were also problems with the form of local government. Indeed these often raised greater passions than 'national' questions. Joseph Parkes, who had played an important role in the 1832 Reform Act, declared that it was less important than the Municipal Corporation Act of 1835. This removed power from parish institutions, often under the control of Anglicans, and allowed towns to establish corporations which provided independence from the surrounding county and formed the basis for government by the propertied electorate.[10] The Poor Law Amendment Act of 1834 threatened another element of traditional local government with the establishment of new Poor Law Boards subject to the central guidelines of the Poor Law Commission. Policing, first in London, then in other towns, and finally in the countryside, was also reformed along uniform lines and under the control of the local government. In all these ways, especially so far as towns were concerned, a structure was established which enabled middle-class dominated governments to play a central role and which created the basis for political party development oriented towards this growing middle-class political opinion. With their stress upon individual achievement, one would expect all these developments to both reflect and promote a liberal movement.

The movement for reform up to 1832 had been a broad, if very diverse and loosely organised one. Catholics, the urban middle class, some groups of working men, great Whig peers, dissenting Protestants, utilitarian and natural rights radicals – all had played some part in the movement which led to reform in 1832. But the very success of the movement, as well as the limits of that success, caused the movement to fragment. Working-class radicals turned from the new Whig Government in disgust for having betrayed them. The Whig Administration, after a number of reforms such as the poor law and municipal government, began to back away from further reforms in a way which alienated utilitarian radicals. The utilitarian measures which were taken provoked popular and Tory opposition, and discomfited the old, county-based liberalism which had stressed local autonomy rather than efficient reform undertaken according to guidelines laid down centrally. The reform impulse in Ireland dried up, especially in the face of opposition from important Whig interests. The Conservative Party in turn began to adapt itself to the new political climate, recognising its need to win middle-class support as early as 1834. It also proved more receptive to taking up some of the ideas Liberals had aired such as retrenchment, financial reform, and reform of tariffs. The liberal impulse, in response, began to break up into single-issue movements concerned with free trade, church questions or administrative or financial reforms. Liberalism as a broad political movement cannot be said to exist after 1833 until it was reconstructed in the 1850s. The task of reorganising the major representative institutions of the state and providing them with more authority against other state institutions had brought together diverse kinds of liberalism, but its very success had then fragmented that fragile coalition.

b) Germany

A very different situation obtained in the German lands. The Congress of Vienna had confirmed much of Napoleon's re-ordering of the area in ways which favoured liberal politics. The temporal powers of the Catholic church were never restored, and neither were the many tiny states or sub-states of the Holy Roman Empire. This meant liberals confronted fewer, larger and more secular states. The view that the larger and more secular the state was, the more favourable it was to liberal purposes was firmly established by 1830. A number of these territorial states were virtually new creations. One way in which the governments of these states sought to integrate their diverse territories, to create new state-wide loyalties, and to build up a barrier against the imposition of political arrangements by the Confederation which Austria and Prussia dominated, was to grant constitutions. Certainly these constitutions conceded little real power to representative institutions. In all cases except Baden those institutions were elected on the basis of legal estates which gave disproportionate power to noble landowners. The constitutions were regarded as gifts from rulers rather than agreements between princes and their subjects. Nevertheless, the very existence of constitutions and representation strengthened the liberal case. However, many liberals already recognised that political arrangements in many ways had a more liberal character than social or economic affairs. The idea of the state as progressive in relation to society, and the idea that the purpose of liberal measures was to provide the state with the power to reform society, had taken hold during the Napoleonic period, and remained a central assumption afterwards. The English arguments of the state as representing sectional interests and of political reform springing from real historical changes at other levels were largely ignored. If England served as a model, it was more in terms of the kind of political structure which should be established rather than in terms of a series of social and economic changes which established liberty firmly on a 'pre-political' basis. Thus, even if German liberalism was grounded in historical arguments about progress, this was always more abstract than such arguments in the English case.[11]

Prussia and Austria had not granted constitutions after 1815 and therefore lacked the type of state-wide representation which could help develop the kind of public and political opinion which could then focus liberal claims upon the government. That is not to say that a great deal of liberal reform had not taken place, especially in

Prussia. Privileged access to high positions in the army and the state bureaucracy had been modified by the insistence on professional qualification and merit. The government had carried out reforms in such areas as Jewish emancipation, guild abolition, and individual land-holding rights. A common argument was that a premature granting of influence to a representative institution would threaten these liberal reforms because it would give rights to still powerful sectional interests hostile to such reform.[12] Only after such reform had begun to alter society and public opinion could one think in terms of rights of political representation. Here, like the Whig argument, representation was seen as something which only made sense at a particular phase of general social development. However, unlike the Whigs, this development was not seen as something natural and pre-political, but rather as a process which the state had to guide. In the meantime, urban self-administration, the meetings of provincial Diets, and the receptiveness of an efficient and cheap administration to liberal ideas, encouraged the belief that Prussia was liberal, or at least becoming liberal, even if not along the same lines as Britain, France or various of the small German states. Indeed, some English liberals who placed their emphasis upon efficient and non-interventionist government providing liberty in non-political areas admired the Prussian state and compared it favourably to the British state.[13]

I very much suspect that at present, for the great mass of the people, Prussia possesses the best government in Europe. I would gladly give up my taste for talking politics to secure such a state of things in England. Had our people such a simple and economical government, so deeply imbued with justice to all, and aiming so constantly to elevate mentally and morally its population, how much better would it be for the twelve or fifteen millions in the British Empire, who, while they possess no electoral rights, are yet persuaded they are freemen, and who are mystified into the notion that they are not political bondsmen, by that great juggle of the "English Constitution" – a thing of monopolies, and Church-craft, and sinecures, armorial hocuspocus, primogeniture, and pageantry.

Nevertheless, the main goal of those who called themselves liberals in Germany around 1830 was to achieve constitutional government in which individuality would be promoted first, by providing civil liberties and equality before the law, and second, by ensuring some measure of political representation. Usually liberals envisaged the way forward as through agreement with rulers, thus avoiding any principled argument about sovereignty. In constitutional states the practical programme was one of removing restrictions on important freedoms such as those of speech and assembly, increasing the powers of representative institutions, and moving from a system of estate representation to one in which individuals (though usually only those holding a substantial amount of property) were represented. In non-constitutional states the first concern was to achieve a constitution.

Some achievements were registered by the early 1830s. Following the first wave of constitutional enactments around 1815, the disturbances following the July revolution in France led to a number of German states granting constitutions in the early 1830s. In some cases governments clearly hoped to divide opposition by granting some concessions to more moderate, propertied elements which felt uneasy by any suggestion of violence and disorder.[14] This, as well as the beginning of repression orchestrated by the Confederation, served to divide an already very weakly organised liberal movement by the mid-1830s.[15] What is more, the coup of the new King of Hannover in 1837 not only involved nullifying the constitution granted in the wake of protest following the July revolution of 1831, but also involved carrying out various populist measures designed to demonstrate the limited support for liberal constitutionalism.[16]

c) Comparisons

English liberals confronted just one state and already had in parliament a national institution on which they could focus their political demands. Although there were some radicals, both natural right and utilitarian, who pressed a rather abstract and theoretical case for reform, the main argument for reform was the claim that important interests were not represented. The prior social and economic changes, the growth of new manufacturing centres and of export trade, provided support for liberalism both in terms of the association of these changes with the growth of individual liberty (liberalism = social progress) and with the need to take political account of new, but inadequately represented interests (liberalism = franchise reform). On this basis a coalition of interests came together in 1830–32, confronting a divided Tory Government which had already dismayed some of its supporters by granting Catholic Emancipation. However, reform had the consequence of dividing that coalition and also providing the basis of a new Tory revival. Instead of liberalism now developing into a broad movement which could support reform-minded governments, it broke up into varied pressure groups which sought to exploit the reformed political system to realise their various objectives.

In Germany liberalism was a weaker and more theoretical movement. It was weaker partly because it had no central point on which to focus. Liberals in various states concentrated their energies upon their particular problems. Admittedly the general repressive policy of the Confederation from the mid-1830s did, in a negative way, force liberals from different states together. But this happened outside institutions, so that liberalism took on the appearance of a publicist, propaganda movement, dominated by writers and speakers, in which representative institutions were used more as mouthpieces of opposition than as practical institutions for advancing a liberal programme. The concern was less with modifying existing institutions in a liberal direction, and more with arguing the case for institutional transformation.

However, at the same time that case was made tentatively as well as theoretically. It was difficult for German liberals to argue that German society had reached an historical stage which made political reform necessary. Indeed the work of a reformed state was often seen as helping society move towards that stage. What is more, the lack of 'liberal' interests in society made many German liberals suspicious of a premature movement towards popular politics, or indeed even of more limited forms of representation. Take the example of urban government reform. We have already seen that in Britain the Municipal Corporation Act of 1835 provided a channel for middle-class political energies. Furthermore, it was achieved by exploiting the political opportunities provided by the 1832 reform. In turn the Act, which was permissive, stimulated a liberal agitation for the incorporation of particular towns. (See above, the essay comparing Hamburg and Manchester.)

By contrast there was less pressure from urban interests in Germany for greater self-government. In the case of Prussia, as is well-known, this came through action taken by the central state bureaucracy. It encountered some resistance from urban interests worried about the effort and responsibility involved. Key powers, for example the running of the police, remained in the hands of the central state.[17] Admittedly, later on the economic growth of some of these towns turned city government into a bastion of the liberal movement.[18] As has been mentioned, the Rhenish cities already had accepted positively the Napoleonic reform of local government and wished to defend that against the Prussian state after 1815. However, the exception proves the rule. Only where there was already a powerful and self-confident commercial middle class does one find a positive attitude towards urban self-government in Prussia. There was more demand for urban autonomy in southern Germany, but the 'liberal' character of this was often suspect because it was linked to attempts to preserve communal restrictions against state government.[19] Until economic development picked up after the mid-century, German liberalism was very much a publicist movement dominated by the educated, often of those in state service, and its programme was much more purely political and theoretical than in England. Recent work has shown a more diverse and petit bourgeois support for 'liberal' causes than was previously thought to be the case, but in numerical terms such support was slight.[20] Above all, the recent consensus about the *mittelständisch* character of early liberalism is, in my view, suspect because of the very problematic character of the liberalism involved. Only further studies of the conflicts within *mittelständisch* groups will make clear which were really committed to extending individual opportunities and which used the catch-words concerning freedom to defend or advance corporate privileges.

Relations between states

a) Germany

The fact that Germany until 1867 consisted of some thirty-nine separate states rather than a single state, even if there was some political coordination through the Austro-Prussian dominated Confederation and economic coordination through the Prussian dominated Zollverein, in part shaped the preoccupation of German governments with international relations. Under the terms of the treaty which established the Confederation, its members could not conduct independent foreign policies in the sense of concluding treaties with non-member states. So far as all states other than Austria and Prussia were concerned, this legal restriction only reflected a real limitation of power. Their principal concern was with responding to the Austro-Prussian domination of the Confederation.

For liberals in these states there were two major consequences of this situation. First, they did not in any sustained sense have to confront problems of inter-state relations. These smaller states had to make a contribution to the Confederal army, but that was something observed largely in the breach. As a consequence liberals in these states could see armies simply as instruments of internal control. It was in the small states that the idea of popular militias to replace standing armies subject to the command of the prince had the most attraction. On the other hand, the very lack of expense of maintaining relatively large armed forces meant that these princes did not have to negotiate with their representative assemblies over the means to pay for soldiers. In the same way many princes wished to join the Zollverein because it would increase their revenue and thereby remove the need to go to any parliament or estate for money. Some liberals opposed entry into the customs union for the same reason.[21] In other words, the dependence for both military protection and money on one or both of the larger German states had the effect of freezing political relationships in the smaller states in favour of the princes. This was most obvious at times of crisis, as in the periods following 1819 and 1830/31, when it was the Austro-Prussian dualism which imposed reaction upon the German states as a whole. That is not to say that the smaller states had *no* resources for handling liberal challenges. The coup of the Hannoverian King in 1837 used an early form of populism to undercut the opposition from educated liberals. In September 1848 it was contingents of the Confederal army from smaller states which put down the riots in Frankfurt in September 1848. On the other hand, the helplessness of the smaller states in the face of relatively restricted protests in March 1848, when Austria and Prussia were too preoccupied with their own internal problems to offer assistance, is an indication of the weakness of these governments.

The consequences were two-fold for liberals in these states. Within their own states they could conceive of politics as a matter of debate and propaganda, demonstrations and petitions. They did not have to confront all the problems of maintaining the authority of a state in a hostile and threatening world. However, they also became increasingly aware that the real obstacles to their objectives lay beyond their states. This encouraged liberals in different states to come together to try to work out common strategies. Liberalism developed as a loose national movement not so much because nationality was at the heart of that liberalism, but because a national orientation was a necessary element in any realistic liberal project. In turn the national dimension had to be seen as one of placing pressure on the Confederation, especially upon Prussia and Austria, so that these states would also accede to liberal demands. Whether that pressure would come from a strong national and popular movement which would compel governments to move in that direction or whether it would be a matter of persuading governments that they stood directly to gain from pursuing a more national policy were to be matters of enduring disagreement amongst liberals from the smaller states.

The situation was perceived rather differently by liberals in Prussia and Austria. From the perspective of these states the Confederation was seen in European rather than German terms. There was not the same constraint upon acting as a European state as existed for the smaller states. The legal ban on members of the Confederation making agreements with non-members was easily sidestepped by Austria and Prussa by having some of their territory outside the Confederation. This meant they were members of the Confederation when it came to applying Confederal rules to others, but non-members when they wished to avoid having those rules enforced upon themselves. The legal provisions simply reflected the realities of power.

For Austria, and especially the major architect of the Confederal solution Metternich, the Confederation allowed indirect Austrian preeminence in Germany, while leaving her own energies free to pursue more direct power politics in areas such as Italy and Hungary. It was part of an elaborate balance of power arrangement. It tied Prussia in to the Confederation (and Prussian acquisitions in western Germany also tied her directly into a defence against France should that prove necessary). That had also in part compensated Prussia for losses to Russia in the east. Metternich saw the continued partition of Poland as essential to European stability and as one instrument for ensuring cooperation between the three partitioning powers. Furthermore, the repression of liberal and national movements in Germany was seen by Metternich to be part and parcel of the repression of such movements throughout Europe. The Confederation was part of a general policy of stabilising European international relations and of maintaining dynastic legitimacy.[22]

The problem for Austrian liberals was that there were features of this settlement they did not wish to challenge. The preeminence of Germans within the Habsburg Empire made it difficult for Austrian liberals to commit themselves to a national programme. For a long period this was not clearly perceived and many imagined they could cooperate in steps to create a more meaningful national arrangement than that of the Confederation whilst preserving the Habsburg Empire. 1848 was to make clear that this was impossible and generally Austrian liberals thereafter supported their government in blocking any 'strong' solution to the national question and focused their attention rather upon modernising reform within the Habsburg Empire.

Prussia, above all, could not avoid the issue of power in international relations. She had virtually been destroyed as a state following her defeat in 1806 and only through an amazing military mobilisation in the war against Napoleon between

1813 and 1815 had she been able to force her way back into the ranks of the major powers. What is more, this process seemed to be accompanied by liberal and national values. It was the Prussian reformers who led the state back to greatness, even if one can argue about the extent of their liberalism and how far it actually contributed to Prussian success. The pressure to concede Polish territories to Russia meant that Prussia had to take territorial compensation wholly within German lands, both in central Germany (northern Saxony) and western Germany (the Rhinelands as well Westphalia).

There was acute awareness of the dangers of Prussia's position, physically divided, holding down part of a potentially rebellious Polish population, and confronted in the west by a still powerful France which in 1830 and then again in 1848 seemed to present a major threat. Although Prussia did allow her army to become weaker, especially after the scare of 1830–31 was over, and relied more upon Metternichian diplomacy, it was regarded as a significant component of Prussian power and one which remained firmly under royal control. Prussian liberals could flirt with a militia idea, namely that embodied in the Landwehr, but unlike small state liberals they recognised the need to combine this with genuine military strength and effectiveness. As a consequence of this, Prussian liberals always appeared more 'realistic' than their small state counterparts. At the same time, more than either their Austrian or small state counterparts, they could see Prussia as the base upon which a more national as well as liberal Germany could be formed. The speed with which the Prussian customs union policy, pursued primarily for financial purposes, was interpreted by Prussian liberals in nation-building terms is one example of how Prussian liberals could take a much more positive view of their own state. The Heppenheim programme of 1847, in which moderate liberals from the Rhineland dominated, made the customs union the vehicle of the national idea. Yet at the same time the Prussian government so frequently disappointed these liberals by refusing constitutional advances and by trailing behind Austria that in many ways liberals in Prussia could be more critical of their government than liberals in other states who eventually came to look to Prussia as the instrument of their ideals. This became apparent when, following the establishment of the North German Confederation in 1867, it tended to be moderate liberals from the states newly annexed to Prussia (Hannover, Hesse, Schleswig-Holstein) which provided the bulk of the National Liberal Party, whereas many liberals in 'old' Prussia continued to oppose Bismarck.

So the different international as well as internal situations of the three German zones – the smaller states, Austria and Prussia – tended to shape liberalism in different ways. It was a publicist movement in the smaller states, not compelled to confront the problem of state power immediately, but also stimulated to move to a national programme quite quickly. It moved to a resistance to any strong national programme in Austria and placed instead its hope on modernising reforms and the leading role of Germans in that progressive tendency. It recognised the powerful state as a possible instrument of a national and liberal development in Prussia, while at the same time often bitterly opposed to the actual government of that state. Obviously these generalisations require qualification. There were divisions within the loose liberal movement in each of the three zones. Rhenish liberals in Prussia tended earlier to a more anti-government line and later to a more pro-government one than their counterparts in East Prussia. These are complexities which cannot be considered here. However, the main point is that the different situation of the states in these three zones in the system of international relations had a major impact on the character of liberalism in those areas.

b) Britain

Liberals in Britain were spared many of these problems because they were able, at least to their own satisfaction, to separate domestic and international issues. The defeat of Napoleon and the settlement at Vienna meant that balance-of-power diplomacy replaced either subsidies to continental allies or direct military intervention as the British way of preventing a single dominant power emerging in Europe. Liberals had found it difficult to criticise a large military expenditure up to 1815. Once the war was over they could quickly reap popularity by demanding retrenchment, by pointing to the corruption and patronage associated with large military expenditure, and by attacking the large national debt and those who benefitted from it. The army was allowed to run down. Most British military effort for the next forty years was focused on non-European areas, was relatively inexpensive and did not arouse too much public concern. The extent of the decay was revealed during the Crimean War when liberals, for a brief period, were once more confronted with the problems of how their state should wage war effectively.[23]

Even the navy was allowed to grow weaker. Britain was in the position, perhaps unique in world history, of being the dominant world power and yet spending very little on military purposes. Of course, this was a matter of relative standing: the British navy was far more powerful than any other. It also became a symbol to many liberals of how security of the state could coexist with the maximum internal freedom. The navy could not interfere in internal affairs and so did not raise the same suspicions as a large standing army would. In its assistance to the cause of the abolition of slavery and its promotion of free trade, the navy could indeed be presented as an instrument of progress. Liberals also argued that Britain's naval role be strictly limited. They wished to see an end to any trace of Britain's mercantilist past and this was finally realised with the end of the Navigation Acts in 1849, i.e. with an end to any British legal monopoly of the carrying trade. Partly this could go through because the argument that Britain needed to maintain a strong mercantile marine in order to reinforce the Royal Navy no longer impressed public opinion which took peace and security for granted. The British government reduced the extent of interference with foreign shipping. For example, there was far less interference with neutral shipping during the Crimean War than there had been during the Napoleonic Wars. Some liberals such as Cobden wanted to go even further and argued that the Royal Navy should be strictly confined to the role of a defence force against possible invasion.[24]

In all these ways international relations, and especially the central issue of war or preparedness for war, could be detached from other economic and political affairs. Liberals even went so far as to criticise the balance-of-power diplomacy pursued by the government (which arguably enabled Britain to run down her military capacity). They then divided between those who argued that Britain should support liberal movements abroad, especially in their struggle against reactionary dynasties such as those of the Habsburgs and the Romanovs, and those who wished Britain to remain completely aloof from all foreign entanglements. Very few liberals, incidentally, objected to a bellicose or interventionist policy on pacifist grounds. But even the 'interventionist' liberals counselled moral rather than military assistance. Britain could serve the cause of progress best by example. This sense of detached superiority was to infuriate many Europeans.

c) Comparisons

In Germany it was impossible for liberals or their opponents to divorce domestic from international concerns. At a European level Metternich and liberals were both clear that the rise of radical liberal movements in France or in Polish areas would have immediate repurcussions in Germany. That they were right was made clear both in 1830–31 and in 1848. What the impact would be was not always clear – for example when German liberals had to weigh the consequences of the war between Austria and France in 1859 or how to respond to the Austro-Prussian war of 1866. The result was not merely high-minded disagreement, as in the British case, but actual political division. A Gladstonian approach to international affairs was unimaginable amongst German liberals who sought to have real political influence.

Furthermore, in the narrower national context German liberals could not leave aside the issue of inter-state relations and, as its ultimate expression, war. German liberals recognised the Confederation had to be replaced. Their preferred method was through reform – agreement between the various states and constitutional negotiations peacefully concluded with monarchs. But the German problem could only be solved by reducing multiple centres of sovereignity to one. That was a basic question of power which could only be settled by force or the credible threat to use force. The end liberals desired could not be achieved through the means they preferred. British liberals confronted no such problem as they operated with a single centre of sovereignty that was fairly secure from external threats. Given that, liberals could confine themselves to pursuing specific goals within a stable and accepted political framework. This again helps to explain the fragmentation of British liberalism into a series of single-issue movements after 1832 at the same time as the divided German liberal movement was beginning to come together more effectively. Why these opposed trends were in turn reversed in the 1860s is something to which we must return.

Economic questions

a) England

In England there had long been a free land market and a general absence of restrictions upon occupational choice and internal movement, even if the longevity of these freedoms has perhaps been exaggerated and recognising that there continued to be restrictions, for example through the operation of a parish-based system of poor relief.[25] Legal economic privileges and restrictions only applied to certain types of colonial trade and were not extended to new external markets in the Americas, Africa, and post-Napoleonic Europe. Unchallenged naval and commercial supremacy and the acceptance of the arguments of political economy made possible the end of the Navigation Acts and an increasingly explicit repudiation of Britain's mercantilist past. As we saw in the previous section, such arguments were also extended into the issues of war and its relationship to trade. The assertion of Goethe's Faust "*Krieg, Handel und Piraterie, Dreieinig sind sie, nicht zu trennen.*" no longer held good. There did remain a range of tariffs. Insofar as these were intended to raise government revenue, liberals argued that a reduction in tariffs might well expand the volume of trade and thereby state revenue. Many liberals did see the need to confront the problem raised by the argument for zero tariffs: that is, either that government expenditure must be further reduced or that other sources of revenue must be created. Peel's income tax was, in part, a means of carrying through tariff reductions.[26]

However, the more contentious question was when tariffs were justified on protective grounds. Although there were other commodities such as sugar which raised passions in this way, the main issue of this kind was presented by the Corn Laws. Admittedly this only became a major political concern at times of poor harvests and high corn prices. It also acquired a particular force during a period of general depression when it could appear to export manufacturing interests that repeal or at least reduction of the corn tariffs offered one chance for foreign economies to earn the income (through exporting food to Britain) to purchase British goods, while at the same time reducing the pressure on wages by bringing down food prices.

It was on this issue that the most formidable liberal political organisation of early Victorian Britain was built, the Anti-Corn Law League (ACLL).[27] By concentrating upon this one issue the ACLL was able to bring together otherwise disparate interests and to prevent a diffusion of energies across a number of objectives. At the same time, it is clear that this issue was invested with far more significance than a narrow question of an inequitable tax. That tax, the 'bread tax' could become a potent symbol. First, to tax the poor man's staple food was regarded as more iniquitous than any other possible tax. Second, the measure was interpreted as an expression of both the continuing political power of the landed aristocracy as well as the inability of that aristocracy to survive the progressive tendencies of the day. Instead it had to block progress by seeking artificially to protect its own position at the expense of the rest of the community. To repeal the Corn Laws would signal a decisive shift of power towards the productive, progressive interests in society. Third, as a major step to free trade, with favourable impacts on the economy of other countries, repeal would help the cause of progress beyond Britain and would remove many of the tensions in the international sphere which provided a justification for wars and the maintenance of expensive and parasitic military establishments. The ACLL was able to combine concentration on a well-defined objective with the argument that this objective had a general significance.

Despite its effectiveness, the ACLL did not monopolise liberal activity in the period 1838–46. Other kinds of liberals focused on their attention on foreign policy, church questions, financial reform, and the extension of the franchise. There were many overlaps between the membership of the different groups involved. At the same time, the particular issues also brought in support from those who did not, in general terms, see themselves as liberals. The most important example was the conversion of Peel and some of his followers to the cause of free trade, tariff reform, and specifically repeal of the Corn Laws.

Peel saw the issue quite differently from the leaders of the ACLL. The Corn Laws had become increasingly difficult to defend. Therefore, in order to make the conservation of many other practices (an established Church, the pre-eminence of the aristocracy, the resistance to further franchise reform) more effective, this particular grievance needed to be tackled. By repealing the Corn Laws, Peel hoped to stabilise the position of the Conservative Party.

In the short run both he and his ACLL opponents turned out to be wrong. He was wrong first because repeal did not come so much as a final step in the well-considered programme of tariff reform, but as a morally motivated act in the aftermath of the Irish famine. The moral significance attached to the Corn Laws helps explain the continued opposition to the repeal within the Conservative Party which led almost immediately to Peel's own downfall and the splitting of the Party in such a way that it would be another twenty years before it could hope to command a majority within the House of Commons. From this angle the equation Cobden made between a reactionary landed interest and the Conservative Party appeared correct. However, the different middle-class interests which had supported the Repeal did not continue to act in a unified way which might have helped the emergence of a party of 'progress'. Instead, repeal led to the removal of any central liberal objective, and after 1846 liberals dispersed their energies in a number of directions. The opponents of the Conservatives, in purely parliamentary terms, did not have to be so effectively organised as when they confronted a united

Conservative Party. The result was an even greater fragmentation of politics. At the same time, Repeal came to be accepted by the mid-1850s as irreversible and a general consensus on liberal financial and fiscal policies was established (at least during peacetime: the Crimean War temporarily reversed these policies). Economic liberalism so clearly made sense for so many interests in mid-century Britain that it ceased to be an issue around which a liberal movement could form. However, whether it made sense because it clearly *did* benefit interests, or because the ideological consensus shaped economic liberalism as the common sense of the day, is a complex question I will have to leave aside. In any case, it would be other issues in the 1860s which permitted a more coherent and organised liberalism to take shape.

b) Germany

The situation was very different in Germany. After 1815 many of the economic restrictions removed during the Napoleonic era were restored. Guilds continued to exercise their privileges in most states, even if they often proved ineffective. Although the Articles of Confederation included an undertaking to allow people to move freely from one member state to another, in fact there were many border controls. Individual states imposed their own tariffs, even if the moves towards the Zollverein reduced the significance of this. Economic privileges continued to carry political rights with them – for example in allowing guild masters a special place on town governments, or by continuing to allow owners of noble estates in Prussia policing and judicial powers as well as sole access to certain institutions of local and regional government.

Given all this, a commitment to economic liberalism would seem to involve a commitment to a wholesale transformation of economic institutions in Germany. The issue was not one which could generate consensus or where there was any obviously powerful existing interest in favour of extensive change. Where such interests might favour liberalisation in one particular area – perhaps reduction in guild privileges, or easier movement from one state to another – they would have little concern with liberalisation in other areas. There was a free trade lobby in German liberalism but it tended to be a rather doctrinaire, academic body fairly detached from any major economic interests.

In any case, the situation made it difficult to see a political opposition movement as the way forward. When Prussian reformers had begun a process of economic liberalisation in the Napoleonic period, they had encountered a good deal of 'popular' resistance. The privileged groups which were threatened by that liberalisation were sufficiently powerful to be able to dominate institutions which provided some representation to 'public opinion'. As a consequence, some economic liberals tended to look to an enlightened, bureaucratic state to dismantle economic privileges and restrictions, in the hope that this would then generate a more prosperous economy in which opinion would come to accept liberal arrangements.

This situation has led some historians to draw a sharp distinction between economic and political liberalism in Germany for at least the period up to about 1860.[28] Economic liberalism is seen as the affair of doctrinaire academics, state officials who are not only convinced by the doctrine of political economy but also motivated by the desire both to reduce political power held by independent corporations such as guilds and aristocracies and to remove the state from an expensive range of economic interventions. There might have been certain economic interests which supported this programme, for example commercial circles in the Rhinelands, but they are seen as elitist, lacking any prospect of popular support. On the other hand, political liberalism which concentrated upon constitutionalism is seen as less concerned with economic liberalisation. Drawing their support from elements of the wide and diverse *Mittelstand*, these liberals could not openly attack many of the privileges and restrictions to which this *Mittelstand* was devoted. Indeed, some historians have argued that the more radical of these liberals actually supported an even more interventionist state and saw the free market and class society of industrialising Britain as something to be avoided rather than emulated.[29]

I think there are problems with these arguments, especially when they also counterpose an early *Mittelstand* liberalism to a later bourgeois liberalism which is more oligarchic and positive about industrialisation. First, we have to keep to some meaningful definition of liberalism. A 'liberal' programme which would impose constitutional restrictions upon the powers of the central state simply in order to substitute the authority of a restrictive, authoritarian, and corporatist community in its place does not fit any characterisation of liberalism which makes the extension of general individual liberty its defining feature.[30]

Second, in fact the two counterposed positions are misleading simplifications. So far as economic liberalism is concerned, it is now coming to be recognised that very few people by 1850 (and this is true of Britain as well) had a clear vision of an industrial society or, if they did, saw this in positive terms. Economic liberalism was far more to do with creating greater efficiency and prosperity within the present range of economic activities. Studies of the Rhenish economic interests which favoured liberalism support this view.[31] It would be more accurate to see the division as between a vision of a corporate and one of a free market society.

On the other side, many political liberals recognised the dangers of too abrupt a move from corporate to free market arrangements (just as they do in many parts of Eastern Europe today). The issue was rather one of a reforming programme. Looked at from this perspective one can see such a programme as one which could obtain significant *Mittelstand* support as well as opposition.[32] The real political distinction is that between liberals and populists, be they conservative or radical in their political values. Liberals, for example, wished to reduce the legal privileges of guilds but to replace them with still influential voluntary associations. The liberals of the Frankfurt Parliament decreed general freedom of movement and of choice of occupation, but then declared that the detailed implementation of such a policy must be left until later. The popular liberals of the 1860s like Schulz-Delitzsch had a great deal of sympathy with economic cooperatives but believed that these could function in a voluntary and free-market way.[33]

The actual character of economic change in this period made such a programme a plausible one. Free masters, journeymen, enterprising peasant farmers as well as practitioners of new economic activities – all stood to gain from this kind of reforming liberalisation. In the 1860s the popular base of liberalism was closely linked to its taking up the causes of free movement from one state to another and freedom of organisation amongst workers. When Lassalle dismissed these as palliatives of no significance, most of the organised labour movement repudiated him. At the same time that movement, as well as many small employers, looked to the associational aspects of popular liberalism with approval.[34]

It was not so much the continuing power of 'corporatists' which made it difficult to develop a Mittelstand liberalism around mid-century, but rather the crisis in which the economy found itself at this time. At such times as the 'Hungry Forties' people were desperate to hold on to what they had and to steer what limited help they thought might be available towards themselves. In these circumstances any argument about liberalisation met with a great deal with hostility, and it was the misfortune of liberals in 1848 to encounter this. However, by the 1860s the more buoyant state of the economy meant that liberalisation was seen as less threatening. Finally, the later move towards a more 'class based' or 'bourgeois' liberalism was actually associated with a move away from policies which favoured free trade as well as free associations and participatory politics. Early liberalism did not involve a commitment to industrialisation; later industrialisation was not associated with the emergence of a new kind of liberalism but rather with a turning away from liberalism. It is within the context of the complex shifts from a corporate to a free market economy that we must situate economic liberalism. From that perspective we can see it as having close links to political liberalism in terms of a reforming programme in which association remains central but on a voluntary basis. Clearly there were then internal divisions about the pace and pattern of reform and these can be related to different interests, but this is very different from juxtaposing an 'economic' to a 'political' liberalism. Rather one should juxtapose this broad, if internally differentiated liberalism, against a corporate populism, both conservative and radical, as well as a doctrinaire but very sectional commitment to complete free trade.

By the 1860s this reform programme promised to become a major factor in creating popular, multi-class support for liberalism. One can trace at an economic level areas of tension. For example, the liberal cooperative movement in practice favoured cooperatives of small traders and manufacturers in areas of credit and raw material purchases as against those of dependent workers in the sphere of production. In turn some of those workers found Lassalle's alternative of state-funded producers' cooperatives more attractive.[35] However, I think one can exaggerate the class division this introduced into liberalism at the time. The failure to maintain its multi-class appeal in what was still a Mittelstand society had less to do with an inappropriate model of economic class divisions and more to do with political and cultural matters. I have considered political issues in the essay 'Liberalism or Social Democracy?' So far as cultural matters are concerned, religious questions were the most important and will be considered in the next section.

c) Comparisons

Economic liberalism in Britain had only a few targets to attack. The most important was the Corn Laws. A powerful movement to repeal the corn laws could develop because this was a definite goal, because a variety of interests could see benefits to be had from repeal, and above all because a general significance could be attached to repeal. By the late 1840s many had accepted the case for free trade, and indeed within another decade it would appear as so commonsensical a position that few could dispute it. What caused free traders like Cobden to despair, however, was that acceptance of this piece of common sense did not bring with it acceptance of the broader liberal values to which he subscribed or to the formation of a dominant Liberal Party drawing for support upon a broad and progressive middle class.

In Germany economic liberalism had too many targets to attack; it became a critique of many internal social arrangements. If pushed in too doctrinaire and laissez-faire a fashion, it came to be detached from any important interests. Rather, liberals had to accept a gradualist reform programme which accorded an important role to associational activity. Liberals also looked to the strong state to realise such objectives as the freedom of movement. The Prussian state, in this as well as in tariff matters, had by far the most liberal record, and this can help account for the fact that both German and foreign liberals such as Cobden, could see that state as an ally of liberalism.

Religion

a) Britain

The major religious questions affecting liberalism in Britain concerned the relationships between the established Church (Anglican in England, Wales and Ireland; Presbyterian in Scotland), Catholicism, and dissenting Protestantism. Secularism as an end in itself (rather than as a means to reduce the advantages enjoyed by other confessions) was of relatively little importance in this period.[36]

Although the treatment of Catholics aroused strong feelings, as the debates at the time about Catholic Emancipation showed, it was an advantage for Liberals that Catholics were concentrated in Ireland and could be treated as a problem somewhat set aside from mainland concerns. The Catholic Church had grown used to having no special privileges, sources of wealth or political power, or drawing support from social elites. Catholics were not so much a confessional group within the nation, as they were in Germany, as a national minority.

As a consequence, when the Catholic Church played a central part in mobilising a popular movement in Ireland in the 1820s and 1830s, a movement associated with the revival of populist religion, this did not lead to a simple Protestant and/or Liberal rejection. Whigs had for some time before 1829 supported the cause of Catholic emancipation on both the principled grounds of civil and religious liberty but also on the pragmatic grounds that Catholic grievances were much more difficult to handle when such discrimination was practised. This latter position was one, in effect, that Wellington and Peel had accepted by 1829.

However, this only affected the political rights of Catholics. It did not address the problem of the Anglican establishment in Ireland. Emancipation changed the balance of power by allowing an Irish Catholic interest to have a voice at Westminster, and the Whig Governments after 1832 were compelled to listen to that voice and make some concessions to it. Nevertheless, by the mid-1830s it had become clear that the Anglican and landed interests within the Whigs would make further concessions difficult. Indeed, it was once again to be Peel and the Conservative Party which took matters further by seeking to promote Catholic education out of state revenue. To complicate matters still further, there did develop from an Anglican point of view the idea that church establishment might actually undermine religious belief, especially where the church in question had only minority support. It was through reasoning of this kind that Gladstone was to move from a High Church Anglicanism which resisted any diminution in the privileges of the Church of England and its connections to the state, to a preparedness to disestablish the Church of Ireland.

Once again, after an initial period of Whig and Catholic cooperation by the mid-1830s the Catholic question fragmented rather than reinforced party divisions. However, when Gladstone took up the matter of Irish church disestablishment in the later 1860s this proved to be a major unifying element for some years within the emergent Liberal Party. It brought in support from dissenting Protestants who welcomed a reduction in the privileges of Anglicanism, from Liberal Anglicans who believed that establishment actually devalued their religion in Ireland, and from some High Church evangelicals like Gladstone himself. When, however, the issue moved on to further questions of land reform, education and home rule, this fragile unity was shattered.[37]

Much more positive for the development of liberalism was the role of dissenting Protestantism. The subject is a very well-known one and there is a good deal of recent literature on it, so there is no need to go into detail. Although some Nonconformist denominations were either politically quietist or even Tory (e.g. many Wesleyan Methodists), most were ready to play an active role in politics. They were especially motivated by the resentment of the privileges of the Church of England. In many parts of England and Wales it was campaigns against church rates, against Anglican influence in schools, and discriminations concerning rights to worship, marry and bury which fuelled popular passions. John Bright, a Quaker who first became involved in Rochdale politics through the church rates issue in the 1830s, recalled later that elections to the parish vestry aroused more interest than parliamentary elections.[38] So long as the Conservative Party defended many of these privileges, and they did throughout this period, such Dissenters would gravitate to supporting their political opponents.

This was to become significant principally because Dissent grew so quickly in the mid-century, as the religious census of 1851 made alarmingly clear to the Church of England. One has to put that into context. There was also something of an Anglican revival, measured in terms of church building and congregations. However, the dissenting expansion was also concentrated in regions and amongst social groups which were becoming politically more influential with franchise reform and the redistribution of seats. The Liberal Party would not have become a party of government without the support it received from areas such as Wales, East Anglia, and parts of the Midlands where Dissent was particularly important, and from groups such as new manufacturers, craftsmen, shopkeepers, skilled workers, and those in mining districts, amongst all of whom there was a disproportionately high Nonconformist element.[39]

Nonconformity also had an important role in animating liberal causes in the period from the late 1830s to the mid-1860s when party divisions were less clearcut. When one looks at liberal pressure groups during this period there is a very prominent role played by Dissenters. John Bright (Quaker) and George Wilson (Sandemanian: a form of Dissent within Scottish Protestantism) in the ACLL; Joseph Sturge (Quaker) in the Complete Suffrage Union: the examples could be multiplied many times. The early trade union leaders with close connections to the Liberal Party from the 1860s were overwhelmingly Dissenters. The Unitarians played a role in Manchester liberalism out of all proportion to their numbers within the city.[40]

This had two major consequences. First, where there was a weakly developed political party, religious affiliations provided an important social bond which enabled people to come together collectively to develop political values, and to support each other in the world of politics. Second, the variety of social groups as well as dissenting denominations involved encouraged a cross-cutting character to politics which made commitment to certain principles, rather than representation of distinct interests, more central. This partly, I think, explains the high-mindedness as well as diverse and popular character of British liberalism.

At the same time it was vital, if liberalism was to have a political impact, that it did not lose significant Anglican support. The bulk of the parliamentary Liberal Party from the mid-1860s were Anglicans. For every major political leader in the liberal camp who was a Dissenter one can name another who was Anglican: Cobden in the ACLL, Beales in the Reform League, and, above all, Gladstone. Liberalism was not so much a movement which sought to mobilise groups, (Vincent rather nicely talks instead of groups projecting their concerns upon the Liberal Party) as a movement which, after pursuing single-issues on a cross-cutting basis, found a series of issues in the later 1860s (franchise reform, Irish disestablishment, educational reform) which could hold these groups together. The role of Dissent was central to that process. However, it also contained tensions, as later divisions on precisely the same issues were to show.

b) Germany

The situation was completely different in Germany. Here there was also a three way relationship to consider but it was between Protestantism, Catholicism and secular liberalism.

Catholics were not a national, nor even for much of the time, a religious minority; in the German Confederation there were more Catholic Germans than Protestant Germans. Only unification reduced them to the status of a large minority. Only the Polish subjects of Prussia constituted a significant group distinguished by nationality as well as Catholicism. German liberals had supported the Polish cause but much more on national than religious grounds.

So far as Germans were concerned there was also no one single area in which one of the confessional groups were concentrated. The complex inheritance of the Reformation and the territorial 'freezing' of confessional affiliations after 1648 meant that Protestants and Catholics lived close to one another in south Germany (e.g. Protestants in Franconia, in Baden and Württemburg), in western Germany (e.g. the Catholic majority in the Prussian province of the Rhineland can be set against the Protestant majority in Westphalia), in eastern Germany (e.g. the Catholics of Silesia), and even in north Germany (some one-fifth of the inhabitants of Hannover were Catholic).

In many ways this mixture had acquired more significance with the territorial reorganisation of Germany under and after Napoleon. Many small states could each have a primarily Catholic or Protestant character. The larger states, formed by amalgamating these smaller states, had a much more mixed character. Bavaria acquired a Protestant population in the Palatinate; Prussia a Catholic one in the Rhineland. On the other hand, this also helped to defuse some of the potential problems. Already by the late seventeenth century religious affiliation was defined geographically rather than by the religion of the prince. Many of the more powerful German princes practised a policy of religious toleration – undertaking to respect the beliefs of new subjects whether acquired by territorial changes or population movement. The Napoleonic generalisation of the territorial dynastic state in Germany also generalised this practice.

At the same time it reduced significantly the temporal powers of the Catholic

Church. It was in Catholic majority areas in south and west Germany that the most territorial amalgamation had taken place and the new princes, whether Catholic or Protestant, were not about to give up their powers. Instead the expropriation of church property and the denial of any temporal powers to the Church meant that a new situation had to be negotiated. In states with a Catholic majority such as Bavaria, agreements with the Papacy led to a church funded out of state revenue and with significant controls on the part of the king. In states with a Protestant majority, the tradition of the state church was continued (though in Prussia the Calvinist and Lutheran confessions were brought together), and after a period of some tension the Catholic church received recognition. There remained many tensions between state and the churches on such matters as education, marriage and confessional strife, but generally speaking the state was not seen as the agent of one particular denomination. Many mid-century British liberals favourably compared the secular character of German states with the Anglican character of the British state. In one sense, therefore, religion was a less politically significant issue in Germany. It would appear that it might not provide a motivating force in an liberal opposition, but neither would it appear likely to weaken liberalism.

However, the Catholic question was to have a major impact upon German liberalism. This was due both to the character of the Catholic revival over this period and its relationship to the question of national unification. Thrown much more upon its spiritual resources after being stripped of wealth and power under Napoleon, the Catholic church came increasingly under the influence of clergy with a religious vocation, often from fairly humble backgrounds, and reacting sharply against what they saw as the enlightenment corruption of belief. It involved itself much more positively in the revival of popular religious practices such as pilgrimages and the display of holy relics.[41] The Trier pilgrimage of 1844, for example, attracted some one million people to Trier cathedral during the month of August to see part of the coat supposedly worn by Jesus at the time of his crucifixion. At the same time as giving expression to popular religiosity, the pilgrimage provoked denunciations from enlightened liberals, including Catholics, and even to the attempt to set up a breakaway German Catholic movement.[42] Even more important, from the mid-century the Catholic Church responded positively to the social and spiritual needs of groups exposed to the problems of rapid economic change. Already in 1848 political Catholicism had demonstrated its political weight (although it has sometimes been exaggerated).

Liberals found it very difficult to respond effectively to these trends. To the social programme of Catholicism they could only offer voluntary association within a basic acceptance of economic growth and the development of free competition. The popular religious practices nurtured within the Catholic Church seemed to them to be superstitious and primitive, and they hoped to remove schooling from reaction-ary clerical influence. Furthermore, the ultramontane character of much of this

Catholic revival aroused their suspicions as nationalists and promoted an image of the Catholic Church as an intolerant hierarchy ultimately loyal to an Italian Pope ruling in Rome.

Nevertheless, there were also areas of potential cooperation. In Catholic minority states such as Prussia both liberals and Catholics argued the case for disestablishment, for the separation of church and state, although they meant different things by this. Catholics could also support moves to greater national unity.

However, as it became increasingly clear that such unity could only come about under Prussian auspices and with the exclusion of Austria from that unity, the Catholic position rapidly became one of opposition. In many ways the tensions between liberal nationalists who looked to Prussia and these Catholics was stronger outside Prussia, because they faced a Catholic society as well as a prince hostile to such unity. Hannoverian and Bavarian liberals were to prove more eager supporters of a policy designed to reduce the influence of the Catholic Church than 'old'-Prussian liberals. The final crisis which led to unification hardened this division.[43] By seeing Catholicism as a cultural question, one in which the secular state had to help undermine a reactionary culture, many German liberals deprived themselves of any understanding for Catholic grievances and of any hope of getting support from Catholics. German liberalism remained a Protestant and a secular movement.[44]

At the same time, dissenting Protestantism had little role to play in German liberalism. Partly this was because a dissenting tradition was far less important in Germany. There was such a tradition and in the 1830s and 1840s it did seem to be a vigorous one.[45] Why it did not match British Dissent thereafter is a complicated question which cannot be considered here. Certainly the defeat of the revolution of 1848 and subsequent repression played an important role. Partly there were not the same grievances as existed in Britain because the state was already more secular. This meant that religious differences tended to be less politicised. Many Dissenters were less interested in political questions, and this in turn made it less important to *organise* Dissent. And of course, dissenting Protestants were notoriously argumentative people who found it difficult to subordinate their individual opinions to the needs of a collective politics. What is more, a good deal of debate about doctrine and church organisation remained confined within the existing churches. Reform Protestantism played its part in liberalism but in a more muted way than that of Dissent.[46]

However, until a good deal more work on Protestantism in nineteenth-century Germany has been undertaken much of this remains speculative. It is a weakness of much comparative history to exaggerate differences and then to spend much time in explaining these. (See Introduction.) There were regions where Dissent was important and it does seem to have helped shape a popular liberal movement. In the Kingdom of Saxony, for example, where both German Catholicism and the 'free

LABOUR AND LIBERALISM IN NINETEENTH-CENTURY EUROPE

communities' (*Freie Gemeinde*) attracted a good following (as well as in Prussian Saxony) there was a strong radical liberal movement in 1848, epitomised in the figure of Robert Blum. The support for the radical liberal rejection of Prussian unification which came from this area can perhaps be related in part to this dissenting tradition. In the same way there were regions in Britain where Dissent did not play an important role in popular politics. This was, for example, the case in London and it can be linked to the relative weakness of popular liberalism in the capital in the 1860s. (See Introduction.)

The net effect, however, was at a national level to deprive liberalism of both the socialising and cross-cutting roles that Dissent played within British liberalism. There was less of a set of 'pre-political' associations upon which German liberalism could build and which gave British liberalism so much of its strength within communities. Instead German liberalism looked to more secular forms of association to provide this support – shooting societies, choral groups, cooperatives, educational associations, and gymnastic clubs.[47] Arguably these could not match the commitments and solidarity generated by common religious beliefs.

At the same time the lack of common beliefs cutting across social divisions meant that those divisions could come to play a much greater role in German politics. British workers had specific labour interests similar to their German counterparts, and in many ways received no more satisfaction from British Liberals. (See the essay 'Liberalism or social democracy?'.) But they were bound to other liberals by agreement on other issues such as Irish disestablishment and the removal of Anglican control of education and this made it easier for them to accept compromises on their own specific interests.

c) Comparisons

It should be emphasised that none of this meant that German liberalism could not become a popular movement. It did attract some Catholic support in the late 1850s and early 1860s. Areas where Dissent did figure as in Saxony were liberal strongholds, and liberalism was managing to build a popular base through its national and reform values and in conjunction with various kinds of associations. However, in retrospect it appears a much more fragile and deliberate achievement than in Britain where central issues, especially in the mid-1860s, served to bring both Catholics and Dissenters around the Liberal Party. By contrast, the crisis of the 1860s alienated Catholics from the liberal nationalist cause, and the lack of the socialising and cross-cutting role played by Dissent meant that German liberalism could not handle the social and regional tensions to which it was subject even in Protestant majority areas. As a consequence German liberalism soon took on a more clearly secular and bourgeois character, anti-clerical rather than anti-establishment. In turn, the developing labour movement also lacked the protestant character of its British counterpart.

Law

I have dealt with this subject in another essay in this book ('Civil society and the labour movement'). Here I will summarise the arguments of that essay. I will also explore further that aspect of the subject which most clearly relates to the politics of liberalism – namely, constitutional questions.

a) England

The argument of that essay briefly summarised was that in England, law, especially statute law, was an instrument of policy. Sometimes this took the form of a very sweeping measure, for example the Poor Law of 1834 and the Municipal Corporation Act of 1835. However, this was an exceptional and recent development. The 1832 franchise reform was innovative in being of a general and systematic kind and clearly elements in government after 1832 had acquired a taste for this kind of legislation. But much law retained a specific and piecemeal character, for example in the new field of urban improvements. There was something of a continuum between the general and the more specific measures. The 1835 Municipal Corporations Act was permissive, and therefore required further action on the part of urban communities before coming into operation. In the field of urban improvements 'model' bills were drafted which provided a basis on which specific measures could be framed.

What was also important was that there was a continuum on how to remedy grievances by changes in the law. In principle, the pursuit of franchise reform was no different from that of changes in laws affecting such matters as the sale of alcohol. The trade unionists who became involved in the passing of the Second Reform Act could easily adjust their methods of agitation to the subsequent campaign to alter the legal framework concerned with industrial relations. The focus throughout was on parliament which was taken for granted as the stable source of law. The rights of individuals were either entrenched in common law or could be created or enhanced by statute. The ideas of the state itself as an abstract legal entity, and of law as a systematic framework for the regulation of affairs, were alien in this context.

What this meant was that English liberals did not concern themselves with broad questions about the form the state should take and the role of law in this. The notion of the judicial function as a separate branch of government, for example, was reduced to the more specific question of the secure tenure of judges. Constitutional questions were reduced to these particular, 'empirical' forms. The exception proves the rule. The one important source of systematic, general thinking about the state and law in early nineteenth-century Britain was utilitarianism. But James Mill, in his *Essay on Government*, deduced the ideal form of the state from psychological principles. Assumptions about human nature preceded any consideration of human rights. The same procedure underpinned Bentham's elaborate legal proposals.

Consequently constitutional issues were never considered of importance within the utilitarian tradition. Paradoxically, therefore, this major attempt at a-historical, systematic regulation of human affairs could be absorbed into the British empirical political tradition. Utilitarians prided themselves on clear and realistic thinking and produced blueprints for legal and administrative reform. Practical politicians could then plunder these blueprints for specific measures. Neither party was concerned with how far such measures conformed to notions of the proper form the state should take, or what limits should be placed on state power.

b) Germany

The situation was very different in Germany. Here the state, except in the eyes of particular kinds of conservatives defending monarchy, was constructed abstractly. Systematic constitutional thought played a major part in liberal thought. The early liberalism of the south German states revolved around questions of civil and political rights. Detailed debates took place on such issues as the relative powers of prince and parliament, the claims of parliaments to approve taxation or even more to scrutinise budgets.[48] In 1847 political debate in Prussia focused on the question of a constitution. And, of course, in 1848 the most cherished achievement of German liberals was the systematic discussion of the legal framework which should define and limit the state. The clash in Prussia in the 1860s revolved around constitutional questions and Bismarck found it necessary to elaborate a particular view of the Prussian constitution to justify his conduct of government without parliamentary consent. The foundation of the North German Confederation in 1867 and then of the German Empire in 1871 were accompanied by the work of constituent assemblies.

Furthermore, general legal codification played a major role in German politics. The major reforms of the Napoleonic period included the introduction of the Code Napoleon into many German territories.[49] This had been preceded in Prussia by the introduction of the *Allgemeine Landesrecht* in 1794.[50] Austrian civil law was codified in 1811. The shift away from a structure of 'feudal' to one of 'bourgeois' property rights involved large-scale legal change. This was most apparent and important in the process of peasant emancipation. Whether this in practice ended up entrenching a system of peasant dominated agriculture or rather dispossessing many small cultivators in favour of larger farmers, in all cases the tangle of shared property rights had to be eliminated. Reform of the guilds also involved sweeping legal changes.

The two areas – constitutions and property rights – cannot be treated separately. For example, where corporate property privileges were attached to the right to participate in the political affairs of a town, the removal of the privileges entailed a redefinition of urban citizenship. In the larger states this increasingly required state-wide regulation, which in turn raised the question of the relationship between local and state political rights.

Around these very real problems there was elaborated the classical liberal theory of law which depended upon a clear and abstract distinction between private and public. Primacy was accorded to the private sphere and to the elaboration of contract law which regulated dealings between equal and free individuals. In some German states the stress upon the individual as the economic agent went so far as to impede the construction of new, corporate legal subjects (such as the limited liability company). Within the public sphere debate focused on civil and political rights, how to define and secure them, and the form the state should take.[51]

c) Comparisons

There are many reasons one can advance for these great differences between Britain and Germany. In the 'private' sphere there already existed a well-developed set of 'bourgeois' freedoms in Britain. People could sell their labour freely, practise whatever occupation they chose, buy and sell property, and move from one area to another without let or hindrance (unless they were very poor). It was not necessary to dismantle a pre-existing set of property relations.

Related to this, there was no formal link between forms of property and political rights. To be sure, franchises even after 1832 were attached to the value of land-holdings in the counties and the wealth of the household in the boroughs. But this was not so much a property as a wealth based franchise, and in turn there were no legal restrictions on who could acquire such wealth. Consequently, after 1832 liberals who believed dependency disqualified people from political rights, could resist further franchise reform.[52] In Germany many liberals strove for such a wealth based franchise. The three-class franchise which was introduced into Prussia after 1848 conformed to such liberal thinking. It was no accident that it had already played a part in Baden and in Rhenish towns, bastions of early German liberalism, and that it was criticised by many conservatives because of the way it paid no heed to the *form* of property involved.

On the public side, what was vital was the territorial and institutional stability of the British state. The institutional aspect should be given the greatest emphasis. There had, of course, been conflicts over the form the British state should take in the seventeenth century. One could argue that once these conflicts were settled in favour of parliamentary monarchy (rejecting both Absolutist forms of monarchy and various non-monarchical forms) then there was little scope for fundamental constitutional debate. Obviously it would be necessary to ask how this state form could adjust to new pressures in such a way as to prevent such debates arising, but that is not something that can be entered into here.

The absence of a parliamentary tradition meant that dissatisfaction with monarchy expressed itself in constitutional forms by the late eighteenth century. The revolutions in America and France coincided with the emergence of this type of political discourse and meant that the construction of new state institutions proceeded through the writing of a constitution. By the early nineteenth century, especially in areas under French control, political change had to be rationalised by means of constitutions. Even the old rulers had to accept this new political rhetoric. Constitutions became not merely ways of breaking with traditional monarchy, but also a means by which princes sought to create legitimacy for themselves.

In the case of Germany they also served to help integrate the diverse territories of new states created by Napoleon and then the Congress of Vienna. Of course, constitutions could have a fairly minimal political role, legitimising existing forms of rule, but in the hands of liberals it was by means of constitutional reasoning that a critique of the status quo could be carried forward.[53]

There was also a sociological connotation. In Germany, as in other states with a strong constitutional tradition, lawyers played a leading role in liberal movements. In America this tended to be lawyers in private practice in a society where 'bourgeois' property rights were well advanced and the state employed few people. In Germany, where private legal practice was less developed but the civil service was larger, more important and prestigious, it tended to be university-trained legal officials who played a prominent role in liberal movements. By contrast, in Britain the legal profession was a notoriously conservative one. Lawyers had an important political role (one only has to look at how many backbench M.P.s were barristers) but not did not take an especially prominent part in the leadership of liberal or radical movements and organisations. Where they did, as for example with William Roberts, Ernest Jones, and Edmund Beales, they often tended to be fairly marginal within their profession; in marked contrast to figures such as Heinrich Simon or Friedrich Dahlmann.

Social questions

a) England

In the case of England what was important was the *separation* of social and political questions, in the sense that poverty and pauperism were not seen as directly relevant to political stability. Poverty was treated as an economic or a humanitarian matter. This lack of political significance is indicated in the manner in which the New Poor Law of 1834 was passed. A doctrinaire and one-sided report served as the basis for an ill-considered measure. However, the criticisms of that measure did not focus on the possibility of political instability as poor people resisted the enforcement of the law, but rather upon what was regarded as faulty analysis or, more often, upon the inhumane character of the law. What political criticism there was concerned itself rather with the way in which the law broke with English political values by imposing a centralised administrative solution. In both this case and the later introduction of police forces, also an unpopular measure, it was the way in which the British state was moving towards a continental model, the 'Prussian' state that excited concern rather than the likelihood that the measures would generate popular opposition.

The measures did, in fact, generate such opposition, and in the case of the poor law this severely limited the extent of its enforcement.[54] What is more, one can establish connections between resistance to the Poor Law and the new police to the rise of Chartism, a mass movement of political opposition. Yet what is remarkable, from a continental perspective, is how *little* political concern this aroused within the ranks of the 'political nation'. Parliamentary debates and the diaries and letters of leading politicians in the late 1830s and early 1840s are more preoccupied with questions such as Ireland, the Church, and tariffs than they are with measures to deal with Chartism. In 1838, for example, Manchester politicians were more engaged over the struggle for incorporation than concerned about Chartist demands. There was some concern in 1842 when political demands were coupled with extensive industrial unrest; and in 1848 when the spectre of revolution on the continent aroused fears, but these were exceptional and short-lived.

In a way the very existence of Chartism helped account for this attitude. The state could monitor the activities of such a comparatively open and well-structured movement. It could calculate when to take repressive measures and when to make concessions. This is not to say that Chartism 'stabilised' British politics: that would be absurd. There were moments of uncertainty, and at such times government forces could panic. There was also repression. The British state did not always respond with negotiations and concessions.[55]

The best example of this came with Ireland. There, a much more 'continental' situation obtained. Government was remote from the populace, ill-informed about popular opinion, worried about underground politics, and faced with unorganised resistance in such forms as attacks on police stations and government officials. Bureaucratic methods and coercion replaced the politics of negotiation.[56] Yet even here, the most pressing social question of all, the famine in Ireland, evoked humanitarian rather than political concern. Perhaps the physical separation from the mainland and the absence of any more general threat from Europe which could ally itself with Irish grievances helped account for this political complacency.

This meant that liberals treated poverty as an economic rather than a political question. In turn they were able to separate various issues such as the labour question (how to handle trade unionism and strikes) from the issue of poverty (see above, 'Civil law and the labour movement'.) The main divisions came over the debate about how far laissez-faire policies would eliminate social problems so far as was possible, or how far particular forms of collective intervention were required. Furthermore, given this lack of political anxiety, it was much easier than on the continent for a largely laissez-faire attitude to be maintained. When this was coupled with fiscal reform which both eased tax burdens and seemed to reduce the presence of central government, such measures could even obtain radical support.[57]

b) Germany

Here the social question up to 1848 had a very different character. No clear economic alternatives appeared attractive in the face of rapid population growth. There was little structural economic change capable of absorbing these extra people. In the countryside there developed a numerous landless and cottager class linked to increased rural industry and more potato cultivation. The towns, though not growing relative to the rural population, maintained their share of the population through immigration. In large towns such as Cologne, Hamburg, Berlin, Breslau, Munich and Vienna there grew a mass of highly visible paupers or casual workers earning below subsistence incomes. The poor harvests of 1844, 1845 and 1846 intensified this situation and created a sense of crisis.

In the debate on the 'social question' various theoretical policies were proposed. Some favoured a return to the restrictions of a corporate society – limiting the right to marriage, restricting the rights of settlement and movement. Liberals, by contrast, argued that only further liberalisation would create the framework for a more efficient economy which could support the larger population. At the level of practice governments showed themselve increasingly paralysed in the face of apparently unmanageable problems.[58]

At the same time there was very little in the way of popular organisation which could give some focus to those suffering from poverty and unemployment. 'Popular' opposition took the form of strikes and riots. Those who claimed to speak for the 'people' might employ a violent and extreme rhetoric, but in part this was a substitute for any popular constituency.[59]

This meant that it was difficult to know how to 'police' discontent. What is more, old-regime monarchies were reluctant to involve civilians in the maintenance of order or even to place much dependency on a police force separated from the military.[60] The dependence of the smaller German states upon Austrian and Prussian backing increased their weakness in the face of any popular opposition that might arise. The military were inept at dealing with riots and strikes and demonstrations, and in any case, especially at times of international tension, had to be kept ready for conventional use against other states.

All this meant that the social question was invested with a huge political significance. This had important consequences for liberals. In sharing the fear of popular upheaval with the governments they opposed, they were constrained in how far they could go in that opposition. They did not feel confident enough to ignore the social issue (which partly explains why German liberals were less inclined to doctrinaire laissez-faire views on the matter compared to their English counterparts). However, neither did they feel confident enough to be able to manipulate social grievances in the way, for example, that Anti-Corn Law League leaders did.

These problems reached their climax in 1848. Faced with what objectively were very limited forms of popular opposition, the governments of the smaller German states, deprived of Austro-Prussian support, capitulated. Given that the popular movements were too ill-organised to take over directly, authority was given to the prominent liberal opposition politicians. In Austria and Prussia there was greater violence before governments capitulated – but it was an exaggerated sense of the domestic upheaval, compounded by fears of challenges from elsewhere (a radical France, opposition in Italy and Hungary) and an inability either to negotiate with popular movements or to repress them efficiently which again led to the assumption of authority, or at least the appearance of authority, by liberals.[61]

Yet those liberals were in turn constrained by their fear and ignorance of popular grievances. Being catapulted into state governments and parliaments as well as the German National Assembly tended to distance them from their local *Mittelstand* 'constituencies'. Rather than working to build up a popular following on the basis of that *Mittelstand* support, liberals tended instead to rely upon the appeal of their general schemes of reform. In fact those schemes had little popular appeal, so that liberals were increasingly forced to look to the old authorities for help. As those old authorities regained confidence, becoming aware of the very real strengths of their own position, so they were able to dispense with liberals.

c) Comparison

One should not exaggerate the contrasts. They become less marked after 1848. Although the events of that year had scarred many German liberals, the rapid economic growth from the mid-1850s did marginalise the social question as a political concern in Germany. Liberals regained confidence and also began to build up something of a popular base amongst a variety of social groups. By the early 1860s a powerful reformist liberal movement was having increasing influence upon the affairs of individual German states. At the same time early trade unionism, workers' educational associations, cooperatives and other popular organisations created the basis for a more organised relationship between liberals and broad sections of the population. However, this never reached anything like the extent it did in Britain, either in the Chartist period or in the 1860s when Gladstone could exploit links to Nonconformity, to trade unions, to political reform movements. Probably within individual states one could have expected the liberal movement in Germany to continue to move towards this English model, especially if parliaments became the centre of real power. What abruptly halted this development was the national question and, above all, the war between Austria and Prussia in 1866. War and the forcible reorganisation of states territorially and institutionally shattered the liberal movement. It remained an important political force, especially in the early years of the Second Empire before broader sections of the population could develop politically, but was never able to rebuild the diverse and popular character it had possessed in the 1860s.

Conclusion

English liberals operated from a more secure position than German liberals. They could take for granted the political context within which they worked. After 1815 the British state was fairly secure from external threats and so the issues of war or control of a powerful army did not complicate the position of liberals. In Germany, the issues of war and control of the army were central liberal concerns, and meant that liberalism could not simply focus on 'domestic' political questions. Territorially the British state was stable which enabled a continuity in political organisation. German liberals faced constant territorial changes which disrupted political organisation. Institutionally a national Parliament provided British liberals with one point of political focus. In Germany a multi-state system, in which until 1848 the most important two states did not have a single parliament, meant liberalism lacked such an institutional focus.

In Britain the system of property rights broadly conceived (that is, including the legal right to practise a trade wherever one wanted) already in many ways conformed to liberal values. In Germany part of the programme of liberalism was concerned with the establishment of such a system of propery rights.

After 1832 in Britain liberals had finally achieved a systematic franchise reform which brought voting rights into conformity with dominant liberal values. Further reforms of municipal government meant they now had secure access to political participation both locally and nationally. By contrast in Germany the reaction against the July revolution and its spread into some German states had led to a reversal of even the limited gains made earlier by liberals.

In Britain liberalism was able to make points of contact with popular movements (in the agitation before 1832, in the Anti-Corn Law League and other single-issue associations, under the leadership of Bright and Gladstone) and never conflated problems of poverty and unemployment with the general issue of political stability. German liberalism was by contrast more isolated from broad sections of the population (which was also less organised and involved in public affairs) and more inclined to invest the social question with general political significance. In Britain the strength of Nonconformity and the territorially separated concentration of Catholics helped create a broad movement in opposition to the Tory defence of the Church of England. In Germany much weaker Nonconformity and the revival of an illiberal Catholicism in many parts of Germany tended to deprive liberals of that broad support and led them to adopt a more secular, anti-clerical position.

As a result, English liberalism tended to break into a series of one-issue movements, often with cross-cutting social support. The focus was upon abolition of the Corn Laws, or disestablishment of the Anglican Church, or an extension of the franchise. To explain why and when liberalism managed to form itself into a broad political movement one needs really to explain why various of these concerns in the country at large could coalesce into support for a particular parliamentary grouping. That would take us too far in this essay.

By contrast German liberals had to focus on the more fundamental questions of how to acquire power (rather than to exert influence) and what kind of state and society would be best suited to the realisation of their values. The more specific questions of how one exercised power came second. There was also less cross-cutting of shared interests across social divisions. Partly one can relate this to particular issues such as the lack of a dissenting Protestantism. More generally it has been argued that within local communities there were rather less contacts between different social groups.[62] This is an interesting idea which needs much more research. I would rather emphasise that the abrupt extensions of political activity from local or state levels to a national level had the effect of breaking what political contacts there had been across social divisions. 1848 too rapidly put liberals into positions of power before they had built up networks of support of corresponding scope. The wars and political reconstruction of 1866–71 had a similar effect. British liberalism, considered in party terms, was rather disorganised and discontinuous, but a stable political framework allowed various movements to form influential coalitions.

Yet in another sense German liberalism was much more clearly definable than English liberalism. Its characteristics included the construction of a political creed which opposed constitutionalism to non-accountable monarchy, which insisted on the need for a written Bill of Rights, on the separation of church from state, which sought to replace systems of shared property rights with one in which property rights were vested in individuals and elaborated the kind of law which would be needed to regulate such a system. All this gave German liberalism a much more clearcut ideological character and made it, in theory at least, a much more radical doctrine. The coherence and radicalism of this position can be seen enshrined in the Imperial Constitution of 1849, and in the sweeping reforms associated with liberalism introduced in the 1860s and early 1870s.

It is this difference which makes it very hard to compare liberalism in the two countries. As a German historian coming to look at the English situation, I found that the historiography seemed very weak on such issues as the ideas of liberal politicians or the social base of liberal movements. The latter point, given that generally English historians are supposed to be more advanced in this kind of area than German historians, was initially surprising. There were studies of the parliamentary composition of the Whig-Liberal party or of the Anti-Corn Law League or even of the electoral support for Liberal candidates, but these were not brought together.[63] The reason soon became apparent. Because the term 'liberal' was so vague, because liberalism was less a movement than a confusion of single-issue groups connected by social ties (and perhaps, though this is under-researched, some broad cultural affinities), it was difficult to decide what generally should be counted as liberal. Given the inability to identify 'liberalism' as a position on the political spectrum, it would in turn be difficult to describe its ideas or social base. Liberalism was not so much a movement as an achieved aspect of English life in many fields (free trade, parliamentary government, more rights for non-Anglicans) leaving a diffuse set of issues on which liberal advances might still be made.

In Germany, by contrast, liberalism, although it too was made up of diverse groups and opinions, occupied a more definite ideological position. It was ranged against clearly illiberal forms of government and also against illiberal forces in society such as revived Catholicism. It was precisely the illiberal character of much of German state and society which helped define sharply the liberal position. The main problem then was, given their embattled position, how German liberals could construct a movement of real power or come to exert any real influence. Before 1848 different emphases were being placed on building up support within society or achieving influence with governments.[64] This tended towards two kinds of liberalism – one an 'associational' liberalism which stressed constitutional reform and the other a state-oriented liberalism which emphasised the role of a reforming administration in clearing away many of the obstacles to liberalism. But with limited popular appeal or governmental influence, neither acquired a clear identity. If anything 1848 undermined both positions, because liberal politicians were distanced from their local constituencies by achieving apparent state and national powers, but at the same time the shift of the old order towards counter-revolution made it more hostile to liberals. The same ambivalent development of a popular base and governmental influence by the early 1860s was potentially stronger, partly because economic liberalism was more acceptable in conditions of greater prosperity, and partly because governments had come to recognise the need for some constitutional concessions to maintain authority. But the civil war of 1866–67 shattered the basis of that movement before it had either become truly popular or acquired real influence in the most important state, Prussia. Liberals could still believe that after 1867 those with whom they formed alliances would gradually become junior partners as progress – economic, political and moral – strengthened liberalism. However, although in certain respects liberal values did become more firmly entrenched (for example, freedom of movement and the right to practise a trade), in other respects their position was undermined. The constitution of 1871 entrenched old political forces associated with particularism more firmly than that of 1867; the onset of depression and then protectionism in 1874 and 1878/79 reduced support for economic liberalism; the re-entry of political conservatism into influence and the rise of political Catholicism and of socialism reduced the predominance of the liberal movement.[65]

One should also note related differences in the ideology of liberalism. There is the well-worn contrast between the abstract rhetoric of German liberalism compared with the empirical tradition of British liberal discourse. That is a valid contrast but needs to be taken further. In both countries there was a similar stress upon progress and civilisation creating the conditions of success for liberalism. The main difference was that in the British case this could be argued in terms of achievements in the present or recent past. In Germany the main stress on this idea of progress came in the post-1848 period and was more future-oriented, even a justification for compromising liberal values in the present.

In both countries particular ideas acquired an almost utopian significance. In the Anti-Corn Law League the notion of free trade could work in this way, and one can find meetings of the ACLL taking place where the specific issue of the corn laws was barely mentioned as these more general hopes predominated. In Germany the notion of the constitution often played a similar role. But the notion of free trade roots itself in the discourse of political economy which had acquired the chararacter of 'common-sense' by the 1850s and which also played down questions about the nature of politics and the state. The notion of the constitution focuses precisely on these questions. It is not actually more 'abstract' but takes on the appearance of being so.

What is more, the specific constitutional reasoning, with its distinction between parliament and the state and its concern with a state defined and bound by law, owes much to the German idealist tradition. Even when the advocates of 'Realpolitik' tried to break with this type of thinking, the actual absence of close connections between economic progress and constitutional advance forced them back to more abstract theorising and demands. In the British case, as I have already emphasised, the equally abstract utilitarian approach ruled out discussions of political principle. In practice political economy was accepted as the economic basis of progress and parliamentary government as the appropriate political form, even if some like James Mill linked that to universal suffrage. Further argument focused on the particular laws which such a government should pass.

What this means is that the lack of a stable political framework in Germany, either territorially or institutionally, tends to make even the apparently 'empirical' and 'Whiggish' elements of liberalism shift back to rather abstract modes of reasoning. By contrast the presence of a stable political framework focused on parliament tends to press even the most abstract and a-historical political ideas in Britain towards an empirical form.

A final point should be made concerning the bourgeois element of liberalism. In a way German liberalism was more obviously bourgeois than English liberalism. It had less support from lower-class groups and also there was really no equivalent of the Whig nobility.[66] Its clearer-cut ideas on constitutionalism, a system of individual property rights, and the secularisation of public life all appear more bourgeois to us than the values of many members of the British Liberal Party. A man such as Gladstone with his religiosity, his belief in the positive role an aristocracy should play in public life, and his huge inherited wealth appears less obviously a bourgeois liberal than the leaders of German liberalism such as Bennigsen, von Gagern, or von Miquel.

Too much emphasis has been placed upon the obvious point that members of the bourgeoisie can be illiberal without ceasing to be bourgeois.[67] The lack of liberal values amongst middle-class Englishmen was something that Cobden and Bright would often bemoan after 1846. More emphasis should be placed upon the converse: members of many non-bourgeois groups can be liberal. Effective political movements are movements which cut across social divides and which attract people by virtue of their apparent ability to realise values in practice. The price they pay for these qualities is diffuseness in ideology. In the case of British liberalism the generally loose character of political organisation meant that it was not even necessary to compensate for this by having streamlined organisation. Liberalism became effective either as a series of one-issue movements or, during the Gladstonian period, by coalescing around a number of such issues under the leadership of an extraordinary individual. The transitional period between a relatively closed world of parliamentary politics and a world of caucus-type parties enabled this politics to be effective for a couple of decades. In Germany the shift from the politics of closed bureaucracies and courts to that of the mass parties proceeded too rapidly for liberalism to achieve a similar position of effectiveness. Liberalism therefore remained more clearly defined but also isolated. It is this which enables us to say much more clearly what liberalism in Germany actually 'was' and at the same time to explain its failure. It is precisely because the ideas, organisation and sociology of British liberalism are so much harder to pin down that it enjoyed so much more success.

Notes

1 Bentley, 1987.

2 Burrow, 1988.

3 Gray, 1986.

4 Lively & Rees, 1984.

5 Brundage, 1988; Finer, 1952.

6 Machin, 1964 and 1977.

7 Moore, 1966; Brock, 1973.

8 Lively & Rees, 1984.

9 Aydelotte, 1954, 1962–63, and 1965.

10 Fraser, 1982, p. 5.

11 Schieder (ed), 1983; Koselleck, 1981.

12 Koselleck, 1981.

13 Cobden, in a letter of 11 September 1838 written in Berlin. The passage is quoted in Muhs, 1988, p. 255, from Morley, 1896, I p. 130. See also Edsall, 1986; and Hinde, 1987.

14 Husung, 1983.

15 Wehler, 1987b.

16 Husung, 1983.

17 Koselleck, 1981.

18 See the studies in Gall, 1990, especially Lenger, 1990.

19 Gall, 1989; Walker,1971; Wehler, 1987b.

20 Schieder (ed), 1983; Langewiesche, 1988.

21 Hahn, 1983.

22 Rumpler (ed), 1990 includes a number of relevant studies of the Confederation.

23 Anderson, 1967.

24 Semmel, 1986.

25 Macfarlane, 1978; Rose, 1976.

26 Gash, 1986.

27 McCord, 1968.

28 Gall, 1975.

29 On the lack of interest in industrialisation see Koch, 1986.

30 Walker, 1971; Matz, 1980.

31 Schieder (ed), 1983; Padtberg, 1985.

32 Sedatis, 1979.

33 Aldenhoff, 1984.

34 Breuilly, 1983.

35 Renzsch, 1980.

36 Machin, 1977.

37 Parry, 1986.

38 Robbins, 1979.

39 Vincent, 1972.

40 Gatrell, 1971.

41 Sperber, 1984.

42 Schieder, 1980; Breuilly, 1980.

43 Windell, 1954; Anderson, 1954.

44 Langewiesche, 1988.

45 Brederlow, 1978; Paletschek, 1990.

46 Von Thadden, 1983; Langewiesche, 1988.

47 Düding, 1984.

48 Wehler, 1987b.

49 Fehrenbach, 1978.

50 Koselleck, 1981.

51 On this whole complex of questions see Grimm 1987, 1988a; and John, 1989.

52 On the links between politics and property in liberal thinking see Ryan, 1984.

53 Berding & Ullman (eds), 1981; Vogel (ed), 1980; Wehler, 1987a.

54 Rose, 1970; Edsall, 1971.

55 Saville, 1987.

56 *Ibid*.

57 Biagini, 1991.

58 Koselleck, 1981.

59 Husung, 1983.

60 Lüdtke, 1989.

61 On the specific issue of handling protests see Langer, 1966.

62 Eisenberg, 1986 and 1988.

63 Aydelotte, 1954; McCord, 1968; Vincent, 1972.

64 Sheehan, 1973 and 1978.

65 Langewiesche, 1988.

66 Dipper, 1988; Muhs, 1988.

67 Blackbourn & Eley, 1984; Kocka, 1987.

8

Conclusion: national peculiarities?

Why did Germany fail to achieve parliamentary democracy by 1914? Was this failure unique amongst those societies in which industry and mass literacy had clearly established themselves? Does this failure point to a special path (*Sonderweg*) in German history?

These questions are at the centre of what is called the 'critical approach' to modern German history. The approach is called critical because it adopts a critical stance towards German history, asking why certain things did not happen rather than contenting itself with an uncritical account of what did happen. The questions also involve theoretical and comparative assumptions. The theoretical assumptions are that in some important sense, and not just a moral one, there is a presumption in favour of the establishment of parliamentary democracy once certain social and economic conditions have been attained. The comparative assumption is that normally these conditions do indeed lead to parliamentary democracy.

So far in these comparative essays I have sought to present a well-documented and rigorous argument about quite specific subjects. In this concluding essay I will present a much more general and speculative argument, building upon those earlier comparisons. I will begin by asking what is meant by the idea of 'national peculiarities', exploring first the meaning of these two words, and then the arguments that have been mounted which claim that the questions of the critical historians are misconceived. Having argued that in fact these questions are both reasonable and important ones, I will go on to suggest that there are problems with many of the answers that have been offered. I will then outline a theoretical approach which can, in my view, provide satisfactory answers, and I will indicate some comparative arguments which support those answers.

In defence of national peculiarities

What is meant by 'national' and what by 'peculiarities'? The first term is usually taken, for western Europe, to mean the nation-state, or the boundaries of that state which define the boundaries of the 'national'. Before going on to ask whether the history of one particular nation-state can be regarded as peculiar, it is necessary to draw attention to the use of the term 'national' in this way. I will confine the argument to the three cases of Britain, France and Germany.

Even with these three there are clearly major differences in the way the idea of a 'nation-state' is employed. France and Britain had single governments ruling the territory of the later nation-state for some time prior to the nineteenth century. Whether those governments should be described as 'national' is a moot point, but at least there was a territorial continuity between monarchical governments which largely excluded popular political participation and later governments, be it of a monarchical or republican or imperial form, which did make provision for such participation. On the other hand, most of the lands loosely known as Germany only came under a single government between 1871 and 1945, and then again since 1990. This raises two problems with regard to Germany. First, insofar as one is dealing with the pre-1871 situation, there is no equivalent unit to compare with that of France or Britain. Second, insofar as comparisons of the post-1871 situation are concerned, it is impossible to forget the novelty of the nation-state.

Within the limitations of these three cases, Germany may appear as the peculiar one (if by this term we mean the odd one out) on this point of comparison. Within a broader framework one could argue the opposite. Most 'nation-states' of the modern era are territorial innovations. Most pre-modern states were either smaller than the nation-state (city-states, ecclesiastical polities, small kingdoms), or larger than the nation-state, above all the great dynastic empires of the Romanovs, the Habsburgs, and the Ottomans. In the New World, the United States of America was a loose and territorially expanding polity still racked by internal conflict over how 'national' it should be as late as the 1860s. Indeed, it may be that in certain respects 'Germany' is closer to Britain and France, at least in there being some cultural if not political sense of being Germany by the early nineteenth century, whereas such a sense seems to be almost wholly absent in the 'small nations' of east-central Europe.

At a political level there is also the question of institutional continuity. In this respect Britain displays the greatest continuity. Apart from the retention of monarchy as its political form since 1660, there is continuity in the central role of a single parliament in which a very exclusive peerage dominates the upper chamber and a very widely defined political nation the lower chamber. There is also continuity in the 'central focus' of British politics, with relatively little independent political power residing in lower level institutions such as the counties and the boroughs. On the other hand, the changes in the franchise for elections to the House of Commons from 1832, the creation of new institutions at the level of municipal government and policing, the reduction in the powers of the monarchy and the Church of England – all sometimes compressed into quite short periods of rapid innovation (e.g. 1832–1835) – point to important changes.

The German states display some institutional continuity even within periods of great territorial change. In the first major territorial upheaval under Napoleon, it was existing dynasties which largely profited, and this was confirmed rather than undone in 1814–15. In the second great upheaval between 1867 and 1871, the deposing of monarchies in northern and central Germany was achieved by extending the rule of the Prussian state (1867), and the south German monarchies were preserved in the new federal structure (1871). The major institutional break came in 1919, not in 1871. There were important and quite sudden institutional innovations such as the granting of constitutional government in Prussia in December 1848, and the creation of federal, later imperial institutions (the Emperorship, the Bundesrat, the Reichstag, and the various imperial ministries and agencies) after 1871. However, the major problem was how to reconcile the functioning of these new institutions with the continuation of the old institutions of monarchy and its civil and military services.

The French case displays, of course, the greatest institutional discontinuity since 1789. Associated with this is the central role of violent internal conflict or revolution as a means of bringing about political change. Apart from the most obvious cases of 1789, 1793, 1830, 1848 and 1871, one must remember that other changes of government (1799, 1814, 1815 (twice), 1851) involved either a coup (1799, 1851), a popular repudiation of the existing government (1815: the first time), or the use of military power by other states to impose their political choice (1814, 1815: the second time). Each conflict brought with it a change of constitutional form between monarchy, republic and empire or a change within the dynastic line (Legitimist, Orleanist). Between 1789 and 1871 there were at least ten such changes (it is difficult to know what counts as a 'change of the form of government' between 1793 and 1800), and eleven if the Commune of 1871 is counted as a form of government: more than one every decade on average.

Yet there were also important institutional continuities. The system of departmental government controlled by prefects appointed from the centre which was consolidated under Napoleon remained largely intact, and has led many historians to argue that the political upheavals after 1814 were in many ways cosmetic, concealing the endurance of a stronger, more centralised system which was largely controlled by the notables of the various regions.

So to come back to the question of what is being compared, I would suggest that instead of taking the unit of 'nation-state' we rather take the units of the British and French states and the states of the German lands, that we leave aside the issue of how 'national' were these polities, and that we note a mixture of continuity and discontinuity at the political levels of institutional forms and territorial control. These can be summarised as follows:

	Continuity		Discontinuity
1 Institutional	Britain	Germany	France
2 Territorial	Britain		Germany
	France		

These comparisons of territorial and institutional continuity at the level of the state can also help us deal with the question of what is meant by peculiarity. If peculiar simply means different, then every history is peculiar. Peculiar simply means particular. Everything is particular. But in normal English usage it would be a nonsense to say that everything is peculiar. The same reasoning would apply to the use of the term unique. The only defence of such a usage is the historicist argument that every historical case must be understood on its own terms, and for its own sake; that it is wrong to employ general concepts in history; that it is wrong to try to understand one epoch in relation to another (teleology) or one history in relation to another. Strict historicism must rule out the possibility of comparison, because there could in principle be no set of terms which could be employed for the analysis of the various cases. In fact, a moment's consideration shows that historians constantly and necessarily employ such common terms (democratisation, bureaucratisation, revolution, industrialisation, etc.) and implicitly set them within comparative perspectives. It is difficult to see how historical work could proceed without such terms and perspectives. Underpinning the historicist argument is a certain metaphysics. There must be 'real' historical objects with their peculiar features. The peculiarity cannot exist in the mind of the historian because then, if historians chose not to think in terms of peculiarities, they would not exist. Therefore, the peculiarity must inhere in the past itself. Conveniently these objective peculiarities are usually taken to exist at the national level. That should rule out any sensible historical work at a lower level (how can a 'unique nation' be made up in turn of 'unique regions' or 'unique localities' or 'unique individuals?') or a higher level (in what sense could the notion of 'European culture' co-exist with the idea of unique national cultures?). However, many historicists never confront these problems squarely and happily follow Herder in proceeding from unique individuals to unique communities to unique nations to an incoherent notion of a common humanity constituted through the principles of uniqueness and diversity. In contrast to this it is necessary to be clear as to the necessary assumptions which inform all good historical work.

First, it is assumed that the historian has access to an understanding of the past by means of the survivals of that past. The idea of access is based not merely on sources but the idea that sources are intelligible. Intelligibility first and foremost involves shared understanding. Shared understanding is based on assumptions about human nature, about how societies work. These assumptions are brought to the past by the historian and are validated by the construction of an intelligible history. In constructing that history the historian has to make more or less explicit those assumptions about human nature and the workings of society. These will be brought to bear upon certain particular activities and sequences of events. The historian will necessarily occupy a different vantage point from that of any of the historical actors. The very construction of a history of industrialisation or national unification or revolution depends upon occupying such a vantage point. But it is equally true of the analysis of a society at a certain moment – the 'snapshot'. This may appear to avoid teleology – that is the understanding of events and situations in relation to what comes afterwards – but the historian still requires some framing concept to identify what is being considered, whether it be a 'society' or an 'epoch'.

This leaves us with only one possible and sensible use of terms such as 'peculiar' or 'unique'. That is that *one particular case* differs in very important respects from *all other cases*. It is important to note the qualification 'in very important respects'. From this angle what matters is what particular aspect of the history of the various cases is regarded as important.

This point is clearly recognised by the 'critical' school of German historical writing. The issue that is regarded as important by these historians is that of parliamentary democracy. So far as comparisons between the three cases are concerned, the crucial issue for these historians is: why did parliamentary democracy establish itself in Britain and France whilst it failed to do so in Germany?

In principle, of course, one could direct attention to some other question which would reserve the term peculiarity or uniqueness for one of the other cases. We can see this when we take the points of comparison I have already made at the political level in trying to identify what we mean by 'national'. Why did France experience political change through a series of revolutions whereas in Germany and Britain political change came about more gradually, without revolution? Why did Britain exhibit such a peculiar degree of territorial and institutional continuity in her politics, compared to the more marked discontinuities of France and Germany? Each question places a different case in the 'peculiar' category.

Clarity about what we mean by the idea of peculiarity is essential to a sensible debate. Those who respond to the critical historians by pointing to various British or French 'peculiarities' are, if they are simply saying that other questions will throw up different kinds of comparison, not engaging in an intelligent argument at all. Instead they are simply changing arguments, although the way in which they do so implies that it is legitimate to talk about peculiarities in the way I have described. It may be that one is not interested in the question of the 'failure of parliamentary democracy in Germany', but not being interested in something is not in itself an argument against the way in which those who are so interested present their case.

More to the point are the arguments that the particular question is in some sense an improper one for historians to raise. There are a number of such arguments. One can quickly be dispensed with: this is that it does violence to historical understanding to ask why something did *not* happen, or to judge one history a 'failure' by comparison with other histories. At one level this is just a re-statement of the historicist case – each history is unique and must be understood in its own terms. So far as the issue of events 'not' happening is concerned, I have in the introduction to this book outlined the legitimate way in which such 'counter-factual' points can be put. What matters is that either the possibility of the other development was consciously raised by contemporaries or that there is a reasonable theory concerning the appropriate conditions for the development of parliamentary democracy. It is clear that contemporaries in Germany did raise the issue of parliamentary democracy and I will argue that there is also a reasonable theory.

Another objection that is often raised is that it is a moral judgement which is being struck with the use of terms such as 'failure' or 'success', and that this is inappropriate in historical analysis. There may, of course, be moral evaluations (though these could and did include extolling German 'constitutionalism' at the expense of 'western parliamentarism'). However, in principle there is no difference between asking why certain countries industrialise while others do not (which no one suggests involves moral judgements) and asking why certain countries achieve parliamentary democracy and others do not. It is only because more people feel sensitive about 'failure' in the latter case that it is thought to be a moral judgement rather than a legitimate comparative historical question.

Two other arguments are more difficult to refute. The first is that the critical historian introduces concerns which are really not significant to the history in question. This objection is not the same as the historicist argument which forbids the use of general concepts and hypotheses, but rather involves the argument that the general terms being employed do not advance historical understanding in that particular case. I would argue against that position on two grounds. First, it is clear that the issue of political democracy figured in political debate and action in nineteenth-century Germany. Clearly to ask why Attila the Hun did not introduce parliamentary democracy would introduce a fairly insignificant historical question for him and his times, but the same case cannot be argued for nineteenth- and twentieth-century Germany. Incidentally, the same points would apply with regard to France and revolution (revolution had become a conscious political category in nineteenth-century Europe) and to Britain and continuity (the idea of this being the essence of British superiority had also become a commonplace). Second, there are important arguments to the effect that the growth of a market economy, of commerce and industry, and of mass literacy in society create conditions which favour the development of parliamentary democracy, and that parliamentary democracy in turn is more 'functional' for such a society than other political arrangements. In other words, in relation to both political consciousness and in underlying objective socio-economic changes, there are important grounds for believing that the issue of parliamentary democracy is as central to modern German history as it is to modern British or French history.

Another important counter-argument is that the approach is 'teleological'. Historians analyse the revolutions of 1848 as a 'failure' in order to answer the questions 'why Hitler?'. I have never understood why it is thought that this is an especially important argument. Historians seek to understand change over time. They cannot wipe from their minds their knowledge of how more recent history relates to more distant history. Nor should they, even if they could, because it would involve tossing away the one advantage the historian enjoys over the historical actors – that is, knowing what comes next. What, of course, is objectionable is the assumption that what comes next had to come next or to analyse earlier situations in terms of the forces 'promoting' or 'hindering' the later events. Butterfield long ago pointed to the dangers of this Whig approach to history. However, his preferred solution – that 'everything' had to be understood in its own terms and that what came next was based on (though not caused by) 'everything' that had happened earlier – is no solution at all. It simply takes us back to the incoherency of historicism. Given that historicism *is* incoherent, the historian either gives up analysing long-term change (focusing instead on snap-shots, vignettes, studies of structures of particular times, etc.) or returns to narrative, which supposedly relates a long-run sequences of events but without smuggling in illegitimate teleological categories. Neither of these positions is tenable.

To give up long-run analysis as impossible but to maintain that other kinds of historical investigation are possible requires the acceptance of some argument to the effect that the categories involved in short-run analysis are different from those involved in long-run analysis, and that these categories alone allow meaningful historical statements to be made. I have never encountered any explicit argument to this effect so do not intend to devote a good deal of energy to constructing such an argument in order to refute it. The *only* possible distinction I can see on which such an argument could be constructed involves drawing a line between the understanding of historical actors and the changes and events which go beyond that understanding. At one level, this is the well-known distinction between intentions and outcomes, but I know of no historian who feels it is possible to ignore unintended outcomes. The issue of how long a sequence of unintended outcomes is considered by the historian is irrelevant. Sometimes, realising that at the level of individuals and events it is impossible to avoid the issue of unintended outcomes, it is instead suggested that the historian should seek to understand 'society' in its own terms. Clearly there are problems with what is meant by 'a society' and 'its own terms'. The idea already admits that one can go beyond the intentions of individuals and that one can construct models (social structures, etc.) for purposes of analysis. Once it is recognised that those models necessarily go beyond the terms employed by contemporaries, and that even the smallest and most apparently consensual of societies is an arena of conflicting and changing interests and values, then the argument loses all force. In principle, there is no difference between analysing change over the long run and events on a large scale and considering short-run change and events on a small scale. Clearly there is more to be taken into account in the first case, and at a certain point the complexity might become too much for the historian to handle, but that can only be judged empirically in each case.

The choice of a narrative of long-run and/or large scale events which avoids all the snares of teleology and of explicit conceptual analysis is also misconceived. The historian has to construct a subject in space and time which acts as the bearer of the narrative. That construction involves theory and that theory should be made explicit. Take, for example, Simon Schama's marvellous narrative history of the French Revolution. First, Schama is compelled to focus on 'politics' and on Paris. The provinces and non-political action appear as background. As a consequence any argument Schama offers against analytic interpretations of the revolution which place a stress upon non-politics or a different focus from that of Paris is, in the terms he puts it, unacceptable because it does not engage with the problems of evidence those historians have had to confront. Even within the focus upon Parisian politics other important conceptual devices are required. The marvellous comparison of Talleyrand and Lafayette works as well as it does because of the introduction of their role in the July revolution of 1830. To depict Talleyrand in the presence of the ageing Voltaire or Lafayette as a hero under the French monarchy because of his involvement in the American rebellion works because of our know-ledge of their later roles in the revolution. The selection of the acts of violence for description and scale of detail employed is based upon the assumption that there is a special kind of violence – revolutionary violence – which is novel and requires special attention. The problem is that it remains an assumption, shaping the narrative but never brought out into the open for proper scrutiny and questioning. There are, as in any good narrative, heroes and villains (Malesherbes is clearly a hero; Robespierre a villain). Schama has the style and verve to make the reader accept this without too much questioning of the assumptions (assumptions about morality, about what kinds of politics are possible in the world) on which the judgement ultimately is based. In other words, Schama handles the problems of unintended outcomes through the employment of teleology (the triumph of revolutionary violence, the later careers of Talleyrand and Lafayette, etc.) and the problem of large-scale action by an arbitrary reduction of the revolution to the political action of Paris-based activists which in turn have to be subject to radical selection. I have no objection to this – Schama's account can only work precisely because such analytic principles underlie it – but I do object if this is somehow presented as an *alternative* to analytical history.

Even within the confines of a biography there are also assumptions about beginning, middle and end. I would not go so far as to argue that narrative is a necessary fiction, because I do believe that certain constructs contain a compelling sense of birth, growth and death (above all, the individual human being) which is not simply contrived by the art of the narrator. But artifice is required to turn those elementary notions of a beginning, middle and end into a story. This artifice necessarily involves assumptions about what is important in shaping change within the story.

Finally, if one accepts that an historical account of long-run and large scale change is as legitimate as any other historical account, and that such an account necessarily involves the use of concepts and models which address our attention to the direction and causality of change, then clearly we should be explicit about those concepts and models. Historians who throw out the terms of critical historians such as modernisation, liberal democracy, and pre-industrial values because they are too large or abstract, find themselves compelled to introduce terms such as 'silent bourgeois revolution' or 'social formation' or 'capitalism' in their stead. The only legitimate way forward then is to make this explicit and to present a case as to why their theoretical terms are preferable.

As a consequence of this philosophical detour I would conclude that it is legitimate to pose the question about the success of parliamentary democracy in France and Britain compared to its failure in Germany, just as it would be legitimate to pose the question about the presence of revolutionary change in France compared to Britain and Germany, or the lack of territorial or institutional discontinuity in Britain compared to France and Germany.

Of course, that does not mean that one accepts the answers critical historians give to this question.

Why is Germany peculiar?

The critical historians suggest that the growth of an industrial and market economy and of a literate society create a presumption in favour of the development of parliamentary democracy. Authoritarian government was associated with an agrarian and hierarchical society in which the privileged landowners, church, and monarchy dominated. The rise of a more industrial and market economy challenged the position of the old landowning elites. The rise of a literate society and the breakdown of traditional ties were associated with a questioning of religious orthodoxy. An increase in social participation led on to a demand for political changes which would reflect the interests of larger numbers of people and to which government would be accountable. The new social groups – manufacturers, merchants, professionals, industrial workers, white-collar workers – made it impossible to impose a single political creed. It became necessary to recognise the legitimacy of competing creeds (liberalism). There was also the demand that government consult the interests of such groups before making decisions (democracy).

However, whereas these political pressures largely led by 1900, in the cases of Britain and France, to constitutional, parliamentary states in which popularly elected parties formed governments, in the case of Germany an authoritarian monarchy, retaining control over the armed forces and the civil administration, remained in power. Only the loss of war, rather than internal conflict, resulted in the overthrow of that monarchy. Furthermore, within fourteen years the German people voluntarily renounced liberal democracy by casting their votes for anti-democratic parties and supporting the suppression of parliament and open political debate and conflict. Once again, only the loss of war led to the overthrow of that totalitarian dictatorship. Liberal democracy once again was imposed by the victors, although in this case only in the western part of Germany.

The contrast can also be put in a more graphic way. Courts, royal power, men in uniform remain prominent in the politics of other European states before 1914, above all in the Habsburg and Romanov empires. But it is clear that these societies lack the modern economic and cultural features of Germany. Germany appears to be the *only* major state in which the influence and panoply of court, monarchy and military coexists with a dynamic economy in which industry dominates and there is a highly educated and literate population. What is the reason for this peculiarity?

Many answers have been suggested. No longer fashionable are those which deploy some idea of 'national character'. Instead critical historians have focused on structures. Central to this is the idea of compression of many different changes into one short period in German history compared to their staged character in British and French history. Britain and France had largely solved the territorial issue by 1800 – the nation-state form was already achieved. Britain had also largely solved her 'constitutional' problems by this time. In the French case rapid economic change came largely in the twentieth century. So, put crudely, the three issues of constitutional, territorial and socio-economic change were solved sequentially in Britain and France (though not in the same order or manner). In the German case they were all compressed into a short period, especially the period c. 1860–1890. In those thirty years Germany became a nation-state, acquired a constitutional political order, and experienced rapid industrial growth.

This had certain consequences for liberalism and democracy. The middle-class groups which were the principal bearers of liberal ideology and politics at a very early stage in their formation were confronted with these simultaneous crises which they felt unable to tackle without a good deal of support from the existing authorities. The revolutions of 1848 and the wars of unification led them to place great dependence on a strong, independent monarchy with a powerful army and civil service. In turn this prevented those middle-class liberals leading a broader political movement for change. Workers and artisans and peasants turned instead to their own special interests, justifying this with resort to various kinds of anti-liberal ideas. Even if these opposed the authoritarian status quo, they often did so in illiberal and anti-democratic ways. As a consequence, the Weimar Republic, borne out of defeat in war, lacked a popular political consensus which could sustain it through a major crisis.

The other side of the equation focuses upon the adeptness and resources of the old order. At key moments (1806–15, 1866–71) conservatives took the helm who were prepared to give up the indefensible in order to defend better the most important of existing institutions. Bureaucratic and military reform contributed to Prussian success against Napoleon. Junker groups manipulated agrarian reforms to their own advantage, also admitting into their ranks newcomers and being prepared to see less able or lucky aristocratic landowners go to the wall. The Prussian state adjusted to 'modern' demands in terms of liberal economic policy and limited constitutionalism. Finally, it used the strength generated by this adaptation to modernity to expel Austria from Germany and to bring the other German regions under its control. This enormously boosted the prestige and power of the successful institutions, above all monarchy and army. By contrast, monarchy gradually withdrew from politics in Britain (especially after Prince Albert's death in 1861) and was finally destroyed in France in 1848. The army never played an important part in British politics after 1815, and its role also markedly declined in France, although at times of crisis military figures (Cavaignac, Boulanger) could still play a central role. However, with the Dreyfus Affair the limits of that role were made clear. In Germany, the middle classes accepted the values proclaimed by these pre-modern institutions. Having carried through a successful modernisation in economic and social spheres, they failed to extend this success to the ideological and political ones. The result was a flawed and 'partial' modernisation.

These arguments have been much contested. Some objections focus specifically on the political; others deal with the various contrasts in the conditions of politics which the critical argument advances.

The political objection would be that too much is made of formal institutional or surface differences. On the one hand, British and French politics remained deeply undemocratic and illiberal. The Dreyfus affair may have revealed the limits of such attitudes but it also revealed their importance in turn-of-the-century France. The social composition of British Cabinets and the attitudes of even 'popular' politicians like Gladstone or Chamberlain hardly reflect the views of the modern liberal democrat. On the other hand, German politics did increasingly take account of popular concerns. By 1900 government could only be carried on if majority support existed in the Reichstag. Military prestige was based on commitment to modernisation (above all in the navy) and the Kaiser in many respects was impatient of tradition.

The same points can then be extended back into a consideration of the conditions of politics. The critical historians often assumed that the failure of liberal democratic politics was associated with the persistence of traditional values in society, relating this to the stubborn maintenance of their position by traditional power-holders.

Again one can develop the argument from two angles. First, one can point to the persistence of traditional values in Britain and France. In a general argument Arno Mayer has maintained that old elites retained their influence in all European countries by 1914. More specifically historians have argued that a peasant dominated agriculture in France as well as the persistent influence of the church and of local notability points in many ways to the survival of traditional values on an even greater scale than in Germany. Wiener has argued that aristocratic and gentry values prevailed in Britain to such an extent that they suffocated more modern bourgeois values of self-help and egalitarianism.

From the other angle of approach it has been powerfully argued that Germany was in many ways a more modern society by 1900 than the surface appearance of politics might suggest. If anything Germany was a more secular society than either Britain or France, where either dissenting Protestantism or still strong Catholicism remained more significant. The architecture of the growing towns, the development of new cultural practices associated with theatre, the creative arts, the use of leisure, the emergence of mass politics, all pointed to a society in many ways emancipated from the traditional values of monarchy, aristocracy and church.

Each point of comparison needs much more careful analysis than they have hitherto received. Notions of 'tradition' and 'modernity' need more explicit definition. In some cases there is rather loose argument ranging from, say, the pronouncements of public school headmasters to the performance of the national economy. What, if any, are the links between cultural modernism and liberal political values? But the arguments have raised two very important points of principle. The first is whether the initial assumptions about what is to be compared are properly stated. Is German politics really less parliamentary and democratic than French or British politics? The second is whether the principal form of the explanation is acceptable. Should 'modernity', measured in such terms as the growth of industrial capitalism and mass literacy be associated with modernity in the political field, and should in turn political modernity be closely linked to liberal democracy?

The arguments are too complex and numerous for any full treatment in an essay. What I want to do here is relate these issues back to the particular comparisons I have made in the preceding essays. Unfortunately, almost all the argument, apart from usually lacking much explicit and sustained comparison, has also focused on the post-1871, or more often post-1890 period. This is understandable given that it is only after then that industrial capitalism extended beyond certain regions, that mass political parties developed as a part of the normal political landscape, that popular nationalism and national rivalry between the major European states took on a central importance. However, it is also necessary to ask how far German political development has already 'diverged' from that of France and Britain by the time a single German state had been constructed. What is more, we can strip away certain issues that complicate the story after 1890. Precisely because industrial production is not as important and mass political participation not yet as advanced, more attention can be focused on the specific issue of liberalism and its relationship to general processes of change.

Liberalism and modernisation

I have already said a good deal about liberalism, both at a national level and in a comparison between Hamburg and Manchester. Much more difficult is the notion of some general process of change to which liberalism can be related. Although many arguments have been levelled against the idea of modernisation I still consider some version of this idea to be indispensable to grasp this general change.

I will use the concept of modernisation to refer to a certain kind of structural change. That is, modernisation does not refer to the process of becoming *more modern*, which is the way it is often used, and which carries with it ideas of growth and expansion of the 'modern' at the expense of the traditional. Rather the term refers to the process of *becoming modern*.

The structure to which I refer is the division of labour within a society in the broadest sense. The process of modernisation involves the formation of a society in which this division of labour is functional. If we consider that there are a range of functions which are carried out in a society – the exercise of power, the inculcation of beliefs, the production and distribution of material goods, the raising and education of children – then a modern society is one in which these various functions are concentrated into the hands of specific institutions. State agencies (the civil service, the armed forces, police, judiciary) and parliaments exercise power in various ways. Churches and other cultural institutions express and communicate beliefs about society. Firms operating in a range of markets (for labour, capital, materials) or under a command system (though that only comes in the twentieth century in some countries) specialise in producing and distributing material goods. Families are charged with the care and upbringing of children, although in modern societies much of their education is compulsorily vested in schools separated from the family. Clearly other societies have carried out these functions without such a division of labour. In many cases the division is rather one between social groups which operate in multi-functional institutions. The ideal-typical guild, for example, had religious, educational, familial, and political as well as economic functions. It was an exemplar of a society based upon a corporate division of labour.

I would argue that by different routes all three countries modernised significantly in the period 1800–70, roughly the period covered by the various essays in this book. In mainland Britain the transformation was, at an institutional level, the least dramatic because at the outset there was less formal expression to such a corporate system. There were no guilds; ownership of land did not in itself confer privileges; beyond a very tightly defined peerage and an established church there was no formal structure of privilege. Whether this meant that England by 1800 was a society of 'individuals' is another matter. In real terms landownership or membership of one of the traditional professions (especially legal) remained a necessary condition for the holding of most political offices. Only during our period was most political office-holding formally separated from membership of the Anglican church. However, this lack of a formal corporate structure meant that modernisation, especially in the area of political functions, often appeared as an extension of participation (widening the franchise, removing religious disqualifications), rather than taking the form of institutional change.

In France and Germany where the major bastion of such a corporate order, agriculture, remained so much more important for much longer, the break was sharper. In France, of course, it took a revolutionary form. The land settlement of the French Revolution, the expulsion of the Catholic Church from any formal role in politics, and the concentration of political power into a rationalised administrative structure were the most important ingredients, and had already taken firm institutional shape under the Emperorship of Napoleon. In Germany Napoleon's influence produced much the same effects, but without an internal revolution. The break was in many ways as deliberate and institutionally as well defined, both in the south German states of Bavaria, Baden and Württemberg as in Prussia, although taking the form of institutional reform rather than revolution. These changes were deepened, certainly at elite and political level, after 1815. In many respects the North German Confederation extended such modern institutions to those parts of non-Prussian northern and central Germany (Hannover, Saxony) which had not undergone modernisation in the Napoleonic and post-1815 phases.

This contrast suggests to me at least two major defects in the arguments of the critical historians. First, there is the argument of a 'compressed' revolution in the German case which had the effect of undermining liberalism. However, the three 'revolutions' – national, socio-economic, and constitutional – are not so clearly compressed in the German case or separated in the British and French cases. We now recognise that industrialisation was a more drawn out and patchy process in all three countries than was once generally believed. At the same time other kinds of economic change – the breakthrough to commercial agriculture operating in a free market, or the spread of capitalism into manufacturing, be it in rural industry or small workshop or domestic production in the towns – have been given more prominence. (See above, the essay on artisans.)

The issue of 'constitutional' change also appears less clearcut. Almost every German state had a written constitution by 1848. If one considers that in the British case the franchise issue in many ways was a proxy for constitutional change, then clearly there was still much to do by this time. Finally 'national' is an ill-chosen word. 'National unification' meant, in the German case, the end of the dualism of the German Confederation, replacing it with much greater Prussian control and a consequent reduction in the autonomy of the remaining German states. What mattered here, and this is a point to which I will return, was that inter-state warfare was the only way of producing this political change. However, the problems of creating popular national identity were still, by 1871, problems for the future, arguably in Britain and certainly in France as well as in Germany.

Another problematic notion used by the critical historians is that of 'partial modernisation'. The term is taken to mean that modernisation took place in some functions (economic, social) but not in others (political, cultural). Within the framework I have adopted, this is difficult to envisage. Once economic functions have been taken over by specialised economic institutions and social functions by specialised social institutions, it almost automatically follows that political and cultural functions will be the province of specialised political and cultural institutions. This appears clearly to be the case: parliaments and bureaucracies, admittedly in conflict with one another, extend their control over the political process, displacing royal courts, churches, assemblies of noblemen, and urban guilds in the process. Theatres, concerts, the use of 'public' spaces, and the satisfaction of a mass-reading public all point to specialised cultural production. Contemporaries were well aware of this. For a modernist like Cobden, for example, the Prussian bureaucracy with its specialised administrative functions was clearly more modern than the English system of vestries, closed corporations, county benches of magistrates confined to Anglican gentry and the like. The problem with critical historians is that they have tended almost to define political modernisation as the construction of parliamentary democracy, and therefore have seen in the autonomies and freedoms offered by a weak central bureaucracy and a dominating House of Commons aspects of political modernity in Britain. But what matters is to pin-point the actual relationship between liberalism and modernisation, not to make liberalism part of the definition of modernisation.

Yet clearly modernisation is never a completed process, and in that sense always partial. I would, however, suggest that its patchiness be understood in spatial rather than functional terms. In regions where large landowners retained control over many traditional institutions (church patronage, policing and judicial powers, etc.) or maintained control in the various 'new' institutions imposed from the centre by a reforming state, then clearly only limited modernisation had taken place. However, significant modernisation in one sphere could rapidly compel corresponding changes in other spheres. For example, once it became easy for agricultural labour in eastern parts of Germany either to emigrate or to move to jobs in the industrialising regions of western Germany, then large landowners were compelled to use more modern political and economic methods (engaging in party politics, agitating in specialised pressure groups, searching out weaker groups in the labour market) to sustain their position.

What this argument suggests, therefore, is that institutional modernisation was marked in both France and Germany between 1800 and 1850 whereas related change in Britain (or rather mainland Britain because Ireland is an altogether more 'continental' case) took the surface form of extending participation rather than making structural changes. However, in the French case conflict took the form of revolution, although there was little fundamental institutional change beyond the centre after 1815. In the German case conflict was resolved through the extension of modernising states at the expense of institutions which defended the corporate world. The partial character of modernisation was not so much between the political and the economic sphere as between more and less modernised regions.

In a short essay I can do no more than baldly state these ideas. If one accepts them, what implications do they have for the development of liberalism in Germany and in what ways will this be a peculiar development?

One area of active recent research is in the field of cultural history, especially insofar as this relates to the idea of the development of a bourgeois society and culture. In the German case the findings point to the construction of a quite sharply defined and regionally well diffused bourgeois culture by 1871. The defence of older privileges sharpened the sense of opposition to establishment culture on the part of bourgeois groups, especially those based on the professions and state service. At the same time the reforming activity of the new territorial states of the Napoleonic and post-1815 era gave this bourgeoisie a centrality which they did not possess in the French or the British cases. The lack of any one dominant cultural centre (eighteenth-century Weimar, the most important location of high cultural activity at the time, had a population of about 6000) but rather the involvement of such a bourgeoisie in innovative cultural activity in a range of towns diffused this culture. At the same time it prevented it acquiring the connotation of 'provincial' which, outside London and to an even greater extent Paris, was the case in Britain and France.

In Protestant regions this cultural activity had a broader significance, involving members of the 'economic' bourgeoisie, often in various voluntary associations of a kind reminiscent of the British pattern and that helped give early German liberalism a potentially popular character. However, the greater weight and importance of a university-educated and professional middle class in Germany meant that these groups took a more prominent part in such cultural activity, and sometimes also set themselves a little self-consciously against the world of trade and industry. Also such activity tended to be highly secular, reflecting the weakness of formal Protestant influences, whereas in many areas of Britain such a culture built upon Protestantism, even if one of liberal Anglicanism, or Dissent, or in areas with Catholic immigrants, populist. In Catholic areas in Germany there was a rather sharper distinction between a bourgeois and secular culture and a still popular religion, just as there also was in Ireland. There appears to be a more self-consciously elitist and modernist bourgeois culture in a city such as Munich compared to Hamburg or Berlin, in part because of this different religious context.

What this meant was that liberalism was much more clearly a part of bourgeois and self-consciously modern culture in Germany than it was in either Britain or France. In Britain an aggressively modernist, oppositional bourgeoisie was based on industry and commerce in a few regions and never acquired the weight, national spread, or access to state institutions to move beyond the status of a ginger group, even if one which occasionally had a good deal of influence. Instead of reflecting a coherent set of underlying values, liberalism rather reflected central practices in British politics such as the shift of political power to central and local elected bodies and away from monarchy, church and privilege, and these practices could bind together different groups in coalitions that agreed on the particular political agenda opened up by this trend of change. In the French case liberalism before 1871 appeared highly elitist and self-serving, and when it took up a popular but also divisive question such as limiting the influence of the Church it had to form links with other politics such as socialism, republicanism and radicalism. Only in Germany can one discern a moment when liberalism appears to be closely integrated with a modern, bourgeois culture.

Yet the manner in which political modernisation came about in Germany also weakened liberalism. It was not the choice between authority or democracy, reform from 'above' and reform from 'below', state or society which was the problem. At times of political stability it seemed possible to combine these elements, above all in the late 1850s and early 1860s. Rather it was that a key element of political modernisation involved territorial change and that could only be brought about by war between states.

Liberalism, especially elitist liberalism, finds it very difficult to cope with war. Liberalism is predicated upon peace. With peace one can run down the military establishment and the machinery and powers of the state. Gladstonian financial liberalism was severely rocked even by the relatively minor problem of the Crimean War; Asquithian liberalism was destroyed by the much bigger problem of the First World War. The tragedy of German liberalism was that only through war could political modernisation proceed – first under Napoleon and then under Bismarck. Yet that left the initiative with institutions – the military, the bureaucracy – which though thoroughly modern by the 1860s were not liberal. At the same time rapidity of change and its very different impact in different regions shattered the construction of a liberal political movement. The consequence was a rather marked division of labour – liberal and middle-class groups could make the running in matters of economic policy or as arbiters of what constituted good taste, but had to leave to authoritarian (though often modern and staffed by the middle-class) institutions decisions about the exercise of political and military power.

I have argued in other essays that a consequence of this was that liberalism gradually lost its attraction to groups whose concern was to influence that political and military power. Middle-class groups operated through pressure groups and informal channels; Catholics and workers moved towards their own political organisations. Yet, liberal and bourgeois influence was at its height in economic and cultural affairs.

As early as the Napoleonic period the Prussian government had accepted many of the arguments of economic liberalism. The need to cut back on government expenditure and also to integrate the different provinces, especially to overcome the physical separation between the two western provinces and the others, help explain why such a policy was pursued after 1815. The same integrative and financial motives persuaded other states to join the Zollverein. Later Austro-Prussian rivalry and the desire to ensure Austria did not enter the Zollverein helped cement that liberal policy. This should not be seen as a pro-industrial policy, as it could disadvantage certain new industries and favour various forms of agriculture. Furthermore the Prussian government in various respects (control over mining, restrictions on limited liability company formation) remained hostile to various kinds of capitalist endeavour at least until the 1850s. Also, one should not see the policy in German terms: it is doubtful if that was even a conscious motive until the 1830s or a leading concern until after 1848; or whether the Zollverein really did help create a national economy or underpin steps to political unification until at least the 1850s. But these policies of economic liberalism were objectively contributions to modernisation because they removed barriers, first to the trend towards a functional division of labour within society and then towards further specialisation within the economic sphere. Thus the basis was laid for the emergence of an economic bourgeoisie with a good deal of freedom of operation.

Second, this bourgeoisie left a strong mark upon the urban culture of Germany by 1871. What is interesting, however, in comparison with France and Britain is the bourgeois rather than intellectual character of this culture and its separation from the worlds of power and production.

I have already mentioned the diffusion of cultural modernism in Germany compared to its concentration in Paris in the case of France. This concentration, the concomitant sense of superiority over the provinces, as well as a sense of superiority over a backward Catholic culture in which peasantry and petty bourgeoisie were mired, helped contribute to the intellectualisation of culture in France. It is interesting to note, for example, the patronising tone with which Paris-based intellectuals treated high cultural endeavours in Lyon, the second city of the country. In turn one finds a constant sense of defensiveness amongst the self-selected cultural spokesman of Lyon. Whereas British and German observers of cultural events organised by bourgeois or intellectual groups tended to worry about how far urban workers were involved or what the attitude of social elites were, one finds French observers commenting on whether bourgeois and peasant groups have been reached and in any way enlightened. It is also the case that Catholicism in quite practical ways marked a great deal of French provincial culture. Business philanthropists funded church building rather than libraries; jewellers and decorators worked on religious objects rather than secular ones. At the same time the involvement of the state in so much cultural activity (a good deal of the best paintings exhibited publicly in Lyon where donations from the government, in turn the product of Napoleonic cultural plunder throughout Europe and the Middle East) reduced the role of voluntary middle-class organisation in cultural activity.

In all these respects mainland Britain and Protestant Germany are more like one another than either are like France. There is no trace of inferiority in the great civic buildings of provincial England as the most superficial observation of Manchester, Sheffield, Liverpool, Leeds, Bradford, Birmingham and many other cities make obvious to this day. But equally it is impossible to imagine the civic elites of

Hamburg, Munich, Frankfurt, Cologne as well as many smaller cities, feeling any sense of cultural inferiority to Berlin; and only the Catholic cities of south Germany might have felt that way towards Vienna.

Yet there is an important difference. In a fascinating but very brief and general study (Nipperdey, 1988), Thomas Nipperdey has suggested the ways in which 'art' and 'life' separated from one another in the nineteenth century (part of the structural process of modernisation), and then how people sought to interpret and give meaning to their lives through aesthetic categories. What has struck me forcibly is how true this is of German bourgeois culture, but how limited is the application of the idea to English bourgeois culture.

Consider the idea and treatment of 'classic' writers, in particular Schiller and Shakespeare who were the subjects of major centenary and tercentenary celebrations in 1859 and 1866 respectively. The Schiller centenary took place at an opportune moment as the 'New Era' had begun in Prussia with the appointment of a liberal ministry by the Regent, later King William I, the successful war by France and Piedmont against Austria, and the formation of the National Verein. Schiller could be celebrated as a great creative writer who embodied in his own life and his works the principles of liberty and nationality. Schiller celebrations were held all over Germany, as well as by Germans abroad, on 10 November, the day of his birth, and on the following days of Friday, Saturday and Sunday. The sheer scale and geographical spread of the celebrations was taken to be proof in itself of the existence of a German national and liberal consciousness.

Three aspects of these celebrations are especially striking. First, middle-class figures, particularly drawn from the professions, were dominant in initiating and running the events. School and college teachers and headmasters used their local prominence, their school buildings, and their pupils to maximum effect. Newspaper editors and journalists publicised the events and wrote many of the speeches and poems which accompanied them. Second, although the general political situation was a crucial ingredient in celebrations, in fact specific national political themes were assiduously avoided. One might see this as caution, though there was little need for that. One might also see it as necessity. To mobilise as wide a range of support as possible one had to avoid raising any divisive political issues. But, and this is the third point, there was the manner in which Schiller was taken into bourgeois culture in mid-century Germany.

Schiller, more than any other figure, symbolised the idea of 'art as religion' of which Nipperdey makes so much. He himself had made quasi-religious claims for art and had made a very clear distinction between art and entertainment, serious and trivial culture, the work of the genius and that of the more or less talented. The veneration of Schiller as genius-hero, of art as transcendence mark the whole celebration. There is a very clear distinction between the 'Monday to Saturday' world of work, domesticity and politics, and the 'Sunday' world of art-as-religion.

The Shakespeare celebrations were very different in tone and content. He was also celebrated as the great national poet and playwright. There was also a tendency to elevate his work, to turn him into an icon of high culture, although that had not been taken as far by the mid-nineteenth century as it has in our own time. There was a far greater range of initiative socially. One finds working men, former Chartists, Reform League activists organising their own celebrations, as well as Whig notables. It was often less the work than the man who was celebrated – a man of the people in the sense both of common origins and of being a popular commercial writer in his own day. (Schiller was not a court writer in the sense of writing for a noble or royal patron, but he did depend upon such patronage.) Shakespeare's art was also seen as more popular; indeed, it was the bawdy and comic in Shakespeare which created problems for those appropriating him for a notion of sacred high culture. There was a more explicit political use of Shakespeare, for example in the close links between a celebration of Shakespeare on Primrose Hill, London and a demonstration in favour of franchise reform and popular access to public places. Yet Shakespeare's work lent itself less well to political exploitation than that of Schiller's. One also gets the strong impression that Shakespeare was not as central in the cultural baggage of any social group in Britain, including middle-glass groups, as Schiller was to middle-class circles in Germany.

What this comparison suggests is that there is a greater degree of middle-class (rather than intelligentsia) definition to the notion of 'national culture' in Germany than in either Britain or France; that this culture is seen in a highly elevated, quasi-religious form, yet abstracted from Christianity; and that the national question, though pre-eminently a political question, is raised somehow above the level of 'mere' politics.

One of the objections levelled at the critical school has been to point to how 'bourgeois' German society and culture had become by the second half of the nineteenth century, conflicting with the idea of the reassertion of pre-modern values. The criticism could continue with the point that the critical historians, by identifying political modernity with liberalism, had failed to see how the bourgeoisie could come to occupy a dominating position. The comparisons I have made above suggest that both sides make valid points but draw invalid conclusions.

First it *is* striking just how influential new middle-class groups were in the urban economy and culture of mid-nineteenth-century Germany. Whether that would continue to be the case after 1871 is actually a moot point: I would suggest that especially the rise of non-German nationalism, political Catholicism and, above all, socialism actually challenged and undermined that cultural centrality and confidence. However, that is another story. The point is: there is in many ways *less* evidence for the continuation of traditional cultural values in many parts of Germany than in France and Britain. To this extent the critical historians have tended to read off economic and cultural meanings from their understanding of political developments, and these readings, certainly at the level of cultural history, have now been persuasively challenged.[1]

Second, and related to this, I would stress the *modernity* of German political institutions. The army, especially after the reforms of the early 1860s, accepted the arguments of merit and performance, of professional training and appraisal, of constant innovation to maintain effectiveness. It is true that a large proportion of the officer corps were of noble origin, but after the reduction in the size of the army after 1815, it was possible to combine that with a meritocratic approach. Again, it may be that complacency set in after 1871 and less adaptation to modern conditions took place, especially as the army was not expanded between the early 1890s and shortly before 1914. Instead the modernist attitude to military affairs was focused upon the navy.

The same points can be made about the bureaucracy, especially following the reforms of the 1806–15 period and then the extension of Prussian practice to much of north and central Germany in 1867, and its infusion into the growing imperial agencies after 1871. In southern Germany there had also been a marked degree of bureaucratic modernisation under Napoleon which continued after 1815.

So Germany modernised thoroughly, in the political and military as well as in the economic and cultural spheres. Where the critics go wrong, however, is in somehow assuming this to be a seamless process which one can refer to as a 'bourgeois revolution', even if one which proceeded without violence, indeed silently. It is the *separation* and *conflict* between the institutions specialising in administration and warfare on the one hand, and those specialising in economic and cultural activity on the other hand which is significant. In Britain the lack of a powerful, administrative layer of officials at the centre, and the relative unimportance of the military in affairs of state prevented such a strong separation taking place. In France there was more such separation, but a less powerful bourgeois position in economy and culture meant that it was rather that the administrative and military elites confronted a more 'traditional' France. Furthermore, military failures in Europe, especially in 1870–71, reduced the political significance of the army.

As a consequence the other element in political life, the element of political representation and public opinion, could come to play a much greater and more positive role in Britain and France, although in the French case this only became routinised and central after 1871. This was not the case in Germany. Constitutionalism became a means of drawing the attention of government to 'public opinion' and of providing representation of distinct interests. Unlike Britain and France it was not the means of actually forming governments and determining policy. It did not matter that high bureaucrats and army officers may have had the same cultural tastes as middle-class professionals and entrepreneurs; what mattered was that they occupied different and separate institutional positions.

The form unification had taken intensified this conflict and separation. Once a lively parliamentary life did take shape, as it did especially with the rise of popular parties with mass support, it became clear that this presented grave problems for the way in which German political life operated. The lack of positive power in

LABOUR AND LIBERALISM IN NINETEENTH-CENTURY EUROPE

representative institutions, as well as the diffusion of public life through state as well as national parliaments, with different responsibilities and electorates, fragmented bourgeois politics and encouraged the politics of agitation at a popular level.

This, therefore, is what is peculiar about German. Its particular form of modernisation enabled a steady growth of middle-class economic and cultural influence in the 'free access' institutions of the market economy and the voluntary cultural activity of the cities. At the same time, the role of administrative reform and warfare at a state-building level provided bureaucracy and army, the props of monarchy, with a much greater degree of independence than was possible in either Britain or France. These modernised institutions had the effect, therefore, of preventing a liberalism based on economic success, cultural confidence and consti-tutional concessions actually managing to make parliament into the central insti-tution of state. Instead, there were two fateful consequences.

First, liberals tended to divide between those who laid the main emphasis upon further restraining the executive in favour of parliamentary power and those who wished to use the executive to continue with their own national and liberal goals. The second kind of 'liberal' could be very modern – favouring active policies of reform in such matters as education and health at urban, state and national level. In a way their liberalism came to reflect the institutions through which they worked: elitist, hierarchical, publicly consensual. In Britain or France where egalitarian and conflict-based institutions (parliaments, free markets) were more central, the appropriate liberalism was more concerned with liberty and control over the executive. Such a liberalism could, in fact, appear in certain ways increasingly archaic by comparison with German middle-class politics when confronted with the social problems of industrialisation.

Second, this bourgeois liberalism, even in parliament, could not make alliances with other political groupings. The reason parliamentary democracy is appropriate to a complex and autonomous civil society of the kind which existed in Germany, is that only through such a parliament do groups with different interests learn to construct coalitions, either within or across political parties, that can implement policies with a broad basis of support. Bureaucracies and pressure groups cannot do this. Political parties which do not have the prospect of power as a consequence of successfully participating in such coalitions cannot do this. That prospect of power is more important than ideological consensus. Right-wing liberals in pre-1914 France and Britain formed coalitions with radicals and even socialists although the ideological gulf was as great as between equivalent political groups in Germany. I have argued a similar case for the differing fortunes of liberalism in Germany and Britain in the 1860s and 1870s.

That inability to form broad-based coalitions was a crucial failure with fateful long-term consequences. The question the critical historians put – why did parlia-mentary democracy fail to establish itself in Germany? – is a legitimate question. It can only be approached by careful comparison. Such comparison suggests that there are problems with some of the answers the critical historians offered, above all the tendency to identify parliamentary democracy with political modernity, to exaggerate the role of pre-modern influences, to stress the problems of a 'compressed revolution', and to use a misleading notion of partial modernisation. But those critics who suggest that it is not legitimate to suggest a *Sonderweg*, or that Germany is just one variant on a theme of the triumph of capitalism and the bourgeoisie, are even more wrong. Both sides in the debate have frequently neglected the most obvious peculiarity in the German case: that territorially new states were created out of war and administrative reform in the two periods 1803–1815 and 1866–71. What is more this was eventually a German achievement (unlike the creation of a united Italy as a by-product of French and Prussian military efforts) and led to the emergence of a new world power by 1900, so that flaws in the political system in Germany had major international consequences. Once those fairly obvious points are taken seriously, it becomes clear that it is the especially autonomous role of the bureaucracy and the military from an increasingly middle-class dominated culture and economy, and the consequent negativity of parliamentary politics to which attention should be paid. This peculiarity is already identifiable by 1871. It is an important peculiarity and one which can be firmly established by means of comparative history.

Note

1 In this very general concluding essay I have refrained from providing references. I do need, however, to refer to the very interesting work in the field of cultural history, especially that concerned with the issue of bourgeois culture. The main impetus has come from a project initiated by Jürgen Kocka at the Centre for Interdisciplinary Research at the University of Bielefeld. This has given rise to a number of publications: Kocka, 1987 and 1988; and Langewiesche, 1988. For work in English see Blackbourn & Evans, 1991.

Bibliography

This is a list simply of published works cited or quoted in the book. Most of the references are to secondary works; some are to published documents. References to primary sources (newspapers, archive materials) are given in full in the text, as are references to some reviews of books.

Ahrens, G. (1982). Von der Franzosenzeit bis zur Verabschiedung der neuen Verfassung 1806–60. In *Hamburg. Geschichte der Stadt und Ihrer Bewonner: Vol. 1* (ed. H. Loose). Hamburg.

Albrecht, W. (1982). *Fachverein-Berfusgewerkschaft-Zentralverband: Organisationsprobleme der deutschen Gewerkschaften 1870–1890*. Bonn.

Aldenhoff, R. (1984). *Schulze-Delitzsch. Ein Beitrag zur Geschichte des Liberalismus zwischen Revolution und Reichsgründung*. Bonn.

Anderson, E. N. (1954). *The Social and Political Conflict in Prussia 1858–1864*. University of Nebraska Studies.

Anderson, M. (1971). *Family Structure in Nineteenth-century Lancashire*. London.

Anderson, O. (1967). *A Liberal State at War: English politics and economics during the Crimean War*. London.

Anderson, P. (1964). Origins of the present crisis. *New Left Review* **23**.

Anderson, P. (1965). Socialism and pseudo-empiricism. *New Left Review* **25**.

Armstrong, A. (1974). *Stability and Change in an English County Town: a social history of York, 1801–1851*. London.

Assmann, K. & Stavhagen G. (1969). *Handwerkereinkommen am Vorabend der industriellen Revolution: Materialien aus dem Raum Braunschweig-Wolfenbuttel*. Göttingen.

Aydelotte, W. O. (1954). The House of Commons in the 1840s. *History* **39**.

Aydelotte, W. O. (1962–63). Voting patterns in the British House of Commons in the 1840s. *Comparative Studies in Society and History* **5**.

Aydelotte, W. O. (1965). Parties and issues in early Victorian England. *Journal of British Studies* **5**.

Baasch, E. (1915). *Die Handelskammer zu Hamburg*, 2 vols. Hamburg.

Balser, F. (1962). *Sozialdemokratie 1848/9–1863. Die erste deutsche Arbeiterorganisation 'Allgemeine deutsche Arbeiterverbrüderung' nach der Revolution*, 2 vols. Stuttgart.

Barrow, L. (1988). *Independent Spirits: spiritualism and English plebeians 1850–1910*. London.

Bavendamm, D. (1969). *Von der Revolution zur Reform. Die Verfassungspolitik des hamburgischen Senats 1849–50*. Berlin.

Bebel, A. (n.d.). *Aus meinem Leben*. Frankfurt.

Beetham, D. (1981). Michels and his critics. *Archives européennes de sociologie* **22**.

Beetham, D. (1983). *Marxists in Face of Fascism*. Manchester.

Beetham, D. (1985). *Max Weber and the Theory of Modern Politics*. London (2nd edn).

Behagg, C. (1979). Custom, class and change: the trade societies of Birmingham. *Social History* **4**(3).

Behagg, C. (1983). An alliance with the middle class: the Birmingham Political Union and early

Chartism. In *The Chartist Experience* (ed. J. Epstein & D. Thompson). London.

Behagg, C. (1990). *Politics and Production in the Early Nineteenth Century*. London.

Beier, G. (1966). *Schwarzkunst und Klassenkampf*. Frankfurt/M.

Beier, G. (1981a). Das Problem der Arbeiteraristokratie im 19. und 20. Jahrhundert. In *Geschichte und Gewerkschaften* (ed. G. Beier). Cologne.

Beier, G. (1981b). Sternberg contra Lenin: Strukturwandel der Arbeiterklasse am Beispiel der Arbeiteraristokratie. In *Fritz Sternberg und die Zukunft des Sozialismus* (ed. H. Grebing). Cologne.

Belchem, J. (1983). 1848: Feargus O'Connor and the collapse of the mass platform. In *The Chartist Experience* (ed. J. Epstein & D. Thompson). London.

Belchem, J. (1985). *Orator Hunt: Henry Hunt and English working-class radicalism*. Oxford.

Benser, G. (1956). *Zur Herausbildung der Eisenacher Partei: Eine Untersuchung über die Entwicklung der Arbeiterbewegung im sächsischen Textilindustriegebiet Glauchau-Meerane*. Berlin (E).

Bentley, M. (1987). *The Climax of Liberal Politics: British Liberalism in theory and practice 1868–1918*. London.

Berding, H. & Ullmann, H. P. (eds) (1981). *Deutschland zwischen Revolution und Restauration*. Königstein/Ts.

Berg, H. von (1981). *Entstehung und Tätigkeit der Norddeutschen Arbeitervereinigung*. Bonn.

Berg, M. (ed) (1983). *Manufacture in Town and Country before the Factory*. Cambridge.

Bergmann, D. (1971). Die Berliner Arbeiterschaft in Vormärz und Revolution 1830–1850. In *Untersuchungen zur Geschichte der frühen Industrialisierung* (ed. O. Büsch). Berlin.

Berridge, V. (1976). 'Popular journalism and working-class attitudes 1859–1886: a study of Reynolds' Newspaper, Lloyd's Weekly Newspaper, and the Weekly Times'. Unpublished Ph.D. thesis, University of London.

Berridge, V. (1978). Popular Sunday papers and mid-Victorian society. In *Newspaper History* (ed. G. Byce, J. Curran & P. Wingate). London/Beverly Hills.

Biagini, E. (1991). Popular Liberals, Gladstonian finance, and the debate on taxation, 1860–1874. In *Currents of Radicalism* (ed. E. Biagini & A. Reid). Cambridge.

Biagini, E. & Reid, A. (eds) (1991). *Currents of Radicalism: popular radicalism, organised labour and party politics in Britain 1850–1914*. Cambridge.

Birker, K. (1973). *Die deutschen Arbeiterbildungsvereine 1840–1870*. Berlin (W).

Blackbourn, D. (1980). *Class, Religion and Local Politics in Wilhelmine Germany: the Centre Party in Württemberg before 1914*. London.

Blackbourn, D. & Eley, G. (1984). *The Peculiarities of German History: Bourgeois society and politics in nineteenth-century Germany*. Oxford.

Blackbourn, D. & Evans, R. J. (eds) (1991). *The German Bourgeoisie: essays on the social history of the German middle class from the late eighteenth to the early twentieth century*. London.

Blanke, T. *et al.* (eds) (n.d.). *Kollektives Arbeitsrecht: Quellentexte zur Geschichte des Arbeitsrechts in Deutschland. Vol. 1: 1840–1932*. Reinbek bei Hamburg.

Blasius, D. (1978). Bürgerliches Recht und bürgerliche Identität. In *Vom Staat des Ancien Regimes zum modernen Parteistaat* (ed. H. Berding *et al.*). Munich & Vienna.

Boberach, H. (1959). *Wahlrechtsfragen im Vormärz: Die Wahlrechtsanschauung im Rheinland 1815–1849 und die Entstehung des Dreiklassenwahlrechts*. Düsseldorf.

Boch, R. (1985). *Handwerker-Sozialisten gegen Fabrikgesellschaft. Lokale Fachvereine, Massengewerkschaft und industrielle Rationalisierung*. Göttingen.

Boch, R. (1989). Die Entstehungsbedingungen der deutschen Arbeiterbewegung: das Bergische Land und der ADAV. In *'Der kühnen Bahn nur folgen wir', I* (ed. A. Herzig & D. Trautmann). Hamburg.

Böhm, E. (1982). Der Weg ins Deutsche Reich 1860–1888. In *Hamburg. Geschichte der Stadt und ihrer Bewohner*. Vol. 1 (ed. H. Loose). Hamburg.

Boldt, W. (1980). Parlamentarismustheorie. Bemerkungen zu ihrer Geschichte in Deutschland. *Der Staat* **19**.

Bolland, J. (1959). *Die hamburgische Bürgerschaft in alter und neuer Zeit.* Hamburg.

Booth, C. (1893). *Life and Labour of the People of London.* London.

Botzenhart, M. (1977). *Deutscher Parlamentarismus in der Revolutionszeit 1848–1850.* Düsseldorf.

Braunthal, J. (1967). *A History of the International,* 1. New York/Washington D.C.

Braverman, H. (1974). *Labour and Monopoly Capital: the degradation of work in the twentieth century.* New York.

Brederlow, J. (1978). *'Lichtfreunde' und 'Freie Gemeinde': Religiöser Protest und Freiheitsbewegung im Vormärz und in der Revolution von 1848/49.* Munich.

Breuilly, J. (1980). *Conflict and Stability in the Development of Modern Europe 1789–1971.* Block I, Part 4. Milton Keynes.

Breuilly, J. (1981). The failure of revolution in 1848. *European Studies Review* **11**.

Breuilly. J. (1982). *Nationalism and the State.* Manchester.

Breuilly, J. (1983). Kontinuität in der hamburgische Arbeiterbewegung von 1844 bis 1863?. In *Arbeiter in Hamburg* (ed. A. Herzig, D. Langewiesche & A. Sywottek). Hamburg.

Breuilly, J. (1984). Nipperdey: Deutsche Geschichte 1800–1866. *Bulletin of the German Historical Institute London* **16**.

Breuilly, J. (1986). The labour aristocracy in Britain and Germany 1850–1914: a review article. In *Arbeiter und Arbeiterbewegung in Vergleich* (ed. K. Tenfelde). Munich.

Breuilly, J. (1987a). The making of the German working class. *Archiv für Sozialgeschichte* **27**.

Breuilly, J. (1987b). The beginnings of German social democracy 1835–1875. In *Bernstein to Brandt: a short history of German Social Democracy* (ed. R. Fletcher). London.

Breuilly, J. (1987c). Eduard Bernstein and Max Weber. In *Max Weber and his Contemporaries* (ed. W. J. Mommsen & J. Osterhammel). London.

Breuilly, J. (1989a). The making of the European working class. In *Probleme der Herausbildung und politischen Formierung der Arbeiterklasse* (ed. H. Konrad). Vienna.

Breuilly, J. (1989b). Weitling und die deutsche Handwerker. In *Wilhelm Weitling. Ein deutscher Arbeiterkommunist* (ed. L. Knatz & H-A. Marsiske). Hamburg.

Breuilly, J. (1990). Nation and nationalism in modern German history. *Historical Journal* **33**(3).

Breuilly, J., Niedhart, G. & Taylor, A. D. (eds) (forthcoming). *British Labour Politics from Chartism to the Reform League: documents selected by Gustav Mayer.*

Breuilly, J. & Sachse, W. (1984). *Joachim Friedrich Martens (1806–1877) und die Deutschen Arbeiterbewegung.* Göttingen.

Briggs, A. (1950). Social structure and politics in Birmingham and Lyons (1825–1848). *British Journal of Sociology* **1**.

Briquet, J. (1955). *Agricole Perdiguier, compagnon du tour et représentant du peuple 1805–1875.* Paris.

Brock, M. (1973). *The Great Reform Act.* London.

Brockhaus, E. (1975). *Zusammensetzung und Neustrukturierung der Arbeiterklasse vor dem ersten Weltkrieg.* Munich.

Brown, K. D. (1982). Trade unions and the law. In *A History of British Industrial Relations* (ed. C. Wrigley). Brighton.

Brundage, A. (1988). *England's 'Prussian Minister': Edwin Chadwick and the politics of goverment growth 1832–1854.* London.

Bry, G. (1960). *Wages in Germany, 1871–1945.* Princeton, N.J.

Burgess, K. (1975). *The Origins of British Industrial Relations: the nineteenth-century experience.* London.

Burgess, K. (1980). *The Challenge of labour: Shaping British Society 1850–1930.* London.

Burns, W. L. (1964). *The Age of Equipoise.* London.

Burrow, J. W. (1988). *Whigs and Liberals: continuity and change in English political thought.* Oxford.

Bythell, D. (1969). *The Handloom Weavers: a study in the English cotton industry during the Industrial Revolution*. Cambridge.

Calhoun, C. (1982). *The Question of Class Struggle: social foundations of popular radicalism during the Industrial Revolution*. Oxford.

Cattaruzza, M. (1984). Schiffszimmerer zwischen Anpassung und Widerstand. Der Übergang vom Holzschiffsbau zur Schiffbauindustrie in Hamburg und Bremen seit der 1860er Jahren. In *Handwerker in der Industrialisierung* (ed. U. Engelhardt). Stuttgart.

Chauvet, P. (1956). *Les Ouvriers du Livre en France de 1789 à la Constitution de la Fédération du Livre*. Paris.

Church, R. A. (1975). *The Great Victorian Boom 1850–1873*. London.

Clapham, J. H. (1932). *An Economic History of Modern Britain, 2*. Cambridge.

Clapham, J. H. (1968). *The Economic Development of France and Germany, 1815–1914*. London.

Clark, J. C. D. (1985). *English Society 1688–1832: ideology, social structure and political practice during the ancien régime*. Cambridge.

Clarke, P. (1971). *Lancashire and the New Liberalism*. Cambridge.

Collins, H. & Abramsky, C. (1965). *Karl Marx and the British Labour Movement*. London.

Coltham, S. (1964–65). George Potter, the Junta, and the Bee-Hive. *International Review of Social History* **IX–X.**

Conze, W. (1965). *Möglichkeiten und Grenzen der liberalen Arbeiterbewegung: Das Beispiel Schulze-Delitzschs*. Heidelberg.

Conze, W. & Engelhardt, U. (eds) (1979). *Arbeiter im Industrialisierungsprozeß: Herkunft, Lage und Verhalten*. Stuttgart.

Conze, W. & Groh, D. (1977). *Die Arbeiterbewegung in der nationalen Bewegung*. Stuttgart.

Cooter, R. (1984). *The Cultural Meaning of Popular Science: phrenology and the organisation of consent in nineteenth-century Britain*. Cambridge.

Corrigan, P. & Sayer, D. (1985). *The Great Arch: English state formation as cultural revolution*. Oxford.

Cottereau, A. (1986). The distinctiveness of working-class cultures in France, 1848–1900. In *Working-class Formation: nineteenth-century patterns in Western Europe and the United States* (ed. I. Katznelson & A. Zolberg). Princeton, New Jersey.

Cowling, M. (1967). *1867: Disraeli, Gladstone and Revolution*. Cambridge.

Crew, D. (1973/74). Definitions of modernity: social mobility in a German town 1880–1901. *Journal of Social History* **7.**

Crew, D. (1979). *Town on the Ruhr: a social history of Bochum 1860–1914*. New York.

Crew, D. (1982). Steel, sabotage and socialism: the strike at the Dortmund 'Union' steel works in 1911. In *The German Working Class 1888–1933* (ed. R. J. Evans). London.

Crew, D. (1986). Class and community. Local research on working-class history in four countries. In *Arbeiter und Arbeiterbewegung im Vergleich* (ed. K. Tenfelde). Munich.

Crisp, O. (1978). Labour and industrialisation in Russia. *Cambridge Economic History of Europe* **2**(2).

Crossick, G. (1976). The labour aristocracy and its values: a study of mid-Victorian Kentish London. *Victorian Studies 19.*

Crossick, G. (1978). *An Artisan Elite in Victorian Society: Kentish London 1840–1880*. London.

Dasey, R. (1981). Family and women's work: women garment workers in Hamburg and Berlin before the First World War. In *The German Family* (ed. R. J. Evans & W. Lee). London.

Davies, A. (1988). 'Leisure and poverty in Salford 1900–1939, British and German working-class culture'. Unpublished conference paper. University of Lancaster, March.

Davies, A. (1991). *Leisure, gender and poverty: working-class culture in Salford and Manchester, 1900–1939*. Milton Keynes.

Davis, S. J. (1985). Classes and police in Manchester 1829–1880. In *City, Class and Culture* (ed. A. Kidd & K. Roberts). Manchester.

Der Kampf . . . (1977). *Der Kampf von Marx und Engels um die revolutionäre Partei der deutschen Arbeiterbewegung.* Berlin (E).

Dipper, C. (1988). Adelsliberalismus in Deutschland. In *Liberalismus im 19. Jahrhundert* (ed. D. Langewiesche). Göttingen.

Ditt, K. (1982). *Industrialisierung, Arbeiterschaft und Arbeiterbewegung in Bielefeld 1850–1914.* Dortmund.

Domansky-Davidsohn, E. (n.d.). *Arbeitskämpfe und Arbeitskampfstrategien des Deutschen Metallarbeiterverbandes von 1891 bis 1914.* Bochum (Diss).

Dominick, R. H. (1982). *Wilhelm Liebknecht and the Founding of the German Social Democratic Party.* Chapel Hill, N.C.

Donajgrudzki, A. (ed) (1977). *Social Control in Nineteenth-century Britain.* London.

Dowe, D. (1989). Einige Bemerkungen zur Berufsstruktur des Lassalleschen Allgemeinen Deutschen Arbeitervereins Ende der 1860er Jahre. In *Der kühnen Bahn nur folgen wir, I* (ed. A. Herzig & G. Trautmann). Hamburg.

Dowe, D. & Offermann, T. (eds) (1983). *Deutsche Handwerker- und Arbeiterkongresse 1848–1852. Protokolle und Materialien.* Berlin & Bonn.

Draper, H. (1972). The concept of the lumpenproletariat in Marx and Engels. *Économie et Société* **15** (December).

Driver, C. (1946). *Tory Radical: the life of Richard Oastler.* New York.

Düding, D. (1984). *Organisierte gesellschaftlicher Nationalismus in Deutschland (1808–1847). Bedeutung und Funktion der Turner- und Sängervereine für die deutsche Nationalbewegung.* Munich.

Dyson, K. (1980). *The State Tradition in Western Europe.* Oxford.

Eccleshall, R., Geoghan, V., Jay, R. & Wilford, R. (eds) (1984). *Political Ideologies: an introduction*

Edsall, N. C. (1971). *The Anti-Poor Law Movement 1834–1844.* Manchester.

Edsall, N. C. (1986). *Richard Cobden: independent radical.* London.

Eger, J. (1973). *Religionskritik als Bedingung der Emanzipation. Arbeiterbewegung und freie Gemeinde in Hamburg vor 1848.* unpublished Examsarbeit: Hamburg.

Ehmer, J. (1991). *Heiratsverhalten, Sozialstruktur, ökonomischer Wandel: England und Mitteleuropa in der Formationsperiode des Kapitalismus.* Göttingen.

Eisenberg, C. (1986). *Deutsche und englische Gewerkschaften. Entstehung und Entwicklung bis 1878 im Vergleich.* Göttingen.

Eisenberg, C. (1988). Arbeiter, Bürger und der 'bürgerliche Verein' 1820–1870. In *Bürgertum im 19 Jahrhundert*, vol. 2. (ed. J. Kocka). Munich.

Eisfeld, G. (1969). *Die Entstehung der liberalen Parteien in Deutschland 1858–71: Studien zu den Organisationen und Programmen der Liberalen und Demokraten.* Hannover.

Elkar, R. (1984). Wandernde Gesellen in und aus Oberdeutschland. Quantitative Studien zur Sozialgeschichte des Handwerks vom 17 bis zum 19. Jahrhundert. In *Handwerker in der Industrialisierung* (ed. U. Engelhardt). Stuttgart.

Emig, D. & Zimmermann, R. (eds) (1977). *Arbeiterbewegung in Deutschland: Ein Dissertationsverzeichnis.* Berlin (W).

Emsley, C. (1979). *British Society and the French Wars 1793–1815.* London.

Endrulat, B. (1860). *Das Schillerfest in Hamburg.* Hamburg.

Engelhardt, U. (1977). *'Nur vereinigt sind wir stark': die Anfänge der deutschen Gewerkschaftsbewegung 1862/63 bis 1869/70.* Stuttgart.

Engelhardt, U. (1978). Gewerkschaftliche Interessenvertretung als Menschenrecht. Anstöße und Entwicklung der Koalitionsrechtsförderung in der preußich-deutschen Arbeiterbewegung 1862/63–1865 (1869). In *Soziale Bewegung und politische Verfassung. Werner Conze zum 31 Dezember 1975* (ed. U. Engelhardt *et al.*) Stuttgart.

Engelhardt, U. (ed) (1984). *Handwerker in der Industrialiserung. Lage, Kultur und Politik vom späten 18. bis ins frühe 20. Jahrhundert.* Stuttgart.

Engels, F. (1976). The true socialists. In *Marx-Engels-Collected works*, 5. London.

Epstein, J. (1982). *The Lion of Freedom: Feargus O'Connor and the Chartist Movement.* London.

Epstein, J. & Thompson, D. (eds) (1982). *The Chartist Experience: studies in working-class radicalism and culture.* London.

Evans, E. J. (1983). *The Forging of the Modern State: early industrial Britain 1783–1870.* London.

Evans, R. J. (1979). 'Red Wednesday' in Hamburg: social democrats, police and lumpenproletariat in the suffrage disturbances of 17 January 1906. *Social History* **4**

Evans, R. J. (1982). Introduction: the sociological interpretation of German labour history. In *The German working-class: 1888–1933* (ed. R. J. Evans). London.

Evans, R. J. (1987). *Death in Hamburg: society and politics in the cholera years, 1830–1870.* Oxford.

Evans, R. J. (ed) (1982). *The German Working Class 1888–1933.* London.

Eyck, F. (1968). *The Frankfurt Parliament 1848–49.* London.

Farnie, D. A. (1979). *The English Cotton Industry and the World Market, 1815–1869.* London.

Faulwasser, J. (1892). *Der grosse Brand und die Wiederaufbau Hamburgs.* Hamburg.

Fehrenbach, E. (1978). *Traditionelle Gesellschaft und revolutionäres Recht. Die Einführung des Code Napoléon in der Rheinbundstaaten.* Göttingen (2nd edn).

Feldman, G. (1981). Streiks in Deutschland 1914–1933: Probleme und Forshchungsaufgaben. In *Streik* (ed. K. Tenfelde & H. Volkmann). Munich.

Fesser, G. (1976). *Linksliberalismus und Arbeiterbewegung: die Stellung der Deutsche Fortschrittspartei zur Arbeiterbewegung, 1861–1866.* Berlin (E).

Finer, S. (1952). *The Life and Times of Sir Edwin Chadwick.* London.

Fischer, W. (1972). *Wirtschaft und Gesellschaft im Zeitalter der Industrialisierung.* Göttingen.

Fischer, W. *et al.* (1982). *Sozialgeschichtliches Arbeitsbuch I: Materialien zur Statistik der Deutschen Bundes, 1815–1870.* Munich.

Foster, J. (1974). *Class Struggle and the Industrial Revolution: early industrial capitalism in three English towns.* London.

Fraser, D. (1976). *Urban Politics in Victorian England.* Leicester.

Fraser, D. (1979). *Power and Authority in the Victorian City.* Oxford.

Fraser, D. (1982). Introduction: municipal reform in historical perspective. In *Municipal Reform and the Industrial City* (ed. D. Fraser). New York.

Fraser, D. (ed) (1982). *Municipal Reform and the Industrial City.* New York.

Fraser, W. H. (1974). *Trade Unions and Society: the struggle for acceptance, 1850–1880.* London.

Freudenthal, H. (1968). *Vereine in Hamburg.* Hamburg.

Fricke, D. (1964). *Die deutsche Arbeiterbewegung 1869–1890.* Leipzig.

Friedensburg, W. (1923). *Stephan Born und die Organisationsbestrebungen der Berliner Arbeiterschaft bis zum Berliner Arbeiterkongress (1840–September 1848).* Leipzig.

Gagel, W. (1958). *Die Wahlrechtsfragen in der Geschichte der deutschen liberalen Parteien, 1848–1919.* Düsseldorf.

Gall, L. (1975). Liberalismus und 'Bürgerliche Gesellschaft'. Zu Charakter und Entwicklung der liberalen Bewegung in Deutschland. *Historische Zeitschrift* **220**.

Gall, L. (1986). *Bismarck: the white revolutionary.* London.

Gall, L. (1989). *Bürgertum in Deutschland.* Berlin.

Gall, L. (ed) (1990). *Stadt und Bürgertum im 19. Jahrhundert.* Munich.

Garrard, J. (1976). *Leaders and Politics in Nineteenth-century Salford: a historical analysis of urban political power.* Salford.

Garrard, J. (1977). Parties, members and voters after 1867: a local study. *Historical Journal* **20**(1).

Garrard, J. (1983). *Leadership and Power in Victorian Industrial Towns, 1830–1880.* Manchester.

Gash, N. (1986). 'Cheap government', 1815–1874. In *Pillars of Government and Other Essays on State and Society c.1770–c.1880*. London.

Gatrell, V. A. C. (1971). 'The commercial, middle class in Manchester, c. 1820–1857'. Unpublished Ph.D. thesis, University of Cambridge.

Gatrell, V. A. C. (1982). Incorporation and the pursuit of liberal hegemony in Manchester 1790–1839. In *Municipal Reform and the Industrial City* (ed. D. Fraser). New York.

Geary, D. (1978). Radicalism and the German worker. In *Society and Politics in Wilhelmine Germany* (ed. R. J. Evans). London.

Geary, D. (1981). *European Labour Protest*. London.

Geary, D. (1982). Identifying militancy: the assessment of working-class attitudes towards state and society. In *The German Working class 1888–1933* (ed. R. J. Evans). London.

Geary, D. (1986). Protest and strike: recent research on 'collective action' in England, Germany and France. In *Arbeiter und Arbeiterbewegung im Vergleich* (ed. K. Tenfelde). Munich.

Gerschrenkron, A. (1976). *Economic Backwardness in Historical Perspective*. Cambridge, Mass.

Gibbon, P. (1975). *The Origins of Ulster Unionism*. Manchester.

Giles, P. M. (1959). The felt-hatting industry, c.1500–1850, with particular reference to Lancashire and Cheshire. *Transactions of the Lancashire and Cheshire Antiquarian Society* **69**.

Gillespie, F. (1927). *Labor and Politics in England 1850–1867*. Durham, N.C.

Goldthorpe, J. *et al.* (1968/69). *The Affluent Worker in the Class Structure*. Cambridge, 4 vols.

Gömmel, R. (1979). *Realeinkommen in Deutschland. Ein internationaler Vergleich*. Nuremberg.

Goodman, G. & Honeyman, K. (1988). *Gainful Pursuits: the making of industrial Europe 1600–1914*. London.

Goodway, D. (1982). *London Chartism 1838–1848*. Cambridge.

Gore, V. (1982). Rank and file dissent. In *A History of British Industrial Relations* (ed. C. Wrigley). Brighton.

Gosden, P. H. (1961). *The Friendly Societies in England 1815–1875*. Manchester.

Gossez, R. (1967). *Les Ouvriers de Paris: l'organisation 1848–1851, 1*. Paris.

Grainger, J. H. (1979). The view from Britain II. In *Intellectuals and Revolution: socialism and the experience of 1848* (ed. E. Kamenka & F. B. Smith). London.

Gramsci, A. (1971). *Selections from the Prison Notebooks*. London.

Gray, J. (1986). *Liberalism*. Milton Keynes.

Gray, R. (1976). *The Labour Aristocracy in Victorian Edinburgh*. Oxford.

Gray, R. (1977). Bourgeois hegemony in Victorian Britain. In *Class, Hegemony and Party* (ed. J. Bloomfield). London.

Gray, R. (1981). *The Aristocracy of Labour in Nineteenth-century Britain*. London.

Grebing, H. (1966). *Geschichte der deutschen Arbeiterbewegung. Ein Überblick*. Munich.

Grebing, H. (1986). *Der 'deutsche Sonderweg' in Europa 1806–1945*. Stuttgart.

Grew, R. (ed) (1978). *Crises of Political Development in Europe and the United States*. Princeton, N.J.

Giressinger, A. (1981). *Das symbolische Kapital der Ehre*. Frankfurt.

Grimm, D. (1987). Bürgerlichkeit im Recht. In *Bürger und Bürgerlichkeit* (ed. J. Kocka). Göttingen.

Grimm, D. (1988a). *Deutsche Verfassungsgeschichte 1776–1866*. Frankfurt.

Grimm, D. (1988b). Die Grundrechte im Entstehungszusammenhang der bürgerlichen Gesellschaft. In *Bürgertum im 19. Jahrhundert* vol. 1, (ed. J. Kocka). Munich.

Groh, D. (1975). *Negative Integration und revolutionärer Attentismus. Die deutche Sozialdemokratie am Vorabend des Ersten Weltkrieges*. Frankfurt.

Grüneberg, A. (ed) (1970). *Die Massenstreikdebatte. Beiträge von Parvus, Rosa Luxemburg, Karl Kautsky, Anton Pannenkoek*. Frankfurt.

Grüttner, M. (1982). Working-class crime and the labour movement: pilfering in the Hamburg docks

1888–1923. In *The German Working Class, 1888–1933* (ed. R. J. Evans). London.

Gugel, M. (1975). *Industrieller Aufstieg und bürgerliche Herrschaft. Sozio-ökonomische Interessen und politischer Ziele des liberalen Bürgertums in Preußen zur Zeit des Verfassungskonflikts, 1857–67.* Cologne.

Gunn, S. (1988). The 'failure' of the Victorian middle class: a critique. In *The Culture of Capital* (ed. J. Wolff & J. Seed). Manchester.

Guttsman, W. (1981). *The German Social Democratic Party 1875–1933.* London.

Hahn, H.-W. (1983). Zwischen deutcher Handelsfreiheit und Sicherung landständischer Rechte. Der Liberalismus und die Gründung des deutschen Zollvereins. In *Liberalismus in der Gesellschaft des deutschen Vormärz* (ed. W. Schieder). Göttingen.

Hall, A. (1977). *Scandal, Sensation and Social Democracy: the SPD press and Wilhelmine Germany 1890–1914.* Cambridge.

Hamburger, J. (1965). *Intellectuals in Politics: John Stuart Mill and the Philosophic Radicals.* New Haven, Ct.

Hamerow, T. (1961). The elections to the Frankfurt Parliament. *Journal of Modern History* **33**.

Hamerow, T. (1967) 1848. In *The Responsibility of Power* (ed. L. Krieger & F. Stern). New York.

Hamerow, T. (1969). *The Social Foundations of German Unification: I.* Princetown, N.J.

Hamerow, T. (1972). *The Social Foundations of German Unification: II.* Princeton, N.J.

Hamerow, T. (1973). The origins of mass politics in Germany, 1866–67. In *Deutschland in der Weltpolitik des 19. und 20. Jahrhunderts* (ed. I. Geiss & B. J. Wendt). Düsseldorf.

Hanagan, M. P. (1980). *The Logic of Solidarity: artisans and industrial workers in three French towns 1870–1914.* Urbana, Ill.

Handke, H. (1989). Sozialgeschichte – Stand und Entwicklung in der DDR. In *Sozialgeschichte im internationalen Überblick* (ed. J. Kocka). Darmstadt.

Hanham, H. (1959). *Elections and Party Management.* London.

Hanham, H. (ed) (1969). *The Nineteenth-Century Constitution 1815–1914: documents and commentary.* Cambridge.

Hanson, C. G. (1975). Craft unions, welfare benefits, and the case for trade union reform, 1867–1875. *Economic History Review*, Second Series **28**.

Hanson, C. G., Thane, P. & Musson, A. E. (1976). Comments on Hanson, 1975. *Economic History Review*, Second Series **29**.

Harrison, J. F. C. (1969). *Robert Owen and the Owenites in Britain and America: the quest for a new moral world.* London.

Harrison, R. (1960). The British working class and the general election of 1868: part 1. *International Review of Social History* **5**.

Harrison, R. (1961). The British working class and the general election of 1868: part 2. *International Review of Social History* **6**.

Harrison, R. (1965). *Before the Socialists: studies in labour and politics, 1861–1881.* London.

Harrison, R. (ed) (1978). *Independent Collier: the coal miner as archetypal proletarian reconsidered.* New York.

Haupt. H.-G. (1986). Staatliche Bürokratie und Arbeiterbewegung. Zum Einfluß der Polizei auf die Konstituierung von Arbeiterbewegung und Arbeiterklasse in Deutschland und Frankreich zwischen 1848 und 1880. In *Arbeiter und Bürger im 19. Jahrhundert* (ed. J. Kocka). Munich.

Heffter, H. (1969). *Die deutsche Selbstverwaltung im 19. Jahrhundert.* Stuttgart (2nd ed).

Hennock, E. P. (1973). *Fit and Proper Persons: ideal and reality in nineteenth-century urban government.* London.

Herzig, A., Langewiesche, D. & Trautmann, G. (eds) (1983). *Arbeiter in Hamburg.* Hamburg.

Herzig, A. & Sachs, R. (1987). *Der Breslauer Gesellenaufstand von 1793.* Göttingen.

Herzig, A. & Trautmann, G. (eds) (1989a). *'Der kühnen Bahn nur folgen wir': Ursprünge, Erfolge und*

Grenzen der Arbeiterbewegung in Deutschland: Vol. I. Entstehung und Wandel der deutschen Arbeiterbewegung. Hamburg.

Herzig, A. & Trautmann, G. (eds) (1989b). *'Der kühnen Bahn nur folgen wir': Ursprünge, Erfolge und Grenzen der Arbeiterbewegung in Deutschland: Vol. II. Arbeiter und technischer Wandel in der Hafenstadt Hamburg*. Hamburg.

Hess, A. (1964). *Das Parlament das Bismarck widerstrebte*. Cologne & Opladen.

Hickey, S. H. (1978). The shaping of the German labour movement: miners in the Ruhr. In *Society and Politics in Wilhelmine Germany* (ed. R. J. Evans). London.

Hickey, S. H. F. (1985). *Workers in Imperial Germany: the miners of the Ruhr*. Oxford.

Hinde, W. (1987). *Richard Cobden: a Victorian outsider*. London.

Hinton, J. (1973). *The First Shop Stewards' Movement*. London.

Hinton, J. (1982). The rise of a mass labour movement: growth and limits. In *A History of the British Labour Movement* (ed. C. Wrigley). Brighton.

Hinton, J. (1983). *Labour and Socialism: a history of the British labour movement, 1867–1914*. Brighton.

Hirst, D. (1975). *The Representative of the People? Voters and voting in England under the early Stuarts*. London.

Hobsbawm, E. (1968). *Labouring Men*. London.

Hobsbawm, E. (1984a). *Worlds of Labour: further studies in the history of labour*. London.

Hobsbawm, E. (1984b). The making of the working class 1870–1914. In *Worlds of Labour*. London.

Hobsbawm, E. (1984c). The formation of British working-class culture. In *Worlds of Labour*. London.

Hobsbawm, E. & Scott, J. W. (1980). Political shoemakers. *Past and Present* **89**.

Hoggart, R. (1957). *The Uses of Literacy*. Harmondsworth.

Hollis, P. & Harrison, B. (1967). Chartism, liberalism and the life of Robert Lowery. *English Historical Review* **82**.

Holton, R. (1976). *British Syndicalism 1900–1914: myths and realities*. London.

Homburg, H. (1978). Anfänge des Taylorsystems in Deutschland vor dem ersten Weltkrieg. *Geschichte und Gesellschaft* **4**.

Homburg, H. (1983). Scientific management and personnel policy in the modern German enterprise 1918–1939: the case of Siemens. In *Managerial Strategies and Industrial Relations* (ed. C. Littler & H. Gospel). London.

Hopkins, E. (1975). Small-town aristocrats of labour and their standard of living, 1840–1914. *Economic History Review* **28**.

Houghton, W. E. (1985). *The Victorian Frame of Mind, 1830–1870*. New Haven, Ct.

Howell, G. (1902). *Labour Legislation, Labour Movements, Labour Leaders*. London.

Huber, E. (1960). *Deutsche Verfassungsgeschichte seit 1789: Vol 2. Der Kampf um Einheit und Freiheit 1830 bis 1850*. Stuttgart.

Huber, E. (1963). *Deutsche Verfassungsgeschichte seit 1789. Vol 3: Bismarck und das Reich*. Stuttgart.

Huber, E. (ed) (1978). *Dokumente zur Deutschen Verfassungsgeschichte, 1*. Stuttgart (3rd edn).

Huck, G. (ed) (1982). *Sozialgeschichte der Freizeit: Untersuchungen zum Wandel der Alltagskultur in Deutschland*. Wuppertal.

Hucko, G. (ed) (1987). *The Democratic Tradition: four German constitutions*. Leamington Spa.

Hughes, A. (1985). The king, the parliament and the localities during the English Civil War. *Journal of British Studies* **24**.

Humphrey, A. W. (1913). *Robert Applegarth: trade unionist, educationist, reformer*. London.

Hunt, E. H. (1981). *British Labour History 1815–1914*. London.

Hunt, E. P. (1973). *Regional Wage Variations in Britain, 1850–1914*. Oxford.

Husung, H.-G. (1983). *Protest und Repression im Vormärz. Norddeutschland zwischen Restauration und Revolution*. Göttingen.

Jacobs, J. (1986). *Cities and the Wealth of Nations: principles of economic life*. Harmondsworth.

Jaeger, R. (1980). *Das hamburger Schiller-Denkmal. Historischer Hintergrund, politische Motive, künstlerliche Probleme und organisatorische Stationen einer bürgerlichen Denkmalsetzung im 19. Jahrhundert*. Hamburg.

John, M. (1989). *Politics and the Law in Late Nineteenth-century Germany: the origins of the civil code*. Oxford.

Johnson, C. H. (1970). *Utopian Communism in France: Cabet and the Icarians*. Ithaca, Ill.

Johnson, C. H. (1975). Economic change and artisan discontent: the tailors' history 1800–1848. In *Revolution and Reaction: 1848 and the Second French Republic* (ed. R. Price). London.

Johnson, P. (1985). *Saving and Spending: the working-class economy in Britain 1870–1939*. Oxford.

Jones, G. S. (1971). *Outcast London*. Oxford.

Jones, G. S. (1973/74). Working-class culture and working-class politics in London 1870–1920: notes on the remaking of a working class. *Journal of Social History* 7 (reprinted in *Languages of Class*).

Jones, G. S. (1975). Class Struggle and the Industrial Revolution. *New Left Review* 90 (reprinted in *Languages of Class*).

Jones, G. S. (1984a). Rethinking Chartism. In *Languages of Class: studies in English working-class history 1832–1982*. Cambridge.

Jones, G. S. (1984b). *Languages of Class: studies in English working-class history 1832–1982*. Cambridge.

Joyce, P. (1982). *Work, Society and Politics: the culture of the factory in later Victorian England*. London.

Joyce, P. (1991). *Visions of the People: industrial England and the question of class 1840–1914*. Cambridge.

Kaelble, H. (1983). Der Mythos von der rapide Industrialisierung in Deutschland. *Geschichte und Gesellschaft* 9(1).

Katznelson, I. & Zolberg, A. R. (eds) (1986). *Working-class Formation: nineteenth-century patterns in Western Europe and the United States*. Princeton, N.J.

Kaufhold, K. (1976). Handwerk und Industrie 1800–1850. In *Handbuch der deutschen Wirtschafts- und Sozialgeschichte, 2* (ed. H. Aubin & W. Zorn). Stuttgart.

Kaufhold, K. (1979). Das Handwerk zwischen Anpassung und Verdrängung. In *Sozialgeschichtliche Probleme in der Zeit der Hochindustrialisierung* (ed. H. Pohl). Paderborn.

Kidd, A. & Roberts, K. (eds) (1985). *City, Class and Culture: studies of cultural production and social policy in Victorian Manchester*. Manchester.

Kirby, R. & Musson, A. (1975). *The Voice of the People: John Doherty, 1798–1854: trade unionist, radical, and factory reformer*. Manchester.

Klessmann, C. (1974). Zur Sozialgeschichte der Reichsverfassungskampagne von 1849. *Historische Zeitschrift 218*.

Klessmann, C. (1978). *Polnische Bergarbeiter im Ruhrgebiet 1870–1945*. Göttingen & Zürich.

Knatz, L. & Marsiske, H.-A. (eds) (1989). *Wilhelm Weitling. Ein deutscher Arbeiterkommunist*. Hamburg.

Koch, R. (1986). Liberalismus und soziale Frage im 19. Jahrhundert. In *Sozialer Liberalismus* (ed. K.Holl, *et al.*). Göttingen.

Kocka, J. (1980). Sozialstruktur und Arbeiterbewegung: die Entstehung des Leipziger Proletariats. *Archiv für Sozialgeschichte 20.*

Kocka, J. (1982). Der 'deutsche Sonderweg' in der Diskussion. *German Studies Review* 5.

Kocka, J. (1983). *Lohnarbeit und Klassenbildung: Arbeiter und Arbeiterbewegung in Deutschland 1800–1875*. Bonn.

Kocka, J. (1986). Problems of working-class formation in Germany: the early years 1800–1875. In

Working-class Formation: nineteenth-century patterns in western Europe and the United States (ed. I. Katznelson & A. R. Zolberg). Princeton, New Jersey.

Kocka, J. (1987). Bürgertum und Bürgerlichkeit als Probleme der deutschen Geschichte vom späten 18. zum frühen 20. Jahrhundert. In *Bürger und Bürgerlichkeit im 19. Jahrhundert* (ed. J. Kocka). Göttingen.

Kocka, J. (1990a). *Weder Stand noch Klasse: Unterschichten von 1800.* Berlin.

Kocka, J. (1990b). *Arbeitsverhältnisse und Arbeiterexistenzen: Grundlagen der Klassenbildung im 19. Jahrhundert.* Berlin.

Kocka, J. (ed) (1987). *Bürger und Bürgerlichkeit im 19. Jahrhundert.* Gottingen.

Kocka, J. (ed) (1988). *Bürgertum im 19. Jahrhundert*, 3 vols. Munich.

Koditschek, T. (1990). *Class Formation and Urban Industrial Society: Bradford 1750–1850.* Cambridge.

Kögler, P. (1974). *Arbeiterbewegung und Vereinsrecht. Ein Beitrag zur Entstehungsgeschichte der BGB.* Berlin.

Kolakowski, L. (1978). *Main Currents of Marxism*, vol. 3. London.

Koselleck, R. (1981). *Preussen zwischen Reform und Revolution: Allgemeines Landrecht, Verwaltung und soziale Bewegung 1791–1848.* Stuttgart (3rd edn).

Kowalski, W. (1962). *Vorgeschichte und Entstehung des Bundes der Gerechten.* Berlin (E).

Kriedte, P. *et al.* (1981). *Industrialisation before Industrialisation: rural industry in the genesis of capitalism.* Cambridge.

Krieger, L. (1957). *The German Idea of Freedom: history of a political tradition.* Boston, Mass.

Krohn, H. (1967). *Die Juden in Hamburg 1800–1850. Ihre soziale, kulturelle und politische Entwicklung während der Emanzipationszeit.* Frankfurt.

Krohn, H. (1974). *Die Juden in Hamburg. Die politische, soziale und kulturelle Entwicklung einer jüdischen Großstadtgemeinde nach der Emanzipation 1848 bis 1918.* Hamburg.

Kuczynski, J. (1962). *Die Geschichte der Lage der Arbeiter unter dem Kapitalismus*, Vol. 2. Berlin (E).

Kumar, K. (1978). *Prophecy and Progress: the sociology of industrial and post-industrial society.* Harmondsworth.

Kutz-Bauer, H. (1988). *Arbeiterschaft, Arbeiterbewegung und bürgerlicher Staat in der Zeit der Großen Depression.* Bonn.

Langer, W. (1966). The pattern of urban revolution in 1848. In *French Culture and Society since the Ancien Regime* (ed. M. Acomb & R. Brown). New York.

Langewiesche, D. (1974). *Liberalismus und Demokratie in Württemberg zwischen Revolution und Reichsgründung.* Düsseldorf.

Langewiesche, D. (1981). Die deutsche Revolution von 1848/49 und die vorrevolutionäre Gesellschaft: Forschungsstand und Forschungsperspektive. *Archiv für Sozialgeschichte* **21**.

Langewiesche, D. (1988). *Liberalismus in Deutschland.* Frankfurt.

Langewiesche, D. (ed) (1988). *Liberalismus im 19. Jahrhundert.* Göttingen.

Lassalle, F. (1921–25). *Nachgelassene Briefe und Schriften*, 6 vols. (ed. G. Mayer). Stuttgart & Berlin.

Lassalle, F. (1970). Offnes Antwortschreiben. In *Reden und Schriften* (ed. F. Jenaczek). Munich.

Lattek, C. (1991). 'German socialists in British exile 1840–1859'. Unpublished Ph.D. thesis, University of Cambridge.

Laufenberg, H. (1911). *Geschichte der Arbeiterbewegung in Hamburg, Altona und Umgegend.* Hamburg.

Lazonick, W. (1979). Industrial relations and technical change: the case of the self-acting mule. *Cambridge Journal of Economics* **111**.

Leeson, R. A. (1979). *Travelling Brothers.* London.

Lehr, H. W. (1919). *Das Bügerrecht im hamburgischen Staat.* Hamburg.

Lenger, F. (1986). *Zwischen Kleinbürgertum und Proletariat. Studien zur Sozialgeschichte der Düsseldorfer Handwerker 1816–1878.* Göttingen.

Lenger, F. (1988). *Sozialgeschichte der Handwerker seit 1800*. Frankfurt/M.

Lenger, F. (1990). Bürgertum und Stadtverwaltung in rheinischen Großstaedten des 19. Jahrhunderts. Zu einem vernachlässigten Aspekt bürgerlicher Herrschaft. In *Stadt und Bürgertum im 19. Jahrhundert* (ed. L. Gall). Munich.

Lenin, V. (1969). *British Labour and British Imperialism: a compilation of writings by Lenin on Britain*. London.

Levenstein, A. (1912). *Die Arbeiterfrage*. Munich.

Leventhal, F. M. (1971). *Respectable Radical: George Howell and Victorian working-class politics*. London.

Levy, C. (1929). 'Die inneren Kämpfe Hamburgs nach dem großen Brande im Spiegel der hamburgischen Publizistik'. Unpublished Ph.D. thesis, University of Hamburg.

Leys, C. (1955). Petitioning in the nineteenth and twentieth centuries. *Political Studies* 3.

Lidtke, O. (1966). *The Outlawed Party: German social democracy, 1878–1890*. Princeton, N.J.

Lidtke, V. L. (1985). *The Alternative Culture: socialist labor in imperial Germany*. Oxford.

Lindemann, M. (1990). *Patriots and Paupers: Hamburg, 1712–1830*. Oxford.

Littler, C. (1982). *The Development of the Labour Process in Capitalist Societies*. London.

Littler, C. & Gospel, H. (eds) (1983). *Managerial Strategies and Industrial Revolution*. London.

Lively, J. and Rees, J. (ed. and introd.) (1984). *Utilitarian Logic and Politics. James Mill's 'Essay on government', Macaulay's critique and the ensuing debate*. Oxford.

Lloyd-Jones, R. & Lewis, M. J. (1988). *Manchester and the Age of the Factory*. London.

Loubère, L. (1961). *Louis Blanc: his life and his contribution to the rise of French Jacobinism–Socialism*. Evanston, Ill.

Low, D. (1977). Introduction. In *Congress and the Raj: facets of the Indian struggle, 1917–1947* (ed. D. Low). Columbia, NY.

Lowery, R. (1979). *Robert Lowery: the selected writings* (ed. P. Hollis & B. Harrison). London.

Lucas, E. (1976). *Arbeiterradikalismus: Zwei Formen von Radikalismus in der deutschen Arbeiterbewegung*. Frankfurt.

Lucas, E., Wickham, J. & Roth, K. (eds) (1977). *Arbeiterradikalismus und die 'andere' Arbeiterbewegung: Zur Diskussion der Massenarbeiterthese*. Bochum.

Lüdtke, A. (1989). *Police and State in Prussia 1815–1850*. Cambridge.

Lützenkirchen, R. (1970). *Der Sozialdemokratische Verin Dortmund-Hörde*. Dortmund.

McCord, N. (1968). *The Anti-Corn Law League, 1838–1846*. London (1st edn 1958).

McCready, H. (1954). The British election of 1874: Frederick Harrison and the liberal-labour dilemma. *Canadian Journal of Economic and Political Science* 20.

McDonagh, O. (1977). *Early Victorian Government, 1830–1870*. London.

Macfarlane, A. (1978). *The Origins of English Individualism: the family, property and social transition*. Oxford.

Machin, G. (1964). *The Catholic Question in English Politics 1820–1880*. Oxford.

Machin, G. (1977). *Politics and the Churches in Great Britain 1832–1868*. Oxford.

Machtan, L. (1978). Zur Streikbewegung der deutschen Arbeiter in den Gründerjahren (1871–73). *Internationale Wissenschaftliche Korrespondenz zur Geschichte der deutschen Arbeiterbewegung* 14.

Machtan, L. (1981a). 'Gibt est kein Preservativ, um diese wirtschaftliche Cholera uns vom Halse zu halten?' – Unternehmer, bürgerliche öffentlichkeit und preußische Regierung gegenüber der ersten großen Streikwelle in Deutschland (1869–1874). *Jahrbuch Arbeiterbewegung* I.

Machtan, L. (1981b). 'Im Vertrauen auf unsere gerechte Sache . . .': Streikbewegungen der Industriearbeiter in den 70er Jahren des 19. Jahrhunderts. In *Streik. Zur Geschichte des Arbeitskampfes in Deutschland während der Industrialisierung* (ed. K. Tenfelde & H. Volkmann). Munich.

Machtan, L. (1983). *Streiks im frühen deutschen Kaiserreich*. Frankfurt.

Machtan, L. & Milles, D. (1980). *Die Klassensymbiose von Junkertum und Bourgeoisie. Zum Verhältnis von gesellschaftlicher und politischer Herrschaft in Preußen-Deutschland 1850–1878/79*. Frankfurt.

Mackenzie, G. (1973). *The Aristocracy of Labour: the position of skilled craftsmen in the American class structure*. London.

McKenzie, R. T. & Silver, A. (1969). *Angels in Marble*. London.

McLeod, H. (1981). *Religion and the People of Western Europe 1789–1970*. Oxford.

McLeod, H. (1982). Protestantism and the working class in imperial Germany. *European Studies Review* **12**.

McLeod, H. (1984). *Religion and the Working Class in Nineteenth-century Britain*. London.

McLeod, H. (1986). Church and class. Some international comparisons. In *Arbeiter und Bürger im 19.Jahrhundert* (ed. J. Kocka).

McWilliam, R. (1991). Radicalism and popular culture: the Tichborne case and the politics of 'fair play', 1867–1886. In *Currents of Radicalism* (ed. E. Biagini & A. Reid). Cambridge.

Maehl, W. (1980). *August Bebel: shadow emperor of the German workers*. Philadelphia, PA.

Mallmann, K.-M. (1981). *Die Anfänge der Bergarbeiterbewegung an der Saar* (1848–1904). Saar-brücken.

Mann, M. (forthcoming). *The Sources of Social Power 2*.

Markovitch, T. (1970). The dominant sectors of French industry. In *Essays in French Economic History* (ed. R. Cameron). Homewood, Ill.

Marsiske, H.-A. (1986). *'Wider die Umsonstfresser'. Der Handwerkerkommunist Wilhelm Weitling*. Hamburg.

Marsiske, H.-A. (1989). Wilhelm Weitling Gesammelte Werke – Ein Editionsprojekt. In *Wilhelm Weitling. Ein deutscher Arbeiterkommunist* (ed. L. Knatz & H.-A. Marsiske). Hamburg.

Martiny, M. (1976). *Integration oder Konfrontation? Studien zur Geschichte der sozialdemokratischen Rechts- und Verfassungspolitik*. Bonn/Bad Godesberg.

Marx, K. (1956). *The Poverty of Philosophy*. London.

Marx, K. (1968). Critique of the Gotha Programme. In *Marx–Engels – Selected Works in One Volume*. London.

Marx, K. (1973). *Grundrisse. Foundations of the Critique of Political Economy* (Rough Draft). Harmondsworth.

Marx, K. (1974). *The First International and After*. Harmondsworth.

Mark, K. (1987). Letter to Engels of 4 November 1864. In *Marx–Engels – Collected Works*, Vol. 42. London.

Marx, K. & Engels, F. (1954). *Karl Marx and Friedrich Engels on Britain*. London.

Mather, F. (1959). Public Order in the Age of the Chartists. Manchester.

Mather, F. (1965). The government and the Chartists. In *Chartist Studies* (ed. A. Briggs). London.

Matsumura, T. (1983). *The Labour Aristocracy Revisited: the Victorian flint glass makers 1850–1880*. Manchester.

Mattheisen, D. J. (1976). Die Fraktionen der preußischen Nationalversammlung von 1848. In *Quanti-fizierung in der Geschichtswissenschaft* (ed. K. A. Jarausch). Düsseldorf.

Matthew, H. C. G. (1979). Disraeli, Gladstone and the policy of mid-Victorian budgets. *The Historical Journal* **22**.

Matthias, E. (1957). *Kautsky und Kautskyanismus*. Tübingen.

Matz, K-J. (1980). *Pauperismus und Bevölkerung. Die gesetzlichen Ehebeschränkungen in den süddeutschen Staaaten während des 19.Jahrhunderts*. Stuttgart.

Mayer, G. (1969). Die Trennung der proletarischen von der bürgerlichen Demokratie in Deutschland, 1863–1870. In *Radikalismus, Sozialismus und Bürgerliche Demokratie* (ed. H.-U. Wehler).

Mayhew, H. (1968). *London Labour and London Poor*, 4 vols. New York.

Mayhew, H. (1971). *The Unknown Mayhew* (ed. E. P. Thompson & E. Yeo). London.

Meacham, S. (1977). *A Life Apart: the English working class 1890–1914*. London.

Melling, J. (1980). Non-commissioned officers: British employers and their supervisory employers. *Social History* 5(2).

Merriman, J. (1978). *The Agony of the Republic: the repression of the left in revolutionary France, 1848–1851*. New Haven, Ct.

Michels, R. (1962). *Political Parties: a sociological study of the oligarchical tendencies of modern democracy*. New York.

Mitchell, B. R. (1978). *European Historical Statistics, 1750–1970*. London.

Mommsen, W. J. (1987). Robert Michels and Max Weber: moral conviction versus the politics of responsibility. In *Max Weber and his Contemporaries* (ed. W. J. Mommsen & J. Osterhammel). London.

Moore, B. (1969). *The Social Origins of Dictatorship and Democracy: lord and peasant in the making of the modern world*. London.

Moore, B. (1978). *Injustice: the social bases of obedience and revolt*. Chapel Hill, N. C.

Moore, D. C. (1966). Concession or cure: sociological premises of the First Reform Act. *Historical Journal* 9.

Moore, D. C. (1975). *The Politics of Deference: a study of the mid-nineteenth century English political system*. Brighton.

Moorhouse, H. (1973). The political incorporation of the British working class: an interpretation. *Sociology* 7(3).

Moorhouse, H. (1978). The Marxist theory of the labour aristocracy. *Social History* 3(1).

More, C. (1980). *Skill and the English Working Class*. London.

Morgan, R. (1965). *The German Social Democrats and the First International, 1864–1872*. Cambridge.

Morley, J. (1896). *The Life of Richard Cobden*, 3 vols. London.

Morris, R. J. (1977). Bargaining with hegemony. *Bulletin of the Society for the Study of Labour History* 35.

Morris, R. J. (1990). *Class, Sect and Party: the making of the British middle class: Leeds, 1820–1850*. Manchester.

Moss, B. (1975a). Parisian workers and the origins of republican socialism 1830–1833. In *1830 in France* (ed. J. Merriman). New York.

Moss, B. H. (1975b). Parisian producers' associations (1830–1850). In *Revolution and Reaction: 1848 and the Second French Republic* (ed. R. Price). London.

Moss, B. H. (1976). *The Origins of the French Labor Movement: the socialism of skilled workers, 1830–1906*. London.

Muhs, R. (1988). Deutscher und britischer Liberalismus im Vergleich. Trägerschichten, Zielvorstellungen und Rahmenbedingungen (ca. 1830–1870). In *Liberalismus im 19.Jahrhundert* (ed. D. Langewiesche). Göttingen.

Müller, D. H. (1976). *Entstehung und Verwendung des Begriffs Arbeiteraristokratie*. Unpublished.

Müller, D. H. (1984). Binnenstruktur und Selbstverständnis, der 'Gesellenschaft' der Berlin Zimmerer im Übergang von der handwerkerkichen zur gewerkschaftlichen Interessenvertretung. In *Handwerker in der Industrialisierung* (ed. U. Engelhardt). Stuttgart.

Musson, A. E. (1954). *The Typographical Association*. London.

Musson, A. E. (1972). *British Trade Unions 1800–1875*. London.

Musson, A. E. (1976). Class struggle and the labour aristocracy. *Social History* 3(3).

Musson, A. E. & Robinson, E. (1969). *Science and Technology in the Industrial Revolution*. Manchester.

Na'aman, S. (1963). Lassalle – Demokratie und Sozialdemokratie. *Archiv für Sozialgeschichte* 3.

Na'aman, S. (1969). *Demokratische und soziale Impulse in der Frühgeschichte der deutschen Arbeiterbewegung der Jahre 1862/63*. Wiesbaden.

Na'aman, S. (1970). *Lassalle*. Hanover.

Na'aman, S. (1976). *Von der Arbeiterbewegung zur Arbeiterpartei: Der Fünfte Vereinstag der Deutschen Arbeitervereine zu Nürnberg im Jahre 1868: Eine Dokumentation.* Berlin.

Na'aman, S. (1983). Die politischen und sozialen Impulse bei der Gründung der organisierten Arbeiterbewegung. In *Arbeiter in Hamburg* (ed. A. Herzig, D. Langewiesche & A. Sywottek). Hamburg.

Na'aman, S. with Harstick, H.-P. (1975). *Die Konstituierung der deutschen Arbeiterbewegung 1862/63: Darstellung und Dokumentation.* Assen.

Nairn, T. (1964a). The English working class. *New Left Review* 24.

Nairn, T. (1964b). The nature of the Labour Party. *New Left Review* 27.

Nairn, T. (1964c). The nature of the Labour Party: Part 2. *New Left Review* 28.

Nettl, J. P. (1969). *Rosa Luxemburg.* Oxford.

Nicolaevsky, B. & Maenchen-Helfen, O. (1973). *Karl Marx: man and fighter* (1st edn 1933). London.

Nipperdey, T. (1983). *Deutsche Geschichte 1800–1866: Bürgerwelt und starker Staat.* Munich.

Nipperdey, T. (1988). *Wie das Bürgertum die Moderne fand.* Berlin.

Nipperdey, T. (1990). The rise of the arts in modern society. *The 1989 Annual Lecture at the German Historical Institute, London.* London.

Nolan, M. (1981). *Social Democracy and Society: working-class radicalism in Düsseldorf 1890–1920.* Cambridge.

Noll, A. (1975). *Sozio-ökonomische Strukturwandel des Handwerks in der zweiten Phase der Industrialisierung unter besonderer Berücksichtigung Arnsberg und Münster.* Göttingen.

Noyes, P. (1966). *Organisation and Revolution: working-class associations in the German revolutions of 1848–49.* Princeton, NJ.

Oberschall, A. (1965). *Empirical Social Research in Germany 1848–1914.* Paris and The Hague.

O'Brien, P. & Keyder, C. (1978). *Economic Growth in Britain and France 1780–1914: two paths to the twentieth century.* London.

Offermann, T. (1979). *Arbeiterbewegung und liberales Bürgertum in Deutschland 1850–1963.* Bonn.

Offermann, T. (1984). Mittelständisch-kleingewerbliche Leitbilder in der liberalen Handwerker- und handwerklichen Arbeiterbewegung der 50er und 60er Jahre des 19.Jahrhunderts. In *Handwerker in der Industrialisierung* (ed. U. Engelhardt). Stuttgart.

Offermann, T. (1988). Preussischer Liberalismus zwischen Revolution und Reichsgründung im regionalen Vergleich. Berliner und Kölner Fortschrittsliberalismus in der Konfliktszeit. In *Liberalismus im 19.Jahrhundert* (ed. D. Langewiesche). Göttingen.

O'Gorman, F. (1989). *Voters, Patrons and Parties: the unreformed electoral system of Hannoverian England 1734–1832.* Oxford.

Padtberg, B. C. (1985). *Rheinischer Liberalismus in Köln während der politischen Reaktion in Preußen nach 1848/49.* Cologne.

Paletschek, S. (1990). *Frauen und Dissens: Frauen im Deutschkatholizismus und in den freien Gemeinden 1841–1852.* Göttingen.

Palmer, A. (1978). Most uncommon commen men: craft and culture in historical perspective. *Labour/Le Travailleur* 1.

Parkin, F. (1979). *Marxism and Class Theory: a bourgeois critique.* London.

Parry, J. P. (1986). *Democracy and religion: Gladstone and the Liberal Party, 1867–1875.* Cambridge.

Parssinen, T. M. (1973). Association, convention and anti-parliament in British radical politics 1771–1848. *English Historical Review* 87.

Parssinen, T. & Prothero, I. (1971). The London tailors' strike of 1834 and the collapse of the Grand National Consolidated Trades Union. *International Review of Social History* 22(1).

Pearson, R. & Williams, G. (1984). *Political Thought and Public Policy in the Nineteenth Century: an introduction.* London.

Pelling, H. (1968). *Popular Politics and Society in Late Victorian Britain*. London.

Penn, R. (1983). Trade union organisation and skills in the cotton and engineering industries in Britain, 1850–1960. *Social History* 8(1).

Perkin, H. (1969). *The Origins of Modern English Society, 1780–1880*. London.

Perkin, H. (1989). *The Rise of Professional Society: England since 1880*. London.

Perrot, M. (1986). On the formation of the French working class. In *Working-Class Formation: nineteenth-century patterns in Western Europe and the United States* (ed. I. Katznelson & A. R. Zolberg). Princeton, NJ.

Perrot, M. (1987). *Workers on Strike: France 1871–1890*. Leamington Spa.

Phelps Brown, E. H. & Browne, M. H. (1968). *A Century of Pay: the course of pay and production in France, Germany, Sweden, the United Kingdom, and the United States of America, 1860–1960*. London.

Place, F. (1972). *The Autobiography of Francis Place* (ed. M. Thrale). Cambridge.

Plumb, J. H. (1969). The growth of the electorate in England 1600–1715. *Past and Present* **45**.

Pohl, H. (ed.) (1978). *Forschungen zur Lage der Arbeiter im Industrialisierungsprozeß*. Stuttgart.

Pollard, S. (1959). *A History of Labour in Sheffield*. London.

Pollard, S. (1980). Review of Zwahr, 1978. *Social History* **5**.

Porter, B. (1979). *The Refugee Question in Mid-Victorian Politics*. Cambridge.

Prelinger, C. (1976). Religious dissent, women's rights and the Hamburger Hochschule für das weibliche Geschlecht in mid-nineteenth-century Germany. *Church History* **45**.

Prelinger, C. (1987). *Charity, Challenge and Change: religious dimensions of the mid-nineteenth century women's movements in Germany*. London & New York.

Price, Richard (1975). The other face of respectability: violence in the Manchester brickmaking trade, 1859–1870. *Past and Present* **66**.

Price, Richard (1980). *Masters, Unions and Men: work control in building and the rise of Labour*. Cambridge.

Price, Richard (1983). The labour process and labour history. *Social History* 8(1).

Price, Roger (1972). *The French Second Republic: a social history*. London.

Price, Roger (1981). *An Economic History of Modern France*. London.

Prothero, I. (1969). Chartism in London. *Past and Present* **44**.

Prothero, I (1971). London Chartism and the trades. *Economic History Review* **24**.

Prothero, I. (1974). William Benbow and the concept of the General Strike. *Past and Present* **63**.

Prothero, I. J. (1979). *Artisans and Politics in Early Nineteenth-century London: John Gast and his times*. Folkestone.

Reid, A. (1978). Politics and economics in the formation of the British working class: a response to H. Moorhouse. *Social History* **3**.

Reid, A. (1979). The labour aristocracy in British social history. *Our History* (Communist Party publication).

Reid, A. (1980). 'The division of labour in the shipbuilding industry 1880–1920'. Unpublished D.Phil. thesis, University of Cambridge.

Reid, A. (1983). Intelligent artisans and aristocrats of labour: the essays of Thomas Wright. In *The Working Class in Modern British History* (ed. J. Winter). Cambridge.

Reininghaus, W. (1984). Die Gesellenvereinigungen am Ende des Alten Reiches. Die Bilanz von dreihundert Jahren Sozialdisziplinierung. In *Handwerker in der Industrialisierung* (ed. U. Engelhardt). Stuttgart.

Renzsch, W. (1980). *Handwerker und Lohnarbeiter in der frühe Arbeiterbewegung. Zur sozialen Basis von Gewerkschaftsbewegung und Sozialdemokratie im Reichsgründungsjahrzehnt*. Göttingen.

Renzsch, W. (1984). Bauhandwerker in der Industrialisierung. In *Handwerker in der Industrialisierung* (ed. U. Engelhardt). Stuttgart.

Repgen, K. (1955). *Märzbewegung und Maiwahlen des Revolutionsjahres 1848 im Rheinland*. Bonn.

Reulecke, J. & Weber, W. (eds) (1978). *Fabrik – Familie – Feierabend: Beiträge zur Sozialgeschichte des Alltags im Industriezeitalter*. Wuppertal.

Rimlinger, G. (1959). International Differences in the strike propensity of coal miners: experience in four countries. *Industrial and Labor Relations Review* 12.

Rimlinger, G. (1967). Die Legitimierung des Protestes. Eine vergleichende Untersuchung der Bergarbeiterbewegung in England und Deutschland. In *Die soziale Frage. Neuere Studien zur Lage der Fabrikarbeiter in den Frühphasen der Industrialisierung* (ed. W. Fischer & G. Bajor). Stuttgart.

Ritscher, W. (1917). *Koalitionen und Koalitionsrecht in Deutschland bis zur Reichsgewerbeordnung*. Stuttgart & Berlin.

Ritter, G. A. (1983). Shlomo Na'aman als Historiker der deutschen Arbeiterbewegung. In *Arbeiterbewegung und Geschichte: Festschrift für Shlomo Na'aman zum 70. Geburtstag* (ed. H.-P. Harstick, A. Herzig & H. Pelger). Trier.

Ritter, G. A. (1985). *Die deutschen Parteien 1830–1914*. Göttingen.

Ritter, G. A. (1989). Die neuere Sozialgeschichte in der Bunderepublik Deutschland. In *Sozialgeschichte im internationalen überblick* (ed. J. Kocka). Darmstadt.

Ritter, G. A. & Tenfelde, K. (1975). Der Durchbruch der Freien Gewerkschaften Deutschlands zur Massenbewegung im letzten Viertel des 19.Jahrhunderts. In *Vom Sozialistengesetz zur Mitbestimmung* (ed. H. O. Vetter). Cologne.

Robbins, K. (1979). *John Bright*. London.

Roberts, R. (1978). *The Classic Slum: Salford life in the first quarter of the century*. Manchester.

Roehl, R. (1976). French industrialisation: a reconsideration. *Explorations in Economic History* 13.

Rose, M. (1970). The anti-Poor Law agitation. In *Popular Movements c. 1830–1870* (ed. J. Ward). London.

Rose, M. (1976). Settlement, removal and the new Poor Law. In *The New Poor Law in the Nineteenth Century* (ed. D. Fraser). London.

Rose, M. (1985). Culture, philanthropy and the Manchester middle classes. In *City, Class and Culture* (ed. A. Kidd & K. Roberts). Manchester.

Roth, G. (1963). *The Social Democrats in Imperial Germany*. Totowa, N.J.

Roth, K. (1974). *Die 'andere' Arbeiterbewegung und die Entwicklung der kapitalistischen Repression von 1880 bis zur Gegenwart*. Munich.

Rothstein, T. (1983). *From Chartism to Labourism: historical studies of the English working class* (1st edn, 1929). London.

Rowntree, B. J. (1901). *Poverty: a study of town life*. London.

Rumpler, H. (ed) (1990). *Deutscher Bund und deutsche Frage 1815–1866*. Munich.

Ryan, A. (1984). *Property and Political Theory*. Oxford.

Salter, S. & Stevenson, J. (eds) (1990). *The Working Class and Politics in Europe and America 1929–1945*. London.

Samuel, R. (1977). The workshop of the world: steam power and hand-technology in mid-Victorian Britain. *History Workshop Journal* 3.

Saul, K. (1974). *Staat, Industrie, Arbeiterbewegung im Kaiserreich. Zur Innen- und Sozialpolitik des Wilhelminischen Deutschland 1903–1914*. Düsseldorf.

Saville, J. (1952). *Ernest Jones: Chartist*. London.

Saville, J. (1987). *1848: the British state and the Chartist movement*. Cambridge.

Schadt, J. (1971). *Die Sozialdemokratische Partei in Baden. Von den Anfängen bis zur Jahrhundertwende* (1868–1900). Hannover.

Schama, S. (1989). *Citizens: a chronicle of the French Revolution*. London.

Schieder, W. (1963). *Anfänge der deutschen Arbeiterbewegung. Die Auslandsvereine im Jahrzehnt nach der Julirevolution von 1830*. Stuttgart.

Schieder, W. (1974). Die Rolle der deutschen Arbeiter in der Revolution von 1848/49. In *Ideen und Strukturen der deutschen Revolution 1848* (ed. W. Klötzer *et al.*), Frankfurt.

Schieder, W. (1980). Church and revolution. In *Conflict and Stability in Europe* (ed. C. Emsley). Milton Keynes.

Schieder, W. (ed) (1983). *Liberalismus in der Gesellschaft des deutschen Vormärz.* Göttingen.

Schildt, G. (1986). *Tagelöhner, Gesellen, Arbeiter. Sozialgeschichte der vorindustriellen und industriellen Arbeiter in Braunschweig.* Stuttgart.

Schmidt, G. (1974). Politischer Liberalismus, 'Landed Interests' und Organisierter Arbeiterschaft, 1850–1880: Ein deutsch-englischer Vergleich. In *Sozialgeschichte Heute: Festschrift für Hans Rosenberg* (ed. H.-H. Wehler). Göttingen.

Schmidt, W. (1983). *Die Revolution von 1848/49 in Hamburg.* Hamburg.

Schmierer, W. (1970). *Von der Arbeiterbildung zur Arbeiterpolitik. Die Anfänge der Arbeiterbewegung in Württemberg 1862/63–1878.* Hannover.

Schofer, L. (1975). *The Formation of a Modern Labour Force: Upper Silesia 1865–1914.* Berkeley & Los Angeles.

Schomerus, H. (1977). *Die Arbeiter der Maschinenfabrik Esslingen. Forschungen zur Lage der Arbeiterschaft im 19.Jahrhundert.* Stuttgart.

Schonhöven, K. (1980). *Expansion und Konzentration. Studien zur Entwicklung der Freien Gewerkschaften in Wilhelminischen Deutschland, 1890–1914.* Stuttgart.

Schorske, C. E. (1983). *German Social Democracy 1905–1917: the development of the great schism.* Cambridge, Mass. (2nd edn).

Schöttler, P. (1986). Syndikalismus in der europäische Arbeiterbewegung. Neuere Forschungen in Frankreich, England und Deutschland. In *Arbeiter und Arbeiterbewegung im Vergleich* (ed. K. Tenfelde). Munich.

Schröder, W. H. (1976). Die Sozialstruktur der socialdemokratischen Reichstagskandidaten 1898–1912. In *Herkunft und Mandat: Beiträge zur Führungspolitik in der Arbeiterbewegung.* Frankfurt.

Schröder, W. H. (1978). *Arbeitergeschichte und Arbeiterbewegung. Industriearbeit und Organisationsverhalten im. 19. und frühe 20.Jahrhundert.* Frankfurt & New York.

Schroeder, W. (1976). Das Berliner Polizeipraesidium und die Gewerkschaftsbewegung 1878 bis 1886. Zur Gewerkschaftspolitik des Bismarckstaates während des Sozialistengesetzes. In *Evolution und Revolution in der Weltgeschichte: Vol. 2* (ed. H. Bartel *et al.*) Berlin (E).

Schröter, A. & Becker, W. (1962). *Die deutsche Machinenbauindustrie in der industriellen Revolution.* Berlin (E).

Schulz, G. (1978). Integrationsprobleme der Arbeiterschaft in der Metall-Papier- and chemischen Industrie der Rheinprovinz 1850–1914. In *Forschungen zur Lage der Arbeiter* (ed. H. Pohl). Stuttgart.

Schuhmacher, F. (1920). *Wie das Kunstwerk Hamburg nach dem großen Brand entstand.* Berlin.

Scott, J. W. (1974). *The Glass Workers of Carmaux.* Cambridge, Mass.

Scott, J. W. (1986). Statistical Representations of Work: the politics of the Chamber of Commerce's 'Statistique de l'Industrie a Paris', 1847–48. In *Work in France: representations, meaning, organization and practice* (ed. S. J. Kaplan & C. J. Koepp). Ithaca, N.Y. & London.

Seal, A. (1973). Introduction. In *Locality, Province and Nation: essays on Indian politics 1870–1940* (ed. J. Gallagher *et al.*) London.

Sedatis, H. (1979). *Liberalismus und Handwerk in Südwestdeutschland. Wirtschafts- und Gesellschaftskonzeptionen des Liberalismus und die Krise des Handwerks im 19. Jahrhundert.* Stuttgart.

Seed, J. (1982). Unitarianism, political economy and the antimonies of liberal culture in Manchester, 1830–1850. *Social History* **7**(1).

Seed, J. (1988). 'Commerce and the liberal arts': the political economy of art in Manchester 1775–1860. In *The Culture of Capital* (ed. J. Wolff & J. Seed). Manchester.

Seidel-Höppner, W. (1961). *Wilhelm Weitling – der erste deutsche Theoretiker und Agitator des Kommunismus.* Berlin (E).

Seidel-Höppner, W. F. Rkitjanski, J. (1985). Weitling in der Revolution 1848/49. Unbekannte Dokumente. *Jahrbuch für Geschichte* **32**.

Semmel, B. (1986). *Liberalism and Naval Strategy: ideology, interest and sea power during the Pax Britannica*. London.

Sewell, W. (1980). *Work and Revolution in France: the language of labor from the old regime to 1848*. Cambridge, Mass.

Sewell, W. (1986). Artisans and Factory workers, 1789–1848. In *Working-Class Formation: nineteenth-century patterns in Western Europe and the United States* (ed. I. Katznelson & A. R. Zolberg). Princeton, NJ.

Sheehan, J. (1973). Liberalism and society in Germany 1815–1848. *Journal of Modern History* **45**(4).

Sheehan, J. (1978). *German Liberalism in the Nineteenth Century*. Chicago, Ill.

Sheehan, J. (1990). *German History 1770–1866*. Oxford.

Shepherd, M. A. (1978). The origins and incidence of the term 'labour aristocracy'. *Bulletin of the Society for the Study of Labour History* **37**.

Siemann, W. (1985). *'Deutschlands Ruhe, Sicherheit und Ordnung'. Die Anfänge der politischen Polizei, 1806–1866*. Tübingen.

Sigsworth, E. (ed) (1988). *In Search of Victorian Values: aspects of nineteenth-century thought and society*. Manchester.

Simon, D. (1954). Master and Servant. In *Democracy and the Labour Movement: essays in honour of Dora Torr* (ed. J. Saville). London.

Skocpol, T. (1979). *States and Social Revolutions: a comparative analysis of France, Russia and China*. London.

Smith, F. B. (1966). *The Making of the Second Reform Bill*. Cambridge.

Spain, J. (1991). Trade unionists, Gladstonian Liberals, and the labour law reforms of 1875. In *Currents of Radicalism* (ed. E. Biagini & A. Reid). Cambridge.

Sperber, J. (1984). *Popular Catholicism in Nineteenth-Century Germany*. Princeton, NJ.

Stadelmann, R. & Fischer, W. (1955). *Die Bildungswelt des deutschen Handwerkers um 1800*. Berlin.

Steffens, H. (1981). Arbeiterwohnverhältnisse und Arbeitskampf. Das Beispiel der Saarbergleute in der großen Streikzeit 1889–1893. In *Streik* (ed. K. Tenfelde & H. Volkmann). Munich.

Steinberg, H.-J. (1976). *Sozialismus und deutsche Sozialdemokratie. Zur Ideologie der Parteien vor dem 1.Weltkrieg*. Berlin/Bonn.

Stephan, C. (1977). *'Genossen, wir dürfen uns nicht von der Geduld hinreissen lassen!' Aus der Urgeschichte der Sozialdemokratie, 1862–1878*. Frankfurt.

Storch, R. D. (1975). The plague of blue locusts. *International Review of Social History* **20**.

Struik, D. (1971). *Birth of the Communist Manifesto*. New York.

Sykes, R. (1982). Early Chartism and trade unionism in south-east Lancashire. In *The Chartist Experience* (ed. J. Epstein & D. Thompson). London.

Taylor, A. D. (1984). 'Ernest Jones: his later career and the structure of Manchester politics, 1861–69'. Unpublished M.A. thesis, University of Birmingham.

Taylor, A. D. (forthcoming). 'Modes of Political Expression and Working-Class Radicalism 1848–1880: the London and Manchester Experience. Unpublished Ph.D. thesis, University of Manchester.

Tenfelde, K. (1979). Linksradikale Strömungen in der Ruhrarbeiterschaft 1905 bis 1919. In *'Glück auf, Kameraden'. Die Bergarbeiter und ihre Organisationen in Deutschland* (ed. H. Mommsen & U. Borsdorf). Cologne.

Tenfelde, K. (1980). Neue Forschungen zur Geschichte der Arbeiterschaft. *Archiv für Sozialgeschichte* **20**.

Tenfelde, K. (1981). *Sozialgeschichte der Bergarbeiterschaft an der Ruhr im 19. Jahrhundert*. Bonn.

Tenfelde, K. (1982). Bis vor die Stufen des Throns. Bittschriften und Beschwerden der Ruhrbergleute 1830 bis 1900. In *Geschichte im Alltag – Alltag in der Geschichte* (ed. K. Bergmann & R. Schoerken). Düsseldorf.

Tenfelde, K. (1988). Überholt von der demokratischen Massengesellschaft: Von Ende und Erbe der Arbeiterkultur. *Frankfurter Allgemeine Zeitung*, 7 March.

Tenfelde, K. (ed) (1986). *Arbeiter und Arbeiterbewegung im Vergleich*. Munich.

Tenfelde, K. & Volkmann, H. (eds) (1981). *Streik. Zur Geschichte des Arbeitskampfes in Deutschland während der Industrialisierung*. Munich.

Thadden, R. von (1983). Protestantismus und Liberalismus zur Zeit des Hambacher Festes 1832. In *Liberalismus in der Gesellschaft des deutschen Vormärz* (ed. W. Schieder). Göttingen.

Thernstrom, S. (1964). *Poverty and Progress: social mobility in a nineteenth-century town*. Cambridge, Mass.

Tholfsen, T. (1971). The intellectual origins of mid-Victorian stability. *Political Science Quarterly* **86**.

Tholfsen, T. (1976). *Working-class Radicalism in Mid-Victorian Britain*. London.

Thomas, J. A. (1950). The system of registration and the development of party organisation 1832–1870. *History* **35**.

Thomas, W. (1979). *The Philosophic Radicals: Nine Studies in theory and practice 1817–1841*. Oxford.

Thompson, D. (1984). *The Chartists: popular politics in the Industrial Revolution*. London.

Thompson, E. P. (1963). *The Making of the English Working Class*. Harmondsworth.

Thompson, E. P. (1965). The peculiarities of the English. In *The Socialist Register. 2* (ed. R. Milliband & J. Saville). London.

Thompson, E. P. (1979). Review of Prothero, 1979. In *New Society*, 3 May 1979.

Thompson, P. (1967). *Socialists, Liberals and Labour: the struggle for London, 1885–1914*. London.

Tilly, C. & Lees, L. (1974). Le peuple de juin 1848. *Annales. Economies, Sociétés, Civilisations* **29**.

Tilly, C. & Shorter, E. (1974). *Strikes in France 1830–1968*. Cambridge.

Trautmann, G. (1983). Das Scheitern liberaler Vereinspolitik und die Entstehung der sozialistischen Arbeiterbewegung in Hamburg zwischen 1862 und 1871. In *Arbeiter in Hamburg* (ed. A. Herzig, D. Langewiesche & A. Sywottek). Hamburg.

Turner, H. A. (1962). *Trade Union Growth, Structure and Policy: a comparative study of the cotton trade unions*. London.

Vernon, J. (1991). 'Politics and the people: a study in English political culture and communication 1808–1868'. Unpublished Ph.D thesis, University of Manchester.

Vetterli, R. (1978). *Industriearbeit, Arbeiterbewußtsein und gewerkschaftliche Organisation*. Göttingen.

Vetterli, R. (1981). Konflikt und Konfliktregelung in einem schweizerischen Großbetrieb 1890–1914. In *Streik* (ed. K. Tenfelde & H. Volkmann). Munich.

Vierhaus, R. (1986). Bürgerliche Hegemonie oder Proletarische Emanzipation: der Beitrag der Bildung. In *Arbeiter und Bürger im 19. Jahrhundert* (ed. J. Kocka). Munich.

Vincent, D. (1981). *Bread, Knowledge and Freedom: a study of nineteenth-century working-class autobiography*. London.

Vincent, J. (1968). The effect of the Second Reform Act in Lancashire. *The Historical Journal* **11**(1).

Vincent, J. (1972). *The Formation of the Liberal Party, 1857–68*. Harmondsworth.

Vogel, B. (ed) (1980). *Preussische Reformen 1807–1820*. Königstein/Ts.

Vogeler, M. S. (1984). *Frederic Harrison: the vocations of a positivist*. Oxford.

Wachenheim, H. (1967). *Die deutsche Arbeiterbewegung 1844 bis 1914*. Opladen.

Waismann, C. H. (1982). *Modernisation and the Working Class: the politics of legitimacy*. Austin, Tex.

Walker, M. (1971). *German Home Towns: community, state and general estate 1648–1871*. London.

Ward, J. (ed) 1970). *Popular Movements c.1830–1850*. London.

Webb, S. & Webb, B. (1920). *The History of Trade Unionism, 1660–1920*. London.

Weber, M. (1924). *Gesammelte Aufsätze zur Soziologie und Sozialpolitik*. Tübingen.

Weber, M. (1978). *Economy and Society: An outline of Interpretive Sociology* (ed. G. Roth & C. Wittich). Berkeley, Cal.

Wehler, H.-U. (1981). 'Deutscher Sonderweg' oder allgemeine Probleme des westlichen Kapitalismus. *Merkur*, 35/5.

Wehler, H.-U. (1987a). *Deutsche Gesellschaftsgeschichte: Vol. 1. 1700–1815*. Munich.

Wehler, H.-U. (1987b). *Deutsche Gesellschaftsgeschichte: Vol. 2. 1815–1845/49*. Munich.

Weisser, H. (1975). *British Working-class Movements and Europe 1815–1848*. Manchester.

Weitling, W. (1969). *The Poor Sinner's Gospel*. London.

Weitling, W. (1971). In *Die Menschheit, wie sie ist und wie sie sein sollte* (ed. W. Schafer). Reinbek bei Hamburg.

Weitling, W. (1974). *Garantien der Harmonie und Freiheit* (ed. A. Meyer). Stuttgart.

White, D. (1976). *The Splintered Party: national liberalism in Hessen and the Reich 1867–1918*. Cambridge, Mass.

Whittaker, P. (1956). 'The growth of liberal organisation in Manchester from the 1860s to 1903'. Unpublished Ph.D. thesis, University of Manchester.

Wieacker, F. (1974). *Industriegesellschaft und Privatsrechtsordnung*. Frankfurt.

Wiener, J. L. (1969). *The War of the Unstamped: the movement to repeal the British newspaper tax, 1830–1836*. Ithaca. N.Y.

Wiener, M. J. (1981). *English Culture and the Decline of the Industrial Spirit 1850–1980*. Cambridge.

Wilson, G. M. (1982). *Alexander Macdonald: leader of the miners*. Aberdeen.

Windell, G. G. (1954). *The Catholics and German Unity 1866–1871*. Minneapolis, Minn.

Wirth, F. (1981). *Johann Jakob Treichler und die soziale Bewegung im Kanton Zürich (1845/1846)*. Basle & Frankfurt.

Wissell, R. (1971). *Des alten Handwerks Recht und Gewohnheit*. Berlin.

Wolff, J. & Seed, J. (eds) (1988). *The Culture of Capital: art, power, and the nineteenth-century middle class*. Manchester.

Wood, G. H. (1909). Real wages and the standard of comfort since 1850. *Journal of the Royal Statistical Society* 72.

Wright, T. (1867). *Some Habits and Customs of the Working Classes*. London.

Wright, T. (1868). *The Great Unwashed*. London.

Wright, T. (1873). *Our New Masters*. London.

Yeo, E. (1983). Some practices and problems of Chartist democracy. In *The Chartist Experience* (ed. J. Epstein & D. Thompson). London.

Zeitlin, J. (1979). Craft control and the division of labour: engineers and compositors in Britain 1890–1930. In *Cambridge Journal of Economics* 3.

Zeitlin, J. (1983). Social theory and the history of work: a review essay. *Social History* 8.

Zerwas, H.-J. (1988). *Arbeit als Besitz. Das ehrbare Handwerk zwischen Brüderliebe und Klassenkampf 1848*. Reinbek bei Hamburg.

Zimmermann, M. (1979). *Hamburgische Patriotismus und deutscher Nationalismus. Die Emanzipation der Juden in Hamburg 1830–1865*. Hamburg.

Zolberg, A. R. (1986). How many exceptionalisms? In *Working-Class Formation* (ed. I. Katznelson & A. R. Zolberg). Princeton, N.J.

Zwahr, H. (1978). *Zur Konstitutierung des Proletariats als Klasse: Strukturuntersuchung über das Leipziger Proletariat während der industriellen Revolution*. Berlin (E).

Zwahr, H. (1985). Zum Gestalwandel von gewerblichen Unternehmern und kapitalabhängigen Produzenten. Entwicklungstypen gewerblicher Warenproduktion in Deutschland. *Jahrbuch für Geschichte* 32.

Zwahr, H. (1989). Arbeiterbewegung in Deutschland innerhalb der Trias von kapitalabhängigen Handwerk, Manufaktur und Fabrik. In *'Der kühnen Bahn nur folgen wir': I* (ed. A. Herzig & G. Trautmann). Hamburg.

Zwahr, H. (ed) (1981). *Die Konstituierung der deutschen Arbeiterklasse von den 30er bis zu den 70er Jahrhen*. Berlin (E).